CHINA AND THE EUROPEAN UNION IN AFRICA

CHINA AND THE EUROPEAN UNION IN AFRICA

China and the European Union in Africa

Partners or Competitors?

Edited by
JING MEN AND BENJAMIN BARTON
College of Europe, Belgium

Routledge
Taylor & Francis Group

LONDON AND NEW YORK

First published 2011 by Ashgate Publishing

Published 2016 by Routledge
2 Park Square, Milton Park, Abingdon, Oxfordshire OX14 4RN
711 Third Avenue, New York, NY 10017, USA

First issued in paperback 2016

Routledge is an imprint of the Taylor & Francis Group, an informa business

British Library Cataloguing in Publication Data
China and the European Union in Africa : partners or
competitors?.
1. European Union--China. 2. China--Foreign relations--
Africa. 3. Africa--Foreign relations--China. 4. European
Union countries--Foreign relations--Africa. 5. Africa--
Foreign relations--European Union countries. 6. Africa--
Strategic aspects.
I. Men, Jing, 1968- II. Barton, Benjamin.
327.5'106-dc22

Library of Congress Cataloging-in-Publication Data
China and the European Union in Africa : partners or competitors? / edited by Jing Men
and Benjamin Barton.
    p. cm.
Includes bibliographical references and index.
ISBN 978-1-4094-2047-7 (hardback)   1. Africa--Strategic aspects.
2. China--Relations--Africa. 3. Africa--Relations--China. 4. European
Union--Africa. I. Men, Jing, 1968- II. Barton, Benjamin.
JZ1773.C45 2010
355'.0326--dc22

2010048575

ISBN 13: 978-1-138-27110-4 (pbk)
ISBN 13: 978-1-4094-2047-7 (hbk)

Contents

List of Figures

List of Tables

Notes on Contributors

Benjamin Barton is Research Assistant for the InBev-Baillet-Latour Chair of European Union-China Relations at the EU International Relations and Diplomacy Studies Department of the College of Europe in Bruges since September 2009. He holds an MA in EU International Relations and Diplomacy Studies from the College of Europe, Bruges (2008–2009), and a BA in European Studies from the University of Sussex, Brighton (2004–2008). He also undertook Erasmus studies at the Institut d'Etudes Politiques (I.E.P) in Strasbourg, France (2006–2007). Before joining the College, Benjamin worked as an Intern, focusing on a Cyber Security Project, in the Worldwide Security Initiative (WSI) at the EastWest Institute in Brussels. Since working at the College, he has published several academic papers in collaboration with Prof. Jing Men and participated in international academic conferences.

Jianxiang Bi is a Lecturer in Chinese Studies at the University of the West of England (UWE), Bristol. Before joining UWE, he taught at Carleton University, St. Mary's University and Dalhousie University in Canada. His research interest is largely focused on international security and Chinese politics, Chinese/East Asian history and politics, with emphasis on culture, technological innovation, economic development and security. Over the years, he has worked on a variety of research projects, such as military modernization, dual-use technology and critical infrastructure protection for the Canadian Department of Natural Resources, the Canadian Department of National Defense, the RAND Corporation, the US Department of Defense, the Center for Naval Analysis and the American Enterprise Institute. He has widely published these aforementioned articles in academic journals such as the *Contemporary Security Policy* journal.

Zhiyue Bo is a Senior Research Fellow at the East Asian Institute of the National University of Singapore. He obtained his Bachelor of Law and Master of Law from Beijing University and his PhD from the University of Chicago. He has taught at Beijing University, Roosevelt University, the University of Chicago, American University, St. John Fisher College, Tarleton State University and the Chinese University of Hong Kong. He was a recipient of the *Trustees' Distinguished Scholar Award* at St. John Fisher College and the inaugural holder of the *Joe and Teresa Long Endowed Chair in Social Science* at Tarleton State University. He is the Author of *Chinese Provincial Leaders: Economic Performance and Political Mobility since 1949* (Armonk, NY: M.E. Sharpe 2002) and *China's Elite Politics: Political Transition and Power Balancing* (Singapore: World Scientific 2007).

Martyn Davies is the Chief Executive Officer of Frontier Advisory (Pty) Ltd. Martyn is also the Director of the Asia Business Centre, Centre for Business and Academic Research at the Gordon Institute of Business Science (GIBS), University of Pretoria, South Africa. Martyn was the (founding) Director of the Centre for Chinese Studies (CCS) that was established under the South Africa-China Bi-national Commission. He has written over 200 articles in academia and the press and is a regular commentator for the international media. He has presented articles for various international conferences. Martyn has chaired both public and private sessions at the World Economic Forum both in Africa and China. In October 2008, he was appointed as an advisor to the Organisation for Economic Cooperation and Development (OECD) for its Global Development Outlook project. Martyn holds a BA degree in Law, an Honours Degree in International Relations, a Master's Degree in International Relations (University of the Witwatersrand), a Diploma in Asian Studies (Yonsei University, Seoul, Korea) and a PhD in International Relations (University of the Witwatersrand).

Joris Larik is a Doctoral Researcher in Law from the European University Institute in Florence, where he has been undertaking his PhD research since August 2009. Since April 2009, he has been working in parallel, as a Postgraduate Intern at the WTO's Appellate Body Secretariat and also as a Junior Visiting Lecturer, where he has been teaching a course at the School of International Studies at the University of Dresden. Between October 2008 and February 2009, he was doing an internship at the European Commission's Legal Service, after having successfully graduated from the College of Europe's International Relations and Diplomacy Masters Studies Programme. He also holds a LLM in International Public Law from the University of Leiden and a BA in International Relations from the University of Dresden.

Anshan Li is a Professor at the School of International Studies, Peking University, the Vice President of the Chinese Society of African Historical Studies and the Director of the Institute of Afro-Asian Studies at Peking University. He has extensively published in the field of Afro-Asian relations and his publication list includes among others *A History of Chinese Overseas in Africa* (Beijing 2000), *British Rule and Rural Protest in Southern Ghana* (New York 2002), *Studies on African Nationalism* (Beijing 2004), *Social History of Chinese Overseas in Africa: Selected Documents, 1800–2005* (Hong Kong 2006). In recent years, he has given speeches on China-Africa relations in numerous countries that range from South Africa, the United Kingdom, Japan, Germany, the United States, Canada, Spain, Norway, Kenya, Botswana, Sweden, South Africa and Zimbabwe. His interest covers African history, China-Africa relations, colonialism, the presence of Chinese citizens overseas, comparative nationalism and development studies. Finally, he was invited as a distinguished guest at the Forum on China-Africa Cooperation (FOCAC) – Beijing Ministerial Conference (2000), the Sino-African Education Ministers Forum (2005) and the FOCAC-Beijing Summit (2006).

Jing Men is the holder of the InBev-Baillet Latour Chair of EU-China Relations at the College of Europe in Bruges. She graduated from Nankai University in Tianjin, China, with a BA (1990) and an MA (1993) in English Language and Literature. She obtained a PhD in Political Science (2004) at the Vrije Universiteit Brussel. She has widely published on EU-China relations, Chinese foreign policy and external relations. She founded the *EU-China Observer* e-journal at the College of Europe in the beginning of 2009. Since then, the e-journal has been published bi-monthly and is widely circulated in both the EU and China among over 5,000 scholars and policy-practitioners.

Eric Kehinde Ogunleye has been working as a Research Fellow for the African Centre for Economic Transformation (ACET) since January 2009. Previously, he was researching as a Postgraduate Intern for the United Nations University's (UNU) World Institute for Development Economics Research in Helsinki between April and May of 2008, and in the same year he worked as a consultant for the United Nations Conference on Trade and Development (UNCTAD), in Geneva, between January and April 2008. Eric has also performed research, via his Doctoral Support, for the World Trade Organisation (WTO). Beforehand, Eric was a lecturer at the University of Calabar, Nigeria. He holds a PhD and an MSc in Economics from the University of Ibadan in Nigeria and a BSc in economics from the University of Calabar. He has widely published in books and journals such as *The African Journal of Economic Policy* or the *African Journal of Contemporary Issues*.

Ian Taylor is a Professor in International Relations at the University of St Andrews' School of International Relations and a Professor in Political Science at the University of Stellenbosch, South Africa. He is also Honorary Professor in the Institute of African Studies, Zhejiang Normal University, China and Joint Professor in the Centre for European Studies, Renmin University of China. He holds a DPhil from the University of Stellenbosch and an MPhil from the University of Hong Kong. Prior to joining St Andrews, he taught African politics at the Department of Political and Administrative Studies, University of Botswana, for four years. Prior to entering academia, Ian worked for the UNHCR in Hong Kong on the Vietnamese Boat People issue. He is primarily interested in Africa's political economy, Africa's international relations and in Chinese foreign policy. He has published a substantial body of work on South Africa's post-apartheid foreign policies. He is the co-editor of the academic journal *African Security* and the *Review of International Studies*.

Sara van Hoeymissen is a PhD Researcher at the Katholieke Universiteit of Leuven Sinology Department, where she has been since 2007. Between 2003–2006, she was Project Manager at the Economic Division of the Taipei Representative Office to the European Union and Belgium, in Brussels. Prior to that, she was a Research and Teaching Assistant at the Sinology Department of the K.U. Leuven. Sara has contributed book chapters and published articles, including the *International Spectator* and the *Journal of Current Chinese Affairs*.

Quentin Weiler is currently the Desk Officer for issues relevant to Small Arms and Light Weapons (SALW) at the European Commission's DG RELEX, the Directorate for External Affairs. He was previously the Political and Security Committee (PSC) Coordinator and Nicolaïdis Counsellor at the French Permanent Representation to the Political and Security Committee of the European Union. He graduated from the Institute of Political Science (I.E.P.) of Lille (2007), where he spent an exchange year at the University of Toronto's Political Science and International Relations department (2005). He also obtained a Masters degree in European Affairs at the Lille 2 University Faculty of Law (2007) and a Master in EU International Relations and Diplomacy Studies at the College of Europe, in Bruges (2008).

Thomas Wheeler works for Saferworld (London), which is an international NGO that aims to reduce violent conflicts in the world. Thomas works on Saferworld's China Programme. He has held this position since June 2009, but he was previously posted in Saferworld's Nairobi Office, working as a Consultant on conflict analysis and peacebuilding. Thomas has also worked as an Intern for both the Conflict Early Warning and Response Mechanism (CEWARN) and the United Nations High Commission for Refugees' (UNHCR) Office in Nairobi. He holds an MA in Conflict, Security and Development (King's College, 2007–2008), and an MA in Politics (University of Edinburgh, 2003–2007), where he also spent a year as an exchange student at McGill University. He has previously published in the academic journal *Global Review*.

Uwe Wissenbach is the Deputy Head of Mission and Head of the Political Section of the European Union's Delegation to South Korea, a position he has occupied since 2009. He has held other positions inside the European Commission, as he was previously Policy Officer responsible for relations with Asian countries at the Commission's Directorate for Development, from 2006–2009. Furthermore, he was Policy Officer responsible for strategic coordination in the Human and Social Development Unit, at the same Directorate General. Prior to this experience, he was First Secretary at the Commission's Delegation in China and Mongolia, where he was responsible for economic cooperation and the Mongolia desk from 2000–2004. He held various other positions inside the European Commission and also at the Council of Europe. His academic record indicates that he has studied three Masters degrees, earned respectively at Mainz University and the Charles de Gaulle University (Lille), the London School of Economics and Beijing Foreign Studies University, in the field of Political Science and European and International Economic Law. He also holds a certificate of Japanese Studies, obtained from the Gutenberg University, in Mainz.

Suisheng Zhao is Professor and Executive Director of the Centre for China-US Cooperation at the Josef Korbel School of International Studies, University of Denver. He is the founding editor of the *Journal of Contemporary China*, a member of the Board of Governors of the US Committee of the Council for Security Cooperation in the Asia Pacific (USCSCAP), a member of National Committee on US-China Relations, a Research Associate at the Fairbanks Centre for East Asian Research at Harvard University, and a honorary professor at Beijing University, Renmin University, China University of International Relations, Fudan University and Shanghai International Studies University. A Campbell National Fellow at Hoover Institution of Stanford University, he was Associate Professor of Political Science and International Studies at Washington College in Maryland, Associate Professor of Government and East Asian Politics at Colby College in Maine, and Visiting Assistant Professor at the Graduate School of International Relations and Pacific Studies (IR/PS), at the University of California-San Diego. He received his PhD degree in Political Science from the University of California-San Diego, his MA degree in Sociology from the University of Missouri and BA and MA degrees in Economics from Peking University. He is the author and editor of an important number of books that concern China's foreign policy.

Xinghui Zhang is a Journalist, working for the *China Youth Daily*, a career he started back in 1996, when he was a correspondent for the newspaper, and where he has published over 700 news stories. Now, he is currently stationed as the Brussels Bureau Chief for the *China Youth Daily*, where he has been working since November 2007. Before moving to Brussels, he was the Editor and Deputy Director of the International News Department for the *China Youth Daily*, in the Beijing Office (2004–2007). He has also worked in Washington, as the *China Youth Daily* Bureau Chief (2000–2004). He holds a Masters in Law and International Relations from Peking University (1993–1996) and a BA in English Language from the Shanxi Normal University (1987–1993). He has also published five articles in Chinese academic periodicals and one book chapter in English.

Acknowledgements

The editors would first like to thank the InBev-Baillet Latour Foundation and the College of Europe for allowing the editors the opportunity to engage in the organization of such projects and for providing the necessary financial and moral support required. Furthermore, the editors are grateful for the generous financial assistance received from the European Commission's Jean Monnet Life Long Learning Programme, without which the book would not have been made possible. On a personal level, the editors would like to thank College of Europe and International Relations and Diplomacy Department staff members for their contribution. In particular, they would like to thank the College of Europe Rector, Prof. Dr Paul Demaret, the Head of the International Relations and Diplomacy Department, Prof. Dr Sieglinde Gstöhl, and our colleagues Prof. Dr Dieter Mahncke, Mrs. Sabine Dekeyser and Ms. Anne-Claire Marangoni for their overall contribution to this project. Finally, they would like also to thank all the contributors and other external participants, without whom this project would not have been possible.

List of Abbreviations

ACP	Africa Caribbean Pacific group
ADB	Asian Development Bank
AfDB	African Development Bank
AMISOM	African Union Mission to Somalia
APEC	Asia-Pacific Economic Cooperation
APRM	African Peer Review Mechanism
ATT	Arms Trade Treaty
AU	African Union
CADFund	China-Africa Development Fund
CASS	Chinese Academy of Social Sciences
CCP	Chinese Communist Party
CDB	Chinese Development Bank
CEIEC	China National Electronics Import-Export Corporation
CMF	Combined Maritime Forces
CMT	Chinese Medical Teams
CNOOC	Chinese National Offshore Oil Company
CNPC	China National Petroleum Corporation
COMESA	Common Market for Eastern and Southern African States
CPA	Comprehensive Peace Agreement
CREC	China Railway Engineering Corporation
CRI	China Radio International
CSCEC	China State Construction Engineering Corporation
CSDP	Common Security and Defence Policy
CSR	Corporate Social Responsibility
DAC	Development Assistance Committee
DRC	Democratic Republic of Congo
EAC	East African Community
ECCAS	Economic Community of Central African States
ECOWAS	Economic Community Of West African States
EDF	European Development Fund
EEC	European Economic Community
EITI	Extractive Industry Transparency Initiative
EPA	Economic Partnership Agreement
EPZ	Export Processing Zones
ESDP	European Security and Defence Policy
ETC	Economic and Technical Cooperation
EU	European Union

EUTM	European Union Training Mission
EXIM	Export-Import Bank of China
FARDC	Forces Armées de la République Démocratique du Congo
FDI	Foreign Direct Investment
FDLR	Democratic Forces for the Liberation of Rwanda
FOCAC	Forum On China-Africa Cooperation
G2	Group of Two
G20	Group of Twenty
GDP	Gross Domestic Product
HIPC	Highly Indebted Poor Country
ICBC	Industrial and Commercial Bank of China
ICC	International Criminal Court
ICCPR	International Covenant on Civil and Political Rights
ICESCR	International Covenant on Economic, Social and Cultural Rights
ICISS	International Commission on Intervention and State Sovereignty
ICMM	International Council on Mining and Metals
ICT	Information and Communication Technology
IDP	Internationally Displaced Persons
IMB	International Maritime Bureau
IMF	International Monetary Fund
IMO	International Maritime Organization
IRTC	Internationally Recommended Transit Corridor
JAES	Joint Africa-EU Strategy
MBA	Master of Business Administration
MDG	Millennium Development Goals
MENA	Middle East and North Africa
MEND	Movement for the Emancipation of the Niger Delta
MFEZ	Multi-Facility Export Zone
MOFCOM	Ministry of Commerce
MONUC	United Nations Organization Mission in the Democratic Republic of Congo
MONUSCO	United Nations Organization Stabilization Mission in the Democratic Republic of Congo
MRAG	Marine Resources Assessment Group
NATO	North Atlantic Treaty Organization
NAVCO	Naval Coordination
NAVFOR	Naval Force
NBF	NEPAD Business Foundation
NCP	National Congress Party
NEPAD	New Partnership for African Development
NGO	Non-Governmental Organization
NPC	National People's Congress

OAU	Organization of African Unity
ODA	Official Development Aid
OECD	Organization for Economic Cooperation and Development
PLA	People's Liberation Army
PLAN	People's Liberation Army Navy
PoA	Programme of Action
PPI	Private Participation in Infrastructure
PPIAF	Public Private Infrastructure Advisory Facility
PRC	People's Republic of China
R2P	Responsibility to Protect
RECSA	Regional Centre on Small Arms
RMB	Renminbi
ROC	Republic of China
SADC	South African Development Community
SALW	Small Arms and Light Weapons
SEZ	Special Economic Zones
SOE	State-Owned Enterprise
SPLM	Sudan Peoples' Liberation Movement
SSA	Sub-Saharan Africa
STP	São Tomé and Principe
TAZARA	Tanzania-Zambia Railway
TFG	Transitional Federal Government
UK	United Kingdom
UN	United Nations
UNAMID	United Nations-African Union Hybrid Operation
UNCTAD	United Nations Conference on Trade And Development
UNDP	United Nations Development Programme
UNICEF	United Nations International Children's Emergency Fund
UNSC	United Nations Security Council
US	United States
USSR	Union of Soviet Socialist Republics
WFP	World Food Programme
WHO	World Health Organization
WTO	World Trade Organization
ZTE	Zhongxing Telecom

OAU	Organization of African Unity
ODA	Official Development Aid
OECD	Organization for Economic Cooperation and Development
PLA	People's Liberation Army
PLAN	People's Liberation Army Navy
PoA	Programme of Action
PPI	Private Participation in Infrastructure
PPIAF	Public Private Infrastructure Advisory Facility
PRC	People's Republic of China
R2P	Responsibility to Protect
RECSA	Regional Centre on Small Arms
RMB	Renminbi
ROC	Republic of China
SADC	South African Development Community
SALW	Small Arms and Light Weapons
SEZ	Special Economic Zones
SOE	State-Owned Enterprises
SPLM	Sudan People's Liberation Movement
SSA	Sub-Saharan Africa
STP	Sao Tome and Principe
TAZARA	Tanzania-Zambia Railway
TFG	Transitional Federal Government
UK	United Kingdom
UN	United Nations
UNAMID	United Nations-African Union Hybrid Operation
UNCTAD	United Nations Conference on Trade And Development
UNDP	United Nations Development Programme
UNICEF	United Nations International Children's Emergency Fund
UNSC	United Nations Security Council
US	United States
USSR	Union of Soviet Socialist Republics
WFP	World Food Programme
WHO	World Health Organization
WTO	World Trade Organization
ZTE	Zhongxing Telecom

Introduction
China and the EU in Africa: Changing Concepts and Changing Policies

Jing Men and Benjamin Barton

China's rise on the international scene over the past few years has correlated with its exponential economic growth. This economic growth has acted as a double edged-sword: China has simultaneously become a possible model for developing nations, whilst acting as a potential rival for developed countries, whether economically, politically or even from a security perspective. China's growth as an economic and political powerhouse is supported by the good relations that it maintains with other developing countries and notably those from the resource-rich African continent. China's 'new march' on Africa is attracting much international attention, criticized by some whilst applauded by others. No matter the criticism or praise, it is commonly recognized that China's increasing engagement in Africa has made a great impact on international politics and China's Africa policy has its own characteristics quite different from that of the West. This uniqueness has been analysed, criticized, extolled and questioned.

In effect, China's relations with Africa dates back to the 1950s, but of late the evolution of these relations has taken on a new dimension, which necessitates careful analysis. This is all the more important since Africa has always been considered as Europe's backyard, owing to former colonial ties and to current-day conditional relations. The European Union (EU), the world's largest development aid provider, has been feeling the heat of Beijing's closer ties with Africa, caused in part by the ineffectiveness of the EU's policy-orientation that is strongly focused on political conditionality. As a result, the EU's overall policy-making towards Africa has suffered from a loss of credibility and this has been further exposed both by the success of China's investments in Africa and by the favourable response that China's investment proposals have received from African leaders.

The EU's Africa Policy

Europe and Africa's bilateral relations represent one of the oldest diplomatic relations in the recorded history of global politics. As neighbouring continents, the two pertain to perhaps the most ambiguous and intertwining diplomatic relationship known to international relations. In effect, given their geographic proximity, their trade and cultural relations have always been strong – and at times, too strong, with many of the EU's older member states often involved in the murkier aspects of African politics. Due to the colonial legacies of many of these member states, relations between the two continents can be seen as a double-edged sword. On the one hand, certain EU member states have been accused of habitually involving themselves in the domestic politics of their former colonies, despite gaining their independence. As a result, the EU's policies have suffered due to this perpetual desire to rekindle political influence in sovereign nations, who were once under the tutelage of these former powers.

On the other hand, this colonial period forged links between the two continents that seem to persist until today. Whether voluntarily or not, relations between Africa and Europe are bound by an infinite, yet not immutable, political link. For the EU, the benefit of this legacy is understated: despite their complicated past, the EU and Africa need to preserve their bilateral relations, in a spirit of reciprocity. It is exactly this spirit which has permitted the EU to revamp the relationship and preserve a form of 'leadership' in terms of acting as Africa's most important exogenous partner. However, this link cannot, and should not, be taken for granted. The EU should indeed realize that the happenings on the African continent are symbolic of the shape that the world order will most probably take in the future. The next few years may be the most crucial ever witnessed between Africa and Europe.

As a separate *sui generis* entity, the EU has sought to distinguish itself from the legacies left by the former colonial powers, by approaching relations with the continent from an unbiased stance, because in itself, the EU and its institutions were not directly involved in the colonization and independence processes.[1] However, despite the EU's unique regional and institutional characteristics, it still remains organically intertwined with the member states and their international political baggage. This symbiotic relation between the member states and the Community was best illustrated during the negotiations on the Rome Treaties, in May 1956, where France demanded that its overseas territories be associated to the future Community (Frisch 2008: 2). This caused quite a stir amongst Germany and the Netherlands, whom were not as involved in African politics as France. Supported by Belgium, France purported a political compromise, by which the colonial powers would relinquish the exclusivity of trade relations with Africa, to the benefit of the Community. Furthermore, joint actions and financial burden-sharing, with regard to Africa's development, would become the order of the day (Djamson 1976: 3).

Although the positive intentions were prominent, the European Economic Community (EEC) was unable to rid itself of connotations to imperialism, most visible in the Community's association with France and Belgium's overseas territories (Bretherton, Vogler 2006: 113). Nonetheless, African states were seeking to preserve their privileged status *vis-à-vis* the Community and the Common

---

1   This, of course, ignores the fact that a country such as Algeria was a *de facto* integral part of the Community at its inception.

Market and this determination resulted in the Yaoundé Convention (1965–1970). The Convention's aim was to institutionalize this privileged access to the Common Market for these African states, by creating a zone of liberalized trade between the two, with commercial preferences extended to many African partners, in order to fasten their economic development (Frisch 2008: 4).

The Yaoundé Convention was hit by a multitude of teething problems, such as financial constraints with regard to development aid, a lack of economic incentives for the EEC member states and political questioning on behalf of the African partners, dissatisfied with the persistence of associationism (Djamson 1976: 4). By this stage, many of the African nations had either won or were fighting for their independence. Therefore, the context for negotiations were no longer as favourable to the EEC, but the realism of no longer dealing with associates, but rather with independent and sovereign nations, forced the hand of the EEC into a change of strategy.

Consequently, by 1975, the Lomé Convention was ratified by both parties, for a period of 5 years. The first major difference concerned the arrival of new actors on both sides of the negotiating table. In 1973, the United Kingdom (UK) had joined the Community and wished to integrate the Commonwealth states – many of which were located in Africa – into the framework. It was at this stage that these dealings became institutionalized: due to the initial desire of preserving its privileged economic relationship with the Community, African states established one of the first pan-African organizations (that included small nations from the Caribbean and the Pacific), entitled the ACP group (African Caribbean Pacific group).

In relation to Yaoundé, preferential market access was further accentuated, to the benefit of the ACP states and development aid was sharply increased. The term association was also dropped (Arts 2003: 128). It was at this stage that the EEC, via the initiatives of the European Commission, was seeking to solidify a European presence in the process so as to simultaneously separate the EEC from the colonial legacy of certain member states, whilst reinforcing the Community's unbiased approach (Frisch 2008: 20). To a certain extent, this explains the thrust of institutionalization visible on both sides, with joint-management and joint-institutions becoming the order of the day.[2] The Lomé Convention was thereafter renewed for three consecutive mandates, but by the time that Lomé III was underway, a change in the tide was impacting upon the Community's approach to its dealings with Africa (European Commission 2010).

With the influence of the neo-liberal wave felt in Western Europe during the late 1980s, the EEC shifted its priorities from a pure and untouched development-oriented strategy towards one focused on attributing resources in a more efficient and structured manner (Bretherton, Vogler 2006: 113). The neo-liberal influence was essentially attempting to redirect and specialize the EEC's funding but this principally entailed cutting back on bureaucratic influence and conditioning access

---

2   Interview with a British academic, Bruges, 2 September 2010.

to funds. This marked the inception of the EU's politically conditioned relationship with Africa – a feature that ever since has been the mainstay of EU-Africa relations. Therefore, in exchange for development aid and trade preferences, African 'recipients' were expected to manage the attributed resources and their political affairs according to standards set by the 'donor'. In this case, the Community was expecting for their African counterparts to develop market liberalization, improve their terms of good governance and accentuate their democratization processes (Bretherton, Vogler 2006: 113).

This incremental shift in attitude was gaining momentum from the 1980s onwards and it gained particular strength throughout the 1990s, with political and security goals slowly gaining ground (European Council 2005). This is perhaps best explained by the general failure of the Lomé and Yaoundé Conventions to pull Africa out of its economic and political misery. A new edge was thus needed so as to preserve the EEC's influence in African affairs. The Maastricht Treaty was not in any way designed to heed to the Union's faulting policies towards Africa, but it did set the legal basis for the Union's development cooperation by converting the latter into a shared competence, between the Community and the member states (Alden, Smith 2005: 5). The Treaty certified the newly-found political nature to the EU's distribution of development aid to Africa and introduced more security-induced instruments to the EU's development toolbox: crisis prevention, crisis management and a focus on security in Africa, as a precondition for development (Alden, Smith 2005: 5).

Poverty reduction, economic and social development or enhanced African integration into the global economy remained priorities, but with the slow demise of communist states in the Community's Eastern neighbourhood – around the time of the Maastricht negotiations – a fundamental policy shift was forced upon the Community. Africa was losing ground to the EU's neighbourhood. Sub-Saharan Africa, in particular, was no longer the unique priority in terms of the distribution of development aid (European Commission 2006). In reaction to the rapidly evolving political environment on the European continent, in the early to mid-1990s, the Union was obligated to respond to the needs of its new neighbours. Once it was agreed to enlarge the Union – by agreeing to the future adhesion of 12 new member states – the EU was tasked with contemplating relations with new neighbours. Most obvious, in this regard, was the Barcelona Process (1995), which institutionalized the EU's relations with North African countries, amongst others (Frisch 2008: 16).

In the year 2000, the final Lomé Convention was teetering towards expiry and a renewal of previous institutional arrangements was needed. It was only after the publication of a Commission Green Paper,[3] that the Cotonou Partnership Agreement set the basis for the EU's desire to boost relations with a group that held a significant place in its foreign policy objectives. Cotonou could no longer benefit from Lomé's informality and change beckoned, as Lomé's legacy was deemed out

---

3   Interview with a British academic, Bruges, 2 September 2010.

of synchronization with World Trade Organization (WTO) principles. It turned out that its unilateral trade preference were not legal according to world trade law. Cotonou's WTO waiver was thus only agreed as part of a package that would force the EU into commencing negotiations with Cotonou members on regional economic partnership agreements (EPAs), which thus far, have proved anything but successful.[4] The Cotonou Agreement further enhanced the dichotomy that had now come to dominate the EU's new approach towards the continent. On the one hand, poverty alleviation was justified as the rationale behind Cotonou, but on the other hand it was accompanied simultaneously by a more prominent demand for good governance, the promotion of democracy and the respect for the rule of law (Avafia 2004). Cotonou certified the EU's political conditionality by including the reciprocal essential and fundamental elements clause – African 'recipients' could no longer dodge political requirements, to the peril of facing potential sanctions (Avafia 2004).

The dynamism that led to Cotonou had not only originated from the EU's internal priority changes, but was also the result of exogenous influences. Firstly, throughout the late 1990s, more emphasis was being placed on helping developing countries overcome their enduring plight of poverty and the repercussions that ensue from living in underdeveloped conditions (Frisch 2008: 44–5). Alternatively, when the EU was poised to welcome its new neighbours, Africa was being partially sidelined. Other actors, most notably China, were quick to profit and the EU suddenly found itself under pressure and under fire in its own supposed 'comfort zone' (Grimm, Makhan 2010). Cotonou also acted as an initial reaction but the context in which its bilateral relations with African states were being held had experienced a fundamental shift, with the emergence of new competitors combined with Africa's political receptiveness to change.

Indeed, the Commission was not blind to these developments and it was quick to muster support from the other EU institutions, in order to provide a reaction.[5] Hence, the EU launched, in 2005, its *EU Strategy for Africa: Towards a Euro-African Pact to Accelerate Africa's Development*, with a markedly changed tone, focusing on mutually beneficial and equal relations. This sudden change of tone represented the greatest indicator that the new competitors on the African continent, and most notably China, were becoming a powerful variable in the EU's decision-making process towards the African continent. In order to further consolidate this approach, two years later, this strategy was followed by a similar agreement in the form of the *Joint Africa-EU Strategy* (JAES). The revamped EU approach became obvious: it shifted its rhetoric towards running the show as partners on equal footing and recognizing Africa as an integral part of the international community, similar to Chinese political rhetoric in Africa (European Union 2007: 2).

---

4   Interview with a British academic, Bruges, 2 September 2010.

5   It can also be envisaged that this reaction served as a timely wake-up call to the Union as a whole.

50 years ago, this type of change in the dynamics of EU-Africa relations would have been unconceivable, but perhaps now more than ever, relations between the two have reached a primordial stage. During the majority of this bilateral relationship, the asymmetry has always favoured the EU, whether in terms of economic or political relations (such as the EU's ability to dictate terms with regards to the Common Agricultural Policy) (Bretherton, Vogler 2006: 125), despite the EU's *sui generis* attempt to undertake business with African partners in an unbiased manner. However, this asymmetry has slowly undermined EU-Africa relations due to the EU's attention being called elsewhere. Africa lost its edge in terms of EU foreign policy, to the benefit of alternative development partners.

These happenings have culminated to the point where it is felt among academic and policy-making circles that the EU is slowly losing its 'leadership' role in Africa (Frisch 2008: 46). It is obvious that the EU's future African strategy will probably be more groundbreaking than ever – in other words, the EU can no longer devise independent and unilateral policies for Africa, if it is to achieve its goal of helping the continent develop. In a sense, the arrival of new competitors on the African continent may yet be held as a blessing for the EU and for its institutions. With the arrival of strong variables such as China, the EU has the opportunity to formulate promises alongside its African partners and then to stick by them. In effect, the EU possesses the capacity to turn its political influence into tangible results with regard to Africa's development. In order for this capacity to produce these tangible results, the EU needs to regain the confidence of the African political elite, by considering its African neighbours as sovereign partners first and foremost. In any case, the EU may no longer hold its destiny in Africa and may be soon forced to ditch the status quo which has haunted its past activities on the African continent.

China's Africa Policy

The People's Republic of China's (PRC) contact with Africa dates back to the mid-1950s. In order to get wide international recognition, Beijing attached great importance to its relations with the developing world. In 1955, the Bandung Conference created an opportunity for the Chinese leadership to meet African leaders. Initiated by the diplomatic relationship established between China and Egypt in 1956, China's Africa policy was developed alongside Africa's anti-colonial struggle in the 1950s and the 1960s, as well as the confrontation between the socialist and the capitalist camps. By emphasizing shared colonial experience and by cultivating a brotherly relationship with Africans nations, the PRC was successful in enlisting support from African countries in order to join the United Nations (UN) in 1971. By focusing on brotherhood and friendship in bilateral relations with African countries, China engaged with Africa politically to support national independence movements, anti-imperialism and the establishment of a new international economic order. Despite the fact that China was a poor country, it was generous in economic assistance to Africa. In order to promote a strong political relationship with African countries, China did not calculate its own economic gains (Men 2010: 125–44). This relationship experienced some changes at the end of the 1970s, when China readjusted its national objectives and made economic prosperity its paramount objective. The changes in domestic policy in China have a direct impact on its foreign policy-making. As a consequence of China's rapid economic development, economic and trade relations between the two sides have become as equally important as political relations. Particularly since the 1990s, when China changed from being an energy exporter to an energy importer, its economic relationship with Africa gained strategic significance in China's external relations. In China's Africa policy, emphasis has switched from paying scant attention to economic cost to emphasizing economic benefits. In other words, China adjusted itself from being Africa's friend to being Africa's partner. As friends, there could be no calculation on economic returns; but as partners, both sides should benefit from cooperation.

When the late Premier Zhou Enlai paid his first visit to Africa between 1963 and 1964, he put forward five principles guiding China's relations with Arab and African countries and eight principles with respect to the distribution of China's foreign aid. These principles became the guiding principles for China in handling its relations with African countries for several decades. Among these principles, China emphasized respect for sovereignty and non-interference, pledged to try its best to help recipient countries and pointed out that experts dispatched by China will have the same standard of living as the experts of the recipient country (China. org.cn 2003). At the end of 1982, Zhao Ziyang, the second Chinese Premier to visit Africa, reaffirmed to his African counterparts the continued importance of Africa to China, explained the reform and development of China to these countries and announced four new principles in China's cooperation with Africa which included 'equality and mutual benefit, pursuing practical result, adopting various ways and seeking common development' (Xinhua News Agency 2004). These principles emphasized common development and encouraged cooperative projects and joint-ventures. In contrast to the previous policy that took no consideration of cost and offered assistance for free, the new policy required strong economic results with less investment, shorter construction cycles and quicker returns with the purpose of enhancing the self-reliance capabilities of both China and Africa (World.people. com.cn 2006).

Since the 1990s, as a result of China's rapid economic growth and a rising need for raw materials and energy, economic and trade relations with Africa have been strengthened remarkably. China-Africa cooperation has been extended from the political field to a more comprehensive partnership with a greater emphasis on economic and trade relations. An important theme emerging in the reform era in China-Africa relations is common development. In his visit to Africa in May 1996, Chinese President Jiang Zemin made a speech at the headquarters of the Organization of African Unity, putting forth the five proposals of sincerity, friendship, equality, unity and cooperation, common development, and facing the future regarding Sino-African relations (Li 2003). In his speech at the

China-Africa summit in 2006, President Hu Jintao pointed out that China has never 'strayed from the principle of enhancing friendship, treating each other as equals, extending mutual support and promoting common development in building our ties' (Newsgd.com 2006).

Established in October 2000, the Forum on China-Africa Cooperation (FOCAC) marked the efforts of Beijing to institutionalize cooperation with Africa. The forum alternates between being held either in Beijing or in an African country and focuses on the issues of assistance, economic development, trade, investment and political partnerships. Under this framework, the Chinese and African delegations meet once every three years. China's *Africa Policy*, an official Chinese government paper, was released in January 2006, and aimed at promoting economic and political cooperation as well as joint energy development (Foreign Ministry of the People's Republic of China 2006). In the same year, the FOCAC summit was organized and 48 African countries sent 1,700 representatives to Beijing including 41 heads of state. Three years later, in November 2009, the fourth forum was held in Egypt to review the implementation of the Beijing summit consensus and to adopt an Action Plan for the coming years.

In the space of six decades, in the history of the PRC, Chinese foreign policy has witnessed a shift in stance from 'war and revolution' to 'peace and development'. China's Africa policy has been adjusted from focusing on political relations, backed by generous economic assistance to emphasizing both political and economic cooperation. Such changes are related to China's economic and reform policy, its de-emphasis of communist ideology, its revision of foreign policy towards pragmatism, its rapid economic growth and its increasing dependence on energy.

In China-Africa relations, the high-profile exchanges of visits have become a noticeable feature. After Premier Zhou Enlai's three visits to Africa, many Chinese leaders have been to Africa. In the 1980s, Chinese Premier Zhao Ziyang, Vice Premiers Huang Hua, Tian Jiyun and Li Peng, Chinese President Li Xiannian, and Chinese Foreign Minister Qian Qichen visited Africa. Since 1991, the first visit abroad of the Chinese Foreign Minister, each year, has always been to Africa (Tu 2008: 333). In the 1990s, apart from Qian Qichen, other Chinese leaders including the late Chinese President Yang Shangkun, Chinese President Jiang Zemin, Chinese Premier Li Peng, Vice Premiers Zhu Rongji and Li Lanqing, Chinese Foreign Minister Tang Jiaxuan visited African countries. In the twenty-first century, Chinese official visits to Africa have become even more frequent. Apart from the current Chinese Premier Wen Jiabao, Chinese Foreign Minister Li Zhaoxing and Chinese Vice President Zeng Qinghong, Hu Jintao has been to Africa six times, first as Chinese Vice President, then as Chinese President. Such high-level and frequent visits by Chinese leaders to Africa cannot be matched by any other country in the world. It indicates that China attaches great importance in pursuing good relations with the African continent. Chinese visits to Africa are reciprocated by African leaders. Since the late 1950s, more than 50 heads of state and over 20 heads of government have visited China, altogether more than 200 times (Tian 2005).

In the wake of the Tiananmen Incident in June 1989, many African countries supported Beijing's domestic policy. During that year, nine leaders from Sub-Saharan countries visited Beijing to express their support for the Chinese leadership. From 1990 to 2007 (except 1991), either an EU member states or the United States (US) had tried annually to introduce a resolution condemning China's human rights practices at the UN Commission on Human Rights meeting in Geneva. Such efforts failed during all these years due to the political support given to China by the developing world, which is composed of numerous African countries. In 2004, for example, the resolution criticizing China, submitted by countries led by the US, was opposed by 28 countries, including 14 African countries (Yang 2006: 6).

When China and Egypt established diplomatic relations in 1956, China-Africa trade amounted roughly to US$12 million. Around that time, certain European governments tried to 'strangle Egypt economically by drastically lowering the price of cotton in the international market'. As 75 percent of Egypt's export revenue came from cotton, Beijing's purchase of 15,000 tons of Egyptian cotton was strategically important to President Gamal Abdel Nasser (El-Khawas 1973: 24). In the 1960s, China bought a quarter of Tanzania's tobacco crop when the country had a huge surplus. It also purchased large quantities of coffee and chocolate from African countries, despite an absence of demand in China, for the purpose of having a more balanced trade with those countries (Segal 1992: 118).

In the reform era, Sino-African trade relations grew rapidly from US$817 million in 1979, to US$1,166.6 million in 1989, to reach US$6,480 million in 1999 (China.org.cn 2000). In the twenty-first century, bilateral trade soared from US$10 billion in 2000, to nearly US$40 billion in 2005 and reached a historic new level of US$106.8 billion in 2008 (Xinhua News Agency 2009). China's top five African trading partners for 2008 were Angola, which accounted for 24 percent of total trade; South Africa, for 17 percent; Sudan, for 8 percent; Nigeria, for 7 percent and Egypt, for 6 percent. Trade with these countries represents 62 percent of China's total trade with Africa (Trade Law Centre for Southern Africa 2009).

Africa's exports to China are composed mainly of petroleum, iron ore and timber, followed by manganese, cobalt, copper and chromium. Oil and natural resources are a major focus of Chinese investment in Africa. Yet, compared to OECD countries, China remains a relatively small player in Africa's oil sector. The energy consultancy, Wood Mackenzie, estimates that Chinese companies hold less than 2 percent of Africa's known oil reserves. Energy demand has significantly helped increase economic cooperation and trade relations between China and Africa. One-third of its oil is imported from Africa (Hanson 2008).

Nevertheless, China's economic ties with Africa are not confined to energy. China has a long history of committing itself to the construction of infrastructure. Between 2002 and 2005, US$9.4 million of Chinese investment and loans were devoted to the field of natural resources extraction/production, whereas US$17.9 million were put aside for the construction and development of African

infrastructure and public works (Lum et al. 2009: 8). According to Chinese Premier
Wen, in the past five decades, China has completed some 900 infrastructure
projects and projects for social development in Africa (Ministry of Foreign Affairs
of the People's Republic of China 2009).

With the title of *Bridges: China's Growing Role as Infrastructure Financier for
Sub-Saharan Africa*, this World Bank report intended to study important Chinese
financial contributions to African infrastructure, which is relatively unknown. The
report pointed out that China's demand for oil and mineral inputs, is matched
by Africa's supply of natural resources, whereas Africa's investment needs,
in its infrastructure, is matched by China's globally competitive construction
industries. Commenting on China-Africa trade, Vivien Foster, a leading World
Bank economist and a co-author of the report, stated that, 'the growing South-
South cooperation is driven by strong economic complementarity between China
and Africa' (Foster et al. 2008).

Since the 1990s, China's foreign aid to Africa has been steadily growing in the
form of government-sponsored investment, concessional loans, grants and debt
cancellation. Between 2002 and 2006, China's aid to Africa amounted to US$15.2
billion (Lum et al. 2009: 7). The most noticeable aid policy was announced by
Chinese President Hu Jintao at the China-Africa summit in November 2006,
where he pledged to double China's assistance to Africa by 2009, to provide
US$5 billion in loans and credits over three years and to create a US$5 billion
China-Africa development fund, to encourage Chinese companies' investments in
Africa. Apart from that, China would help train 15,000 Africans, send 100 senior
agricultural experts to Africa, build 30 hospitals and 30 malaria treatment centres,
provide Chinese-made anti-malaria drugs, send 300 youth workers to Africa, build
100 schools and increase scholarships for African students (Ministry of Foreign
Affairs of the People's Republic of China 2006). Reacting to Hu's announcement,
Mandisi Mahlwa, South Africa's Minister of Trade and Industry, was quoted as
saying at the forum:

> I believe China understands where we are coming from, as it has long been
> a supporter of our struggle for freedom. I believe China understands that we
> must redress the imbalances of our past through broad-based black economic
> empowerment and rapid skills development in order to be successful. I also
> believe that China is willing and able to assist us through investment, technology
> and skills transfer, and constructive partnership (Naidu, Mbazima 2008: 748).

One major problem in terms of Africa's economic development is the issue of
crippling levels of debt. In order to help the Africans out of poverty, at the first
FOCAC summit in October 2000, in Beijing, the Chinese government pledged to
write off the 156 overdue African debts, totalling US$1.3 billion, over two years,
which was fulfilled ahead of schedule (Yang 2007: 9). At the China-Africa summit
in November 2006, the Chinese government again pledged to waive the repayment
of interest-free loans amounting to more than US$1.3 billion, overdue by the end

of 2005 (He 2006). China offers hope to African economic development. In 2006, China pledged to more than double bilateral trade from US$40 billion in 2005 to US$100 billion by 2010. This goal was realized two years ahead of schedule. China also announced that the number of African exports subject to Chinese duty-free treatment would increase from 190 to 440. African countries were impressed by China's offer. A South African diplomat told IRIN, the humanitarian news and analysis service of the UN Office for the Coordination of Humanitarian Affairs: 'We are very excited about these offers – this means a lot for Africa. It will especially make a huge difference for the poorest countries in the region' (IRIN 2006).

Changes from Concepts to Reality

By developing and consolidating political and economic cooperation with Africa, China has become an influential actor in Africa. In its external relations, China adheres to the principle of non-interference. China's respect for sovereignty and territorial integrity resonates with most African leaders. In China's economic cooperation with African countries, no conditions are added concerning human rights and economic liberalization, which goes against the requirements of most Western countries and international financial organizations. This 'allows projects to be implemented quickly, with visible and often immediate results' (Cooke 2009: 27). In view of the Senegalese President, Abdoulaye Wade, 'China's approach to our needs is simply better adapted than the slow and sometimes patronizing post-colonial approach of European investors, donor organizations and non-governmental organizations. In fact, the Chinese model for stimulating rapid economic development has much to teach Africa' (Cooke 2009: 31). As Jennifer Cooke noted, China's economic engagement in Africa is regarded by Africans as 'more pragmatic and in line with African priorities' (Cooke 2009: 27).

China's approach to promoting economic development was branded by Joshua Cooper Ramo as the 'Beijing Consensus', in his 2004 publication. Since then, the 'Beijing Consensus' has been compared with the 'Washington Consensus'. The 'Washington Consensus' refers to neo-liberal design for economic and political development 'policed' through the International Monetary Fund (IMF), the World Bank and the WTO, with loan and grant conditionalities linked to democracy, good governance, decentralization, anti-corruption and transparency. For many African countries, Western interference is 'characterized by arrogance, failure, widening inequalities and a profound loss of sovereignty' (Mawdsley 2007: 413). In contrast, some contend that 'the Beijing Consensus offers hope for the world' (as quoted in Liang 2007: 141). As Liu Guijin, China's Ambassador to South Africa noted, China's rise will 'provide an alternative market, a new source of economic assistance and a new development approach' (as quoted in Liang 2007: 141). China's model serves as a credible alternative with regard to Africa's development and political economic reforms. Contrary to the interventionist approach promoted by the West in their relations with developing countries in general, the Chinese leadership does not want to oblige other countries to follow the Chinese model. As early as 1980, Deng Xiaoping stated, 'We should respect other parties and peoples in the search for solution to their own concerns. We resolutely object to others giving orders to us, we should neither give orders to others. This is an important principle' (Deng 1980). Beijing's emphasis on state sovereignty and non-interference earns respect from African leaders and elites who are reluctant to implement the economic or political reforms demanded by the West (Thompson 2005: 1).

China's approach is in conflict with the Western approach. The question is: between national sovereignty and human rights, which is more important? Should the international community interfere in the domestic affairs of those states which have human rights problems? Or should those states be left alone for their governments to maintain their absolute sovereign control? Such debates have been running on for some years, but there is no agreement between the two positions. Therefore, should China continue its non-interference policy in its cooperation with African countries? Or should China cooperate with the US and European countries, in order to promote good governance in Africa?

The largest Chinese investment in Africa is in Sudan, the government of which is widely condemned as responsible for genocide. Most recently, the International Criminal Court (ICC) issued a request for the indictment of Omar al-Bashir, Sudan's President. Based on the policy of non-interference and respect for sovereignty, China opposed the decision of the ICC together with a number of other African leaders, including Jean Ping, chair of the African Union Commission (Cooke 2009: 32). Although China's efforts in persuading Omar al-Bashir to accept the UN peacekeeping forces in Darfur were positively evaluated, China's economic activities are accused of indirectly worsening the humanitarian crisis in the country. Against this background, certain Europeans called for a boycott of the Beijing Olympic Games in 2008.

China's investments in Angola are confronted by a similar problem. The IMF intended to exert pressure on Angola for reforms in transparency and governance with conditions attached to its loans. China's EXIM (Export Import) Bank first offered Angola US$2 billion in 2004 and then another US$2 billion in 2007 to fund reconstruction of its infrastructure. While China's assistance is extremely important to Angola's post-war reconstruction, China's relaxed loan policies have been questioned by the IMF.

Zimbabwean President Robert Mugabe is widely criticized for his abuses against opposition activists. Since the independence of Zimbabwe in 1980, Mr Mugabe has held office. His oppressive regime in Zimbabwe has faced rising opposition in the country and during the 2008 Presidential election, Mr Mugabe was behind Mr Tsvangirai in the first round polls. The US and European countries called for increased sanctions against the Mugabe regime, but China and Russia vetoed the sanctions at the UN Security Council. Currently, China has been criticized for its irresponsible attitude towards the human rights issue in Zimbabwe and also because of its arms sales to the regime.

Since 2001, Beijing has become involved in peacekeeping operations in Africa. In April 2003, about 175 Chinese solders and a medical team of 42 personnel were deployed to the Democratic Republic of Congo on a peacekeeping mission. In December 2003, 550 peacekeeping soldiers were sent to Liberia. By the first half of 2008, more than 10,000 Chinese peacekeepers had taken part in missions in countries including Congo, Libya, Lebanon and Sudan (China Daily 2008). To date, China has sent five groups of peacekeepers to Sudan. The first group was sent in May 2006, to join the UN's peacekeeping efforts in the war-torn region of Darfur. More recently, a Chinese warship has been deployed to patrol the waters off the Somali coast, so as to help combat piracy.

The review of China's Africa policy in the past decades and its differences from the prevalent Western norms and values, indicate the changes and continuities in the understanding of some key political concepts in the field of international relations. The concept of sovereignty was developed in the seventeenth century as a consequence of the emergence of modern states in Europe. Between 1648 – when the Peace of Westphalia was signed – and 1948, when the Universal Declaration of Human rights was adopted, the world experienced great changes. In 1648, the great powers in Europe agreed among themselves that sovereignty should be respected. Territorial integrity and non-intervention have then since been maintained as the two basic norms of sovereignty: 'Existing states, as sovereign members of the decentralized, state-centric international community, are entitled to recognition and respect and to the right of political autonomy [...]' (Amstutz 2005: 129). Thanks to the Peace of Westphalia, states are understood as legally equal entities which work to maintain international peace, via a range of widely accepted treaties, agreements, conventions and declarations.

State sovereignty and human rights are considered as two fundamental values in international relations. Traditionally, the state is regarded as the basic unit of international relations. Against the anarchical international system, the 'defining feature of the state is sovereignty, its absolute and unrestricted power' (Amstutz 2005: 76). Anarchy obliges each state to take care of its own national security and property. Without world government, it is difficult for states to give much concern to the rights of individuals, when faced with intense national competition from others (Hoffman 1981). Imbued with high autonomy, states are supposed to respect each other's independence (Jackson, Sorensen 2006: 133).

While the Treaty of Westphalia set principles for states to act in international relations, states have responsibilities to protect the basic rights of its people and to allow individuals to enjoy freedom within legal boundaries. International relations are ultimately relations between human beings. Human rights impose limitations on the scope of authority a state can exercise over its citizens (Krasner 1995: 140). States, which are considered as internationally legitimate, may not be necessarily domestically legitimate. McMahan proposed two criteria for domestic legitimacy: a state should be a representative of the political community or communities, within its territorial boundaries; it should enjoy the support and approval of the mass of its citizens (McMahan 1987: 85). In today's world, the rights of human beings in each individual state are given increasing concern as a result of globalization and growing interdependence between states.

Following the line of the UN, human rights can be distinguished between civil and political rights, and economic and social rights. The Universal Declaration on Human Rights expressed a liberal ideal of human rights where the individual is the basic unit, whereas the state should be the result of the creation of its citizens. However, liberalism is not the only contemporary conception of human rights. Debates on human rights between the liberal-minded market economy states and most of the Third World states have been ongoing for decades. In the first two decades following the foundation of the UN, debates focused overwhelmingly on civil and political rights. As a consequence of the independence of a large number of former European colonies, the Third World states secured a majority in the UN which diverted the discussion more towards the economic and cultural rights. Against such a background, the UN General Assembly passed a resolution, in 1977, stating that it was impossible to have political and civil rights without providing for economic, social and cultural rights first (Krasner 1995: 162–4).

Noticeably, there is a tendency that human rights are becoming internationalized. Based on the Universal Declaration of Human Rights, both the UN treaties including the International Covenant on Civil and Political Rights (ICCPR) and the International Covenant on Economic, Social and Cultural Rights (ICESCR) were created in 1966 and entered into force in 1976. The issue of human rights is 'no longer a matter always or necessarily within the state's domestic jurisdiction' (Forsythe 2000: 4). Attention to human rights seems to have become part of international governance (Forsythe 2000: 5). The violation of human rights is often criticized worldwide. States are requested to be responsible for the treatment of their citizens.

The concept of sovereignty was only introduced to China after Western colonial powers established their concession areas in Chinese territory. Against the background of revitalizing the nation against Western colonization and exploitation, the Chinese always put sovereign rights ahead of human rights. State sovereignty and national security are always listed on top of its national interest. Accustomed to defending sovereignty and group rights, the Chinese government was not prepared for the Western attack on its human rights record in the post-Cold War era. It took some time for Beijing to develop a human rights policy as part of its foreign policy. Apart from its dialogue with major Western countries on the issue of human rights and active efforts in the UN to block the resolutions criticizing China, the Chinese government has since 1991, published about 70 white papers, with a majority of them on human rights. The two most important UN human rights documents, the ICESCR and the ICCPR, have been respectively signed by China, in 1997 and 1998. China ratified the ICESCR in 2003.

Together with its developing human rights policy, China has also been more active in international intervention. While sovereignty stays as the top national interest and non-interference is held as the basic principle in its foreign policy, China quietly changed from strongly opposing intervention organized by the

West, to supporting and participating in such activities, as long as it perceived them as legitimate according to international rules and law. When the report on the Responsibility to Protect (R2P) principle was published by the International Commission on Intervention and State Sovereignty, in 2001, China was suspicious and 'worried that this concept would be used to justify unwarranted military intervention by the United States or some European powers' (Pang 2008), but it gradually changed its attitude. As a rising power and serious international player, China should accept and perform its international responsibility for peace and security. Therefore, in both 2005 and 2006, China endorsed the R2P principle at the UN, once at the World Summit, and also in Security Council Resolution 1674. Since then, China has demonstrated clarity in its support for the R2P principle (Teitt 2008: 2). Nevertheless, such support is not without condition: China maintains that such R2P actions should be fully backed by relevant regional organizations or states. This attitude is based on China's emphasis on sovereignty in international relations, but somehow there have been quiet yet noticeable moves towards increased Chinese participation in international interventions. China's peacekeeping mission in Sudan, for example, was only dispatched after approval from the Sudanese government. China's changing attitude demonstrates the evolution of the concepts of sovereignty, human rights and non-interference which reveals the new interesting development of these concepts and the process of bringing them into practice.

Organization of the Book

Following the changing policies of both the EU and China in Africa, it is essential to understand how these changes would affect Africa's development. This book will serve that purpose by not only further examining China's rising influence in Africa, but also by analysing if and how the EU should adapt to the impact of China's rising influence. This book will offer an innovative framework for research by focusing on the changes brought by China to Africa and the ensuing reactions that have emerged in the EU, in terms of security issues, humanitarian intervention, evolving norms and models of social and economic development – areas where limited research has been accomplished thus far. The book is divided into five parts, which bring to the fore relatively new areas of study. The first part of the book takes an integrated approach to conceptualizing how China's 'march' on Africa is perceived primarily from a Chinese perspective. The articles are all written by Chinese scholars, but their individual analysis raises interesting questions because they take into consideration how Western pressure affects the Chinese perception of the Middle Kingdom's growing implication in Africa.

Part II provides an interesting account of the recent military cooperation between the EU and China, on two very specific case studies: maritime cooperation in the fight against piracy off the coast of Somalia and collaboration in the fight against the proliferation of Small Arms and Light Weapons (SALW). These constitute state of the art research areas, as there have been no published studies, of yet, on the cooperation and competition between the EU and China in their first respective overseas naval missions or with regard to SALW policies promoted in Africa.

The third part of the book will be dedicated to the underlying competitiveness that exists between the EU and China in relation to their respective normative power aspirations. It will provide specific case studies that relate to the normative evolutions in terms of human rights, national sovereignty and the responsibility to protect (R2P principle). Debates on human rights between China and the EU have lasted for several decades. The interesting feature of this part concerns the fact that these chapters link the human rights issue to China's principle of non-interference and then studies how China's adherence to non-interference and absolute state sovereignty are evolving, towards a more limited approach to sovereignty and humanitarian intervention. Under pressure, China would like to present a positive international image, as a responsible power.

Part IV will concentrate on economic development in Africa and the competition between China and the EU on development aid distribution to Africa. The research on the strong correlation between China's economic growth and Africa's economic growth should convince readers that the most important question concerning China's rising influence in Africa is not to ask whether China affects African development but how China affects such development and with which means sustainable development can be maintained in Africa. Development aid is indispensable to African development. However, whether Chinese concessional loans or European conditional aid is more appropriate to African development is worthy of analysis. This section will thus further examine whether China and the EU are purely competitors in terms of African development or whether they can actually establish cooperation to jointly finance development projects in Africa.

The last part of the book will outline the future for cooperation or competition between the EU and China in Africa and will take a look at how future relations between the three actors might pan out. The chapters will analyse concrete examples of how cooperation should be established, by providing policy proposals and by simultaneously exposing the various obstacles that currently form stumbling blocks to relations between the three.

All in all, this book offers a comprehensive overview of the interaction that takes place between the three actors, in the framework of the evolving international political system. It is not a study of the EU, China or Africa's respective policies, but an analysis of how the interaction between the three holds the key to solving one of the world's most challenging issues. The study of this book brings to light the necessity for all three actors to understand how important their interactions are in Africa and how this will affect their bilateral and trilateral relations. There is a need for the three not only to talk about each other, but also to talk to/at each other. This book serves as a solid platform upon which all the major points of accord/discord are examined. Each chapter of this book will increase the mutual understanding between the three, which in turn, will reduce the countercyclical policies conducive to developing a truly win-win-win situation.

Bibliography

Book References

Amstutz, M.R. 2005. *International Ethic: Concepts, Theories, and Cases in Global Politics*. Lanham: Rowman and Littlefield Publishers.

Bretherton, C. and Vogler, J. 2006. *The European Union as a Global Actor*. Volume 2. Oxon: Routledge.

Djamson, E.C. 1976. *Dynamics of Euro-African Co-operation: An Analysis and Exposition of Institutional, Legal and Socio-Economic Aspects of Association/ Co-operation with the European Economic Community*. The Hague: Martinus Nijhoff.

Forsythe, D.P. 2000. *Human Rights in International Relations*. Cambridge: Cambridge University Press.

Hoebink, P. and Stokke, O. 2005. *Perspectives on European Development Cooperation*. London: Routledge.

Hoffman, S. 1981. *Duties Beyond Borders: On the Limits and Possibilities of Ethical International Politics*. Syracuse: Syracuse University Press.

Jackson, R. and Sorensen, G. 2006. *Introduction to International Relations: Theories and Approaches*. New York: Oxford University Press.

Liang, J. 2007. *What Drives China's Growing Role in Africa?*. Washington, D.C.: International Monetary Fund.

Ramo, J.C. 2004. *The Beijing Consensus*. London: The Foreign Policy Centre.

Sutton, M. 2007. *France and the Construction of Europe, 1944-2007: The Geopolitical Imperative*. New York and Oxford: Berghahn.

Book Chapters

Alden, C. and Smith, K.E. 2005. Strengthening democratic structures and process in Africa: a commentary on the role of the European Union, in *Os Desafios das Relaçoes Europa-Africa: Uma Agenda de Prioridades* (*The Challenge of Europe-Africa Relations: An Agenda of Priorities*), edited by the Instituto de Estudos Estrategicos Internacionais. Lisbon: IEEI, 83–90.

Cooke, J.G. 2009. China's soft power in Africa, in *Chinese Soft Power and Its Implications for the United States: Competition and Cooperation in the Developing World*, edited by C. McGiffert. Washington, D.C: Centre for Strategic and International Studies, 27–44.

Krasner, S.D. 1995. Sovereignty, regimes, and human rights, in *Regime Theory and International Relations*, edited by V. Rittberger and P. Mayer. Oxford: Oxford University Press, 139–67.

McMahan, J. 1987. The ethics of international intervention, in *Political Realism and International Morality: Ethics in the Nuclear Age*, edited by K. Kipnis and D.T. Meyers. Boulder: Westview Press, 75–101.

Men, J. 2010. China and Africa: old friends, new partners, in *Dancing with the Dragon: China's Emergence in the Developing World*, edited by D. Hickey and B. Guo. Lanham: Rowman and Littlefield-Lexington, 125–44.

Yang, F. 2006. Fayang Zhongfei chuantong youyi zaizhu huihuang (Giving full play to the traditional China-Africa friendship to bring it to a new high), in *Tongxin ruojin: Zhongfei youhao guanxi de huihuang licheng (Golden Friendship: A Review of China-Africa Friendly Relations)*, edited by M. Lu et al. Beijing: World Affairs Publishing House, 3–7.

Journal Articles

Arts, K. 2003. ACP-EU relations in a new era: the Cotonou Agreement. *Common Market Law Review*, 40(1), 95–116.

Avafia, T. 2004. Political conditions in the Cotonou Agreement: economic and legal implications. *Nepru Working Paper*, 93, 1–13.

El-Khawas, M.A. 1973. China's changing policies in Africa. *Issue: A Journal of Opinion*, 3(1), 24–28.

Mawdsley, E. 2007. China and Africa: emerging challenges to the geographies of power. *Geography Compass*, 1(3), 405–21.

Naidu, S. and Mbazima, D. 2008. China-African relations: a new impulse in a changing continental landscape. *Futures*, 40(8), 748–61.

Segal, G. 1992. China and Africa. *The Annals of the American Academy of Political and Social Science*, 519(1), 115–26.

Thompson, D. 2005. China's soft power in Africa: from the 'Beijing Consensus' to health diplomacy. *China Brief*, 5(21), 1–5.

Tu, J. 2008. Sino-African relations: historical development and long-term challenge. *China: An International Journal*, 6(2), 330–43.

Wei, L. 2007. China: globalization and the emergence of a new status quo power?. *Asian Perspective*, 31(4), 125–49.

Websites

allAfrica.com. 2008. *Africa: export to China rises to US$22 billion, says report*. [Online]. Available at: http://allafrica.com/stories/200807140914.html [accessed: 9 September 2009].

China Daily. 2008. *China's UN peacekeepers exceed 10,000 in Sudan*. [Online]. Available at: http://www.chinadaily.com.cn/china/2008-06/30/content_6807441. htm [accessed: 10 September 2009].

China.org.cn. 2003. *Chinese leaders on Sino-African relations*. [Online]. Available at: http://www.china.org.cn/english/features/China-Africa/82054. htm [accessed: 22 August 2009].

China.org.cn. 2005. *50 years of Sino-African friendly relations*. [Online]. Available at: http://www.china.org.cn/english/2000/Oct/2547.htm [accessed: 23 August 2009].

European Commission. 2006. *EU donor atlas 2006 volume I*. [Online]. Available at: http://ec.europa.eu/development/body/publications/docs/eu_donor_atlas_ 2006.pdf [accessed: 22 September 2010].

European Commission. 2010. *The Lomé Convention*. [Online]. Available at: http:// ec.europa.eu/development/geographical/cotonou/lomegen/lomeitoiv_en.cfm [accessed: 9 September 2010].

Foster, V., Butterfield, W., Chen, C. and Pushak, N. 2008. *Building bridges: China's growing role as infrastructure financier for Sub-Saharan Africa*. [Online]. Available at: http://siteresources.worldbank.org/INTAFRICA/Resources/ Building_Bridges_Master_Version_wo-Embg_with_cover.pdf [accessed: 26 August 2010].

Frisch, D. 2009. *The European Union's development policy: a personal view of 50 years of international cooperation*. [Online]. Available at: http://www.ecdpm.org/Web_ECDPM/Web/Content/Download.nsf/0/ E745463054C3EC41C12574D00048D329/$FILE/PMR15eng%20Final%20n ew%20version%20nov%2008.pd [accessed: 9 September 2010].

Grimm, S. and Makhran, D. 2010. *Opinion: revising the Cotounou Agreement – Nothing new?*. [Online]. Available at: http://www.dw-world.de/dw/ article/0,,5755848,00.html [accessed: 9 September 2010].

Hanson, S. 2008. *China, Africa and oil*. [Online]. Available at: http://www.cfr. org/publication/9557/ [accessed: 13 August 2009].

He, W. 2006. *China's loans to Africa won't cause debt crisis*. [Online]. Available at: http://www.chinadaily.com.cn/opinion/2007-06/06/content_888060.htm [accessed: 13 August 2009].

IRIN. 2006. *China to double aid to Africa*. [Online]. Available at: http://www. worldpress.org/africa/2554.cfm [accessed: 13 August 2009].

Li, Z. 2003. *Forging a new chapter in Sino-African friendship and cooperation*. [Online]. Available at: http://www.china.org.cn/english/features/China-Africa/82204.htm [accessed: 23 August 2009].

Lum, T., Fischer, H., Gomez-Granger, J. and Leland, A. 2009. *China's foreign aid activities in Africa, Latin America, and Southeast Asia*. [Online]. Available at: http://www.fas.org/sgp/crs/row/R40361.pdf [accessed: 24 March 2010].

Ministry of Foreign Affairs of the People's Republic of China. 2006. *Beijing summit opens as China pledges package of aid to Africa*. [Online]. Available at: http://www.fmprc.gov.cn/zflt/eng/tptb/t404219.htm [accessed: 23 August 2009].

Ministry of Foreign Affairs of the People's Republic of China. 2006. *Transcript of Premier Wen Jiabao's press conference in Cairo*. [Online]. Available at: http:// www.mfa.gov.cn/eng/wjb/zzjg/xybfs/gjlb/2813/2815/t258665.htm [accessed: 21 August 2009].

Newsgd.com. 2006. *President Hu Jintao delivers speech at China-Africa summit*. [Online]. Available at: http://www.newsgd.com/news/chinakeyword/ focac/200611040019.htm [accessed: 20 August 2009].

Pang, Z. 2008. *Playing by 'the rules' is China a partner or ward?.* [Online]. Available at: http://www.spiegel.de/international/world/0,1518,584758,00 [accessed: 11 July 2009].

Teitt, S. 2008. *China and the responsibility to protect.* [Online]. Available at: http://www.responsibilitytoprotect.org/files/China_and_R2P%5B1%5D.pdf [accessed: 11 July 2009].

Tian, P. 2005. *China and Africa in a new period.* [Online]. Available at: http://www.cpifa.org/en/Html/2005121145747-1.html [accessed: 5 July 2009].

Trade Law Center for Southern Africa. 2009. *Africa-China trading relationship – Update 2009.* [Online]. Available at: http://www.tralac.org/cause_data/images/1694/Africa-China09.pdf [accessed: 5 July 2009].

World.people.com.cn. 2006. *Zhongguo tichu Zhongfei jingji jishu hezuo yuanze (China puts forward principles on economic and technology cooperation between China and Africa).* [Online]. Available at: http://world.people.com.cn/GB/8212/72927/73386/4988583.html [accessed: 11 July 2009].

Xinhua News Agency. 2004. *Zhongguo gongchandang dashiji 1982 (Big event of the Chinese Communist Party 1982).* [Online]. Available at: http://news.xinhuanet.com/ziliao/2004-10/15/content_2094021_3.htm [accessed: 6 July 2009].

Xinhua News Agency. 2009. *Chinese-African trade volume hits all time high to reach US$106.8 billion.* [Online]. Available at: http://news.xinhuanet.com/english/2009-01/19/content_10684845.htm [accessed: 3 June 2010].

Command Papers

The European Consensus on Development. 2005. Brussels: Council of the European Union.

The Joint Africa-EU Strategic Partnership. 2007. Brussels and Addis Ababa: European Union and the African Union.

PART I

PART I

Chapter 1
China's Design of Global Governance: The Role of Africa

Zhiyue Bo

Introduction

In the past six decades, China has been through three different stages in terms of its design of global governance. In the era of Mao Zedong, China was a revolutionary state. As a visionary revolutionary, Mao envisioned a world of three different forces. In his view, the most dangerous threat to China's security and world peace in general came from the competition between the two superpowers (the United States and the Soviet Union), consisting of the First World. Developing countries in Africa, Asia and Latin America belonged to the Third World, an important force against hegemonism. Japan, Canada, Australia and European countries constituted the Second World, an important ally for the Third World. African countries, in turn, represented important political allies for China, as they helped restore China's seat at the United Nations (UN).

In the era of Deng Xiaoping, China became a status quo state. Since economic development was the top priority for China, the country opened up to the West and accepted established international norms. African countries became less relevant in this context, and some often attempted to play off the People's Republic of China (PRC) against the Republic of China (ROC).

In the new century, China is becoming an active participant in international affairs and a responsible stakeholder. China is no longer a passive receiver of the international political and economic order but an active contributor to the emergence of a new world of peace, prosperity and harmony. Africa is again very important for China, not only as a source of natural resources but also as a comprehensive strategic partner.

Mao Zedong's Revolutionary World View

Mao Zedong, the founder of the PRC, was a visionary revolutionary. In the heydays of the Cultural Revolution, he envisioned a new world free of hegemonism and strived to be a leader in the fight against global hegemonism.

In the early years of the PRC, the Chinese leaders adopted a 'leaning-to-one-side' policy. China's friends were mostly communist countries. By April 1955,

China had established diplomatic relations with 23 countries. Among them, 12 were communist countries. Others included six European countries (Sweden, Denmark, Switzerland, Liechtenstein, Finland and Norway) and five Asian countries (India, Indonesia, Myanmar, Pakistan and Afghanistan) (Ministry of Foreign Affairs of the People's Republic of China 2008: 359–60). No African countries then held diplomatic relations with China. China was a junior partner of the Soviet Union and was willing to follow the lead of its elder brother on the international stage.

The Bandung Conference of April 1955 marked a turning point. China decided to participate in the conference to expand its united front. At the conference, Premier Zhou Enlai proclaimed a principle of '*qiu tong cun yi*' ('seeking commonalities and avoiding differences') that gained further respect for China from other Asian and African countries. As a result, China expanded its diplomatic relations with Asian and African countries. Between August 1955 and December 1964, China extended diplomatic relations to 27 countries, including seven Asian countries and 18 African countries (Ministry of Foreign Affairs of the People's Republic of China 2008: 360–2).

In particular, 1964 was coined the year of Africa. Premier Zhou Enlai made a historical visit to the continent from 13 December 1963 to 5 February 1964 (Qian, Wang 1999), where he visited ten countries, a record in the PRC's history. The countries he visited included Egypt, Algeria, Morocco, Tunisia, Ghana, Mali, Guinea, Sudan, Ethiopia and Somalia. In 1964, six African countries established diplomatic relations with China. They were Tunisia, the Republic of Congo, Tanzania, the Central African Republic, Zambia and Benin. Zhou Enlai visited Africa three more times in 1965 (Qian, Wang 1999).

African countries played a very important role in restoring the position of the PRC at the UN and at expelling the 'representatives of Chiang Kai-shek'. Among the 17 countries that requested on 15 July 1971 to discuss the question of the 'restoration of the lawful rights of the PRC to the UN', nine were from Africa. Among the 23 countries that submitted a draft resolution (A/L. 630 and Add. 1 and 2) on 25 September 1971, 11 were African countries (Qian, Wang 1999). Among the 76 countries that supported the adoption of A/L. 630 and Add. 1 and 2 as Resolution 2758 on 25 October 1971, 26 (more than one third of the total supporters) were from Africa (Qian, Wang 1999).

Following the PRC's entry to the UN, many more countries established diplomatic relations with the 'new China'. Within a period of two years (1971 and 1972), 38 countries established (or restored) diplomatic relations with the PRC.

Mao Zedong subsequently put forth a new theory of global governance in 1974. It was during his meeting with President Kenneth David Kaunda of Zambia on 22 February 1974 that Mao provided his classification of world countries into three categories, as previously observed. In April 1974, Deng Xiaoping announced this theory in his speech to the UN (Sun 1994).

Mao's theory of the three worlds, it should be noted, was not offensive but defensive. He was not seeking to create a new world of communism. He simply wanted to fend off the danger of hegemonism. The most serious danger in the world, in his view, was the competition between the two superpowers for world hegemonism. The primary task of the Third World countries, therefore, was to oppose hegemonism. In the global fight against hegemonism, the Third World countries (in particular African countries) were most important forces and the Second World countries were potential allies of the united front. As part of the Third World, it was deemed that China should work with other Third World countries against hegemonism.

In Mao's United Front against world hegemonism, the Soviet Union was singled out as the most serious danger to China's security and to world peace. Mao developed rapprochement with the United States, another superpower, and worked with it against the Soviet Union.

China Under Deng Xiaoping: From a Revolutionary State to a Status Quo State

China's world outlook experienced a fundamental shift under the leadership of Deng Xiaoping. Mao Zedong worried about an imminent war first with the United States and later with the Soviet Union. He relocated industries from coastal areas to inland areas in preparation for the worst outcome. For a period of 14 years, China invested RMB205.2 billion in the third front construction, involving 13 provinces and autonomous regions in the inland areas.[1]

After Deng Xiaoping returned to power again in 1977, he began to entertain the possibility of delaying the breakout of a major war. At a Plenary Meeting of the Military Commission of the Central Committee of the Chinese Communist Party (CCP) on 28 December 1977, Deng talked about the possibility of gaining 'some additional time free of war' (Deng 1977). In his view, prolonging the peace was possible for two reasons. On the one hand, China was a major force for peace; on the other hand, neither the Soviet Union nor the United States was ready to start a world war.

One year later, in December 1978, the CCP leadership decided to shift its attention from politics to economic development at the CCP's Third Plenum of the Eleventh Central Committee. The Chinese central government subsequently took the decision in 1979 to establish four special economic zones along the coast: Shenzhen, Zhuhai, Shantou and Xiamen. Since China's economic development requires a peaceful international environment, promoting world peace became a top priority in China's foreign policy.

In 1980, Deng Xiaoping produced a list of three major tasks for China in the new decade. They were:

1. to oppose hegemonism and work to safeguard world peace
2. to strive for China's reunification and particularly for the return of Taiwan to the motherland

---

1   For further information, see http://baike.baidu.com/view/798186.htm.

3. to accelerate socialist modernization. The key, however, remaining
    economic development (Deng 1994b).

Economic development, as Deng clearly pointed out, is at the core of all these three
major tasks because it is the essential condition for solving China's domestic and
external problems. China's economic growth would substantially boost its capacity
in international affairs and would make the reunification with Taiwan easier. The
two tasks of opposing hegemonism and reunifying the country by achieving the
return of Taiwan to the motherland both required that China successfully managed
its economic development.

In 1982, he modified the order in which these three tasks were presented to
better reflect his priorities. In his opening speech to the Twelfth Party Congress on
1 September 1982, the three tasks were:

1. to accelerate socialist modernization
2. to strive for China's reunification and particularly for the return of Taiwan
    to the motherland
3. to oppose hegemonism and work to safeguard world peace (with economic
    development again remaining the key).

'It is the basis', in his words, 'for the solution of our external and internal problems'
(Deng 1982).

In this sense, it was imperative for China to subsist in a peaceful international
environment. In 1977, Deng Xiaoping believed that China could gain some
additional time (*duo yi dian shijian*) for its military modernization and estimated
it to be somewhere between ten and 20 years. In 1984, he hoped that there would
be longer-lasting peace for China's modernization drive and that China would
need another 30 to 50 years in the twenty-first century (Deng 1984).

Under this guiding principle, China developed its relations with major powers
in the world. China established diplomatic relations with the United States in 1979
and normalized its relations with the Soviet Union ten years later. China opened
its door to the West and began to embrace the established international norms,
becoming a status quo state instead of a revolutionary state.

In this context, African countries became important allies for safeguarding
world peace. High-level exchanges between China and African countries
accelerated in the 1980s. The visits by heads of state from African countries
increased from 33 times in the 1970s to 51 times in the 1980s. Chinese Premier
Zhao Ziyang visited 11 countries in Africa from 20 December 1982 to 17 January
1983. The countries he visited included Egypt, Algeria, Morocco, Guinea, Gabon,
Zaire (later the Democratic Republic of the Congo), the Republic of the Congo,
Zambia, Zimbabwe, Tanzania and Kenya (Qian, Wang 1999). During his trip,
Zhao stressed China's commonalities with African countries and downplayed the
role of ideology in China's interactions with them. China would no longer base its
relations with African countries on whether they were allies of the Soviet Union or

the United States. In 1986, President Li Xiannian visited three African countries, the first such trip in China's history. He visited Egypt, Somalia and Madagascar from 17 to 27 March 1986.

In the aftermath of the Tiananmen Incident, Western countries imposed diplomatic and economic sanctions against China. Yet, it was African countries that showed their support for China. After the Incident, the first visit by a Foreign Minister of a foreign country was from São Tomé and Príncipe, an African state. Premier Li Peng met this foreign minister in Beijing on 29 June 1989.[2] The first head of state was from Burkina Faso. The President of Burkina Faso, Blaise Compaoré and his wife visited China from 7 to 12 September 1989.[3] The first country the Chinese President visited in the aftermath of the Tiananmen Incident was also an African country. In his second trip abroad and first foreign trip after June 1989 as President of China, Yang Shangkun visited Egypt as his first stop in a four-country tour in December 1989 (Yang 2001).

Nonetheless, the 1990s witnessed the worst period in China-Africa relations. Out of the 13 countries that interrupted their diplomatic relations with the PRC in the decade, ten were African countries. They were Lesotho, Guinea Bissau, the Central African Republic, Niger, Burkina Faso, Gambia, Senegal, São Tomé and Príncipe, Chad and Liberia. Notably, both São Tomé and Príncipe and Burkina Faso switched allegiance to Taiwan. The Central African Republic and Liberia acted in similar fashion – both of them breaking their ties with the PRC twice. The Central African Republic had established diplomatic relations with the PRC on 29 September 1964 but cut its ties with the PRC on 6 January 1966. The two countries restored their relations on 20 August 1976. The Central African Republic broke its ties again with the PRC on 8 July 1991 and then restored its relations with the PRC again on 29 January 1998. Similarly, Liberia established diplomatic relations with the PRC on 17 February 1977 but interrupted its ties with China twice: once on 10 October 1989 and once on 9 September 1997. As the PRC and the ROC were competing to win their diplomatic support, these countries took full advantage of this situation for their own benefit.

In the 1990s, China's diplomatic efforts were, therefore, focused on Asian countries. China restored its ties with Indonesia and established diplomatic relations with Singapore in 1990; then established diplomatic relations with Brunei and South Korea in 1991 and 1992, respectively. In the meantime, China also re-established diplomatic relations with members of the former Soviet Union, members of the former Yugoslavia, and both the Czech Republic and Slovakia after the dissolution of Czechoslovakia.

---

2 São Tomé and Príncipe established diplomatic relations with the PRC on 12 July 1975, but unfortunately, it established diplomatic relations with the ROC on 6 May 1997. The PRC suspended its relations with the island country on the same day.

3 Burkina Faso established diplomatic relations with the PRC on 15 September 1973 but switched its diplomatic relations to the ROC on 2 February 1994. The PRC suspended its relations with the country two days later.

In the aftermath of the Tiananmen Incident, Deng Xiaoping's advice to the new leadership was to adopt a low profile and never take the lead in international affairs. He said,

> Some developing countries would like China to become the leader of the Third World. But we absolutely cannot do that – this is one of our basic state policies. We can't afford to do it and besides, we aren't strong enough. There is nothing to be gained by playing that role; we would only lose most of our initiative. China will always side with the Third World countries, but we shall never seek hegemony over them or serve as their leader (Deng 1989).

In his view, China should focus on its own economic development in the framework of a peaceful international environment and a stable domestic climate. Initially, the new leadership under Jiang Zemin failed to heed Deng Xiaoping's advice and did not promote reform and liberalization to the outside world. Deng then had to take dramatic measures by conducting a Southern tour to push for reform. Subsequent to Deng's Southern tour of 1992, China entered into a new era of rapid economic development.

As a result, China's Gross Domestic Product (GDP) increased from RMB2.2 billion in 1991 to RMB9.9 billion in 2000; and its GDP per capita rose from RMB1.9 to RMB7.9 billion in the same period. In constant prices, for the year 2000, China's GDP and GDP per capita were respectively 2.4 and 2.3 times those of its 1991 levels (China Statistical Yearbook 2007).

China in the Twenty-First Century: From a Status Quo State to a Responsible Stakeholder

China's world outlook experienced another fundamental shift in the new century. In his initial advice in the aftermath of the Tiananmen Incident, Deng Xiaoping also urged Chinese leaders to contribute to international affairs. He stated,

> Nevertheless, we cannot simply do anything in international affairs; we have to make our contribution. In what respect? I think we should help promote the establishment of a new international political and economic order. We do not fear anyone, but we should not give offence to anyone either. We should act in accordance with the Five Principles of Peaceful Coexistence and never deviate from them (Deng 1990).

After 15 years of negotiations, China was accepted to the World Trade Organization (WTO) in November 2001, representing the country's formal integration into the world economic system. China's economy has continued its rapid growth in the new century, and China's trade has also expanded substantially. After having taken over Germany as the third largest economy in the world in 2007, China overtook

Japan to become the second largest economy in 2010. China also replaced Germany as the largest exporter in the world in 2009 (CNN Asia 2009).

Moreover, China has accepted the suggestion made by then-United States' Deputy Secretary of State Robert Zoellick to become a responsible stakeholder in the international system along with the United States and other countries. China has now become an active participant in international affairs, making its own contribution to world peace and development according to its own conditions and abilities.

China has actively participated in activities of various international organizations and developed bilateral and multilateral relations with many countries in the world. China has been a major player in the Six-Party Talks on the nuclear issue concerning the Korean Peninsula; has worked with the United States and other countries over the Iran nuclear issue; and has been a contributor to UN peacekeeping forces around the world.

Most recently, China has worked with other members of the G20 in stabilizing the global economic environment and reforming the international financial system. China has also engaged with the United States, the European Union and Japan on climate change issues and committed to cut its carbon intensity by 40 to 45 percent by 2020, from its 2005 level.

In the eyes of Chinese leaders, although the world political and economic order is still dominated by the West, the emergence of major developing countries such as China and India is reshaping world governance. In this context, China should become an active participant in establishing a new world order, contributing to world economic development, world peace and taking responsibilities for dealing with global issues such as the financial crisis, climate change, food security, public health issues and natural disasters. In President Hu Jintao's terms, China should work with other countries to build a 'harmonious world', which requires countries of the world to promote political democratization in international relations; to promote economic globalization that is balanced and beneficial to all; to seek the resolution of international disputes through peaceful means and safeguard world peace; to work together to protect the earth – the common home of mankind (Zhang 2009).

From this perspective, China's relations with Africa have also changed significantly. China's new policies in Africa have followed its economic and political logic. Economically, China is looking for natural resources to satisfy its increasing demand. Politically, China wants to consolidate its traditional friendship with developing countries in Africa, as in other developing regions of the world.

Technically, Africa is not a single unit for China in terms of trade. A larger unit for China is Western Asia and Africa. In the Ministry of Commerce, there is a Department of Western Asian and African Affairs. Three divisions under the department deal with different parts of this unit: Division I works with countries in Western Asia and Northern Africa; Division II, countries in Central and Western Africa; and Division III, countries in Eastern and Southern Africa.

China's trade with African countries fluctuated in the early years but increased substantially in the past two decades. China's trade with all African countries was

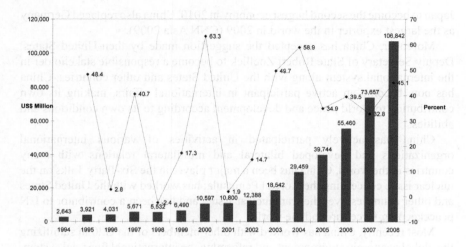

Figure 1.1   China's trade with Africa

Source: http://zhs.mofcom.gov.cn.

only US$12 million in 1950. Twenty years later, it increased to US$177 million. The bilateral trade declined in the 1980s. It went from US$960 million in 1980 to only US$935 million in 1990. However, bilateral trade increased in the 1990s and substantially expanded in the first decade of the twenty-first century.

China's trade with Africa increased more than 41 times from 1994 to 2008. The bilateral trade passed the ten billion mark in 2000, registering a total of US$10.6 billion. In 2000, trade between China and Africa jumped by 63.3 percent in comparison to 1999. From 2000 to 2008, China's trade with Africa increased another tenfold, reaching US$106.8 billion in 2008. For six consecutive years, from 2003 to 2008, China's trade with Africa expanded by more than 30 percent annually. Of course, China's trade with Africa is only a small fraction of China's total foreign trade. The former is only 4.2 percent of the latter, which totalled US$2.6 billion in 2008 (China Statistical Yearbook 2009).

China's trade with African countries as a whole is more or less balanced but its trade with individual countries tends to vary. China's total trade with Africa was US$106.8 billion in 2008, including US$56 billion in imports and US$50.8 billion in exports. China held a US$5.2 billion trade deficit with Africa in 2008 (China Statistical Yearbook 2009). Among its top ten trading partners in Africa, China had trade deficits with Angola, South Africa, Sudan, Congo, Libya and Equatorial Guinea; and trade surpluses with Nigeria, Egypt, Algeria and Morocco.

Angola is China's number one trading partner in Africa. In 2008, bilateral trade increased by 79.3 percent in comparison with 2007, reaching US$25.3 billion. Angola's trade surplus was US$19.5 billion because its exports to China equated to US$22.4 billion and its imports from China only represented US$2.9 billion

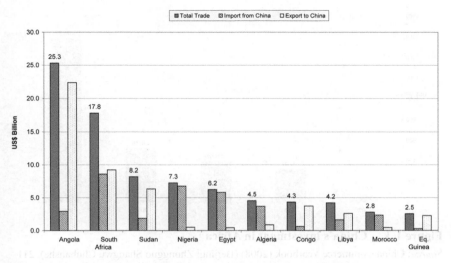

Figure 1.2   China's top ten trading partners in Africa (2008)

Source: http://zhs.mofcom.gov.cn.

(China Statistical Yearbook 2009). Angola was the second largest supplier of oil to China in 2008, providing 596,000 barrels per day to China (US Energy Information Administration 2009). In 2009, Saudi Arabia, Angola and Iran were the three largest oil sources for China, providing 41.9 million tonnes, 32.2 million tonnes and 23.2 million tonnes, respectively (CCPIT 2010). Angola replaced Saudi Arabia as China's most important crude oil supplier in the first half of 2010 (Peakoil.com 2010).

Sudan's trade with China follows a similar pattern. Sudan was China's third trading partner in Africa in 2008, with a total trade of US$8.2 billion. Sudan's trade surplus with China was US$4.5 billion with US$6.3 billion in exports to China and US$1.9 billion in imports from China. Sudan is also a major supplier of oil for China (China Statistical Yearbook 2009).

Similarly, RD Congo, Libya and Equatorial Guinea also enjoyed trade surpluses with China because of their oil supplies. In 2008, RD Congo, Libya and Equatorial Guinea had trade surpluses with China which amounted to US$3.1 billion, US$1 billion, and US$2 billion respectively (China Statistical Yearbook 2009).

In contrast, Nigeria, China's fourth largest trading partner in Africa, possessed a huge trade deficit with China. In 2008, the bilateral trade equalled US$7.3 billion – an increase of 67.7 percent when compared to 2007. Nigeria's trade deficit, however, was US$6.3 billion because its imports from China totalled US$6.8 billion and its exports to China only approximated US$0.5 billion. Nigeria is the largest producer of oil in Africa, but it is not a major supplier of oil to China (China Statistical Yearbook 2009).

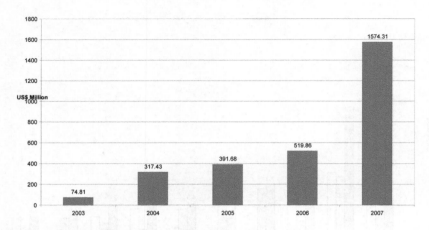

Figure 1.3   China's investment in Africa

Source: China Commerce Yearbook (2008) (Beijing: Zhongguo Shangwu Chubanshe), 211.

China is also a major investor in Africa. China's investment in Africa expanded very rapidly in recent years. In 2003, China's investment was only US$74.8 million. It increased more than three times in 2004, reaching US$371.4 million. After increasing more than 20 percent in the two following years, China's investment in Africa doubled from 2006 to 2007, reaching US$1.5 billion (China Commerce Yearbook 2008).

However, China's investment in Africa is only a small percentage of its overall foreign investment. China's cumulative investment in Africa amounted to US$4.5 billion by 2007, totalling only 3.8 percent of China's overall foreign investment portfolio.

China's major investment destinations in Africa include South Africa, Nigeria, Sudan, Zambia, Algeria and Niger.

Investment in Angola, China's number one trading partner in Africa, has increased very rapidly in the past few years. From 2003 to 2005, China's investment in Angola was no more than half a million US dollars. The investment jumped to more than US$22 million in 2006 and further to US$41.2 million by 2007. By the end of 2007, China's cumulative investment represented US$78.5 million (China Commerce Yearbook 2008).

Along with these mutually beneficial economic relations, China has also established a strategic partnership with Africa. During his six-country visit to Africa in May 1996, President Jiang Zemin proposed to establish long-term stable and comprehensive cooperative relations with African countries in the twenty-first century (Zhong 2006). According to Jiang, China would like to become all-weather friends with African countries based on the principle of non-interference and thus develop mutually beneficial economic relations with African countries. China would continue to provide assistance to African countries without the pressures of

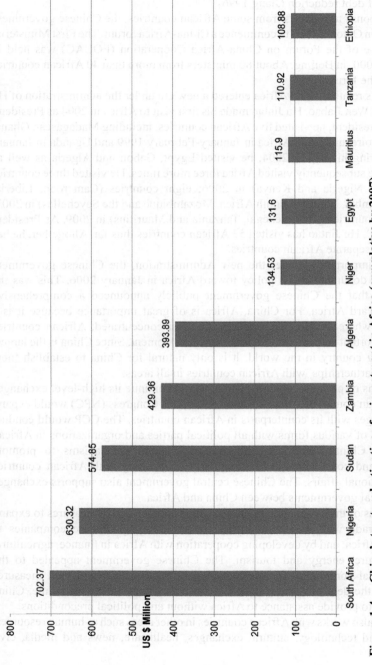

Figure 1.4   China's top ten destinations for investment in Africa (cumulative by 2007)

Source: China Commerce Yearbook (2008) (Beijing: Zhongguo Shangwu Chubanshe), 214–215.

conditionality (except Taiwan) and would speak up on behalf of African countries in terms of debt reduction (Jiang 1996).

In response to requests from some African countries, the Chinese government proposed in October 1999 to commence a China-Africa forum. The First Ministerial Conference of the Forum on China-Africa Cooperation (FOCAC) was held in October 2000, in Beijing. About 80 ministers from more than 40 African countries attended the forum.

China's relations with Africa entered a new era under the administration of Hu Jintao and Wen Jiabao. Hu Jintao made his first visit to Africa in 2004 as President. As Vice President, he visited five African countries, including Madagascar, Ghana, Cote D'Ivoire and South Africa in January-February 1999 and Uganda in January 2001. During his trip in 2004, he visited Egypt, Gabon and Algeria as well as France. He subsequently visited Africa three more times. He visited three countries (Morocco, Nigeria and Kenya) in 2006; eight countries (Cameroon, Liberia, Sudan, Zambia, Namibia, South Africa, Mozambique and the Seychelles) in 2007; and four countries (Mali, Senegal, Tanzania and Mauritius) in 2009. As President of the PRC, Hu Jintao has visited 53 African countries thus far. Altogether, he has visited 22 separate African countries.

More importantly, under the new Administration, the Chinese government released a document on its policy toward Africa in January 2006. This was the first time that the Chinese government publicly announced a comprehensive policy toward Africa. For China, Africa is of great importance because it is a continent where developing countries are most concentrated; African countries are an important force for world peace and development. Since China is the largest developing country in the world, it is only natural for China to establish 'new strategic partnerships' with African countries in all areas.

In terms of political relations, China would continue its high-level exchanges with African countries. China's National People's Congress (NPC) would expand its exchanges with its counterparts in African countries. The CCP would conduct exchanges of various forms with all political parties and organizations in African countries. China would establish various bilateral mechanisms to promote dialogue and consultation, whilst regularly cooperating with African countries in international affairs. The Chinese central government also supports exchanges among local governments between China and Africa.

In terms of their economic relations, China adopted active measures to expand bilateral trade with African countries; by encouraging Chinese companies to invest in Africa; and by developing cooperation with Africa in finance, agriculture, infrastructure, energy and tourism. The Chinese government appealed to the international community for the reduction of African debt and took measures to reduce the debt of African countries towards China. In the meantime, China continues to provide assistance to Africa without any political preconditions.

China also works with African countries in other areas such as human resources, science and technology, cultural exchanges, healthcare, news and media, civil service, non-government exchanges, environmental protection, security and non-traditional security.

Subsequently, the FOCAC forum held its first summit meeting along with the third ministerial meeting in Beijing, in November 2006. In his opening remarks at the summit, President Hu Jintao reiterated China's desire to work with African countries in five areas of political relations, economic cooperation, cultural exchanges, balanced global development and international cooperation in order to develop a new strategic partnership with Africa (Hu 2006).

Hu also promised to adopt eight policy measures to promote China-Africa cooperation. Hu's pledges included the doubling of China's aid in 2009 in relation to the aid disbursed in 2006, preferential loans amounting to US$3 billion, preferential buyer's credits of US$2 billion within three years and the establishment of a China-Africa Development Fund of US$5 billion for Chinese companies to invest in Africa (Hu 2006). China promised to assist in building a conference centre for the African Union (AU) and cancel all the government interest-free loan debt that matured at the end of 2005, owed by the heavily indebted poor countries (HIPC) and the least developed countries in Africa that have diplomatic relations with China (Hu 2006). China would further open up its market to Africa and increase zero-tariff commodities from the least developed African countries having diplomatic relations with China from 190 to more than 440, whilst establishing three to five economic and trade cooperation zones in Africa (Hu 2006). Finally, China would train 15,000 African professionals in the next three years, send 100 senior agricultural experts to Africa, establish ten special agricultural technology demonstration centres in Africa, build 30 hospitals, provide a grant of three billion RMB for setting up 30 malaria prevention and treatment centres, dispatch 300 youth volunteers, build 100 rural schools and increase government scholarships for African students from 2,000 per year to 4,000 per year by 2009 (Hu 2006).

In his speech at the opening of the Fourth Ministerial Conference of the FOCAC, Premier Wen Jiabao announced eight new measures to strengthen China-Africa cooperation. According to Wen, China would work with African countries on climate change as well as science and technological cooperation (Wen 2009). China would assist Africa in building 100 clean energy projects, carry out 100 joint demonstration projects on scientific and technological research with Africa, and train 100 African post-doctoral fellows (Wen 2009). China would provide another US$10 billion in concessional loans to African countries and cancel debts associated with interest-free government loans due to mature by the end of 2009 for the HIPC and least developed countries in Africa having diplomatic relations with China (Wen 2009). In further opening its market to African products, China would phase in zero-tariff treatment for 95 percent of the products from the least developed African countries having diplomatic relations with China, starting with 60 percent of the products within 2010 (Wen 2009). China would further assist Africa with regard to agriculture, increasing the number of agricultural technology demonstration centres in Africa, sending 50 agricultural technology teams to Africa, and training 2,000 agricultural technology personnel (Wen 2009).

China would also work closely with Africa on issues such as healthcare, human resources development, education and cultural exchanges. China would train 3,000 doctors and nurses, build 50 China-Africa friendship schools and train 1,500 school principals and teachers, whilst increasing the number of Chinese government scholarships to African students (Wen 2009).

Clearly, China's partnership with Africa has become comprehensive and strategic. They are no longer simply political and economic partners but comprehensive strategic partners.

Concluding Remarks

In the past six decades, China has twice experienced fundamental shifts in terms of its design of global governance. In Mao Zedong's era, China was a revolutionary state, aiming to create a united front against hegemonism. In Mao's view, the international community was composed of 'three worlds': the First World of two superpowers, the Second World of fence sitters and the Third World of developing countries. China's goal, therefore, was to work with Third World countries (such as African countries) and unite the Second World countries (such as Japan, Australia and European countries) against the hegemonism of First World powers.

Under the leadership of Deng Xiaoping, China experienced the first fundamental shift in the 1980s and 1990s, from a revolutionary state to a status quo state. China no longer challenges the existing international order. Instead, it tries to work within the existing world order for its own benefits. Since then, China's top priority has become economic development for which a peaceful international environment is imperative. Instead of opposing the two superpowers, China established diplomatic relations with the United States in 1979 and normalized its relations with the Soviet Union ten years later.

China's design of global governance experienced another fundamental shift under the leadership of Hu Jintao: from a status quo state to a responsible stakeholder. With the rise of China as an economic and financial power, China's leadership has decided to play a more active role on the international stage as a responsible stakeholder. China is aiming at building a world of peace, prosperity and harmony.

Africa has played different roles in China's design of global governance during these different periods. During Mao's era, African countries were China's political partners. Many African countries established diplomatic relations with the PRC in the 1960s and they were the main supporters for the PRC's bid to accede to the UN. Thanks to their strong support, the PRC regained its seat at the UN and the ROC representatives were expelled in October 1971.

Africa's significance declined somewhat in the era of Deng Xiaoping when China pursued economic development and worked more closely with the West. In the 1990s, a number of African countries played off the PRC against the

ROC. They switched their diplomatic relations back and forth in order to gain economic returns in this same period.

Africa has become an important partner with China again in the new century. With the surge of China's demand for natural resources, China has developed closer ties with Africa. With the inauguration of the FOCAC in 2000, the bilateral relationship entered a new stage. China and Africa have since become comprehensive strategic partners, where they have worked together in many areas of political cooperation, economic development, environmental protection, social reforms and cultural exchanges.

Bibliography

Book References

Qian, Q. and Wang, T. 1999. *Xin Zhongguo Waijiao Wushi Nian* (*The 50 Years of the New China's Diplomacy*). Volume 2. Beijing: Beijing Press.

Yang, S. 2001. *Yang Shangkun Huiyilu* (*Yang Shangkun Memoirs*). Beijing: Central Archive Press.

Zhong, Z. 2006. *Weile Shijie Gengmeihao: Jiang Zemin Chufang Jishi* (*For a Better World: Jiang Zemin's Foreign Visits*). Beijing: World Knowledge Press.

Book Chapters

Deng, X. 1993a. We must safeguard world peace and ensure domestic development (29 May 1984), in *Selected Works of Deng Xiaoping*. Volume 3. Beijing: People's Press, 56–57.

Deng, X. 1993b. With stable policies of reform and opening to the outside world, China can have great hopes for the future (4 September 1989), in *Selected Works of Deng Xiaoping*. Volume 3. Beijing: People's Press, 315–21.

Deng, X. 1993c. Seize the opportunity to develop the economy (24 December 1990), in *Selected Works of Deng Xiaoping*. Volume 3. Beijing: People's Press, 363–5.

Deng, X. 1994a. Speech at a plenary meeting of the Military Commission of the Central Committee of the Communist Party of China (28 December 1977), in *Selected Works of Deng Xiaoping*. Volume 2. Beijing: People's Press, 72–78.

Deng, X. 1994b. The present situation and the tasks before us (16 January 1980), in *Selected Works of Deng Xiaoping*. Volume 2. Beijing: People's Press, 239–73.

Deng, X. 1994c. Opening speech at the Twelfth National Congress of the Communist Party of China (1 September 1982), in *Selected Works of Deng Xiaoping*. Volume 3. Beijing: People's Press, 1–8.

Mao, Z. 1999. Guanyu sange shijie huafen wenti (On the classifications of the three Worlds – 22 February 1974), in *Mao Zedong Wenji* (*Collections of Mao Zedong*). Volume 8. Beijing: People's Press, 441–42.

Journal articles

Zhang, X. 2009. Hu Jintao shidai guan de Zhongguo zhuzhang (Hu Jintao's world view and China's role in international affairs). *Liaowong* (*Outlook Weekly*), 47.

Websites

CCPIT. 2010. *Saudi Arabia, Angola, Iran remain top three oil suppliers to China.* [Online]. Available at: http://www.ccpitnb.org/tpl/en/detail.php?id=68945 [accessed: 10 June 2010].

CNN Asia. 2009. *China passes Germany in economic rankings.* [Online]. Available at: http://edition.cnn.com/2009/WORLD/asiapcf/01/15/china.economy/index. html?iref=topnews [accessed: 10 June 2010].

Hu, J. 2006. *Hu Jintao zhuxi zai zhongfei hezuo luntan Beijing fenghui kaimushi shang de jianghua (President Hu Jintao's speech at the opening ceremony of the Beijing summit of the Sino-African cooperation forum).* [Online]. Available at: http://news.xinhuanet.com/world/2006-11/04/content_5289040. htm [accessed: 10 June 2010].

Peakoil.com. 2010. *Angola becomes China's largest crude oil source.* [Online]. Available at: http://peakoil.com/production/angola-becomes-chinas-largest-crude-oil-source/ [accessed: 10 June2010].

Sun, D. 1994. *Sange shijie huafen de zhanlue sixiang yu xinshiqi waijiao zhengce de tiaozheng (The strategic idea of three world classifications and the adjustment of China's foreign policy in the new era).* [Online]. Available at: http://cpc.people.com.cn/GB/69112/70190/70194/5235123.html [accessed: 10 June 2010].

US Energy Information Administration. 2009. *China energy data, statistics and analysis.* [Online]. Available at: http://www.eia.doe.gov/cabs/China/Oil.html [accessed: 13 September 2010].

Wen, J. 2009. *Wen Jiabao tichu baxiang jucuo tuijin zhongfei hezuo (Wen Jiabao put forth eight measures to promote Sino-African cooperation).* [Online]. Available at: http://news.xinhuanet.com/world/2009-11/08/content_12411492. htm [accessed: 10 June 2010].

Newspapers

Jiang, Z. 1996. Establishing a new historical monument for Sino-African friendship. *Renmin Ribao*, 14 May, 6.

Command Papers

China Commerce Yearbook. 2008. Beijing: Ministry of Foreign Affairs of the People's Republic of China.

China Statistical Yearbook. 2007. Beijing: China Statistics Press. National Bureau of Statistics of China.

China Statistical Yearbook. 2009. Beijing: China Statistics Press. National Bureau of Statistics of China.

Chapter 2
Cultural Heritage and China's Africa Policy

Anshan Li

Introduction

China's African studies have made some progress, especially since 1978. However, it has by no means echoed the rapid expansion of China's engagement in Africa in recent years (Li 2005). One of the missing subjects is the linkage between culture and China's Africa policy. This is without doubt a very interesting yet difficult subject. It is interesting because all foreign policy embodies historical tradition, social values as well as political ideology of the nation-state concerned – it therefore has a direct linkage with the culture of that country. It is also difficult simply because 'culture' is a rich and ambiguous term, and has countless interpretations. The author's intention is neither to argue against the various definitions of 'culture', nor to explain the characteristics of Chinese culture.

Regarding the definition of 'culture', as early as 1952, A. Kroeber and Clyde Kluckhohn attempted to catalogue and classify all the definitions proposed by anthropologists, sociologists and social psychologists, and list as many as 169 definitions exemplifying a dozen distinct conceptual approaches (Kroeber, Kluckohn 1952). Yet they failed to include the definitions provided by historians or political scientists. P. Bagby once defined 'culture' as being 'regularities in the behaviour, internal and external, of the members of a society, excluding those regularities which are clearly hereditary in origin' (Bagby 1958: 84). In addition, he stated that in virtue of being 'the patterned or repetitive element in history' (Bagby 1958: 95), 'culture is history's intelligible aspect' (Bagby 1958: 124). As a political scientist, Samuel Huntington later considered that language and religion are two major factors of any culture or civilization. In his view, 'The central elements of any culture and civilization are language and religion' (Huntington 1996: 59). It is meaningless to challenge this view, yet I will not discuss these two key elements at further length in this chapter.

In order to make the subject-matter clearer, I would like to narrow down the meaning of 'culture' to a more concrete one. Following the tradition of 'culture-values', 'culture' in my understanding means specifically 'values', thus it is closely associated to what cultural anthropologist Richard A. Shweder thinks about culture: 'community-specific ideas about what is true, good, beautiful and efficient' (Shweder 2000: 163).

China's 'new march' to Africa is attracting much international attention; some have criticized it while others have applauded it. No matter the criticism or praise, two facts have been noticed about China-Africa relations. Firstly, it is commonly recognized that China's increasing engagement in Africa has made a great impact on international politics. This has been dealt with by many scholars, either distinguished Africanists, famous sinologists, by a younger generations of China-fans, or by 'one-day experts', meaning those who know neither Chinese nor African affairs, but become the fast producer of piles of literature covering China-Africa relations since they have found the topic a fashionable business and as an easy way of receiving funding (Large 2008: 45–61).

Secondly, many scholars also noticed that China's Africa policy has its own characteristics quite different from that of the West. This uniqueness has been analysed, criticized, extolled and questioned (Strauss, Saavedra 2009). Chinese scholars consider China's Africa policy as positive, whether it is effective remains another question (Yang 2007, Li 2008). Western authors generally take a negative view of the role played by Chinese factors in Africa, although of late, there seems to be a change towards a milder tone employed (Eisenman, Kurlantzick 2006: 223, Brautigam 2009). African leaders usually think China's involvement in Africa is constructive and they have highly praised its contributions to African development (Wade 2008, allAfrica.com 2009). However, the opinions of African academia and Non-Governmental Organizations (NGOs) differ regarding China's engagement in Africa (Manji, Marks 2007, Guerrero, Manji 2008, Ampiah, Naidu 2008, Harneit-Sievers, Marks, Naidu 2010).

Deborah Brautigam, an American scholar who has launched research on Chinese aid to Africa since the 1990s, recently published a book entitled *Dragon's Gift*, which challenges many stereotypes and *clichés* regarding recent literature on China-Africa relations causing a serious debate among academia and policy-makers. She clearly stated the differences of approach between China and the West in terms of aid distribution:

> Where the West regularly changes its development advice, programmes and approach in Africa (integrated rural development in the 1970s, policy reform in the 1980s, governance in the 1990s, and so on), China does not claim to know what Africa must do to develop. China has argued that it was wrong to impose political and economic conditionality in exchange for aid, and that countries should be free to find their own pathway out of poverty. Mainstream economists in the West today are also questioning the value of many of the conditions imposed on aid over the past few decades (Brautigam 2009: 308).

Her observation deserves notice.

What factors have shaped China's Africa policy? The making of foreign policy is surely a result of a mixed combination of reactions to external challenges and reflections on diplomatic affairs. It is, however, also influenced by internal affairs, such as the political system, the ideological orientation, policy choices, the public media, think-tanks or different interest groups, such as the business sector (Hao, Lin 2007). It is also realized that culture has impacted on development and some believe that culture can play a decisive role in this process. We can trace this view to Tocqueville and Max Weber. Tocqueville argued that democracy could exist in the United States (US) because of its cultural heritage, while Weber believed that capitalism in its essence is a phenomenon of religious culture. However, there is little study of the cultural impact on foreign policy.

China has a long history of being considered as a great civilization, yet is there any linkage between Chinese culture and China's policy towards Africa? It seems there is no systematic study on this subject. In this chapter, I would like to analyse the positive impact of the historical heritage on China's diplomatic behaviour and more specifically, I intend to answer the following questions: what kind of 'community-specific ideas about what is true, good, beautiful and efficient' shape China's Africa policy? In order to provide a thorough answer, I will concentrate on four notions of Chinese values, which represent the principles or rules regarding human relations, for example, *ren*, (benevolence, 仁), *shu* (forbearance, 恕), *xin* (trustfulness, 信) and *pingdeng* (equality, 平等). By analysing the linkage between these four Confucian notions and China's contemporary foreign policy, we may discover the extent of the cultural impact on China's external relations.

Essence of *Ren* (仁, Benevolence or Humanity)

Ren, signifies, to a certain extent, benevolence or humanity in English. As the Chinese character indicates, *Ren* presents two people. Confucius once said, 'A benevolent person loves people (*ren zhe ai ren*)', which really shows the humanitarian nature of *Ren*. As the key notion of Confucianism, *Ren* has caused a lot of debates in Chinese academia. However, the criticism mostly targets the fact that the ruling class exercised this notion in contradiction with the notion itself. The following section will permit an analysis of the application of *Ren* in China's policy towards developing countries, particularly Africa.

The typical example of *Ren* indicated in foreign policy is Chinese medical cooperation with developing countries, especially concerning the dispatchment of Chinese Medical Teams (CMT) since 1963 to the world, and more specifically African countries (Li 2009). In July 1962, after the victory of the liberation movement and the withdrawal of French medical staff, the Algerian government called out to the international community for medical assistance. The Chinese government received the message through two channels, the Red Cross and the Algerian Minister for Health. In January 1963, China was the first to express its willingness to provide medical assistance to Algeria, marking the beginning of China medical dispatchments abroad (*People's Daily* 1963). Until the beginning of 2009, 45 CMTs have worked in 44 different African countries.

About 900 members are now working in about 100 hospitals or health centres in Africa. The total figure for CMT person/time – the total number of times that personnel have been sent on such missions – is 16,000 and about 26 million Africans have been served by CMT. It is not unusual for Chinese doctors to transmit their blood in order to save African patients (Wang 2006: 307).

Table 2.1   Chinese medical teams in Africa (1963–2008)

African Country	Dispatched Province	Start Date	Various Changes
Algeria	Hubei	Apr. 1963	Withdrew in Feb.1995 due to war, and re-dispatched in 1997.
Zanzibar	Jiangsu	Aug. 1964	-
Somalia	Jilin	June 1965	Withdrew in 1991 due to civil war.
Congo (Brazzaville)	Tianjin	Feb. 1967	Withdrew in 1997 due to civil war, and returned in Dec. 2000.
Mali	Zhejiang	Feb. 1968	-
Tanganyika (Tanzania)	Shandong	Mar. 1968	-
Mauretania	Heilongjiang	Apr. 1968	-
Guinea	Beijing	June 1968	-
Sudan	Shanxi	Apr. 1971	-
Equatorial Guinea	Guangdong	Oct. 1971	-
Sierra Leone	Hunan	Mar. 1973	Withdrew in 1993 due to war, and re-dispatched in Dec. 2002 formally.
Tunisia	Jiangxi	June 1973	To help to set up the first acupuncture centre in 1994.
D.R. Congo (Kinshasa)	Hebei	Sept. 1973	Withdrew in 1997 due to war, and returned in June 2006.
Ethiopia	Henan	Nov. 1974	Interrupted in Sept. 1979, and returned in Dec. 1984.
Togo	Shanghai	Nov. 1974	-
Cameroon	Shanghai	June 1975	Interrupted in Jan. 1979, and dispatched by Shanxi in 1985.
Senegal	Fujian	July 1975	Withdrew in 1996, and re-dispatched in Sept. 2007.*
Madagascar	Gansu	Aug. 1975	-
Morocco	Shanghai	Sept. 1975	Jiangxi Province joined in 2000.
Niger	Guangxi	Jan. 1976	Withdrew in July 1992 and re-dispatched in Dec. 1996.
Mozambique	Sichuan	Apr. 1976	-
São Tomé and Príncipe (STP)	Heilongjiang Sichuan	June 1976	Withdrew in 1997 after diplomatic relationship was suspended.
Burkina Faso (Upper Volta)	Beijing	June 1976	Withdrew in 1994 after diplomatic relationship was suspended.
Guinea-Bissau	Guizhou	July 1976	Withdrew in 1990 and re-dispatched by Sichuan in 2002
Gabon	Tianjin	May 1977	-
Gambia	Tianjin	May 1977	Dispatched by Guangdong province instead in 1991, and withdrew in 1995.
Benin	Ningxia	Jan. 1978	-

Zambia	Henan	Jan. 1978	-
The Central African Republic	Zhejiang	July 1978	Withdrew in July 1991, re-dispatched in Aug. 1998.
Chad	Jiangxi	Dec. 1978	Withdrew in 1979 and re-dispatched in 1989; withdrew in 1997 and re-dispatched in 2006; withdrew in Feb. 2008 due to the war and re-dispatched in May.
Botswana	Fujian	Feb. 1981	-
Djibouti	Shanxi	Feb. 1981	-
Rwanda	Inner Mongolia	June 1982	-
Uganda	Yunnan	Jan. 1983	-
Zimbabwe	Hunan	May 1985	-
Libya	Jiangsu	Dec. 1983	Contract expired in 1994 and not renewed.
Cape Verde	Heilongjiang	July 1984	Province change to Sichuan in Feb. 1998, and late changed to Hunan.
Liberia	Heilongjiang	July 1984	Withdrew in 1989 and returned in 2005.
Seychelles	Guangxi	May 1987	Guangdong recruited 5 CMT members as a Chinese volunteer project in 2007.
Burundi	Guangxi	Dec. 1986	The dispatched province was changed to Qinghai.
Namibia	Zhejiang	Apr. 1996	-
Comoros	Guangxi	1994	-
Lesotho	Hubei	June 1997	-
Eritrea	Henan	Sept. 1997	-
Malawi	Shanxi	June 2008	-
Angola	Sichuan	2007	Postponed since the accommodations were not prepared in time in Angola.
Ghana	Guangdong	2008	-

Notes: *The reason for withdrawal of CMT is usually due to the rupture of diplomatic relations, unless an explanation is provided.

Source: *People's Daily*, 1964–2008.

On 26 January 1965, an Algerian woman lost much blood while giving birth and was in a very critical situation. Dr Shen Xingzhi and Dr Xu Zexian immidiately transmitted their blood to the woman and saved her life (*Xinhua News Agency* 1993: 33). A Tanzanian woman was very weak after a serious operation and needed a blood transfusion. Dr Liu Fangyi gave 250cc of blood to the woman. Dr Liu who had been to Africa three times finally died in Tanzania and was praised by President Julius Nyerere as 'Doctor-Ambassador of friendship and kindness'

(Liu 1998: 62–3). Forty-five CMT members died in Africa during their service (Bo 2007). Their humanitarian service brought them much merit and many honours: more than 600 CMT members received different top awards from different countries where they worked for more than 40 years (Department of International Cooperation of the Ministry of Health 2003: 16). What is more, their service was extended to diplomats and others, besides the country they were working in. For example, CMT in Algeria served not only Algerians, but also diplomats and other people from more than 60 countries (*Xinhua News Agency* 1993: 12). The same can be applied to CMT in Tunisia, Mali and other countries.

Ren is also expressed in other fields besides CMT. China's humanitarian assistance to Africa includes anti-malaria campaigns, humanitarian efforts, building hospitals, schools and elderly community centres. For example, in Liberia, through the series of bilateral cooperation agreements signed with China, the latter has expanded teaching facilities at the University of Liberia's Fendell Campus, established an anti-malaria treatment centre at the JFK hospital in Monrovia, set up a modern hospital in Tappita (Nimba County), and constructed primary and secondary schools across Liberia. Furthermore, Chinese goodwill was also expressed in the construction of roads and streets across Liberia (allAfrica.com 2009).

Tropical diseases and epidemics represent a major threat towards the health and lives of African people. A recent United Nations International Children's Emergency Fund (UNICEF) report disclosed that five million children under the age of five died in Africa in 2006. Malaria is the number one killer and about one million children die of malaria annually in Africa (Thompson 2005: 1–4, Shinn 2006: 14–16, Siringi 2003: 456). To fight against malaria in Africa, the Chinese government adopted several measures simultaneously, namely CMT, training programmes, anti-malaria projects, donation of facilities and drugs, and the building of anti-malaria centres. In 2006, during the China-African summit, President Hu promised to continue China-African medical cooperation and offered to help build 30 anti-malaria centres in Africa (Table 2.2).

In the run-up to the Fourth Forum On China-Africa Cooperation (FOCAC) meeting, the work on these projects was progressing smoothly. A very effective anti-malaria medicine Cotecxin is now the most widely used medication in Africa, which has become one of the most welcome gifts presented by the Chinese leaders whenever they are on official visits to African countries (Lu 2008).

China has also constantly supported the Sudanese people with humanitarian aid. China's aid helps to target the root of the conflicts – poverty. China has provided infrastructure development such as schools, hospitals and water projects for Sudan. Aside from offering help to Sudan to develop its oil industry and infrastructure, China has sent several shipments of humanitarian aid, including tents, blankets, medical and agricultural equipment. Since 2004, China has sent five shipments of material for humanitarian aid to Darfur. The fourth shipment, worth RMB20 million (US$2.6 million), left for Sudan on 16 August 2007, and

Table 2.2   China supported anti-malaria centres in Africa

Country	Date	Location
Liberia	1 February 2007	Monrovia
Chad	28 December 2007	Ndjamena (Ndjamena Freedom Hospital)
Burundi	27 March 2008	Bujumbura
Uganda	15 May 2008	Kampala (Mulago Hospital)
Congo (Brazzaville)	13 August 2008	Brazzaville
Gabon	28 September 2008	Libreville (China-Gabon Cooperation Hospital)
Guinea-Bissau	10 December 2008	Bissau
Togo	7 January 2009	Lomé
Mali	13 February 2009	Bamako (Kadi Hospital)
Cameroon	26 March 2009	Yaoundé (Women and Children Hospital)

Sources: *People's Daily* (until April 2009).

included pumps, tents and blankets to help residents in the Darfur region improve their living conditions (FOCAC 2007). The fifth batch of aid material, valued at RMB40 million, was shipped on 25 August 2007 and included board-houses for at least 120 schools, generators, vehicles and pumps (Focac.org 2007). Until July 2007, China had already provided US$10 million in humanitarian aid and promised to offer more (China Daily 2007). China had also provided humanitarian aid by sending peacekeeping forces to four African countries, all of which are involved in engineering or medical assistance.

Sense of *Shu* (恕, Forbearance)

When his student, Zi Gong, asked him about the most important doctrine in life, Confucius answered, 'That should be "forbearance", for example, what you do not want done to yourself, you should not do to others' (as cited in Yang 2005: 166). As an important principle of social relations in the daily life of the Chinese people, this doctrine has also left its print on China's foreign policy. For recent years, the most criticized policy in China's relationship with African countries is the no-strings-attached principle or in other terms, the absence of political conditionality. Indeed, China follows its own principle of non-interference, thus attaches no political condition to its assistance to Africa. However, certain countries criticize others for their own interests, be it economic, political and cultural. And the criticism is usually carried out under the cover of 'universal values' or 'international standards', implying Western doctrines or principles as universal. That practice has worked for some time in modern history, but is no longer effective (Li 2007: 8–12).

The idea of *Shu* or forbearance definitely affects China's foreign policy. China learnt hard lessons when receiving conditioned assistance from other countries. In 1958, when the Union of Soviet Socialist Republics (USSR) provided aid to China, it also proposed that China should agree with the USSR to the establishment of a long-wave transceiver by the USSR and its allied fleet. Chairman Mao Zedong realized that the two issues belonged to the realm of China's internal affairs and that any concession would jeopardize Chinese national defence: thus Mao resolutely refused the proposal. This explains why China has always set self-reliance as the first principle of development with foreign aid as a subsidiary, and China would thus never allow the aid donor to interfere with its internal affairs.

When China offers assistance to African countries or other developing countries, it would not attach political conditions, whilst Western countries usually do so regardless of the process or the stage of development. The typical example is the criticism targeted at the Chinese government for its role in the Darfur crisis. The Darfur issue is a very complicated case, with historical origins, national integration, religious conflict, refugee migration and poverty, all playing a role. Firstly, the crisis in Darfur is mainly caused by environmental degradation, as pointed out by the United Nations Environment Program report issued in 2007 (United Nations Environmental Programme 2007: 329, Mohammed 2004).[1] Secondly, Darfur is a regional tragedy that affects many people and disastrously impacts upon the region. However, apart from the US, neither the United Nations (UN), regional organizations nor other countries use the term 'genocide' to describe the situation in Darfur (Auteserre 2006, Apps 2007).[2]

Thirdly, the crisis in Darfur is related to development and can only be solved through development. Fourthly, the Darfur crisis is expressed as a conflict between different groups inside Sudan. Nation-building is a difficult process for all countries. For example, after more than 80 years of independence, the US undertook a Civil War to prevent the secession of the nation, resulting in about 600,000 deaths (Gilpin Faust 2008). The same holds true regarding the nation-building process in Europe (Blanning et al. 2000, Berger 2009). Yet, this seemed to escape most people's attention when the Sudanese government was put to blame. The international community should give the Sudanese people time to solve this

---

1 The Programme's report provided the following explanation: 'Environmental degradation, as well as regional climate instability and change, are major underlying causes of food insecurity and conflict in Darfur – and potential catalysts for future conflict throughout Central and Eastern Sudan and other countries in the Sahel belt'. See also the Programme's Post-Conflict and Disaster Management Branch website at http://postconflict.unep.ch. This view on the role of environmental degradation is not new but has been neglected by the outside world. The Sudanese Ambassador to the US provided the same explanation in his speech at the National Press Club in Washington, D.C., on 30 May 2007, when addressing the Bush Administration's new sanctions against the Sudanese government.

2   It is noteworthy that a much more serious disaster in the neighbouring Democratic Republic of the Congo did not elicit as much attention from the US.

problem. In most cases, interference from outside has only worsened fragile political situations, such as in Iraq and Afghanistan. The recent independence of Southern Sudan, as voted for by popular consent, may yet prove to be another example of such a fragile environment.

China's policy of non-interference does not equate to ignoring humanitarian disasters, rather China respects the sovereignty of nations and acknowledges its limits in solving such crises. In diplomatic discussions with African nations, China does make suggestions on issues of governance and intra-state affairs. What distinguishes Chinese suggestions from Western interventions is that they are provided in a friendly rather than a coercive manner. China has used its ties with Sudan to persuade the Sudanese government to cooperate with the United Nations (UN) (Chutian Metropolis Daily 2007). Since there is mutual respect and trust, China can work with the Sudanese government to find a solution agreeable to all parties to alleviate the suffering of the Sudanese people. Recently, the Sudanese government accepted a 'hybrid peacekeeping force' in Darfur (Xinhua News Agency 2007).

Another good example to describe *Shu* is the forbearance shown by the recipient towards others' decisions or choices which may not benefit the recipient. In 2003, a Canadian oil firm decided to sell its interest in a Sudanese consortium that also involved Chinese and Malaysian firms. The Chinese company wanted to buy the Canadian share, but was refused by the Sudanese government. Instead, Sudan awarded the share to an Indian firm with a higher bid, in order to multiply the investors (The Hindu 2002). This shows two facts: China and Sudan are equal partners, who can make decisions on their own, without the need to be complimentary or complicit.

With China's investment and support, Sudan has transformed from an oil-importing country to an exporting one, and has built a complete infrastructure for exploration, production, refining, transport and sales of crude oil, gasoline or petrochemical products.

Belief in *Xin* (信, Trustfulness, Good Faith)

Confucianism always employs *Xin* as one of the most important principles for human beings, either in terms of governance or in one's personal life. Meaning trustfulness or good faith, '*Xin*' was mentioned 24 times in Confucius' *Analects*, thus indicating how seriously Confucius and his followers regarded this principle. Confucius once put good faith, at first, in governance, when he discussed how to run the administration of a state. In order to govern a state, the leader should 'Work earnestly and live up to your words' (*Jing shi you xin*) (Yang 1980). He once said, 'I do not know how a man without truthfulness is to get on' (*Ren er wu xin, bu zhi qi ke ye*). His student Zi Gong also illustrated his idea by stating 'to be true to one's words' or 'To live up to one's words' (*Yan er you xin*) (Yang 1980). All these sayings indicate that once a person has promised something, he/she has to live up to it, and he/she should be a trustful person, especially towards friends.

China has followed this principle in its cooperation with African countries. During his visit to African countries, Premier Zhou Enlai heard on the way the news of an unsuccessful *coup d'état* against Presdent Nkrumah on 2 January 1964 in Ghana – the next destination of his tour. Chairman Liu Shaoqi and Premier Zhou Enlai both immediately sent a telegraph of comfort to Nkrumah. The Chinese leadership hesitated whether to push ahead with the visit and there was a heated debate among the members of the delegation. Some of them suggested that the visit should be cancelled owing to the political instability and the dangerous situation in Ghana. Yet Premier Zhou thought the delegation should go as planned since President Nkrumah, more than ever, needed moral support at this critical moment. Premier Zhou thus sent Mr Huang Zheng and Mr Huang Hua to pay an official visit, first, to convey his sincere solicitude to President Nkrumah, who was injured during the coup. Considering Nkrumah's situation, Premier Zhou also suggested that all the official etiquette be cancelled and Nkrumah should hold neither welcome ceremony at the airport, nor an outdoor banquet. Nkrumah did not expect that the Chinese Premier would continue the visit as planned. He was moved by the two telegraphs, yet showed a desire to get a letter from Chairman Mao Zedong. When Zhou arrived in Accra, he brought the letter from Chairman Mao and enjoyed a very successful visit in Ghana. It was here that he put forward the eight principles of foreign economic cooperation (Li 2001: 310–1, Huang 2007: 122–6).

Confucius once emphasized that a good person is 'to be trustworthy in word and resolute in deed' (*Yan bi xin, xing bi guo*). TAZARA (Tanzania-Zambia Railway) is a good example of the practice of *Xin*. This is one of the biggest aid projects which China has ever undertaken in terms of development aid. After both Tanzanian President Nyerere and Zambian President Kaunda failed to receive financial support from the West and the USSR, they then turned to China for assistance, who decided to help the two countries build the railway (Zhang 1999, Yu 1975). The 1,860-kilometre-long rail-road begins in Dar Es Salaam (Tanzania) in the East and ends in Kapri Mposhi (Zambia) in the West. Chinese experts and engineering technicians did all the exploration work, surveying and designing. They also assisted the Tanzanian and Zambian governments in organizing the execution of the construction. During the Cultural Revolution, China's economic relations greatly suffered. Although in a very difficult situation, the Chinese leaders continued to support their African friends, via this 'poor helps poor' model.

During the period of the TAZARA construction, China was experiencing very difficult times. The economy was strongly impacted by the political chaos and people were suffering from food shortages and the rationing of daily goods. There were also unimaginable difficulties in the building of the TAZARA, such as the mountainous regions and the tropical diseases, or building bridges and tunnels on swampy mud and quick sand. Many Chinese experts or technicians were injured and 65 Chinese died during the construction (Zhang 1999). Running through mountains, valleys, torrential rivers, dense and primitive forest, this railway required about US$400 million long-term interest-free loans from China,

30,000–50,000 Chinese railway experts, and took about ten years to accomplish. Notwithstanding the motives, to live up to one's words and help one's friends were the most important drivers behind this operation. In order to fulfil the promise, China even bought 98 Japanese bulldozers (worth about US$1.7 million) from Komatsu Manufacturing in Japan and transported them directly to Dar Es Salam, which eventually arrived in early 1970 and were put to use in the construction of the TAZARA (Yu 1975: 140–1, Monson 2009).

During the early 1990s, the West largely neglected Africa after the Cold War. China's Foreign Minister has made his visits to African countries the first official stop every year since 1991 (Qian 2003: 255–7). China also insists on using influence without interference – respect to others is vital to finding solutions in international politics.

The recent financial crisis testified to China's determination to fulfil its promise while many Western countries failed to realize their Official Development Aid (ODA) pledges to Africa. Although China suffered immensely during the *Wen-chuan* earthquake – as its economy was severely hit especially in terms of exports. China kept its word and tried by every means to finish the projects President Hu put forward during the China-Africa summit. After great efforts and close cooperation from both sides, China's promise was fulfilled before the fourth FOCAC summit (Xinhua News Agency 2010).

Principle of *Pingdeng* (平等, Equality)

Pingdeng or 'equality' is a modern concept, and one of the most important concerns in social movement and human history. In world history, the realization of the principle of equality was not only one of the major aims of the revolutions in Great Britain, France and the US (amongst others), but is a term which is highly praised in the West. However, in international politics, it seems that the 'might is right' approach reigns supreme and that equality is never mentioned.

The principle of equality has been understood as equivalent to that of socialism and is also claimed as the guiding principle of the Chinese Communist Party (CCP). However, the concept was always embodied in ancient Chinese philosophy, expressed in various ways and became another historical heritage embodied in China's diplomacy. Zi Xia, one of Confucius' students once said 'All men under Heaven are brothers' (*Sihai zhi nei, jie xiongdi ye*) and there is a strong sense of equality throughout Confucianism. Confucius himself claimed this principle as his educational philosophy: 'Education for all', or 'To teach everybody without prejudice' (*You jiao wu lei*). In another case, he even treated teacher and student as equals, by stating that 'teaching and learning improve each other' (*Jiao xue xiang zhang*). As another Confucian thinker and a typical equalitarian, Mencius was famous for his ideology of a *min ben* (people oriented) community. He once described his ideal society by saying, 'Treat your elders as elders, and extend it to the elders of others; treat your young ones as young ones, and extend it to the young ones of others' (*Lao wu lao yiji ren zhi lao, you wu you yiji ren zhi you*) (Yang 1960). It is noticeable that in this scenario every elder is equal, so is every youngster. In this philosophical approach, human beings must care for each other and treat others as equal, as their own family, which represents the incarnation of an ideal world.

This idea seems to be utopian but has a real meaning in China's foreign policy-making. For example, these four following characteristics are often used to describe China-African relations: summit diplomacy, sense of equality, mutual benefits and mechanism of cooperation (Li 2006: 11–13). Both China and Africa share a similar history, as they suffered from the ill-effects of the colonial era and this shared experience underpins the ideas of equality and respect for sovereignty that each highlight in their approach to international relations. The Eight Principles of Economic Cooperation and Technological Aid made it clear that China would guarantee that technicians in recipient countries would be able to master relevant technology when technical assistance is provided by Chinese experts, who despite working on specific missions abroad, are restricted from enjoying any privileges, thus they are to receive the same treatment as the local experts (People's Daily 1964).

Since the 1960s, the meetings between top leaders in China and Africa have become a key mechanism in establishing direct communication at the highest level of government and have set the tone for relations and bilateral politics. This 'summit diplomacy' has created mutual trust between heads of state and demonstrated mutual respect between China and African countries. Premier Zhou Enlai's visit to Africa during the early 1960s left a rich legacy in the framework of China-Africa relations. It was during Premier Zhao's 1982 visit to Africa that he put forward the four principles which emphasized mutual benefits.

In the same light, Chairman Mao Zedong always emphasized the equal status of Chinese and African citizens. When talking with African friends, he mentioned that Chinese and Africans citizens are both coloured, not only have the same historical experiences, but are also despised by the West and bullied by imperialists. China and African countries are thus considered equal: 'The mutual relations between us is that of brotherhood, not father-son relations' (Mao 1994: 490–2, Li 2001: 432–8). Deng Xiaoping held the same attitude with African leaders. In 1989, he met the Burundian President at the age of 85 and called the President his 'young friend'. He met Ugandan President Museveni in the same year, and talked about the exchange of experiences (Deng 1993: 289–90). Jiang Zemin visited Africa four times and made an important speech at the Organization of African Unity (OAU) on the consolidation of equal partnership. President Hu Jintao visited many African countries and expressed Chinese willingness to entertain friendly relations with Africa. The principle of equality in China's dealings with other countries represents more than just a slogan. It is noticeable that although the concept is largely the norm between individuals, it has never been effectively applied to the realm of international relations. Powerful nations have always made the rules in the global community. China's practice in Africa will challenge this reality and may offer an alternative model for intra-state behaviour.

Among ordinary people, this attitude of equality also exists. Jamie Monson, an American historian and TAZARA-expert described the situation:

> During TAZARA's construction, the Chinese railway technicians did indeed labour 'side by side' with African workers, camping out with them in some of the most remote and rugged areas of the East African interior. They did not stand aside shouting out instructions, but taught the African recruits by example. They did not confine themselves to handling complex engineering technology, but were willing to pitch in on the most basic tasks. Chinese technicians remember assisting their young African friends with fatherly advice on matters ranging from saving their wages to repairing their shoes (Monson 2009: 7).

It is worth noticing that China has never used concepts such as 'donor-recipient'. The Chinese government stresses that China pursues a philosophy different from the West; it does not view aid as an instrument of political conditionality and understands assistance as a relationship based on mutuality. This is explained due to the fact that the term of 'donor-recipient' itself implies unequal positions, for example, rich and poor, top and bottom, superior and inferior or arrogant and humble.

As early as 1964, Premier Zhou Enlai put forward the Eight Principles of Economic Cooperation and Technological Aid. The principles are the following:

1. The Chinese government always bases itself on the principle of equality and mutual benefit in providing aid to other countries. It never regards such aid as a unilateral grant, but as mutual help
2. In providing aid to other countries, the Chinese government strictly respects the sovereignty of the recipient countries, and will never attach any conditions or ask for any privileges
3. In order to lighten the burden of the recipient countries, China will provide economic aid in the form of interest-free or low-interest loans and extend the time limit for repayment when necessary
4. The purpose of the Chinese government's aid to other countries is not to make the recipient countries dependent on China but to help them embark step by step on the road of self-reliance and independent development
5. The Chinese government will try its best to help the recipient countries build projects which require less investment while yielding quicker results, so that the recipient governments may increase their income and accumulate capital
6. The Chinese government will provide the best-quality equipment and material of its own manufacture at international market prices. If the equipment and material provided are not up to the agreed specifications and quality, the Chinese government undertakes to replace them

7. In providing any technical assistance, the Chinese government will see to it that the personnel of the recipient country fully master such techniques

8. The experts dispatched by China to help with construction projects in the recipient countries will have the same standard of living as the experts of the recipient country. The Chinese experts are not allowed to make any special demands or enjoy any special privileges (People's Daily 1964).

Zhou Enlai's Eight Principles of Economic Cooperation and Technological Aid are impressive in several aspects. Firstly, they figure as self-disciplined rules rather than regulations on bilateral relations. Secondly, the first principle directly outlines that Chinese aid should not be considered as a unilateral aim, but as mutual help. Thirdly, several principles can be considered as lessons learnt by a recipient country from its dealings with previous donors; more specifically, it highlights the lessons that China learnt from the aid formerly provided by the USSR. Finally, the eighth principle concerning Chinese experts is also a reflection of China's experience with Russian experts, who had asked for many privileges when working on projects in China, which caused a great deal of trouble and dissatisfaction from many Chinese citizens.

With Premier Zhao's visit to Africa in 1982, China's new policy was issued. Zhao announced the 'Four Principles on Sino-African Economic and Technical Cooperation' – including equality, bilateralism, effectiveness and co-development – which emphasizes mutual benefits and co-development (People's Daily 1983). Zhao's 'Four Principles' were a supplement to Zhou's 'Eight Principles', yet both follow the principle of equality. While the 'Eight Principles' guaranteed that China would provide the most favoured assistance to Africa, with additional restraints on Chinese aid personnel. The 'Four Principles' stressed bilateral cooperation and co-development.

In the field of aid and economic cooperation between China and Africa, we can also trace the influence of cultural heritage. 'Transparency' is a hot issue which has caused much criticism from the West. Yet, we can also find the cultural origin of this policy. According to Chinese values, people should cherish others' help, but should not talk of his or her assistance to others. A Chinese saying goes, 'If others have helped me, I should never forget; if I have helped others, I should forget' (Zhu 1985). It is common sense that the helped do not like others to frequently mention the help they received. It is the same logic for China's assistance to Africa – even if there may be other practical reasons as well (Li 2008: 21–49). China's assistance to Africa also emphasizes the traditional philosophy of 'Teaching others to fish is better than giving others fish'. That could explain why the Chinese are busy building infrastructure on the African continent.

However, three points must be stressed here. First, it is by no means to indicate that culture is the only factor to make its print on foreign policy; on the contrary, culture influences diplomatic affairs together with various alternative factors. Secondly, it is obvious that Chinese culture has had different impacts on China's foreign policy, both in a positive and negative sense. Thirdly, China's policy is not necessarily always consistent. For example, this can be applied to the non-interference policy. During the Cultural Revolution, some revolutionary measures were exported to countries, and this happened to interfere with the latter's political affairs, as demonstrated by the works of certain Chinese scholars that explored the cases of China's interference during the Cultural Revolution (Wang 2000, Long 2000). This topic has also been progressively covered by Western scholars (Taylor 2006).

Conclusion

There is a linkage between Chinese culture and China's policy towards Africa. In order to understand China's Africa policy, we should try to appreciate Chinese culture. The European Union and China have different cultural traditions, yet they both want to develop good relations with Africa. Mutual criticism will not lead to this ideal, whereas the exchange of ideas and lessons from their own process of development would increase their mutual understanding.

China's engagement in Africa may be considered as an experiment: an experiment taken from China's culture and China's own development, which still remains unimaginable for many in the West, who will need time to fully understand this process. In concluding her *Dragon's Gift*, Deborah Brautigam states:

> At the end of the day, we should remember this: China's own experiments have raised hundreds of millions of Chinese out of poverty, largely without foreign aid. They believe in investment, trade, and technology as levers for development, and they are applying these same tools in their African engagement, not out of altruism but because of what they learned at home. [...] These lessons emphasize not aid, but experiments; not paternalism, but the 'creative destruction' of competition and the green shoots of new opportunities. This may be the dragon's ultimate, ambiguous gift (Brautigam 2008: 312).

Her statement is somewhat true. It is possible to reach a win-win situation, even for different partners engaged in a fight against poverty and in the fulfilment of humankind's destiny, and yet, in order to achieve such an end, it is essential for both partners to attempt to forge greater cooperation.

Bibliography

Book References

Ampiah, K. and Naidu, S. 2008. *Crouching Tiger, Hidden Dragon? Africa and China*. Cape Town: University of KwaZulu Natal Press.

Autesserre, S. 2006. *Local Violence, International Indifference? Post-Conflict 'Settlement' in the Eastern D.R. Congo (2003–2005)*. New York University: PhD Dissertation.

Bagby, P. 1958. *Culture and History*. London: Longmans.

Brautigam, D. 2009. *Dragon's Gift: The Real Story of China in Africa*. Oxford: Oxford University Press.

Deng, X. 1993. *Selection of Deng Xiaoping*. Volume 3. Beijing: People's Press.

Guerrero, D.G. and Manji, F. 2008. *China's New Role in Africa and the South: A Search for a New Perspective*. Nairobi, Oxford and Bangkok: Pambazuka Press.

Hao, Y. and Lin, S. 2007. *Chinese Foreign Policy Making: An Analysis of Societal Factors*. Beijing: Social Sciences Academic Press.

Harneit-Sievers, A., Marks, S. and Naidu, S. 2010. *Chinese and African Perspectives on China in Africa*. Nairobi, Oxford and Bangkok: Pambazuka Press.

Health Department of Hubei Province. 1993. *Famous Doctors in North Africa*. Beijing: Xinhua News Agency.

Huang, H. 2007. *Witnesses and Experiences: Huang Hua's Memoir*. Beijing: World Affairs Press.

Huntington, S.P. 1996. *The Clash of Civilizations and the Remaking of World Order*. New York: Simon and Schuster Paperbacks.

Kroeber, A. and Kluckhohn, C. 1952. *Culture: A Critical Review of Concepts and Definitions, Papers of the Peabody Museum of American Archaeology and Ethnology*. First Edition. Cambridge, MA: Harvard University Press.

Li, J. 2001. *Big Events in the History of Foreign Affairs of the People's Republic of China*. Volume 2. Beijing: World Affairs Press.

Liu, J. 1998. *Chinese Medical Teams in Tanzania*. Health Department of Shandong Province.

Manji, F. and Marks, S. 2007. *African Perspective on China in Africa*. Nairobi and Oxford: Pambazuka Press.

Mao, Z. 1994. *Mao Zedong on Diplomacy*. Beijing: Documentation Office of Communist Party of China Central Committee Publisher and World Affairs Publisher.

Monson, J. 2009. *Africa's Freedom Railway: How a Chinese Development Project Changed Lives and Livelihoods in Tanzania*. Bloomington and Indianapolis: Indiana University Press.

Qian, Q. 2003. *Ten Notes on Diplomacy*. Beijing: World Affairs Press.

Strauss, J.C. and Saavedra, M. 2009. *China and Africa: Emerging Patterns in Globalization and Development*. Cambridge: Cambridge University Press.

Taylor, I. 2006. *China and African: Engagement and Compromise*. Abingdon and New York: Routledge.

Yang, B. 1960. *Menzi Yizhu* (孟子译注). Beijing: Zhonghua Shuju Book Company.

Yang, B. 1980. *Lunyu Yizhu* (论语译注). Beijing: Zhonghua Shuju Book Company.

Yu, G. 1975. *China's African Policy: A Study of Tanzania.* New York: Praeger Publishers.

Zhang, T. 1999. *Road of Friendship*: *Report of Building of TAZARA.* Beijing: China Foreign Economy and Trade Press.

Zhu, Z. 1985. *Zhanguo Ce Ji Ju Hui Kao* (战国策集注汇考). Yangzhou: Jiangsu Guji Chubanshe.

Book Chapters

Li, A. 2008. China's new policy towards Africa, in *China Into Africa: Trade, Aid, and Influence*, edited by R. Rotberg. Washington, D.C.: Brookings Institute Press, 21–49.

Long, X. 2000. A study on China-African relations in 1966–1969, in *China and Africa*, edited by the Centre for African Studies. Beijing: Peking University, 72–86.

Shweder, R.A. 2000. Moral maps, 'First World' conceits, and the new evangelists, in *Culture Matters, How Values Shape Human Progress*, edited by L.E. Harrison and S.P. Huntington. New York: Basic Books.

Wang, L. 2006. Great achievements in China-African medical cooperation, in *Unity as Treasure as Gold-Glorious History of China-African Relation of Friendship*, edited by M. Lu, S. Huang and Y. Lin. Beijing: World Affairs Press, 308–13.

Wang, Q. 2000. A setback of China-African relations, in *China and Africa*, edited by the Centre for African Studies. Beijing: Peking University Press, 59–71.

Journal Articles

Berger, B. 2006. China's engagement in Africa: can the EU sit back?. *South African Journal of International Affairs*, 13(1), 115–27.

Department of International Cooperation of Ministry of Health. 2003. To strengthen the implementation of new strategy of reform of medical aid in Africa. *West Asia and Africa*, 5, 15-18.

Eisenman, J. and Kurlantzick, J. 2006. China's Africa strategy. *Current History*, 105(691), 216–24.

He, W. 2007. The balancing act of China's Africa policy. *China Security*, 3(3), 23–40.

Large, D. 2008. Beyond 'dragon in the bush': the study of China-African relations. *African Affairs*, 107(426), 45–61.

Li, A. 2005. African studies in China in the twentieth century: a historiographical survey. *African Studies Review*, 48(1), 59–87.

Li, A. 2006. China-African relations in the discourse on China's rise. *World Economics and Politics*, 315(11), 7–14.

Li, A. 2007. Africa in the perspective of globalization: development, assistance and cooperation. *West Asia and Africa*, 7, 5–14.

Li, A. 2008. Studi africanistici in Cina all'inizio del XXI secolo (African studies in China in the twentieth century). *Afriche e Orienti (China in Africa)*, 2, 88–101.

Li, A. 2009. Chinese medical teams abroad: a history of medical cooperation. *Foreign Affairs Review*, 26(1), 25–46.

Mohammed, A. 2004. The Rezaigat camel nomads of the Darfur region of Western Sudan: from cooperation to confrontation. *Nomadic Peoples*, 8, 230–40.

Shinn, D.H. 2006. Africa, China and health care. *Inside AISA*, 3–4, 14–16.

Siringi, S. 2003. Africa and China join forces to combat malaria. *The LANCET*, 362(9382), 456.

Thompson, D. 2005. China's soft power in Africa: from the 'Beijing Consensus' to health diplomacy. *China Brief*, 5(21), 1–4.

Yang, L. 2006. Africa: a view from China. *South African Journal of International Affairs*, 13(1), 23–32.

Websites

2007. *Humanitarian aid from China leaves for Sudan's Darfur.* [Online]. Available at: www.focac.org/eng/zxxx/t353371.htm [accessed: 20 December 2007].

AllAfrica.com. 2009. *President Sirleaf hails Sino-Africa partnership, says it increases continent's chances.* [Online]. Available at: http://allafrica.com/stories/200911091586.html [accessed: 10 November 2009].

Apps, P. 2007. *Watch your facts, UK ad watchdog warns campaigners.* [Online]. Available at: http://www.alertnet.org/thenews/newsdesk/L14822855.htm [accessed: 20 December 2007].

Bo, Z. 2007. *The life of foreign aid of doctors from Hubei.* [Online]. Available at: http://www.africawindows.com/bbs/thread-9931-1-1.html [accessed: 20 December 2010].

China Daily Newspaper. 2007. *Confrontation over Darfur 'will lead us nowhere'.* [Online]. Available at: http://www.chinadaily.com.cn/2008/2007-07/27/content_5445062.htm [accessed: 20 December 2010].

Focac.org. 2007. *Humanitarian aid from China leaves Sudan's Darfur.* [Online]. Available at: http://www.focac.org/eng/zxxx/t353371.htm [accessed: 16 September 2010].

Lu, C. 2006. *Cotecxin – tie of Sino-African friendship.* [Online]. Available at: http://qkzz.net/magazine/1003-5303B/2006/06/1849404.htm [accessed: 30 June 2008].

Mohan, R. 2002. *Sakhalin to Sudan: India's energy diplomacy.* [Online]. Available at: http://www.hinduonnet.com/thehindu/2002/06/24/stories/2002062404201100.htm [accessed: 24 June 2002].

Xinhua News Agency. 2007. *Sudan government deals with Darfur issue with a light pack.* [Online]. Available at: http://news.xinhuanet.com/world/2007-07/15/content_6377969.htm [accessed: 15 July 2007].

Xinhua News Agency. 2010. *Chinese Foreign Minister Yang review FOCAC achievements in the past three years*. [Online]. Available at: http://www.focac. org/chn/zxxx/t625612.htm [accessed: 10 January 2010].

Newspapers

1963. Chinese medical team went to Algeria. *People's Daily*, 7 April.
1964. Premier Zhou answered questions of the news reporter of Ghana news agency stating a new independent powerful Africa will appear in the world and China will support the newly rising countries develop their independent national economy strictly according to the eight principles. *People's Daily*, 18 January.
1983. Premier Zhao talked about how his visits to ten African countries had reached the expected purpose at the Dar es Salaam press conference. *People's Daily*, 15 January.
2007. What kind of issue Darfur is: a special interview with the Special Representative of the Chinese government. *Chutian Metropolis Daily*, 8 July.

Command Paper

Sudan Post-Conflict Environmental Assessment. 2007. Nairobi: United Nations Environment Programme.

Chapter 3

China's African Relations and the Balance with Western Powers

Suisheng Zhao

Introduction

China's rise has come with global activism. Outside of Asia, nowhere else is China's footprint more visible than in Africa. Investing billions of dollars in mineral projects across Africa, China is expanding its development assistance and building massive infrastructure projects. Chinese leaders have made regular visits to the continent and thousands of Chinese servicemen and police officers are on the ground serving in United Nations (UN) peacekeeping missions. China's fast-growing African engagement has caused concerns and criticisms from many in the West as if a benign, postcolonial West has been outfoxed and marginalized by a ruthless and unscrupulous authoritarian power. As the influence of former colonial powers is waning, they decry Beijing's condition-free approach to investing in corrupted African states in the name of non-interference, worry about China's rush into the exploitation of natural resources on the continent, and criticize China's insensitive business and labour practices.

To what extent are these concerns justifiable? What are the implications of China's foray in Africa? How has China responded to Western concerns? This chapter seeks to shed light on these questions by examining China's engagement with African countries in the context of its relations with Western powers. It argues that while China has found some niches and effectively mobilized its diplomatic, cultural and financial resources to pursue its interests, China has failed to design a grand strategy towards the continent. To serve its interests in the region while avoiding diplomatic and strategic confrontation with the Western powers on a broad range of controversial issues, China has constantly made adjustments to achieve a delicate balance between ensuring a reliable supply of resources from Africa to fuel its burgeoning economy and maintaining relations with Western powers. This chapter is divided into three parts. It first starts with a discussion of the Western factor in China's African engagement. The second part looks at Western criticisms of China's African foray. The third part examines China's response.

The Western Power Factor in China's African Engagement

The United States (US) and European powers have been a factor in China's relations with African countries since the mid-twentieth century. The strategic interest of breaking the diplomatic isolation imposed by Western powers was the initial motivation for China to venture into Africa in the early 1950s. African countries played a decisive role in Beijing's 1971 entry into the UN. Driven by the ideology of Third World solidarity in the 1960s–1970s, Beijing built the costly railway to link from Tanzania to Zambia, and constructed stadiums for football matches and political rallies in many African countries that supported Mao's anti-imperialist struggle.

Launching market-oriented economic reform in the 1980s, while the rhetoric of Third World solidarity persisted, Beijing was no longer sure whether it could benefit from relations with economically stagnant African countries and moved its foreign policy priority toward Western countries. The 1980s thus became a decade of neglect for Africa in China's foreign policy (Taylor 1990). This 'neglect' was corrected after the Tiananmen Incident in 1989, motivated by the strategic interest of working with its Third World allies to resist Western sanctions and reinforced by the economic incentives of securing energy and other natural resources to sustain China's phenomenal growth. China's political stability depends on continued economic growth, which is fuelled by readily available and affordable supplies of natural resources imported from foreign sources. Therefore, China rediscovered Africa, as one of the few places in the world where so many resources are still available to China. Rich in diamonds, oil reserves, hydroelectric power and forests, Africa holds 90 percent of the world's cobalt, 90 percent of its platinum, 50 percent of its gold, 98 percent of its chromium, 64 percent of its manganese, and one-third of its uranium (Behar 2008b). Africa's vast deposits of copper, bauxite, cobalt, iron ore, gold and other mineral resources have become even more attractive as prices of natural resources continue to soar in the new century.

Driven mostly by the quest for African resources to feed its economic boom, China has become part, since the late 1990s, of a global race to tap the continent's energy resources and mineral wealth, when Beijing embarked on a 'Going-Global' policy of helping Chinese companies' international competitiveness. China's interest in Africa is basically similar to those of the European powers who arrived on the continent several centuries earlier. While Africa's traditional business partners have either abandoned or found many problems operating in Africa in recent decades, many Chinese companies have taken advantage of this opportunity and established the three following advantages when competing with Western powers in Africa.

Firstly, Chinese workers are not only very diligent and disciplined but are also less expensive than their Western counterparts. Living together in barracks with their spouses and children, Chinese managers and workers do not normally ask for the comfort and expenses that Western expatriates often demand. Chinese equipment and materials are also cheaper. In addition, China's market-oriented economic reform has created a frenzy of entrepreneurialism among the Chinese looking for adventure and the opportunity to set up businesses in Africa. Given their energies and talents for profit-making, the Chinese have engaged in ruthless competition, which creates a virtually unbeatable price and efficiency. In comparison, it is difficult for Europeans and Americans to do what the Chinese have done. As Edward Friedman (2009) noted,

> Coming from richer countries, they insist on better living conditions and bigger profit margins. While Chinese may cluster in Chinatowns and spark a racist backlash, they work harder in harsher circumstances. They accept smaller margins. Their numbers are also infinitely greater than the handful of Euro-Americans moving to Africa. Backed by a government with a seemingly bottomless pool of foreign exchange and a serious commitment to succeeding in Africa, China's energies can transform the continent. The subsidies, cheap money and assistance to business in Africa from the Chinese government will have a huge impact because of the efforts of hard working, globally mobile, entrepreneurial Chinese. Therefore, whereas satisfied European and American investors saw few profit-making opportunities in Africa, entrepreneurial Chinese have found plenty of possibilities.

Secondly, compared with Western powers, China has no history of enslavement, colonization, financing coups against unfriendly African regimes or deploying military forces in support of its foreign policies. Chinese involvement in African resource extraction, thus, not only provides a welcome infusion of competition to raise prices for African resources and reduce prices for the construction projects on which many Chinese firms bid, but also presents the continent with an opportunity for development through the Chinese packages of infrastructure construction for extraction rights. China has made a spate of resource acquisitions by signing agreements to build infrastructure projects in exchange for minerals. Although much of the infrastructure is crucial to China's ability to operate effectively in the country, it can also provide a much-needed stimulus to the local economy because the infrastructure deficit is a major impediment to growth and Western investors have failed to fill this massive investment gap. This constructive partnership thus serves the continent well in creating a platform for future development and wealth creation in Africa (Edinger 2008). The resources for infrastructure deals have provided China with a competitive advantage along with increased trade and investment opportunities on the continent.

Thirdly, while Western companies have come under increasing pressure and oversight from shareholders and regulators to improve their ethical and environmental performance, Chinese business has operated without such pressure. While the Americans and Europeans pressure their African partners into abiding by Western conditions, the Chinese have followed a policy of non-interference in domestic affairs and impose no political conditions before signing business contracts. This is a welcome relief after years of Western investment and assistance inconveniently offering premises on high benchmarks about environmental damage, human rights, transparency and good governance. China's no-strings-attached approach has, therefore, espoused a new business model with none of the meddling so common among Western business practices. Many African governments welcome Chinese investors because they see poverty rather than liberal concerns as their top priority. While only three decades ago, China was as poor as some of the poorest African countries, China has lifted hundreds of millions of their own people out of poverty without dramatic social and political disorder that often comes with democratization. According to Loro Horta (2009),

> China's model of a strong government and its focus on economic growth is looked upon by many African despots, and even some democratic leaders, as an example to follow. Frustrated with decades of instability and corruption, which many African elites tend to blame on the West and its liberal democratic model, the continent's elites are fast embracing the Chinese model.

With these competitive advantages, China has launched a multifaceted effort to mobilize its diplomatic, cultural and financial resources in Africa. Diplomatically, building the largest number of Embassies and Consulates, Chinese leaders have made one Bono-like tour after another of Africa. No other major power has shown the same interest, muscle and ability to connect with African leaders. Culturally, while the Chinese government has pressed hard to build Confucius Institutes in Africa, Chinese universities have offered a growing number of degrees in international Master of Business Administration (MBAs) and similar courses for many African students and young professionals. Financially, China's development assistance is an effective tool to cement alliances, secure access to natural resources and drum up business for its companies. African governments have received multi-billion dollar deals in return for mining, timber or oil rights, and for the purchase of goods from China. In this way, the Chinese companies have a great advantage over companies from other countries that cannot access such facilities from their governments. To further help Chinese companies' African ventures, the Chinese government has built a framework of multilateral institutions with the Forum on China-Africa Cooperation (FOCAC) that held its first summit meeting in October 2000. Its importance came into the spotlight when more than 50 African heads of states gathered in Beijing at the FOCAC summit meeting in 2006.

China's policy has paid huge dividends. While the US still reigns in terms of cumulative direct investment on oil resources in a few countries, China has gained ground and is growing fast, spreading its investments across many resources and infrastructure projects in less than a decade. Cutting a swath across the entire continent and securing access to much-needed raw materials, the Chinese government has offered debt relief and interest-free loans, taught the Chinese language to African students and provided Chinese businesses with information and technical support to lower their cost of doing business, in return. There is now barely an African country that does not have a sizeable Chinese presence. With its involvement in oiling, mining, timber, fishing and digging for precious stones for its resource hungry economy, China has been credited with building crucial infrastructure and providing easy loans and assistance for some of the world's poorest nations as well as internationally condemned dictators.

Criticism of China's African Foray

Redrawing the global geo-economic and political map, China's foray into Africa has attracted wide international attention. China's dealings with some of the most disreputable governments have raised concerns among some in the US and Europe that China is not only challenging their historic dominance on the continent but also undermining Western efforts to promote democracy, good governance and human rights, thereby damaging Western interests and values. China's relations with African countries have, therefore, become an issue in China's relations with many Western countries. The Western criticism, which is echoed by some in Africa, has focused mostly on four issue areas:

1. human rights
2. corruption
3. natural resources exploitation
4. labour practices.

Human Rights

While China played a critical role in supporting African decolonization struggles, its *laissez-faire* policy has raised questions about its moral and ethical commitment to Africa's sustainable socio-economic and political development. China's no-strings-attached investment is criticized by Western nations but commended by some African nations for making business deals with corrupt and ruthless African governments, whilst threatening to wipe out the efforts made by global institutions to push African governments into improving their protection of human rights and government transparency. In particular, China's relationships with the so-called rogue states, particularly Sudan and Zimbabwe, have been tackled with vigour in the international media.

Sudan has become an international pariah and for years was out of bounds for Western companies because of its policy in Darfur, where hundreds of thousands of people were killed, countless numbers raped and tortured, and millions displaced. Chinese state oil companies, nevertheless, have no qualms about doing business in Sudan, which now pumps hundreds of thousands of barrels of oil a day from its Red Sea port into Chinese vessels. In the midst of what many Americans and Europeans have dubbed as genocide in Darfur, China continues to be not only the biggest importer of Sudan's oil, but also its main supplier of weapons, including ammunition, tanks, helicopters and fighter aircraft used by the government forces and militia against rebellious forces (Moyo 2008). While it is arguable whether China's close relations with Sudan have allowed the regime in Khartoum to carry out atrocities, China did threaten a veto when Great Britain and the US pushed in 2004 for a punitive UN Security Council resolution against Sudan for the mass killing of civilians in Darfur.

China has also avowed to an all-weather friendship with the Mugabe government in Zimbabwe, another rogue state under Western sanctions. While the Chinese government argues that its support for Zimbabwe is based on close historical ties dating back to the struggle for independence, Chinese companies have clinched lucrative deals in mining, aviation, agriculture, defence and other sectors. China's veto, together with Russia, against the UN sanctions on the Mugabe regime, for its human rights violations in the midst of an election crisis, in June 2008, angered those who worked for substantive political change in Zimbabwe. It is from this perspective that Moyo (2008) described China as 'shrewd, selfish, calculating, greedy and primitive because it prioritizes its economic and political interests over ordinary people's human rights in its dealings with African countries'.

China is also blamed for enabling human rights abuses in other African countries. One example is of a multi-billion dollar deal struck by China's International Fund for oil and mineral extraction rights in Guinea, a country run by a military junta (Berger 2009). The deal came just weeks after the 28 September 2009 massacre, in which soldiers opened fire on protesters who took to the streets against Captain Camara's announcement to run for presidency. Killing 157 people and raping women in the streets, the incident drew international condemnation and prompted renewed international pressure for the junta to relinquish power to elected civilians. International protest at Guinea's repressive military regime escalated into an embargo. While Guinea became a no-go area for reputable companies, China sensed an opportunity to enhance its position in Guinea which has the world's largest deposits of bauxite, as well as gold, diamonds, uranium and iron ore (Berger 2009). While the Chinese government spokesman insisted that the deal was of a corporate nature and 'as a developing country, China has South-South Cooperation with Guinea based on equality, mutual benefit, international norms and market rules' (Berger 2009), critics said that China's deal would potentially throw the regime a lifeline, raising fresh questions about the willingness of China to prop up rogue African governments (Burgis, Wallis 2009).

Corruption

Although China, as a fast-rising economic power is known for lifting millions of people out of poverty with unimaginable speed, it is also known for its widespread corruption, most apparent during the reform years. The lack of transparency in China's business deals is also a source of corruption in Africa. Embracing preferential loans from the Chinese government for a host of unmet needs, such as building new roads, power plants and telecommunications networks across the African continent, many African nations have to cope with China's practice of secret government-to-government agreements and the requirement that foreign aid contracts be awarded to Chinese contractors, through a closed-door bidding process. Competitive bidding is discouraged and China pulls a veil over vital data such as project costs, loan terms and repayment conditions. Compared with Western loans, which require strong measures against corruption, China's attempts to prevent corrupt practices by its companies overseas are weak because China has no specific law against bribing foreign officials and the government is not eager to investigate or punish companies that have engaged in shady practices overseas.

While the murky nature of China's practice has caused concerns, China's position is that transparency will come only after economic might has worked its magic. As Li Ruogu, the head of China's Export-Import (EXIM) Bank told an audience in Cape Town, 'Transparency and good governance are good terminologies, but achieving them is not a precondition of development; it is rather the result of it' (Behar 2008a). Such secrecy, however, invites corruption and puts much of the wealth China injects into Africa, into the pockets of either the Chinese companies or the local corrupted elite.

Natural Resource Exploitation

Cutting deals and securing supplies of oil, copper, timber, natural gas, zinc, cobalt, iron and other natural resources, China's investment and development assistance in Africa are most often tied to business deals in resource-rich countries. Chinese acquisition of resources in Africa's mountains, forests and offshore waters has increasingly become a concern for Western powers who criticize China for taking advantage of the investment needs of African countries and for providing financing, in return for natural resource extraction rights.

It is not difficult to find evidence to support this criticism. In Zimbabwe, China pledged a US$5 billion loan to obtain 50 percent equity in a US$40 billion platinum concession (Guchu 2009). Given Western sanctions on Zimbabwe, Mugabe was forced to deal with the Chinese over its extensive platinum reserves in exchange for credit and cash. Therefore, 'The Zimbabwean loan has raised serious allegations of President Robert Mugabe's regime mortgaging the country for generations to come' (Guchu 2009). In Mozambique, Chinese companies pushed deeper into its forests while China introduced widespread logging bans at home, in 1999, to stop the deforestation that was blamed for soil erosion and severe flooding. Mozambique is now China's leading source of wood in East Africa and most of this timber leaves the country as raw, unprocessed logs, essentially subtracting its value from one of the world's poorest economies and adding it to what is becoming one of the richest. From this perspective, one observer argues that China's log exporting from Mozambique has become an exploitative 'gold rush' (Behar 2008b). China has few large-scale copper mines of its own, so its enormous smelting industry relies on raw copper from abroad. China, therefore, has also established a huge operation in Zambia, which has the second-largest reserves of raw copper in Africa. With global copper prices at record levels, Zambians have grown furious, complaining that the Chinese bought the reserves at lower levels and have lined their pockets at the expense of the Zambians (Behar 2008c).

As a result, some Western countries have tried to put pressure on African countries to alter their deals with China. In 2008, a US$9 billion mineral for infrastructure deal China negotiated with the Democratic Republic of Congo (DRC), by which a consortium of Chinese companies agreed to build roads, railways, hospitals and universities in return for the right to develop a copper and cobalt mine. Concerned that the deal would give the Chinese consortium unprecedented state financial guarantees, including some that earmark government revenues and transform China into a privileged creditor, the Paris Club of creditors and the International Monetary Fund (IMF) raised objections to specific provisions of the deal. The Paris Club claimed it would not offer relief on the cash-strapped Congolese government's US$11 billion debt, if it accepted Chinese financing on commercial terms. To address Western donors' concerns, the Congolese deal with China was eventually scaled back. One *Financial Times* report commented that 'it could mark a turning point in China's quest for resources, which has threatened to marginalize Western donors' (Jopson 2009).

Insensitive Labour Practices

Chinese companies' labour practices have also been subject to Western criticism. In contrast with Western companies that rely primarily on local labour, Chinese companies have tended to keep local hiring to a minimum and to recruit mostly their own professionals and labourers for construction projects. In Angola, for example, Chinese companies bring 70 to 80 percent of their labour from home. While nearly 90 percent of Chevron's workers are Angolan, including specialized personnel such as engineers and managers – whereas less than 15 percent of staff in Chinese oil companies are Angolan and they are usually located at the lower end of the pay scale (Horta 2009). The Chinese are therefore criticized not as investors but as invaders, in Africa (Hitchens 2008).

Despite China's growth and new-found wealth, it still suffers gravely from having a hugely under-employed and unemployed rural population. After a visit to Ethiopia and Guinea, to explore possibilities for agricultural cooperation, a delegate from the Zhangjiakou Academy of Agricultural Sciences in Hebei province proposed at the annual session of China's National People's Congress (NPC) that Africa's vast land and underdeveloped agriculture could provide employment for up to 100 million Chinese labourers. The delegate suggested Beijing draft a long-term strategy of dispatching Chinese labourers to Africa in order to solve two of China's greatest challenges – food security and unemployment (Bezlova 2009). Although his proposal was not officially endorsed, hundreds of thousands of Chinese nationals, drawn from poor rural communities, are now working in Africa. Most of them live on site, thereby saving on rent while earning more than they would in China. There are Chinese restaurants, Chinese clinics and Chinese housing. As many Chinese tend to live in isolation with little or no contact with the local population, they do not have strong incentives and opportunities to learn the local languages or culture, and therefore, are insensitive to local concerns. Spending a few years in Africa, the Chinese journalist, Liu Zhirong, recorded in his blog (Liu 2009) the many conflicting issues between Chinese workers and the locals populace. In Ethiopia, one local official told him that when Chinese workers came to build a road, they ate all of the pigs in the area (Liu 2009). He also found that the Chinese disrupt markets. Their bids are often one third the price of a bid by a French competitor, to the fury of the French bidders (Liu 2009). The Chinese companies often pollute heavily, use poor materials or renege on their contracts. Africans are often angry at being outbid by the Chinese, who they see as forcing them out of their own market (Liu 2009).

When Chinese companies do hire locals, they tend to flout local laws, disregard atrocious safety records, provide no welfare, and pay less than the country's prescribed minimum wage. Chinese employers do not allow their workers to join labour unions and the workers are not given adequate leave days. In 2004, the Zambian authorities had to ask Chinese managers at the Zambia-China Mulungushi Textiles Ltd. Company to stop locking workers in the factory at night. They also shut down Collum Coal Mining Industries in Southern Zambia, saying miners had been forced to work underground without safety clothing and boots. The government said the mine would re-open only after it was satisfied that conditions had improved. In 2005, Zambians who worked at the Chinese owned Chambishi Mine, rioted and demanded higher wages and better working conditions after an industrial accident killed 46 workers. The workers also demanded an end to exploitation and the adherence to established safety regulations. Similar riots also erupted in a suburb of Algiers in August 2009, after Chinese workers were accused of not respecting Muslim customs and of taking jobs from locals (Faucon, Swartz 2009).

China's Balancing Act

China's reaction to Western criticism has been very measured. Citing a bias against China, Beijing has launched a counter-offense to dismiss the criticism. At the 2009 FOCAC summit, China's Assistant Foreign Minister told the media that China was not seeking to impose its 'hegemony' and would not 'practice colonialism in Africa'. He claimed that unlike Western powers, 'China will not treat Africa in an imperialist way. China will not be pointing fingers or bullying African countries' (Bezlova 2009). China also charged the US and European powers with hypocrisy, considering that their own engagements in Africa were not especially benevolent or historically exemplary. The Chinese believe that a cross section of Africans in key states have a very favourable opinion of China because they come to Africa as equals, and with no aspirations of practising colonialism. Since Western investments and assistance have failed to lift African countries out of poverty, China's business model may provide an alternative opportunity for

Africans. Beijing has never hesitated to showcase the FOCAC process in which China won applause from its African friends, for its no-strings-attached approach, and was held as an example for development worth emulating by countries around the world (Sautman, Yan 2009).

Denying the charge that it harbours any intention of replicating Western colonialist expansion, Beijing has also taken cautious actions to adjust its practices in the recent years mostly due to the following two considerations. Firstly, China's relations with the US and European powers can no longer be disentangled from certain difficult issues involving China's relations with African countries. Therefore, it must address the Western call for taking more international responsibility. Secondly and more importantly, with its increasing investment in resource rich but often politically unstable African countries, helping maintain political stability and good governance is now in China's own interest for protecting its investment. As a result, China has made adjustments to refrain from investing in politically unstable countries, thus becoming more cautious in its dealings with oppressive regimes, and moving beyond its strategy of simply 'grabbing resources'.

Avoiding Politically Unstable Countries

Although China's quest for natural resources and trade has not stalled, Chinese companies are now avoiding some of the most chaotic corners of the continent. For about one decade, with its no-strings-attached approach and a strong appetite for taking risks, China seemed to offer Africa a complete economic and political alternative to the heavily conditioned aid and economic restructuring that Western countries and international aid agencies pressed on Africa. Polgreen (2009) notes, however, that 'as global commodity prices have plummeted and several of China's African partners have stumbled deeper into chaos, China has backed away from some of its riskiest and most aggressive plans, looking for the same guarantees that Western companies have long sought for their investments: economic and political stability'.

China learned this lesson the hard way. For example, when Royal Dutch Shell was at loggerheads with the Nigerian government, the China National Offshore Oil Company (CNOOC) bought a 45 percent stake in the Akpo oilfield and signed more than US$10 billion of contracts with Nigeria in 2006 (Timberg 2006). With the change in government the following year, and the new Nigerian government's lack of commitment to these deals, it thus became impossible to enforce them. In addition, Chinese companies were exposed to militant attacks on personnel, pipelines and other infrastructure. In May 2006, the militant Movement for the Emancipation of the Niger Delta (MEND), located in Nigeria's volatile oil-producing region, detonated a car bomb targeted at Chinese investors. The spokesman of the movement specifically warned 'the Chinese government and its oil companies to steer well clear of the Niger Delta. Chinese citizens found in oil installations will be treated as thieves. The Chinese government by investing in stolen crude places its citizens in our line of fire' (Timberg 2006). The warning came after Chinese President Hu Jintao's week-long tour of Africa in which he reached a series of deals securing access to oil and other resources, including one signed with former Nigerian President Obasanjo that offered China four oil exploration licenses (Timberg 2006).

As a result, Chinese companies began to bargain-hunt for deals in more stable countries. For example, although the Guinean government sought a multi-billion dollar deal from China to build a desperately needed hydroelectric dam in exchange for access to reserves of bauxite and iron ore, in 2009, China backed away from what Guinean officials portrayed as a done deal because of the unstable political situation (Polgreen 2009). Another similar example is of China's 2008 US$9 billion deal signed with the Democratic Republic of Congo, for access to its giant trove of copper, cobalt, tin and gold in exchange for developing roads, schools, dams and railways which were needed to rebuild a country shattered by more than a decade of war. This deal came in to question in early 2009, partially because of the pressure from Western powers and partially because the Congo's political and ethnic turmoil remained deep and its economy was near collapse. These examples illustrate the recent shift in Chinese investment strategy as neither Western pressure, nor political instability were cause for Chinese concerns just a few short years ago (Jopson 2009).

Cautious with Repressive Regimes

China has increasingly adopted a more nuanced perspective in dealing with unpopular African regimes such as those in Sudan and Zimbabwe. One study by Kleine-Ahlbrandt and Small (2008) finds that although China is often accused of supporting a string of despots and genocidal regimes, in recent years, 'Beijing has been quietly overhauling its policies toward pariah states [...]. China is now willing to condition its diplomatic protection of pariah countries, forcing them to become more acceptable to the international community', because 'China's fears about a backlash and the potential damage to its strategic and economic relationships with the United States and Europe have prompted Beijing to put great effort into demonstrating that it is a responsible power'.

A major buyer of Sudanese oil and a partner in large-scale infrastructure projects, China is one of the few countries with influence to affect the situation in the desolate war zone. For many years, human rights organizations criticized China for failing to convince Khartoum to accept the presence of peacekeeping forces or the organization of negotiations to find a political solution to the conflict, after Darfur's black African population rebelled, in 2003, against the Arab-run government. Some US and European activists even called for a boycott of the 2008 Olympic Games in Beijing, because of China's lack of forcefulness regarding the situation. When the volume of complaints rose, the Chinese government began making public statements urging for more cooperation from the Sudanese while privately pressuring Khartoum for a solution to the Darfur crisis. President Hu quietly tried to persuade the Sudanese government to agree to the deployment of the peacekeepers in his February 2007 visit to Sudan. Meanwhile, he publicly called on the Khartoum government to cooperate in the swift deployment of international peacekeeping forces and to help end humanitarian abuses in the embattled Darfur region, at his meeting with visiting Sudanese Vice President Ali Taha, in June 2008. Reported on the front page of *People's Daily*, Hu told Taha that 'It is necessary to push forward the relevant parties to carry out a comprehensive cease-fire and constantly improve the humanitarian and security situation according to the account to allow people there to reconstruct their homeland'. A Western report saw the official portrayal of Hu's meeting as a departure from China's usual style of quiet diplomacy and ritual proclamations of friendship (Cody 2008).

Beijing also put pressure on Mugabe to hold a meeting with Morgan Tsvangirai, the leader of the opposition Movement for Democratic Change, for the first time in ten years, in July 2008, after signing a memorandum of understanding mediated by South Africa's President to form a government of national unity. Although the meeting appeared to be a triumph for South African diplomacy, 'the power behind the curtain is China. Mugabe was told in clear terms by his Chinese friends that he has to behave and act in a way that will help dampen international outrage over the recent elections in the run-up to the Olympics' (Evans 2008). China exerted diplomatic pressure on Mugabe for the protection of its own interests, given the threat and risks of their economic investments in the country. Beijing has many sources of leverage on Mugabe because it has been his most important economic partner and has helped train Zimbabwean military forces for more than two decades. At a news conference in June 2008, the spokesman for the Chinese Foreign Ministry, Liu Jianchao, told reporters that while China respected the integrity of domestic affairs in Zimbabwe, 'we hope the political parties will act in such a way as to put the interests of the people of Zimbabwe first through engaging in further dialogue. We believe that through increased and further dialogue a peaceful solution to the problems in Zimbabwe is possible' (Appel 2008). This explains Mugabe's sudden change of heart.

Moving beyond the Resource Grab

China has brushed off accusations regarding its investment in Africa and has pledged to help African countries sustain development, overcome poverty and fight new threats like climate change. In response to the charge that China has imposed unmanageable new debt burdens on impoverished African nations, the FOCAC made debt relief one of its top agenda issues. China has also taken an important step by joining the list of World Bank donors and other international institutions that channel grants and concessional loans to the poorest countries. In a trip to China in 2007, Robert Zoellick, the President of the World Bank, acknowledged that 'From statistics I have seen, China has paid attention to debt sustainability'. He saw this effort as evidence of 'China being a stakeholder in the field of development' (Wheatley 2007). At the 2009 FOCAC summit, Chinese Premier Wen Jiabao proposed to establish a China-Africa partnership for addressing climate change as the first among the eight new measures the Chinese government would undertake to strengthen China-Africa cooperation. As reported by the *Xinhua News Agency* (2009), he announced that 'China would enhance cooperation on satellite weather monitoring, development and utilization of new energy sources, prevention and control of desertification and urban environmental protection. China has decided to build 100 clean energy projects for Africa covering solar power, bio-gas and small hydropower'.

The Chinese government has made other efforts to demonstrate that its expansion in Africa is not solely driven by the interests in the continent's vast natural resources. One such effort is to encourage a growing number of Chinese entrepreneurs to set up manufacturing on the continent. In a December 2009 interview, Robert Zoellick found that the Chinese government had shown a 'strong interest' in 'moving some of the lower-value manufacturing facilities to Sub-Saharan Africa', helping the continent to develop a manufacturing base and boost its economy (Branigan 2009). This is a response to the complaint that the flood of cheap Chinese imports has undercut Africa's weak manufacturing base and that Africa may never get the chance to fully develop if cheap household goods continue to emanate from China's competitive manufacturing sectors.

In an early 2009 article, Edward Friedman praised this effort for following the underlying logic of globalization and producing a subsequent 'flying geese' effect of development. The flying geese pattern of development occurs when a rapid increase in technology and value-added production allows a country to outsource its lower-end production to other countries, which in turn develop technology and market shares, and lower-end production is again moved to countries with lower price labour. This idea was promoted by the Japanese when it began outsourcing its lower-end production to other Asian countries. Increasing wages, costs and a higher valued currency in China have begun to force the workshop of the world to outsource much of its lower-end production. In this way, the flying geese of Japan's Asia can become the flying geese of China's Africa. Plugging into Chinese dynamism, African nations can continually move up the value-added chain and take advantage of the opportunities inherent in China's rise to join the flock of flying geese. From this perspective, Friedman (2009) believes that poor Africans can be lifted out of poverty by Chinese investment and benefit from playing a role in a world economy largely structured by an Asian motor.

Beijing has also responded sensitively to Western criticisms of China promoting its model of development, characterized by the combination of authoritarian politics and market-oriented economy. Chinese Premier, Wen Jiabao, at the fourth FOCAC summit, argued that neither the 'Washington Consensus' nor the 'Beijing Model' offered prescriptions for Africa's development. It should instead be based on its own conditions and should follow its own path, that is, the African Model. All countries must learn from other countries' experience in development, while simultaneously following a path suited to their own national conditions and based on the reality of their own country. A Western report commented that:

Wen's carefully diplomatic comments do underscore China's sensitivity about its role in Africa, and how careful the government is in not being seen to dictate terms to poorer developing nations. He has to tread carefully as China's increasingly extensive financial business relationship with Africa is generating much debate in society there. Wen's remarks also reflect a genuine lack of dogmatism among Chinese economic policymakers, and a resistance to pre-packaged solutions from the West or anywhere else (Batson 2009).

In this case, China would become less of a model and more of a catalyst for African development.

Conclusion

After China began actively securing mineral rights in Africa to fuel its burgeoning economy, phrases such as the 'new scramble for Africa's riches', 'voracious, ravenous and insatiable appetite for natural resources', and 'profiting from states with problematic human rights records', have been typical descriptors of China's engagement in the continent. In contrast, the operations of Western companies are described with anodyne phrases such as 'development', 'investment', 'employment generation'. It seems that the African continent is in the process of being devoured by China although its operations remain smaller than Europe's and the US's (Ghosh 2008). Whether there is hypocrisy or even conspiracy, these perceptions have emerged largely because China's way of doing business in Africa differs from Western practices. In order to respond to Western criticism, as well as to serve its evolving interests, Beijing has taken pains to make delicate adjustments in its policy practice to balance its relationships with Western powers with its engagements with African countries.

In this process, China has made positive reforms in response to Western concerns on some issues, but the most important motives underlying China's policy adjustments are China's geo-economic and political interests, rather than simple reactions to Western criticism. That is why China is still hesitant to make significant changes on the issues of transparency, anti-corruption and labour practices. For example, although the lack of transparency surrounding much of Beijing's expansion in Africa is heavily criticized by the Western powers, Beijing has not taken decisive actions to alter its practices in this regard because the secret nature of economic transactions continues to serve Chinese companies' interests in sealing business deals. Corruption has not only accompanied their growth in profit but also become a driving force of at least a considerable part of Sino-African relations. In this case, China's advance on the continent has appeared and will continue to appear as *ad hoc*, without any sign of the implementation of a grand strategy at least in the foreseeable future. Although China's African foray looks enthralling and unnerving, the Chinese government and Chinese companies are still struggling to find their place on an increasingly crowded African continent.

Bibliography

Journal Articles

Kleine-Ahlbrandt, S. and Small, A. 2008. China's new dictatorship diplomacy. *Foreign Affairs*, 87(1), 38–9.
Sautman, B. and Yan, H. 2009. African perspectives on China-Africa links. *China Quarterly*, 199, 728–59.
Taylor, I. 1990. China's foreign policy towards Africa in the 1990s. *Journal of Modern African Studies*, 26(3), 443–60.

Websites

Appel, M. 2008. *China commits 320 military engineers to Darfur*. [Online]. Available at: http://www.buanews.gov.za/view.php?ID=08062710451003&coll=buanew08 [accessed: 20 July 2010].
Batson, A. 2009. *China's Wen forswears 'Beijing Model' for Africa*. [Online]. Available at: http://blogs.wsj.com/chinarealtime/2009/11/11/chinas-wen-forswears-beijing-model-for-africa [accessed: 20 July 2010].
Behar, R. 2008a. *China surpasses US as leader in sub-Sahara*. [Online]. Available at: http://www.fastcompany.com/magazine/126/endgame-hypocrisy-blindness-and-the-doomsday-scenario.html [accessed: 20 July 2010].
Behar, R. 2008b. *China saps Mozambique of timber resources*. [Online]. Available at: http://www.fastcompany.com/magazine/126/mozambique-a-chain-saw-for-every-tree.html [accessed: 20 July 2010].
Behar, C. 2008c. *Mining copper in Zambia*. [Online]. Available at: http://www.fastcompany.com/magazine/126/zambia-china-mine-shaft.html [accessed: 10 September 2010].
Berger, M. 2009. *Deal with Guinea raises questions about Chinese role*. [Online]. Available at: http://ipsnews.net/news.asp?idnews=48897 [accessed: 20 July 2010].
Bezlova, A. 2009. *China – latest Africa foray: altruism or hegemony?*. [Online]. Available at: http://www.ipsnews.net/news.asp?idnews=49191 [accessed: 20 July 2010].
Branigan, T. 2009. *China wants to set up factories in Africa*. [Online]. Available at: http://www.guardian.co.uk/world/2009/dec/04/china-manufacturing-factories-africa [accessed: 20 July 2010].
Burgis, T. and Wallis, W. 2009. *China in push for resources in Guinea*. [Online]. Available at: http://www.ft.com/cms/s/0/87afaf4e-b693-11de-8a28-00144feab49a.html [accessed: 20 July 2010].
Cody, E. 2008. *China steps up pressure on Sudan over Darfur*. [Online]. Available at: http://www.washingtonpost.com/wp-dyn/content/article/2008/06/12/AR2008061200902.html [accessed: 20 July 2010].

Edinger, H. 2008. *Colonial ambitions?*. [Online]. Available at: http://newmatilda.
    com/2008/08/11/colonial-ambitions [accessed: 20 July 2010].
Evans, I. 2008. *Robert Mugabe forced into talks with opposition after China
    told him 'to behave'.* [Online]. Available at: http://www.telegraph.co.uk/
    news/worldnews/africaandindianocean/zimbabwe/2461693/Robert-Mugabe-
    forced-into-talks-with-opposition-after-China-told-him-to-behave.html
    [accessed: 20 July 2010].
Faucon, B. and Swartz, S. 2009. *Africa puts breaks on China oil search in
    the continent.* [Online]. Available at: http://africanewsonline.blogspot.
    com/2009/09/africa-puts-breaks-on-china-oil-search.html [accessed: 20 July
    2010].
Friedman, E. 2009. *China-driven development, as China pours billions into
    Africa, other countries are trying to keep up.* [Online]. Available at: http://
    www.bjreview.com/world/txt/2009-02/01/content_176304.htm [accessed: 20
    July 2010].
Guchu, W. 2009. *China-Africa deal a lose-lose situation.* [Online]. Available at:
    http://www.informante.web.na/index.php?option=com_content&task=view&
    id=4496&Itemid=100&PHPSESSID=8d9e1176ecb2ff808ba0e7504cb8aefe
    [accessed: 20 July 2010].
Hitchens, P. 2008. *How China has created a new slave empire in Africa.* [Online].
    Available at: http://www.dailymail.co.uk/news/worldnews/article-1063198/
    PETER-HITCHENS-How-China-created-new-slave-empire-Africa.html
    [accessed: 20 July 2010].
Horta, L. 2009. *China and Africa.* [Online]. Available at: http://www.asiasentinel.
    com/index.php?option=com_content&task=view&id=2154&Itemid=422
    [accessed: 20 July 2010].
Jopson, B. 2009. *Donors press Congo over US$9 billion China deal.* [Online].
    Available at: http://www.ft.com/cms/s/0/f4d34d3a-f6d9-11dd-8a1f-0000779fd2ac.
    html [accessed: 20 July 2010].
Liu, Z. 2009. [Online]. Available at: http://blog.scol.com.cn/zuoguantianxia/
    archives/212561.html.
Moyo, L. 2008. *China's role in African politics appalling.* [Online]. Available
    at: http://www.howardwfrench.com/archives/2008/07/23/chinas_role_in_
    african_politics_appalling [accessed: 20 July 2010].
Polgreen, L. 2009. *As Chinese investment in Africa drops, hope sinks.* [Online].
    Available at: http://www.nytimes.com/2009/03/26/world/africa/26chinaafrica.
    html?hpw [accessed: 20 July 2010].
Wheatley, A. 2007. *World Bank eyes joint Africa projects with China.*
    [Online]. Available at: http://www.reuters.com/article/idUSPEK151636200
    71218 [accessed: 20 July 2010].
Xinhua News Agency. 2009. *Chinese Premier announces eight new measures to
    enhance cooperation with Africa.* [Online]. Available at: http://news.xinhuanet.
    com/english/2009-11/08/content_12411421.htm [accessed: 20 July 2010].

Newspapers

Ghosh, N. 2008. China's African ventures: no sinister aim. *The Straits Times*, 10 July.
Timberg, C. 2006. Militants warn China over oil in Niger delta. *Washington Post*, 1 May.

PART II

PART II

Chapter 4

Going Naval in Troubled Waters:
The EU, China and the Fight against Piracy
off the Coast of Somalia

Joris Larik and Quentin Weiler

Introduction

Since early 2009, two kinds of gold-starred flags can be spotted on the horizon off the coast of Somalia, one on a blue background, one on a red background. Participating in the international community's efforts to combat an upsurge of piracy in these waters, both the European Union (EU) and the People's Republic of China (PRC) have ventured into naval military operations far away from their home shores. Next to various other navies and international coalitions, the Chinese have maintained a flotilla of three ships, two warships and a supply ship in the Gulf of Aden, while the EU's operation EU Naval Force (NAVFOR) *Atalanta* involves around ten ships and several maritime reconnaissance aircrafts. Despite the limited size of both deployments, there is indeed something historical about them. As the *Xinhua News Agency* underlined, this 'will be the first overseas deployment for Chinese maritime forces since the fifteenth century' (Hao 2008), referring to the expeditions of Admiral Zheng He's Treasure Fleet under the Ming Dynasty. While for the EU member states, naval operations are not a distant historical memory, it is nevertheless remarkable that this is the first time the EU itself has conducted a naval operation. What started out as a largely introvert economic integration project, half a century ago, now appears to have developed into a fully-fledged international actor, capable of undertaking credible military operations on land and on sea.

Being more than a historical curiosity, these two missions also have important geopolitical implications for Africa, and for the international order of the twenty-first century in general. It is here that three developments – that have received heightened academic and wider public attention – converge. The first development is the emergence of the piracy threat off the coast of Somalia, which has to be placed in the wider context of the problems that the international community, at large, currently has to deal with, as a result of the failed state situation prevailing in Somalia (Boot 2009, Ndumbe Aynu, Moki 2009, Middleton 2008). The second is the rise of China as an international player (Goldstein 2005), which takes place against the backdrop of the real, desired or loathed multipolarization of international relations, a process in which the EU, itself a non-state *sui generis* entity, also seeks to assert itself (Fox, Godement 2009, Grant, Barysch 2008, Men 2007). The third is the role both these entities play in particular on the African continent, with the EU having largely followed in the historical footsteps of the member states in Africa, but with China being ever more present, which in turn leads to the discussion of the nature of the relationship between both (Fox, Godement 2009: 59–61, Grant, Barysch 2008: 82–9, Davies 2008). China and the EU's respective anti-piracy operations demonstrate that this relationship is not just defined in economic and investment related terms, but has also acquired a distinct security dimension. In particular, it allows us to scrutinize – beyond abstract theorizing on the multipolarization of the international order – how this intricate relationship works out in practice, all the way from Brussels and Beijing to the troubled waters off the coast of Somalia.[1]

This chapter will therefore assess to what extent both powers, in view of their motivation and operational approaches, can be seen rather as partners or competitors. The first section will provide a brief description of the political context leading up to the extremely fragile situation in Somalia and off its coast. Subsequently, the second part will look at the underlying motivations of the EU and China for launching their respective operations, which includes both the protection of their economic interests as well as tending to their respective great power aspirations. The third part will then analyse the operational approaches employed by the EU and China and assess the practical coordination and cooperation between them, which reveals a number of difficulties that originate from the divergent views on the kind of multipolar international order that both powers pursue. In the final section, we conclude that this case demonstrates how the system of international crisis management in Africa and beyond, is at a crossroads between the traditional system of balance of power – or 'walled' international system – and the cooperative kind of multipolarity the EU is promoting. The great challenge for the EU will be to facilitate China's integration, without giving up its own prominent position.

Background: Troubled Land, Troubled Waters

In order to fully understand the nature of the relationship between the two aspiring powers in Africa and beyond, it is worth recalling the main developments that led to the current crisis in the Horn of Africa, which in turn prompted both China and the EU to launch their first modern overseas maritime operations.

---

1   In the course of the research for this chapter, the authors conducted a number of interviews with officials in Brussels throughout November and December 2009 as well as January and May 2010. Due to the sensitive nature of the information received, the sources have to remain anonymous.

Somalia: The Forgotten State

The issue of piracy in the Gulf of Aden and the broader political and security context in the Horn of Africa had been neglected by the international community since the mid-1990s, despite the dramatic humanitarian situation that has been prevailing in Somalia. After the collapse of the dictatorial regime of General Bassié in 1991, the country descended into a civil war with extremely violent inter-ethnic conflicts and became a so-called 'failed state'. In this context, concerns about a potential spread of fundamentalist Islamist influence and a new-found interventionism to guarantee the stability of the international order after the Cold War, prompted the US to launch the United Nations (UN)-backed operation *Restore Hope*, in Somalia. It resulted in a major failure and a retreat of the American troops by 1995. This experience durably affected the American volition – both among the political leadership and in public opinion – to get directly involved in the Horn of Africa (Menkhaus 2004).

In the aftermath of 9/11, the United States (US) pushed its agenda on the 'war on terror', concentrating on this priority in certain designated areas, first and foremost Afghanistan, and later Iraq. In this new geopolitical context, Somalia was seen as a potential safe haven for Al-Qaeda terrorists rather than a priority area for concrete Western political involvement. The Islamist-led bomb attacks against the US Embassies in Kenya and in Tanzania, in 1998, confirmed the looming threat of Al-Qaeda in the Horn of Africa. Still, both the US and the EU continued to show little political interest for this region. The situation in Somalia worsened when the Islamic Courts Union took power in Mogadishu in 2005 and it is only after the Ethiopian military intervened in 2006 that the Transitional Federal Government (TFG), which is recognized and supported by the international community, assumed power in a very fragile situation (Dagne 2009).

Currently, the TFG's authority hardly extends beyond Mogadishu, while there exist in parallel a number of *de facto* independent provinces, such as Puntland and Somaliland in the North. Despite efforts to bolster the TFG, such as the joint United Nations-European Union-African Union (AU) international donors' conference for Somalia on 23 April 2009, where US$213 million were pledged (Phillips 2009b), the country has remained in a state of lawlessness and the lack of effective governmental control has lasted for 15 years, with no end in sight as of yet.

The Coast of Somalia: A New Kingdom for Pirates of the Twenty-First Century

In view of this lack of order, the country has descended into a breeding ground not only for terrorists, but also for organized crime, which recently manifested itself in the form of piracy. The upsurge in piracy is also linked to a certain degree to external abuse of the absence of effective state authority, most notably in the form of foreign fishing activities. Legally, this is an opaque matter, with fishing licences being granted by internationally unrecognized entities such as Puntland

and Somaliland, as well as by local tribes and warlords. In any event, foreign competition represented a significant burden for the already poverty-stricken Somali fishermen. Following the breakdown of the central government in 1991, fleets of hundreds of foreign fishing vessels, often heavily armed, have been harvesting maritime resources off the Somali coast (Daly 2009, Lehr, Lehmann 2007: 12–13). This included a certain number of European companies, in particular French, Greek and Spanish-owned vessels, often flying flags of convenience, at least until 2005. It even prompted the UN Special Representative in Somalia, Ahmedou Ould-Abdallah, to state that 'Europe does indeed have a lot to answer for' (Phillips 2009a). A 2005 report from the Marine Resources Assessment Group (MRAG) puts as a 'conservative' estimate for Somalia's economic losses at US$94 million per year, due to illegal, unregulated and unreported fishing (2005: 166–7). With their source of income thus limited, it has been argued that some local fishermen turned to piracy as an alternative source of income (Ndumbe Anyu, Moki 2009: 104). As Muammar Gaddaffi, then-chairman of the AU was quoted as saying: 'It is not piracy. It is self-defence, and it is defending Somali children's food. It is a response to greedy Western nations who invade and exploit Somalia's resources illegally' (Perry 2009). Others, even though sympathetic to the Somali fishermen's plight, caution 'not to romanticise the pirates as some Robin Hoods of the waves' (Phillips 2009a).

Indeed, the piracy phenomenon in this region has taken on a dynamic of its own, with the number of pirate attacks 'growing at an alarming rate' in recent years (Boot 2009: 94). According to the International Maritime Bureau (IMB) Piracy Reporting Centre, 51 pirate attacks took place in 2007, a figure that more than doubled in 2008 with 111 attacks. In 2009, 217 pirate attacks had been carried out off the coast of Somalia, which represents more than half of all reported pirate attacks worldwide.[2] In these 217 attacks, 74 vessels had been hijacked successfully and 867 crewmembers taken hostage. About half of these took place in the Gulf of Aden. However, pirate activity has spread increasingly to surrounding areas, up to 1,000 nautical miles into the Indian Ocean (IMB 2009: 5–6, 21). In the first half of 2010, another 100 incidents were reported (IMB 2010: 21). These attacked ships included high-profile targets such as the Ukrainian freighter MV *Faina* carrying a reported 33 Soviet made tanks, or the Saudi supertanker MV *Sirius Star* shipping two million barrels of oil. Armed rescue operations have also captured the headlines, such as that of the US cargo ship MV *Maersk Alabam* or the French yachts *Le Ponant* and *Tanit*. In most cases, however, ransoms have been paid, adding up to a total of over US$100 million in recent years, 'making piracy one of the most lucrative industries and pirates one of the biggest employers in Somalia' (Flintoff 2009). Consequently, with its 3,700 kilometres of coastline, Somalia has made the surrounding waters the most dangerous in the world. As

---

2   These figures refer to attacks in the Gulf of Aden, the Southern Red Sea, off the Somali coast, the Arabian Sea, the Indian Ocean and off the coast of Oman, which the IMB Piracy Reporting Centre attributes to Somali pirates.

a response, the UN Security Council passed a number of resolutions calling on states to protect ships chartered by the World Food Programme (WFP) bringing humanitarian aid to Somalia and to suppress piracy, if necessary, also in Somali territorial waters and soil.[3]

There have also been allegations that the pirates are becoming intertwined with terrorist groups operating in Somalia. Even though the pirates in the Horn of Africa do not have a political agenda, like some of their counterparts in the Gulf of Guinea, they evidently constitute a considerable 'potential source of financing' for terrorist activities (Ndumbe Anyu, Moki 2009: 116, Lehr, Lehmann 2007: 11). While a direct nexus with terrorist groups like Al-Qaeda has not been established, there are profit-motivated links between pirates and terrorist groups such as the Alliance of the Re-Liberation of Somalia, led by the Al-Shahaab, which is fighting the TFG (Bruton 2009: 82, Pham 2008). Moreover, the wider area around the Gulf of Aden has long been a theatre for terrorist and counterterrorist measures, notably with a maritime dimension, as the attack on the USS *Cole* in Yemen, in 2000, and the presence of Task Force 150, as the maritime component of operation *Enduring Freedom* illustrates. The spotlight on Yemen, since January 2010, as a breeding ground for terrorism just on the other side of the Gulf further highlights this dimension (Cohen 2010).

Shared Motivation: Safe Trade and Great Power Aspirations

As the first benchmark in determining the nature of the EU-China relationship in the fight against Somali pirates, the motivations behind the respective deployments of naval forces will be assessed. We argue that both share strong economic incentives, but that these alone cannot explain the decision to 'go naval'. In addition, both share great power aspirations, for which to display this case presented a formidable opportunity. In both respects, the EU and China are in the same boat together, and thus partners at large.

Economic Stakes of Two Major Trading Powers

Both for the EU and China, the economic interests at stake in combating piracy in the Gulf of Aden are evident. The Gulf of Aden is one of several 'chokepoints' in international trading routes, through which about 20,000 ships pass every year, transporting about 12 percent of the world's commerce, including 30 percent of global crude oil shipments (Ndumbe Anyu, Moki 2009: 103, Struye de Swielande 2009: 7).

---

3   See UN Security Council resolutions 1814(2008), 1816(2008), 1838(2008), 1846(2008) and 1851(2008), 1863(2009), 1897(2009). On the high seas, according to international law, any state can pursue, arrest and prosecute pirates, see United Nations Convention on the Law of the Sea, Article 105.

For Europeans, it is a strategic transit area, since goods to and from Asia are shipped through the Suez Canal and the Gulf of Aden. Of particular importance is the fact that about 30 percent of Europe's crude oil supplies pass through here (Reuters 2008). Moreover, the European fishing industry, primarily from Spain and France and to a lesser extent from Italy and Greece, is also involved in the area, with their ships representing easy targets for pirates using increasingly sophisticated means.[4] Consequently, the economic costs of operating in this area, including insurance fees, rose for both commercial and fishing vessels. Some companies decided to use an alternative route along the Cape of Good Hope to avoid the piracy threat but it has not proven to be a cost-effective alternative (Ndumbe Anyu, Moki 2009: 115). With public awareness raised by European media reporting on high-profile hijackings, pressure from the fishing and ship-owner industries, especially the French and Spanish ones, European decision-makers were compelled to discuss the issue in the wider context of the political situation in Somalia. France and Spain therefore called, at the EU Political and Security Committee, for concrete steps to deter piracy off the coast of Somalia by presenting a so-called non-paper at the beginning of the French Presidency of the EU.[5] This joint initiative contributed to raising awareness among other member states and kicked off the work to devise an appropriate European response.

For China – also a major trading power that has surpassed Germany as the world's largest exporter in 2009 (Inman 2010) – there is a similarly strong economic interest in keeping the Somali waters safe. By taking into consideration, on the one hand, the fact that the EU is China's first trading partner and that China is the EU's second most important trading partner (Kaufman 2009: 8), and on the other hand that 80 percent of international maritime trade in the Gulf of Aden is to or from Europe (US Department of Transportation 2008), this makes the strategic importance of securing this sea lane apparent. Moreover, as part of the complex strategic competition that exists between South East Asian countries and China over the Malacca Strait (Ross 2009: 70), one of the future priorities in regard to China's security interests lies in its capacity to secure other strategic sea lanes in order to guarantee a safe passage for its ever growing oil and gas imports, which in large part have to pass through the Gulf of Aden. The same is true for China's strategy of direct access to the continent's natural resources (Fiott 2009), in particular in Somalia, as the 2007 deal for a Chinese company to drill for oil in the Puntland region illustrates.[6] China has devoted increasing attention to the Horn of Africa in recent years in terms of trade and investment (Simons 2009), as well as military cooperation and arms sales related-issues (Shinn 2005), turning itself into 'one of the Horn of Africa's main partners' (Bertollo et al. 2009: 415).

---

4   Interview by the authors, Brussels, 8 December 2009.

5   Interview by the authors, Brussels, 8 December 2009.

6   The Chinese state oil giant, Chinese National Offshore Oil Company (CNOOC), signed an agreement in 2007 with the TFG for the exploitation of oil resources in the Northern part of Somalia, despite the extremely volatile security situation (Jopson 2007).

Great Power Aspirations

Trade and economics is but one side of the coin. What both the EU and China also share is the aspiration to become global players, not only by wielding economic power, but also by accumulating the full spectrum of attributes needed in order to attain world power status, which includes remote maritime power projection capabilities.

The EU, for its part, has been developing rather rapidly a stronger and more autonomous Common Security and Defence Policy (CSDP),[7] as exemplified by the numerous missions of both a military and civilian character (Howorth 2007). The launching of its first ever naval military operation represents a notable innovation in this process. Operation *Atalanta* can be seen as a more assertive form of engagement since it is, first and foremost, an international police mission warding off a direct threat to European vessels, citizens and interests (Gros-Verheyde 2009a), next to providing protection to ships of the WFP for the delivery of food to Somalia. It thus goes further than crisis management as initially defined in the 1992 Petersberg tasks (comprising humanitarian and rescue tasks, as well as peacekeeping and peacemaking), and could even be described as a form of collective defence against non-state actors. It also contributes to giving more credibility to the CSDP by adding an aero-naval dimension to its spectrum of activities in an operation with few military and political risks. Last but not least, it bolsters the role of the EU as a responsible and active power on the global stage fully assuming its declared objective to 'lead a renewal of the multilateral order' (Council of the European Union 2008). The EU's initiative and leadership managed to draw attention to the issue of piracy, as China or the North Atlantic Treaty Organization's (NATO) subsequent involvement demonstrates. Overall, the EU's endeavours to adopt a comprehensive approach in addressing the root causes of piracy highlight its willingness to promote a 'distinctive European approach to security and foreign policy'.[8] From being considered solely as a civilian soft power, the EU has in many ways evolved into a *normative power with teeth*.

For China, it has been argued that its implicit grand strategy now goes beyond securing the country's 'peaceful rise' in terms of economic development and trade. As the then US Director of National Intelligence put it, 'China's international behaviour is driven by a combination of domestic priorities, primarily maintaining economic prosperity and domestic stability, and a long-standing ambition to see China play the role of a great power in East Asia and globally' (Pham 2009). This second aspect contributes to the transformation of the still unipolar international order into a multipolar one, with China itself considered as one of the poles, if not the leading one. According to Goldstein, this represents a cautious 'strategy of transition' (2005: 38), but with far-reaching ulterior motives aimed at increasing

---

7　Before the entry into force of the Lisbon Treaty this was known as the European Security and Defence Policy (ESDP).

8　Interview by the authors, Brussels, 8 December 2009.

'the country's international clout without triggering a counterbalancing reaction' from other powers that have become anxious about China's rise (2005: 12).

With regard to the anti-piracy mission, this caution is well-reflected in the fact that Chinese strategists first 'raised the idea of a possible deployment in the media to gauge the international reaction' (Weitz 2009a: 36–7). Subsequently, Chinese diplomats floated the idea at the UN, and finally announced officially China's intentions 'with high-profile public relations campaigns' (Li 2009b). Chinese officials stressed that the action was legally justified by UN Security Council Resolutions, commercially justified by China's trade interests falling victim to piracy and politically justified in view of other countries' deployments already in place (Li 2009b). China thus went at great lengths to appear as a responsible power, being very concerned about not appearing to act recklessly or as a threat to others (Weitz 2009a: 28). As the Deputy Director of the Chinese Naval Bureau at the time stated, China has 'to fulfil [its] international obligations and act as a responsible country internationally' (Pomfret 2009). In the less solemn words of *The Economist*, 'for China, the deployment in the Gulf of Aden is as much about flying the flag and showing solidarity with a multinational effort as it is about making a real difference to the security of Chinese shipping in the region' (2009).

The decision to launch an anti-piracy operation far from its own shores could also be considered as an expansion of the Chinese definition of its national interests, such as to include not only matters of immediate national-security, but also interests pertaining to the country's future development (Lam 2009). The People's Liberation Army (PLA) and the People's Liberation Army Navy (PLAN) would be the operational arm of this new strategy of projection, aimed at protecting 'a more diverse set of national interests that are not defined by geography' (Kaufman 2009: 4). This analysis reflects the scope of the new 'historic missions' as defined by President Hu Jintao in December 2004, and later enshrined in the Chinese Defence White Paper (Chinese Government 2009). These missions assign four principal tasks to the PLA, namely to consolidate the power of the Communist Party, to ensure continued national development by guaranteeing China's sovereignty, territorial integrity and internal security, to safeguard China's expanding national interests and to help maintain world peace (Cooper 2009: 3). The last two priorities imply a more important role devoted to the PLA and a capacity to project forces where Chinese interests are at stake. Even though this does not amount to any Clausewitzian use of war, it constitutes nonetheless a considerable extension of the tasks of the military, which is now to be used in so-called 'Military Operations Other Than War', that is 'to maintain maritime, space and electromagnetic space security and to carry out the tasks of counter-terrorism, stability maintenance, emergency rescue and international peacekeeping' (Chinese Government 2009) – a sort of Chinese Petersberg tasks.

In order to logistically sustain such a policy, much attention has been devoted to the Chinese strategy of the so-called 'Pearl String', which consists of concluding bilateral agreements, from the South China Sea to the Indian Ocean, with a view to establishing commercial and military bases (Zajec 2009). While this strategy was initially conceived to cope with political tensions with the US over Taiwan, it seems to have extended into the Indian Ocean, thus allowing China to break through the perceived (US-imposed) 'blockade wall', obstructing its free access to the oceans (Ross 2009: 74–5). From 2005 onwards, China reinforced cooperation with several countries along the coasts of the Indian Ocean. These include Burma (Myanmar), Sri Lanka, Bangladesh, the Maldives, Pakistan (with the port of Gwadar as the main strategic base for the Chinese navy in the area), the Seychelles and Mauritius (Zajec 2009). Yin Zhuo, admiral and senior researcher at the PLAN's Equipment Research Centre, even suggested that China should build an additional naval base in the Gulf of Aden to support its ships deployed in the anti-piracy operation (IOL 2009). The 'Pearl String' could then add one more pearl to its collection – with the official justification being the anti-piracy efforts in this area. From this angle, the Chinese anti-piracy operation could be seen as a test case for further projection of the PLAN, to defend broader national security interests outside the East and South China Sea. It could also be a means to justify further expansion of Chinese naval bases in the Indian Ocean without raising international concerns.

Lastly, next to geopolitics, there is also an internal, but certainly non-negligible motivation for both China and the EU, namely using maritime power to cater to public opinion. The EU has long been plagued by a general disinterest of its citizens in its activities. Operation *Atalanta* now poses the opportunity to disseminate the image of the EU being a very visible actor on the international stage to which ordinary citizens can relate, fostering the image of an 'EU fleet' (Norton-Taylor 2008), fighting for the protection of EU citizens.[9] China, for its part, is using its operation in a similar fashion. Unlike the EU, however, it is not faced with a disinterested public that needs to be reminded of the existence of its role in international security. Instead, it is catering to vivid nationalist feelings. These, if not catered for adequately, could eventually call into question the legitimate claim to power of the Chinese Communist Party and thus undermine the first objective of the 'historic missions'. Indeed, it has been observed that there is a veritable 'naval nationalism' present among the entire spectrum of Chinese society, with as its epitome the acquisition of an aircraft carrier, regardless of its strategic usefulness (Ross 2009: 54–60). Naval power is seen as the ultimate attribute of global power, which China ought to possess in order to live up to its deserved place among the leading powers of the twenty-first century.[10] Of course, China's first out-of-area maritime operation has further kindled that discussion and, according to Ross, has 'stimulated even greater mass interest in an aircraft carrier' (2009: 63).

---

9 After the entry into force of the Lisbon Treaty, the Treaty on European Union specifically states that the Union shall 'uphold and promote its values and interests and contribute to the protection of its citizens' on the international scene (Article 3, paragraph 5).

10 This appears to be influenced *inter alia* by the 1890 work by Alfred T. Mahan, 'The Influence of Seapower upon History, 1660–1783', which enjoys great popularity in China today (Ross 2009: 62).

Divergence: Revelations from Practice

In the following, we will turn to the respective naval operations as they have been carried out since the end of 2008. While both China and the EU, as described above, have largely convergent motives, a closer look at the implementation of the missions reveals differences in the EU's and China's approaches and the lack of coordination in this field. Whereas the first indicates divergence in terms of values and long-term vision, the second reveals the highly political character of these operations, the geopolitical stakes underlying them and the potential for both future rivalry and cooperation.

Approaches: Comprehensive Security versus 'Traditionalism'

The EU has a long-standing comprehensive understanding of security, for example, the interlocking of different threats and the need to employ military as well as civilian means, using multilateral institutions and acting in conformity with the rule of law. The 2003 European Security Strategy already pointed out state failure as one of the key threats, which in turn 'can be associated with [other] obvious threats, such as organized crime or terrorism' (Council of the European Union 2003: 4). Furthermore, it stressed maritime piracy as a 'new dimension to organized crime which will merit further attention' (2003: 5). The 2008 Report on the Implementation of the European Security Strategy expressly stated that piracy 'is also a result of state failure' (Council of the European Union 2008: 8).

This comprehensive and rule-based approach is already reflected in Operation *Atalanta*'s mandate as established by Joint Action 2008/851/CFSP. According to Article 2, the operation is to be carried out '[u]nder the conditions set by the relevant international law' and the relevant UN Security Council resolutions. It also mandates *Atalanta* to 'liaise with organizations and entities, as well as states, working in the region to combat acts of piracy and armed robbery off the Somali coast'. This is best illustrated by the EU's approach towards the treatment of captured piracy suspects, which is a crucial issue, given that *Atalanta* has captured by far the largest number of piracy suspects among all actors in the region (521 by May 2010, Gros-Verheyde 2010a). As Commodore Pieter Bindt, then Force Commander of Operation *Atalanta*, put it: '[...] we like to have due process in legal issues' (BBC News 2009b). Hence, according to Article 12 of the Joint Action, captured piracy suspects shall be transferred either to the competent authorities of the flag state that captured them, or 'if that State cannot, or does not wish to exercise its jurisdiction', the detainee can be allocated to another state that does want to press charges. This clarifies that piracy suspects cannot simply be released when there is reluctance to bring them, for constitutional or political reasons, before the courts of the state responsible for the capture – a practice also shown by EU member states.[11] More importantly, it is further stipulated in Article 12 of the Joint Action that individuals may only be transferred to a third state under conditions which are 'consistent with relevant international law, notably international law on human rights'. In particular, 'no one shall be subjected to the death penalty, to torture or to any cruel inhuman or degrading treatment', which constitutes a form of export of the EU's own legal order. Hence, EU member state vessels operating in the framework of *Atalanta* are prohibited from transferring captured persons to states or regimes with a questionable human rights record, like Puntland, to which France used to transfer captured piracy suspects (Middleton 2009: 6). Instead, from the outset of this operation, the EU has strived to conclude transfer agreements with countries of the region for the prosecution of captured pirates, being well aware that this issue could jeopardize the success of the mission itself.

Thus far, the EU has concluded such agreements with Kenya in March 2009 and the Seychelles in December 2009. These stipulate the conditions under which the transferred persons are to be treated, prosecuted and tried. To secure their support, the EU offered assistance packages to the judiciary and penitentiary systems of these countries in order to help them carry out their obligations under the agreements. However, given the very limited judicial and prison capabilities of the Seychelles and the reluctance of other countries in the region to prosecute pirates, the long-term sustainability of the EU's approach has been strained. The Kenyan authorities, being increasingly displeased to receive the lion's share of piracy suspects from international forces deployed in the area (134 as of June 2010, Gros-Verheyde 2010b), decided to call off the transfer agreement with the EU in March 2010 (with six months notice before cancellation). The EU therefore undertook an extensive public diplomacy campaign to convince other countries to accept prosecuting suspected pirates. This was illustrated by the visit in the region, in May 2010, of the EU High Representative for Foreign Affairs and Security Policy, Baroness Ashton, which resulted in the adoption of the non-binding Victoria statement on piracy, signed by Djibouti, Kenya, Mauritius, Mozambique, the Seychelles and South Africa, calling for strengthening the capacities of the countries in the wider region with regard to the prosecution and imprisonment of pirates (President of the Republic of Seychelles 2010). Whilst no new formal agreement has been concluded thus far – and with the agreement with Kenya still on hold – the issue definitely raises the question of the EU's capacity and credibility to sustain a comprehensive approach in line with its declared objectives.

Further indications of the EU's comprehensive engagement are its role as the largest donor to Somalia, its support to the TFG, to the African Union's Mission in Somalia (AMISOM) (EU Council Secretariat 2010), as well as to the implementation of the International Maritime Organization's (IMO) Code of Conduct to repress acts of piracy and armed robbery against ships, adopted by regional states on

---

11   See, for example, the case of the Dutch frigate *De Zeven Provinciën*, operating in the framework of NATO, that released a group of Somali pirates in April 2009 (Labott 2009).

26 January 2009. Furthermore, the EU supports the establishment of a regional training and documentation centre in Djibouti and a regional information-sharing centre in Yemen.[12] As the latest step, the Council of the EU adopted, on 15 February 2010, Council Decision 2010/96/CFSP initiating a military training mission for the Somali security forces (EUTM Somalia), to contribute to the consolidation of the TFG. This 14-month mission aims at training TFG military forces in Uganda for a six-month period before they return to Mogadishu. It further demonstrates the EU's willingness to promote stability in Somalia, while not being directly engaged in its domestic affairs.

Concerning the Chinese mission, no such comprehensive approach can be discerned. Rather, its approach is reminiscent of its traditional understanding of international law, stressing state sovereignty and the principle of non-interference. As of yet, China has not concluded any transfer agreements. Furthermore, the mandate of its operation is primarily to 'protect and escort Chinese ships carrying strategic cargos, such as crude oil' (Hao 2008). Upon request, the fleet would also come to the help of ships from other countries, as well as those of the WFP (Weitz 2009a: 34). After one year of being present in the area, it was reported that the Chinese flotillas had 'escorted more than 1,300 merchant ships, including 405 foreign vessels' (Li 2009a). However, apart from escorting, the Chinese navy does not seem to be prepared to engage the pirates. In this sense, it avoids both using force and having to face the problem of prosecuting or transferring captured piracy suspects (Sakhuja 2009). In the case of the captured *De Xin Hai* merchant vessel, the first which was both Chinese-flagged and composed of an all-Chinese crew, the Chinese media only stated that it had been 'successfully rescued' without going into detail (People's Daily 2009). Western media suggested that a ransom had been paid (BBC News 2009a). Firstly, there is an image-driven explanation for this. It is plausible that China shows itself hesitant when it comes to using force 'as a botched operation would be an embarrassment for a navy that earlier this year celebrated its sixtieth anniversary with much hoopla' (The Economist 2009). Secondly, it raises the question whether the Chinese navy is actually capable of reacting promptly in the field to an urgent situation when all decisions must be cleared with the Central Command in Beijing (Weitz 2009b).

Furthermore, in practice, this operation did not turn out to be a huge break with the traditional Chinese foreign policy stance. Interestingly, when discussing a draft resolution on piracy at the UN Security Council in May 2008, the Chinese initially had strong reservations regarding phrasing which included the possibility of entering the territorial waters of Somalia, in order to repress piracy.[13] The subsequent UNSC Resolutions (1846 and 1851) eventually noted the 'primary role of the TFG in rooting out piracy and robbery at sea' and authorize states and regional organizations 'to undertake all necessary measures' (in other words, also

---

12 Interview by the authors, Brussels, 4 December 2009.
13 Interview by the authors, Brussels, 28 November 2009.

to use force) only 'pursuant to the request of the TFG'.[14] This explicit authorization by the UN Security Council as well as the reference to the TFG 'mean[s] that Chinese leaders can participate in the military operations off Somalia's coast [...] without compromising their doctrine of non-interference in other countries' affairs' (Weitz 2009a: 31).

However, more importantly than showing China's concerns for Somalia's (largely fictitious) sovereignty, this approach safeguards, and indeed underlines, China's own calls for respect of its sovereignty and non-interference into what it perceives to be its internal affairs, most notably concerning Taiwan. The impact on cross-Strait relations has become manifestly present in China's operation since, during the first year of its deployment, the Chinese flotilla has also protected 18 ships 'from Taiwan province' according to *People's Daily* (Jie 2009). This put the Taiwanese government in a delicate situation, as it was criticized by the opposition, for letting the PRC bolster its sovereignty claims over the island. The government, however, noted that a Taiwanese deployment would be logistically difficult given the lack of recognition by most other countries (Weitz 2009a: 33–4).

Finally, the Chinese deployment may also be seen as indirectly asserting Chinese sovereignty claims in the South China Sea (Weitz 2009a: 36). Considering the operation also as a test case for 'the long-distance capability of China's inchoate blue-water navy' or even a 'trial run for China's future aircraft carrier battle group' (Lam 2009), China's deployment appears a lot more worrisome in geopolitical terms than the EU's. The former is not connected to any claims for 'lost territories' or pursued to accommodate nationalist feelings calling for military symbols of great power status. In any event, China's operation is prone to create more anxiety in its neighbouring region than the EU's ever could in its respective environment,[15] and generally reveals the different visions of both powers for the future international order.

Coordination: The 'Walled Sea' and Zero-Sum Games

The EU and China's differing visions become even more apparent when turning to the issue of military coordination, which reveals an underlying potential for future rivalry while paving the way for innovative forms of cooperation. The Gulf of Aden has indeed become the first theatre to gather all great powers at the same time, in the same area, to combat the same threat. In addition to the EU and China, NATO with operation *Ocean Shield*, the multinational Combined Maritime Forces (CMF), individual EU member states as well as India, Iran, Japan, Malaysia, Russia, Saudi Arabia, South Korea and the US have all deployed military assets in the area. The issue of tactical coordination therefore became a pressing concern

---

14   UN Security Council resolution 1851(2008), paragraph 6; for Somalia's territorial waters, see UN Security Council resolution 1846(2008), paragraph 10.

15   In this context, it should be noted that a number of European non-EU countries have made contributions to *Atalanta*, such as Norway, Croatia and Montenegro.

in terms of avoiding wasting the limited resources available to fight piracy. At the political level, a Contact Group on Piracy off the Coast of Somalia was created under the auspices of the IMO in January 2009, gathering no fewer than 42 participants, including the EU and China, to discuss coordination, legal protection and information issues related to the fight against piracy. At the operational level, the growing number of actors involved generated a need to establish concrete *ad hoc* multilateral coordination mechanisms.

As one of the first actors involved in the area, the EU played an active role in this field and contributed to elaborate innovative solutions. Before operation *Atalanta* was launched in December 2008, the EU had first adopted, on 19 September 2008, Council Joint Action 2008/749/CFSP, establishing a fairly light operation called EU Naval Coordination (NAVCO). It consisted of a coordination cell located in Brussels gathering information on the activities of military ships in the Gulf of Aden, from EU member states, as well as from third countries with a view to providing improved escorting of the WFP ships. EU NAVCO also established a website, the Maritime Security Centre for the Horn of Africa, on which private ships can register in order to be tracked and allowed to cross the Gulf of Aden alongside military vessels.[16]

When the EU then formally launched EU NAVFOR *Atalanta*, coordination with other forces deployed in the area (CMF, later NATO and China) was considered a necessity to ensure the efficiency of the operation. In this context, at the request of the deputy Commander of CMF, a meeting entitled 'Shared Awareness and Deconfliction' (*Shade*) was convened with EU NAVFOR in Bahrain, in December 2008, to discuss information exchange, coordination issues and the protection of ships in the Gulf of Aden. It was then decided to hold *Shade* meetings on a monthly basis in Bahrain and later to invite other countries with forces deployed in the area. In terms of procedure, CMF invited EU NAVFOR in April 2009 to co-chair the *Shade* meetings, while other countries (Russia, China, Japan), as well as representatives from the shipping industry, took part as observers. These resulted in a number of concrete and innovative outputs:[17]

1. Coordination: *Shade* participants agreed to the promulgation of the International Recommended Transit Corridor (IRTC) defining a single transit route in the Gulf of Aden according to specific coordinates that military ships would follow to perform the escorts on a rotating basis.
2. Protection: CMF, EU NAVFOR and NATO designed the IRTC Coordination Guide setting out recommendations to protect merchant ships.
3. Communication: Participants agreed to use a single means of communication, the EU NAVFOR-designed Mercury system, to facilitate contacts between one another.

---

16   See website of the Maritime Security Centre for the Horn of Africa: http://www. mschoa.eu/.

17   Interview by the authors, Brussels, 28 November 2009.

4. Information: A 'Counter Piracy Planning Chart' has been circulated among the shipping industry to provide information on the military efforts.

In this context, there appeared to be a mutual interest for China, the EU and the US to coordinate with one another, both operationally and politically speaking. On the one hand, the three Chinese warships present in the area were providing protection for Chinese-flagged ships five miles away from the agreed transit corridor, which created a potential for duplication or overlap with EU NAVFOR and CMF escorts. The Chinese themselves realized the advantages of the single corridor to increase the protection of their merchant ships. On the other hand, there was a strategic interest for both the US and the EU to test maritime cooperation with China in the framework of a multilateral mechanism, while it was an opportunity for the Chinese to gain experience in maritime affairs and to bolster their status as a responsible stakeholder. Yet, *Shade* initially gave rise to Chinese reluctance mainly due to the fact that it was perceived as a US-led initiative, an impression reinforced by the circumstance that these meetings originally took place in a US military compound in Bahrain.[18]

China therefore promoted alternative coordination arrangements to the *Shade* mechanism. Firstly, the Chinese supported a stronger role for the UN with a view to creating a universal coordination mechanism, run by a UN Commander, where all nations would be treated on an equal basis. However, the UN did not have forces deployed in the Gulf of Aden and did not wish to assume such a responsibility given that there already existed well-functioning mechanisms.[19] Secondly, China advocated for a division of the Gulf of Aden into geographical zones where one state/organization would be individually responsible for all ships passing through.[20] This approach, somewhat reminiscent of the Allied sectors of Berlin during the Cold War, neatly illustrates the Chinese preference for a policy of non-interference between international powers even in a context of multilateral cooperation. This Chinese brand of sectorization has been dubbed the 'Walled World' by Leonard, such as a worldview where the sovereignty of each power is not to be scrutinized by the others while assuming international responsibilities (Leonard 2008). This proposal has been straightforwardly rejected by all other parties for numerous reasons, including the willingness to operate in the whole area without depending on one country. Thereafter, the EU undertook mediating efforts to convince China to step up its contribution to *Shade*, including the organization of a Chinese visit to *Atalanta*'s Operational Headquarters.[21] A crucial argument to persuade the Chinese consisted in underlining that the *Shade* mechanism is a tactical instrument rather than a political forum. As defined in its terms of reference, it only makes

---

18 Interview by the authors, Brussels, 28 November 2009. The location of Shade meetings was changed eventually to the 'British Club' in Bahrain.
19 Interview by the authors, Brussels, 29 November 2009.
20 Interview by the authors, Brussels, 29 November 2009.
21 Interview by the authors, Brussels, 8 December 2009.

non-binding recommendations on coordination-related issues to participating states/organizations without affecting the national chain of command.[22] Under these conditions, it provided an opportunity for China to explicitly declare its willingness to assume greater responsibilities commensurate with its great power status. The Chinese 'requested that the co-chairman positions [in *Shade*] should be rotated, making clear that, on occasions, they would also be willing to co-chair' (Pflanz 2009), thus abandoning their plan for a 'Walled Sea' and replacing it by their goal to take a leading role in the multinational coordination efforts. In the solemn words of a Chinese Defence Ministry Spokesman, 'China is always open to boosting international patrolling cooperation [and] wishes to cooperate, bilaterally and multilaterally, with all nations involved' (Zhang 2009).

To this end, the Chinese decided to hold a conference in Hong Kong on 6 and 7 November 2009 to enhance international cooperation in the Gulf of Aden (Zeenews 2009). This conference offered an opportunity to devise a way for fully-fledged Chinese participation in *Shade*, but at the price of EU-US unity: the deputy Commander of CMF suggested that the Chinese could replace EU NAVFOR as a co-chair of the *Shade* mechanism. While this was a conceivable option for the Operation Headquarters of *Atalanta*, as they perceived it in a strictly military and technical sense, it was strongly rejected by representatives from the General Secretariat of the Council of the EU and later by the member states during a meeting of the contact group on piracy.[23] For them, the possible removal of EU NAVFOR from *Shade* and the modalities of concrete cooperation with China had an important political dimension. As a result, the Chinese claim to play a greater role in the Gulf of Aden had generated tensions between the Americans and the Europeans. While the US was eager to test maritime cooperation with China without giving up its own status, the European 'eviction' was thus seen as a lesser of two evils. In any event, neither of the three was willing to give up their seat, effectively turning the *Shade* chairmanship into a zero-sum game – an unenviable situation that all three parties sought to avoid on a strategic level (Kaufman 2009: 9).

In an attempt to find a mutually agreeable solution to this issue, EU NAVFOR and CMF eventually proposed an alternative idea involving the creation of a third rotating chair, backed by the two permanent co-chairs CMF and EU NAVFOR. This new chair, rotating on a monthly basis and filled by countries/organizations having sufficient technical capacity and operational means, would assume the task of coordinating the IRTC system in the Gulf of Aden.[24] At this stage, only EU NAVFOR, CMF, NATO and China have signalled readiness to assume this role. In June 2010, the EU also tried to convince India to assume this responsibility. However, India not only expressed reluctance to do so in the short-term, but it also contested the Chinese legitimacy to become a co-chair, being extremely concerned

22 Interview by the authors, Brussels, 12 May 2010.
23 Interview by the authors, Brussels, 29 November 2009.
24 Interview by the authors, Brussels, 8 December 2009.

about what it perceives to be important operational as well as political implications of this assignment (Mitra 2010). In practice, it means that China could assume this responsibility once every four months and that EU NAVFOR or CMF could act as a rotating chair whilst simultaneously holding the position of co-chair.[25] This somewhat peculiar proposal demonstrates the difficulties in reaching a consensus on designing a tactical and military mechanism incorporating a multitude of great powers, given the underlying political implications. For the EU, it highlights both the risk and the opportunity of Chinese participation in *Shade*. In line with its strategy of effective multilateralism, the EU strived to play a mediating role to include China but it could have ended up in US-China cooperation with the EU being sidelined. In this respect, the EU's attempt to include India in the game, while unleashing explicit tensions between the two great Asian powers, can be seen to form part of the strategy to engage all strategic partners and to overcome a limited US-China dialogue. While recalling some aspects of the traditional diplomatic struggles between great powers, the case of the *Shade* mechanism eventually reveals the potential for innovative multilateral arrangements and solutions that avoid slipping back into the zero-sum game logic.

Conclusion: Beyond Chess and Checkers, Towards the 'Go' Game

The first deployment of naval forces by the EU and China – alongside the US, NATO, Russia, India and Japan – to fight the upsurge of piracy off the coast of Somalia represents an unprecedented phenomenon with tremendous political ramifications. While the EU is conducting the largest operation in the area and contributed to propel an international dynamic, China's deployment is more modest but no less groundbreaking. These naval operations have a common objective that is linked to the willingness to (forcefully) protect the respective fundamental economic interests of the EU and China, especially in and around Africa. Moreover, they serve as essential acid-tests for the new military dimension that both players have added to their foreign policy toolkits, as well as an opportunity to assert themselves as major, yet responsible actors, on the global stage.

However, while their motives seem to largely converge, their actual deployment reveals diverging approaches and visions for the future world order. For the EU, this operation is in line with its declared strategy to take a leading role in effective multilateralism addressing today's threats and challenges in cooperation with all relevant partners in a rule-based system. *Atalanta* adds a new facet of its foreign and security policy spectrum to its ongoing comprehensive approach to improve the political situation in Somalia, while the recent EUTM Somalia military training mission illustrates additional efforts to promote stability. It is, however, questionable whether its engagement will effectively address

---

25   Interview by the authors, Brussels, 8 December 2009.

the root causes of piracy – yet, at least, it is leading by example. For China, it epitomizes a shift in its traditional policy of non-interference and territorial defence towards a more active approach to defend its national interests beyond its borders. In this case, this happens to overlap with an international priority, which in turn helps to bolster its image as a responsible stakeholder. However, its initial reluctance to engage in anything beyond escorting and its 'Walled Sea' proposal, highlight the difficulty it is still experiencing in fully acclimatizing itself to multilateral cooperation. Nonetheless, its future accession as a co-chair of the *Shade* mechanism reveals a new attitude towards multilateralism for China, whilst its actual deployment clearly demonstrates that the third and fourth priorities of the Chinese 'Historic Missions' – that relate to safeguarding national interests and promoting world peace and mutual development – are now occupying a far greater place in China's strategic policy, at least *vis-à-vis* Africa. As stressed by a researcher of the Chinese Naval Command Academy, 'the escort operation to the Gulf of Aden and Somali waters reflects and starts the transformation of our military strategy, [...] the Chinese navy will conduct more long-distance escort missions in the future' (Weitz 2009b).

This strategic change offers a chance for the EU to further cooperate with China, in Africa and beyond, albeit in an environment of greater strategic competition between two great powers vying to establish their own visions of multipolarity. For the EU, this indeed poses the double-challenge of integrating China into the multilateral order it seeks to promote, as well as preserving its own prominent position as opposed to being left out in a future US-China 'G2'. This has been foreshadowed in the politically charged discussions over the co-chairing of *Shade*. In sum, this case study can be seen as the tip of the iceberg of the complexity of the future multipolar order. This new strategic situation may well be compared with the complex Chinese game 'Go', where the players aim at gaining ground, but without destroying each other. It appears that in strategic terms, we are well beyond chess and checkers.

Bibliography

Book References

Fox, J. and Godement, F. 2009. *A Power Audit of EU-China Relations*. London: European Council on Foreign Relations.

Goldstein, A. 2005. *Rising to the Challenge. China's Grand Strategy and International Relations*. Stanford: Stanford University Press.

Grant, C. and Barysch, K. 2008. *Can Europe and China Shape a New World Order?*. London: Centre for European Reform.

Howorth, J. 2007. *Security and Defence Policy in the European Union*. Basingstoke: Palgrave Macmillan.

Leonard, M. 2008. *What Does China Think?*. New York: Public Affairs.

Menkhaus, K. 2004. *Somalia: State Collapse and the Threat of Terrorism*. Oxford: Oxford University Press.

Book Chapters

Davies, M. 2008. Military and security relations: China, Africa, and the rest of the world, in *China Into Africa: Trade, Aid, and Influence*, edited by R. Rotberg. Washington, D.C.: Brookings Institute Press, 155–96.
Lehr, P. and Lehmann, H. 2007. Somali pirates' new paradise, in *Violence at Sea: Piracy in the Age of Global Terrorism*, edited by P. Lehr. New York: Routledge, 1–22.

Journal Articles

Bertollo, M., Appolloni, O., Bustamente Izquierdo, J.P., De Angelis, F., Lelli, E. and Vesenjak, S. 2009. China and the different regional approaches in Africa. *Transition Studies Review*, 16(2), 404–20.
Boot, M. 2009. Pirates, then and now. How piracy was defeated in the past and can be again. *Foreign Affairs*, 88(4), 94–107.
Bruton, B. 2009. In the quicksands of Somalia. Where doing less helps more. *Foreign Affairs*, 88(6), 79–94.
Dagne, T. 2009. Somalia, prospects for a lasting peace. *Mediterranean Quarterly*, 20(2), 95–104.
Gros-Verheyde, N. 2009a. Atalanta : l'UE à l'abordage des pirates. *Europolitique*, 3761, 12–22.
Men, J. 2007. The EU-China strategic partnership: achievements and challenges. *University of Pittsburgh European Policy Paper Series*, 12, 1–22.
Ndumbe Anyu, J. and Moki, S. 2009. Africa: The piracy hot spot and its implications for global security. *Mediterranean Quarterly*, 20(3), 96–121.
Ross, R. 2009. China's naval nationalism. Sources, prospects, and the US response. *International Security*, 34(2), 46–81.
Weitz, R. 2009a. Operation Somalia: China's first expeditionary force?. *China Security*, 5(1), 27–43.

Websites

BBC News. 2009a. *Chinese ship crew 'rescued' from Somali pirates*. [Online]. Available at: http://news.bbc.co.uk/2/hi/asia-pacific/8432111.stm [accessed: 28 July 2010].
BBC News. 2009b. *Can Somali pirates be defeated?*. [Online]. Available at: http://news.bbc.co.uk/2/hi/africa/8371139.stm [accessed: 28 July 2010].
Chinese Government. 2009. *China's national defence in 2008*. [Online]. Available at: http://www.gov.cn/english/official/2009-01/20/content_1210227.htm [accessed: 27 July 2010].

Cohen, J. 2010. *Islamist radicalism in Yemen*. [Online]. Available at: http://www.
cfr.org/publication/9369/islamist_radicalism_in_yemen.html [accessed: 27 July
2010].

Cooper, C. 2009. *The PLA navy's 'new historic missions'; expanding capabilities
for a re-emergent Maritime Power. Testimony presented before the US-China
Economic and Security Review Commission on 11 June 2009*. [Online].
Available at: http://www.rand.org/pubs/testimonies/2009/RAND_CT332.pdf
[accessed: 27 July 2010].

Daly, J. 2009. *Somalia: pirates at the Gulf*. [Online]. Available at: http://www.
isn.ethz.ch/isn/Current-Affairs/Security-Watch/Detail/?id=97585&lng=en
[accessed: 30 July 2010].

EU Council Secretariat. 2010. *EU engagement in Somalia*. [Online]. Available
at: http://consilium.europa.eu/uedocs/cms_data/docs/missionPress/files/
100407%20FACTSHEET%20EU%20ENGAGEMENT%20SOMALIA%20-
%20version%208_EN01.pdf [accessed: 28 July 2010].

Fiott, D. 2009. *China's PLAN: securing supplies and sailing into blue-waters?*.
[Online]. Available at: http://www.madariaga.org/articles/articles-2009/242-
chinas-plan-securing-supplies-and-sailing-into-blue-waters [accessed: 27 July
2010].

Flintoff, C. 2009. *A record year for pirate attacks*. [Online]. Available at: http://
www.npr.org/templates/story/story.php?storyId=122066185 [accessed: 27
July 2010].

Gros-Verheyde, N. 2009b. *L'Evertsen libère 13 pirates faute de pays d'accueil,
un bug?*. [Online]. Available at: http://bruxelles2.over-blog.com/article-l-
evertsen-libere-13-pirates-faute-de-pays-d-accueil-un-bug--41359338.html
[accessed: 28 July 2010].

Gros-Verheyde, N. 2010a. *Bilan des opérations anti-piraterie (EUNAVFOR
Atalanta, CTF, Otan, Russie)*. [Online]. Available at: http://bruxelles2.
over-blog.com/pages/_Bilan_des_operations_antipiraterie_EUNAVFOR_
Atalanta_CTF_Otan_Russie_Exclusif-1169128.html [accessed: 30 July
2010].

Gros-Verheyde, N. 2010b. *Comment les pirates arrêtés sont jugés?*. [Online].
Available at: http://bruxelles2.over-blog.com/article-comment-sont-juges-les-
pirates-arretes-le-point--42673756.html [accessed: 30 July 2010].

Hao, Y. 2008. *China ready to send warships to Somalia for escort mission, fleet
commander*. [Online]. Available at: http://news.xinhuanet.com/english/2008-
12/25/content_10559690.htm [accessed: 26 July 2010].

Inman, P. 2010. *China becomes world's biggest exporter*. [Online]. Available at:
http://www.guardian.co.uk/business/2010/jan/10/china-tops-germany-exports
[accessed: 27 July 2010].

IOL. 2009. *Call for Chinese naval base in pirates' den*. [Online]. Available at:
http://www.iol.co.za/index.php?set_id=26&click_id=2227 [accessed: 27 July
2010].

Jopson, B. 2007. *Somalia oil deal for China.* [Online]. Available at: http://www.ft.com/cms/s/2/20a8a430-3167-11dc-891f-0000779fd2ac,dwp_uuid=9c33700c-4c86-11da-89df-0000779e2340.html [accessed: 27 July 2010].

Kaufman, A. 2009. *China's participation in anti-piracy operations off the Horn of Africa: drivers and implications.* [Online]. Available at: http://cna.org/sites/default/files/Piracy%20conference%20report.pdf [accessed: 27 July 2010].

Labott, E. 2009. *Clinton says releasing pirates sends 'wrong signal'.* [Online]. Available at: http://edition.cnn.com/2009/POLITICS/04/20/clinton.pirates/index.html [accessed: 28 July 2010].

Lam, W. 2009. *China flaunts growing naval capabilities.* [Online]. Available at: http://www.jamestown.org/programs/chinabrief/single/?tx_ttnews[tt_news]=34334&tx_ttnews[backPid]=25&cHash=82d69dfe0f [accessed: 27 July 2010].

Li, J. 2009a. *A year of protection against pirates.* [Online]. Available at: http://www.chinadaily.com.cn/china/2009-12/29/content_9239796.htm [accessed: 28 July 2010].

Li, M. 2009b. *China's Gulf of Aden expedition and maritime cooperation in East Asia.* [Online]. Available at: http://www.jamestown.org/programs/chinabrief/single/?tx_ttnews[tt_news]=34335&tx_ttnews[backPid]=25&cHash=2901bda83a [accessed: 27 July 2010].

Marine Resources Assessment Group. 2005. *Review of impacts of illegal, unreported and unregulated fishing on developing countries, final report.* [Online]. Available at: http://www.dfid.gov.uk/pubs/files/illegal-fishing-mrag-report.pdf [accessed: 27 July 2010].

Middleton, R. 2008. *Piracy in Somalia. Threatening global trade, feeding local wars.* [Online]. Available at: http://www.chathamhouse.org.uk/publications/papers/download/-/id/665/file/12203_1008piracysomalia.pdf [accessed: 26 July 2010].

Middleton, R. 2009. *Pirates and how to deal with them.* [Online]. Available at: http://www.chathamhouse.org.uk/publications/papers/download/-/id/733/file/13845_220409pirates_law.pdf [accessed: 28 July 2010].

Mitra, D. 2010. *EU asks India to co-chair anti-piracy group.* [Online]. Available at: http://www.southasianews.com/544147/EU-asks-India-to-co-chair-anti-piracy-group-.htm [accessed: 30 July 2010].

Norton-Taylor, R. 2008. *Britain to lead fleet of EU warships to tackle pirates.* [Online]. Available at: http://www.guardian.co.uk/world/2008/nov/19/piracy-somalia-eu-operation-atalanta [accessed: 27 July 2010].

People's Daily. 2009. *Hijacked Chinese bulk carrier rescued.* [Online]. Available at: http://english.people.com.cn/90001/90776/90883/6853134.html [accessed: 28 July 2010].

Perry, A. 2009. *Muammar Gaddafi shakes up Africa.* [Online]. Available at: http://www.time.com/time/world/article/0,8599,1878339,00.html [accessed: 27 July 2010].

Pflanz, M. 2009. *China wants a lead role in fight against Somali pirates*. [Online]. Available at: http://www.telegraph.co.uk/news/worldnews/piracy/6538997/ China-wants-a-lead-role-in-fight-against-Somali-pirates.html [accessed: 28 July 2010].

Pham, J. 2008. *Time to hunt Somali pirates*. [Online]. Available at: http:// worlddefensereview.com/pham092308.shtml [accessed: 27 July 2010].

Pham, J. 2009. *The Chinese navy's Somali cruise*. [Online]. Available at: http:// worlddefensereview.com/pham031209.shtml [accessed: 27 July 2010].

Phillips, L. 2009a. *The European roots of Somali piracy*. [Online]. Available at: http://euobserver.com/9/27966 [accessed: 26 July 2010].

Phillips, L. 2009b. *Somalia wins over US$200 million in Brussels donors' conference*. [Online]. Available at: http://euobserver.com/9/28001 [accessed: 26 July 2010].

Pomfret, J. 2009. *China to boost efforts in fighting Somalia piracy*. [Online]. Available at: http://in.reuters.com/article/worldNews/idINIndia-4391392009 1113?pageNumber=2&virtualBrandChannel=0&sp=true [accessed: 27 July 2010].

President of the Republic of Seychelles. 2010. *Joint communique, Seychelles regional conference on piracy*. [Online]. Available at: http://www.statehouse. gov.sc/index.php?option=com_content&view=article&id=203:conference-on-piracy&catid=36:the-press-room&Itemid=64 [accessed: 30 July 2010].

Reuters. 2008. *Somali pirates risk chocking key world trade route*. [Online]. Available at: http://www.alertnet.org/thenews/newsdesk/LD681364.htm [accessed: 27 July 2010].

Sakhuja, V. 2009. *Is the Chinese navy reluctant to use force against Somali pirates?*. [Online]. Available at: http://www.jamestown.org/single/?no_ cache=1&tx_ttnews[tt_news]=35861&tx_ttnews[backPid]=13&cHash=3ed4 ae03f8 [accessed: 28 July 2010].

Shinn, D. 2005. *Dueling priorities for Beijing in the Horn of Africa*. [Online]. Available at: http://www.jamestown.org/programs/chinabrief/single/?tx_ ttnews%5Btt_news%5D=30972&tx_ttnews%5BbackPid%5D=195&no_ cache=1 [accessed: 27 July 2010].

Simons, B. 2009. *Masked motives in China's anti-piracy push*. [Online]. Available at: http://www.atimes.com/atimes/China/KA15Ad01.html [accessed: 27 July 2010].

Struye de Swielande, T. 2009. *La piraterie maritime: un nouveau rapport de force dans l'Ocean Indien*. [Online]. Available at: http://www.uclouvain.be/cps/ucl/ doc/pols/documents/Note-analyse-1-INBEV.pdf [accessed: 27 July 2010].

The Economist. 2009. *Cash and carry. China's navy off to Somalia*. [Online]. Available at: http://www.economist.com/world/asia/displaystory.cfm?story_ id=14745027 [accessed: 27 July 2010].

US Department of Transportation. 2008. *Economic impact of piracy in the Gulf of Aden on global trade*. [Online]. Available at: http://www.marad.dot.gov/

documents/HOA_Economic%20Impact%20of%20Piracy.pdf [accessed: 27 July 2010].

Weitz, R. 2009b. *Priorities and challenges in China's naval deployment in the Horn of Africa.* [Online]. Available at: http://www.jamestown.org/programs/ chinabrief/single/?tx_ttnews[tt_news]=35795&tx_ttnews[backPid]=459&no_ cache=1 [accessed: 28 July 2010].

Zajec, O. 2009. *Actualité et réalité du 'collier de perles'.* [Online]. Available at: http://www.diploweb.com/Actualite-et-realite-du-collier-de.html [accessed: 27 July 2010].

Zeenews. 2009. *China hosts meeting on Somalia piracy.* [Online]. Available at: http://www.zeenews.com/news576634.html [accessed: 28 July 2010].

Zhang, H. 2009. *Team anti-piracy fight urged.* [Online]. Available at: http://www. chinadaily.com.cn/china/2009-11/20/content_9007337.htm [accessed: 28 July 2010].

Command Papers

A Secure Europe in a Better World. European Security Strategy. 2003. Brussels: Council of the European Union.

Report on the Implementation of the European Security Strategy. Providing Security in a Changing World. 2008. Brussels: Council of the European Union.

Piracy and Armed Robbery Against Ships, Annual Report, 1 January–31 December 2009. 2009. London: International Maritime Bureau.

Piracy and Armed Robbery Against Ships, Report for the Period, 1 January–30 June 2010. 2010. London: International Maritime Bureau.

Chapter 5

Tackling the Proliferation of Small Arms and Light Weapons: An Opportunity for EU-China Cooperation

Thomas Wheeler

Introduction

The People's Republic of China's (PRC) relationship with African countries has historical origins in the establishment of political ties with many newly independent states in the 1950s and 1960s. More recently the economic relationship has deepened substantially, as Africa's exports to China, most notably in natural resources, have increased by nearly 40 percent every year between 2001 and 2006 (Aning, Lecoutre 2008: 42). In 2008, trade hit US$107 billion (China Daily 2009), surpassing expectations and despite the slowdown caused by the financial crisis, the rate of this growth seems set to continue over the long run. For example, after having established diplomatic ties only ten years ago, China has recently become South Africa's largest export market. However, as the scholar Li Weijian (2008) points out in his appraisal of the 2006 Forum on China-Africa Cooperation (FOCAC) summit, challenges for the China-Africa relationship are by no means absent. Li highlights the fact that 'Africa still faces enormous challenges in the area of security and development' and that despite the fact that 'Africa's security situation is generally improving', a few countries 'are still facing grave internal conflicts' while 'some countries are facing more urgent issues like the post-conflict rebuilding' (Li 2008: 30).

Just as it is significant to European Union (EU)-Africa relations, it is important to consider challenges surrounding conflict and insecurity when assessing the China-Africa relationship. As two outside actors with established relations within Africa, the potential for EU-China cooperation in this area is worth examining.

This chapter aims to highlight a potential area where closer partnership between the EU, China and their African partners would be of great benefit to improving security on the continent. The first section provides an overview of some of the different manifestations of conflict and insecurity on the African continent, highlighting that small arms and light weapons (SALW) proliferation is a problem that links them all. The second section – which establishes the context for cooperation – outlines some of the commitments China has made to support African security and explores the degree to which these pledges have been met. Some of the key factors and interests that drive China's engagement on these issues and the depth to which this engagement will grow in the future is examined, illustrating that although expectations should be limited, there is both a need and an opportunity for closer Africa-China-EU cooperation. The third section looks more specifically at commitments made by both China and the EU to assist African countries in tackling SALW proliferation and stresses that confronting the problem presents an opportunity for closer cooperation. Examples, of where practical joint initiatives could be implemented alongside African partner states and regional organizations, are given. In addition to this, it is argued that bilateral China-EU dialogue needs to focus upon finding agreement, in the area of responsible arms transfers, for the simple reason that nearly all of Africa's SALW originate from outside the continent. In conclusion, it is suggested that while there are significant obstacles to Africa-China-EU cooperation, agreeing upon areas for practical joint action on the ground, may serve as an effective entry point to broader cooperation.

African Security Challenges

While it holds only 14 percent of the world's population, 38 percent of the world's armed conflicts were being fought in Africa from 1990–2003 (UNDP 2005). In 2006, nearly half of all high-intensity conflicts were fought there (HIIK 2006). A host of factors challenge both the security of states and the human security of citizens across Africa. Conventional inter-state conflicts are not common but are also not absent, as the case of Ethiopia and Eritrea illustrated from 1998–2000. The conventional confrontation between these two states formally ended but they have continued to clash indirectly through supporting and sponsoring opposing armed groups across the region. Indeed, this indirect and unconventional form of inter-state proxy conflict is far more of the norm and can be seen elsewhere across the continent, for example, between Chad and Sudan, who have intervened in one another's domestic conflicts through supporting anti-government rebel groups. While the incidence of civil war has fallen across Africa since 2000, it remains a latent threat in many countries with often catastrophic consequences when realized.

    In Somalia, for example, the Transitional Federal Government (TFG) has only partial control over small areas of the country. At the same time, 3.6 million Somali citizens – half the population – depend on aid for survival while 1.6 million are displaced, in what is now becoming one of the most challenging humanitarian crises in the world (Reuters 2009a). Peace in many of the countries that have recently emerged from prolonged civil war remains fragile, as is the case in Sudan, where the peace agreement continuously comes under serious strain from many directions. West African countries that have emerged from civil war such as Sierra Leone, Liberia and Côte D'Ivoire also face instability. Elsewhere, armed insurgencies have become embedded and persistently destructive, as the multitude of rebel groups in the Eastern Democratic Republic of Congo (DRC) or the continued fighting in Nigeria's Niger River Delta region illustrates. The Lord's Resistance Army has unleashed its unique form of instrumentalized mayhem across borders spanning Uganda, Sudan, DRC and the Central African Republic. Yet violence is often far more localized, as is the case of small-scale communal clashes over water, pasture and cattle between different pastoralist groups in arid regions of Kenya, Uganda, Ethiopia and Sudan. In some countries, such as Kenya and Zimbabwe, violence has erupted during highly contested election periods. Terrorism is a serious threat in North Africa and Eastern Africa. Crime, ranging from armed robbery to banditry or piracy is also a serious security challenge faced by governments and citizens alike.[1]

The causes behind these different manifestations of violence are equally varied and complex. There are historical, political, economic, global, social and cultural factors which drive these conflicts, all of which have their own unique characteristics. Without exploring the nature of this violence more deeply, one factor that has a bearing on them all can be highlighted: the proliferation of SALW across the African continent is a thread which ties all types of conflict and insecurity together. Such weapons are obviously not a direct cause of conflict and insecurity. They can, however, be considered to be a proximate cause of violence, through fuelling both its lethality and its duration. Drawing from experience, the ex-Kenyan Foreign Minister makes this clear:

> Conflict is part of the history of mankind. My part of the region is no exception to this historical fact. There are enough reasons to cause conflict, like religious, ethnic and clan difference. Poor people tend to have even more causes for conflict. But when guns get into the calculus then it becomes a recipe for disaster (Tuju 2006).

SALW, such as the Kalashnikov-type assault rifle, are the most commonly used weapon, responsible for the majority of direct conflict deaths and injuries. SALW are found in all typologies of conflict and insecurity, by flowing across porous borders, following and then fuelling violence. SALW are used by smaller insurgent and rebel groups and are integral to their ability to challenge the state's authority and territorial control. Indeed, their excessive accumulation by one group can have a destabilizing effect in a fragile environment (IANSA, Oxfam, Saferworld 2007). In post-conflict environments, the proliferation of SALW means that the state's supposed monopoly on the means of violence – a core component of any functioning state – is continually challenged, undermining state-building efforts. Peacekeepers find their work much harder, especially when continued proliferation undermines the difficult task of disarmament, demobilization and rehabilitation. In Southern Sudan, SALW proliferation amongst civilians and non-state groups

---

1   Added to these more traditional security threats are non-traditional security threats such as disease, natural disasters and climate change.

is central to understanding the high-levels of violence that continue to threaten stability and the peace agreement.

It is not only in conflict-afflicted countries that SALW proliferation threatens security. In Northern Kenya, for example, the state's security agencies are often out-gunned by well armed pastoralist groups that continue to clash with one another. Elsewhere in the country, armed criminals inflict great costs upon civilians and day-to-day life in urban areas. After the election-related violence of 2008, reports that some groups may be arming themselves with SALW in preparation for future rounds of political violence are especially worrying.[2] Since SALW proliferation fuels violence and insecurity, there are negative knock-on effects related to human rights violations, humanitarian assistance, illegal trading routes and socio-economic development in general.[3]

One cannot, of course, isolate an analysis of the effects of SALW proliferation from the wider factors that create a demand for these relatively cheap, transportable, easy to use and above all highly effective weapons. All along the spectrum of insecurity, ranging from conventional war to criminal activity, where there is demand, there is supply. As such, through reducing the demand for weapons in the first place, it will require a comprehensive approach to address the root causes of insecurity that will have an effective and sustainable impact on stemming proliferation. Yet a complex inter-dependency is at play: in order to better contain violence and to better support security, efforts to tackle the supply-side of proliferation must be part of the toolbox of any such comprehensive approach.

Outside Interests in Africa's Challenges

Especially in the past decade, Africa's peace and security challenges have become a central theme in the EU's financial and technical support to the continent which has been delivered through a myriad of initiatives such as the European Development Fund, the Instrument for Stability, the Africa Peace Facility and other bilateral channels instigated by individual European countries. In 2007, peace and security cooperation was made a priority in the Joint Africa-EU Strategy (JAES), which established a framework through which the EU supports its African partners. Without glossing over historical, geopolitical, economic and core security interests that Europe has in Africa, the prioritization of peace and security assistance stems from the acknowledgement, by both African and EU actors, that continued insecurity is a restraint on economic and social development.

In contrast, peace and security issues are not at the forefront of China's relations with Africa, which primarily focuses on deepening economic relations and lacks some of the contextual factors that shape the EU-Africa relationship. Despite this, some pledges to support African peace and security have been made, with President

2   See for example *BBC News* (2009).
3   See for example Small Arms Survey (2003) or Muggah, Batchelor (2002).

Hu stating, for example, in 2009 that China 'will play a constructive role of settling conflicts and hot issues and maintaining peace and security in Africa' (Hu 2009b). China's *Africa Policy* (2006) outlines several areas of support, including military cooperation, peacekeeping contributions and utilizing its Security Council position to bring African conflicts to the United Nations' (UN) attention. The FOCAC is an important arena for the agreement and public announcement of Chinese commitments to Africa, which are captured in three-year Action Plans. Drawn from the first FOCAC meeting in 2000, the *Beijing Declaration* (2000) stressed the need for international mediation in conflicts.

The second FOCAC's *Addis-Ababa Action Plan 2004–2006* (2003: 2.2–2.4.2), was somewhat more expansive and included Chinese commitments to peacekeeping and support to the African Union (AU), including subregional organizations. The *Beijing Action Plan 2007–2009* (2006: 4.7–4.9) called for cooperation on tackling terrorism and non-traditional security threats, pushing the international community to focus its attention on conflicts in Africa and a commitment that China 'will enhance cooperation with Africa in the prevention, management and resolution of regional conflicts'. In 2009, the *Sharm El Sheikh Action Plan 2010–2012* (2009: 2.6–2.6.4) re-iterated China's commitment to UN peacekeeping missions with a new reference to assistance in post-conflict reconstruction. It explicitly stressed China's belief in the practice of 'Solving African Problems by Africans', committing further support to the AU and regional organization, whilst pursuing dialogue through the newly-appointed Special Representative for African Affairs.

There are several areas in which China has followed through and implemented these commitments. Due to its sensitive nature, it is difficult to assert the nature, detail and depth of bilateral military cooperation between China and African countries. Although cooperation exists, it is often made public in the form of ambiguous statements declaring a deepening of military relations.[4] It is known that the Chinese military has directly assisted the DRC military with training, outside of the UN security sector reform initiatives (Reuters 2009b: 1). The Chinese government also built a US$5.5 million army barrack for the Liberian military (The Informer 2009: 1). In 2007, China launched a de-mining assistance programme for eight countries in Africa,[5] providing training for de-mining personnel and landmine removal devices.[6] The only known case of joint military exercises is Operation Peace Angel, which was a humanitarian and medical training operation between the Chinese and Gabonese military in 2009 (PLA Daily 2009: 1). However, overall, Jonathan Holslag (2008: 10) highlights that only 15 Chinese Embassies have

---

4   See for example *Xinhua News Agency* (2010: 1) and *China Radio International* ((CRI) 2010: 1).

5   Angola, Burundi, Chad, Guinea-Bissau, Egypt, Ethiopia, Mozambique and Sudan have all received assistance with de-mining.

6   See Information Office of the State Council of the People's Republic of China's National Defence in 2008.

military *attachés*, reflecting the fact that in reality, military-military cooperation remains thin.

China has lent support to the AU and subregional bodies. In 2000, China gave US$300,000 to the AU's Peace Fund and in 2006, US$400,000 was given to support the AU's peacekeeping mission in Darfur, with a more substantial US$3.5 million being donated in June in terms of budgetary support and humanitarian emergency aid. The Economic Community Of West African States (ECOWAS) has also received financial and technical support for peace and conflict prevention initiatives. Despite the fact that the sums in question are relatively small when compared to other areas of Chinese assistance to Africa, these tentative steps suggest that China, like the EU, is willing to directly fund and build the capacity of African peace infrastructures.

China has also rapidly increased its participation in peacekeeping missions, increasing contributions of personnel ten-fold since 2001. In 2009, China had 2,155 Chinese peacekeepers stationed in ten mission areas (People's Daily 2009). Three quarters of Chinese peacekeepers are operating in seven of the eight UN missions in Africa, including the DRC, Ethiopia/Eritrea, Mozambique, Liberia, Sierra Leone, Sudan and Western Sahara. Furthermore, China is taking steps towards leadership positions within peacekeeping missions and, despite some problems, their 'peacekeepers are consistently rated among the most professional, well-trained, effective and disciplined in UN peacekeeping operations' (Gill, Huang 2009: vii). Beijing has not only voiced its willingness to take a larger role in the UN's peacekeeping missions at the headquarter level in New York, but also to work more closely with the UN Peacebuilding Commission. This reflects Beijing's intention to widen its participation beyond conventional peacekeeping through partaking in more complex post-conflict reconstruction and peacebuilding efforts (Wang 2010: 2). China's naval contributions to the anti-piracy initiatives in the Gulf of Aden also reflect China's growing multilateral engagement on what is a new area of security challenges.

In the DRC, Chinese diplomats engaged multilaterally with other external actors through joining the International Committee Supporting the Transition, and in Sudan a special envoy was appointed by Beijing to focus on the Darfur crisis. Nonetheless, as Dan Large (2008) points out, this in-country national level multilateralism is by no means the norm, and instead most of China's diplomatic engagement has been taking place at the UN level. There have been occasions when China has also used its position in the UN Security Council to bring the focus of the international community towards conflicts in Africa. For example, the Chinese UN delegation played an important role in the resolution for sanctions and the establishment of a peacekeeping operation in Somalia, in 2006 (Gill, Huang 2009: 15). China provided strong initial support for a French resolution on Chad in 2007 (Holslag 2008). Critics have pointed to previous cases where China has prevented UN resolutions over the conflict in Sudan from being passed, an issue which has been a continuous diplomatic challenge for Beijing. In 2006, China refused to support Resolution 1706 (which would extend the UN's Sudan peacekeeping mission in Darfur) without consent from Khartoum. However, China was later credited with using diplomatic means to persuade the Khartoum government to accept UN peacekeepers and Kofi Annan's three phase plan. In 2007, China voted alongside the other UN Security Council members for Resolution 1769 that deployed a 26,000-strong joint AU-UN hybrid mission, which was accepted by the Khartoum government. The UN Under-Secretary-General for Peacekeeping Operations concluded that China had ultimately played 'a key and constructive role' in securing the approval (Yu, Wang 2008: 89).

China's growing engagement in security issues in Africa means progress, although incremental in nature, has been made in meeting some of the commitments made to Africa. There are several reasons why China has an interest in African security issues that might drive it to deepen its engagement. Firstly, the Chinese government maintains that it is committed to promoting growth and development in Africa. However, without including crime and other forms of insecurity, it is estimated that the cost to African economic development due to armed conflicts, from 1990–2007 is US$248 billion (IANSA, Oxfam, Saferworld 2007). Economic development, not only for countries but entire regions, cannot be achieved in the absence of security and peace. As with the EU, China's commitment to African development also necessitates a commitment to African peace and security. Secondly, China's own prosperity is to a degree linked to Africa's. African markets are a potential growth area for Chinese goods, which is an important consideration in Beijing's desire to sustain high domestic growth rates through expansion into new global markets (He 2007: 23). Another dimension of the economic relationship is investment opportunities, such as the US$5.6 billion purchase of a 20 percent stake in South Africa's successful Standard Bank by the Industrial and Commercial Bank of China (ICBC) (Reuters 2007). By some estimates, China invested more in Africa, from 2005–2009, than in any other region in the world (Foreign Policy 2010). Yet without growing prosperity on the African continent, markets will never meet their full potential for Chinese goods and investments. To paraphrase Deng Xiaoping, safeguarding African peace may contribute to China's domestic development.

While resources are by no means the only component of China-Africa economic relations, China's access to energy and minerals in Africa have been, and will continue to be, of great importance. China's unparalleled and rapid economic growth over the last three decades has created a demand for energy and mineral resources from outside China. Chris Alden and Ana Christina Alves (2009: 5) illustrate how energy security is an important aspect of Chinese foreign policy and that 'in this regard Africa has assumed a critical role in achieving this objective'. There are a host of examples of Chinese investments in energy and mineral extractions across the continent, with a significant proportion being made in areas afflicted by instability and insecurity. Recently, a Chinese state-owned oil enterprise was in talks with the Nigerian government 'to buy large stakes in some of the world's richest oil blocs in a deal that would eclipse Beijing's previous efforts to secure crude oil overseas' (Burgis 2009: 1). While such an acquisition aims to promote China's energy security, it is estimated that 'at least one-third of Nigeria's oil capacity is shut because of attacks by militants' (Burgis 2009: 1), most notably by the tenacious Movement for the Emancipation of the Niger Delta (MEND). A Chinese gas exploration project in Ethiopia's turbulent Ogaden region was set back due to rebel attacks while investments in Sudan have faced similar disruptions (BBC News 2007). In short, China's global quest for energy security has necessitated a local confrontation with African insecurity. As with all economic entanglements, confronting these problems often necessities a non-economic response.

Chinese citizens themselves have been directly targeted. In 2007, MEND kidnapped nine Chinese oil workers, a practice inflicted on Western oil workers over the previous years (People's Daily 2007). Chinese citizens have also become violently entangled in civil conflicts elsewhere. Nine Chinese workers were killed and seven kidnapped when an Ethiopian rebel group attacked after warning foreigners to stay out of the Ogaden region (BBC News 2007). Oil installations have been attacked in Darfur, where nine workers were kidnapped and four killed, as recently as 2008 (BBC News 2008). Chinese nationals have become a security concern for Chinese Embassies elsewhere in Africa: for example, after clashes in the Chadian capital in 2008, the Chinese government evacuated 212 compatriots (Ministry of Foreign Affairs of the People's Republic of China 2008).

Although often overstated, even the most localized of security threats can have ramifications for global security. The example of piracy in the Gulf of Aden, which has roots in the perpetual security crisis inside Somalia itself, shows that trade routes are threatened in a way that impacts on multiple countries, a fact not lost on Beijing. Shi Yinhong (2008: 26) notes that 'international responsibility has become the primary keywords to China's grand strategy'. As China rises as a global power, there has been a realization in Beijing that it must shoulder international responsibilities and provide international public goods (Smith, Wheeler, Mariani 2009). Global security is one of these public goods and, as the Somali case makes clear, African security issues often have global externalities.

In the context of its rapidly deepening engagement, some Western activists and media have vocally criticized China's role in Africa. For example, Beijing's relations with the ruling regimes of Sudan and Zimbabwe during periods of violent instability led to claims that China was failing to act as a responsible power. While some of this criticism has been unnecessarily confrontational, and occasionally reflected knee-jerk reactions rather than sound analysis, the damage to China's international image aroused significant concern in Beijing. Yet, of even greater concern, is the fact that African civil society actors have also voiced their dissatisfaction with China's role in conflict afflicted countries, threatening its image on the continent.[7] Such criticism generates further impetus for Beijing to take more of an interest in its own role in Africa's security concerns and at least be seen to be utilizing its power responsibly.

---

7   See for example Kendo (2008).

Lastly, and more broadly, China's foreign policy is seen through the view that great powers are the key, that the Asia-Pacific region or periphery nations are the priority and that the Third World, including Africa, is the foundation. Gill, Huang and Morrison (2007: 4) note that 'Africa is seen as integral to Beijing's strategic ambition to advance a "new security concept" that can ensure China's peaceful rise as a global power and strengthen relations with key neighbours and regions'. Wang Wei (2010: 3) argues that in the wider context of China-Africa relations, Chinese support for African peace and security 'has become an important part of the strategic cooperation and will lay a solid foundation for the development of mutual political trust between the two'. Strengthening political relations with African states in pursuit of China's global strategic ambitions may include support to cement stability: if the foundation shakes, the rest of the international environment shakes with it.

While peace and security may not be at the forefront of China-Africa relations, China's deepening relationship with African countries has meant that it has inevitably become enmeshed in local, domestic and regional conflicts through its very presence. In turn, these issues impact upon China. Yet to what degree will these factors mean that China's engagement on peace and security issues will deepen? In reference to the challenges of Darfur, Yu and Wang (2008: 88) argue that Beijing's change in policy 'indicates that China's diplomacy in Africa has entered a new stage'. When China supported a UN resolution for a peacekeeping mission in Chad, a Chinese diplomat argued that it showed Beijing's 'awareness on the increasing complexity of conflicts in Africa grows' (Holslag 2008: 142). While Beijing continues to stress the primacy of governments in solving national problems, Chinese policy may have begun to move away from past methods of unilaterally supporting partner regimes in Africa, to supporting regional (especially AU) initiatives as well as deeper participation in UN-level action. Indeed, in recent years, several observers have noted that China is gradually favouring more cooperative and multilateral policies of engagement.[8] These developments suggest that in the near future, the EU may find opportunities to engage with China on their mutual roles in relation to African security.

Conversely, the degree to which these policy developments will become normalized and established, is open to observation over the long run. Firstly, what is deemed cooperative and responsible by others may not always be what China sees to be in its national interest, which, as with all external powers in Africa, will often take priority. Secondly, there are clear tensions between deeper engagement and Beijing's ideological insistence on respecting sovereignty, including non-interference in domestic conflicts. Furthermore, there still exists a weariness of taking high-profile leadership positions in multilateral initiatives. More fundamentally, China has little experience of engagement on overseas conflict issues and holds little developed capacity or resources to do so. Lastly, China has

---

8 For example see Bates, Huang and Morrison (2007), Holslag (2009), Raine (2009) and Teitt (2009).

far less political influence in Africa than is often assumed (Large 2008). Clearly expectations of China's role in the future need to be somewhat limited.

Expectations also need to consider that effective and sustainable solutions to African peace and security threats are to be found within the continent itself, in the hands of governments, politicians and civil society who proactively utilize state institutions, regional structures and activism for peaceful ends. No matter their commitment or influence, external actors can only ever seek to support this process. This applies to the EU's relations with Africa. Despite the prioritization of peace and security in EU-Africa relations, the success of such assistance will greatly depend on factors beyond the EU's control. This same reasoning also applies to China. For example, in specific reference to China and the Darfur crisis, Large (2008) dispels the popular myth that China alone can somehow magically solve the conflict. Taking this into account, the most important factor that will determine the depth of Chinese engagement on peace and security issues will be the extent to which African actors, especially governments, request and utilize its assistance.

What can perhaps be stated with more certainty is the fact that any future support to Africa from outside actors will be more useful when it is delivered in a cooperative and coordinated manner. Cooperation would build trust and strengthen relations while at the same time, and most importantly, lead to a more effective delivery of assistance and so improve the capacity of African actors to solve their pressing problems. There is a case for closer Africa-China-EU discussion on how this could best be accomplished. A closer trilateral dialogue should explore the relative success of past experiences and allow for an exchange of perspectives on what are the priorities for support. The optimal result of such a dialogue would be the identification of common areas where the EU, China and Africa could cooperate. One such area, which is central to African peace and security, could be jointly confronting SALW proliferation.

SALW: An Area for Cooperation?

African states have demonstrated leadership in international efforts to address SALW proliferation, making important contributions to the development and agreement of the UN Programme of Action (PoA), which serves as an international framework for the implementation of initiatives to combat the illicit proliferation of SALW at various levels (International Alert, Saferworld, The University of Bradford 2006). States have developed regional Common Positions (*The Bamako Declaration* of December 2000 and the *African Common Position* of December 2005), and have also signed a number of subregional agreements on small arms control, including legally binding instruments in Southern Africa (the *South African Development Community Protocol*), the Great Lakes Region and the Horn of Africa (the *Nairobi Protocol*). More recently, in April 2010, the 11 member states of the Economic Community of Central African States (ECCAS) validated a draft Convention on SALW (UNREC 2010). Many states have established national coordination bodies to combat SALW and have developed national strategies or action plans. Currently, the AU is developing a continent-wide SALW strategy. Despite progress, the depth and strength of SALW initiatives varies considerably between different African subregions and countries, with some agreements being implemented faster and more effectively than others (International Alert, Saferworld, The University of Bradford 2006). This reflects the fact that some countries have accorded greater priority to the issue than others.

The EU has also taken a leading international role in combating SALW proliferation and made clear commitments to this end. In 2006, the Council of the EU formed the *Strategy to Combat Illicit Accumulation and Trafficking of SALW and their Ammunition*, which clarifies the EU's 'compelling obligation to act' through a series of internal and external initiatives at the national, regional and international level, including support for regions such as Sub-Saharan Africa. The EU Commission's (2005) *Strategy for Africa* also makes similar statements, while its successor, the JAES, highlights this as an important area for cooperation and joint action. Part of its work has included cooperating with the AU on an Africa-wide SALW strategy. On the international level, EU member states' participation in initiatives such as the UNPoA reinforces these commitments.

Beijing too has made commitments on combating SALW proliferation. China's *White Paper on Arms Control* (2005) notes that 'firmly combating illegal activities in the field of small arms and light weapons is of great importance'. China became the forty-sixth signatory of the *UN Protocol Against the Illicit Manufacturing of and Trafficking in Firearms*, though it has not yet ratified the document. By 2007, China had implemented a marking system in adherence to the International Instrument on Identifying and Tracing Illicit SALW (Ministry of Foreign Affairs of the People's Republic of China 2010: 17). Beijing claims to be actively implementing the UNPoA domestically, as well as lending support internationally to SALW initiatives, via the Shanghai Cooperation Organization and the Organization of American States' respective initiatives.[9] There have also been recent commitments made specifically to Africa. China's *Africa Policy* (2006) calls for 'closer cooperation in combating terrorism, small arms smuggling, drug trafficking, transnational economic crimes, etc'. Both the *Beijing Declaration* (2000) and the *Addis Ababa Action Plan* (2003) make reference to closer cooperation on SALW. Most explicitly though, the *Beijing Action Plan* (2006) stated that China would continue to support: 'the effort to combat illicit trade in small arms and light weapons. It will provide financial and material assistance and related training for African countries within its capacity'.

While a substantial amount of FOCAC commitments have been met, SALW objectives are yet to be addressed. The fact that in 2009, SALW seemed to drop off the agenda in the fourth FOCAC ministerial meeting in Egypt, with no specific

---

9   See the *National Report of the People's Republic of China on the Implementation of the United Nations Programme of Action* (2010) for full details.

references to SALW made in the *Sharm El Sheik Action Plan*, suggests that the issue is less of a priority in terms of the China-Africa dialogue. This is by no means purely due to a lack of interest or incentive by Chinese policy-makers and officials, as a host of factors – including the willingness of African leaders – need also to be taken into account. Whatever the reasons, in assessing the implementation of China's security commitments to Africa, SALW proliferation sticks out as an area in which pledges have not been entirely met.

Despite these setbacks, and given that both the EU and China have made commitments to support Africa, there is, in principle, a foundation for future cooperation. Indeed, the EU SALW strategy (2006) explicitly notes that the strategic dialogue with China should include discussions on tackling SALW proliferation. There are some practical areas where the EU and China could jointly support African partners on the ground. For example, joint funds and initiatives could provide resources for training, stockpile management, destruction of surpluses, computerized record-keeping and border control mechanisms in those African countries that require such assistance. Providing technical assistance on developing and strengthening national legislation is a further avenue for cooperation.

Arms control best practices could become established as part of any future joint military exercises between Chinese, EU and African countries, and exchange trips could be organized for officials to share information and experiences. Chinese peacekeepers, who have a growing role on the continent, could partake in more disarmament initiatives and experienced EU member states could assist Chinese forces by providing the adequate training to be able to carry out these often complex operations. Both China and the EU are financially supporting the AU's peace and security institutions as well as subregional groupings, such as ECOWAS. More joint EU-China support could be focused on developing AU SALW initiatives, while there exist organizations on the subregional level – for example, the East Africa's Regional Centre on Small Arms (RECSA), which already receives some EU funding – that require support and assistance. Joint commitments to regional initiatives and agreements such as the *Nairobi Protocol*, the *South African Development Community (SADC) Protocol* and the *ECOWAS Convention* present further opportunities. Lastly, clearer information exchange and communication between the EU and China would, at the very least, avoid duplication of efforts. All of these practical and largely uncontentious recommendations would simply fulfil commitments already made by both China and the EU. There are several African states who have diverted serious attention to tackling SALW and who would welcome much needed resources and assistance in order to improve security both within and across their borders.

Despite efforts in Africa to combat proliferation on the ground, one cannot ignore the fact that over 95 percent of Africa's most commonly used conflict weapons come from outside the continent (IANSA, Oxfam, Saferworld 2007: 3). Effectively controlling this supply of SALW requires international action, which should also be on the agenda of any Africa-China-EU dialogue. Firstly, international debates, such as those within the framework of the UNPoA, have focused overwhelmingly on combating illicit transfers, but more has to be done to recognize that most illicit weapons have an origin in the licit market. Furthermore, while both EU member states and China have supported the UNPoA, much more could be done by both to improve implementation at the national, regional and international levels.[10] One international item that has been specifically highlighted by the UN Secretary-General is transparency: 'of all transparency measures on weapons systems, those on small arms are the least developed' (United Nations Office of the Secretary-General 2008). As such, regular reporting on SALW transfers to the UN Register on Conventional Arms is required by all states. Beyond this, control of arms brokering, support for tracing instruments, standardizing end user-certificates, tighter controls to prevent diversion and better enforcement of UN embargoes are all issues that should be raised in any dialogue on how Africa, the EU and China could cooperate at the international level.

Since they are both exporters of weapons, there is a specific area for bilateral EU-China dialogue which is more contentious: arms export controls. The EU's arms transfer controls, as established in the now legally binding Common Position on Arms Export Controls, lay out eight criteria for responsible exports and establishes a significant degree of transparency over arms transfers from member states. Beijing claims that it too improved its arms exports controls in 2002, through amending and updating its export control rules (White Paper on Arms Control 2005). China only exports military weapons to state entities and does not allow unauthorized re-export, an especially important criterion which not all arms exporting countries meet (Ministry of Foreign Affairs of the People's Republic of China 2010: 14). There are three main criteria that must be observed in exporting arms, which are the following: that they are used for legitimate national self-defence, that they do not threaten regional or international security and that there is no interference in the affairs of the recipient country (Ministry of Foreign Affairs of the People's Republic of China 2010: 14). Not withstanding the principles behind these rules, they appear somewhat too generic and leave too much scope for different interpretation. There are, in fact, some critical issues with China's export controls, namely that gaps and loopholes exist and that the focus remains overwhelmingly on tackling the illicit trade, rather than better regulating the licit trade or improving inter-departmental policy co-ordination, transparency and dialogue with other exporting countries.[11] However, steps taken since the mid-1990s suggest that China is starting to take more seriously policies on arms transfer controls to fulfil its role as a responsible actor (Smith, Wheeler, Mariani 2009).

Despite the difficulty in accessing reliable and measurable data, China's share of arms exports to Africa, especially in SALW, has grown markedly in recent decades.[12] Many of the countries which have received weapons from China – for example Uganda – have also been supplied by EU member states, the United

10   See for example: Biting the Bullet Project and IANSA (2006).
11   See Teitt (2009: 21–2) and Raine (2009: 166–9).
12   See Small Arms Survey (2009) and Shinn (2009).

States (US) and other large arms exporters. However, Chinese exports to sensitive destinations, such as Zimbabwe and Sudan, have led to substantial criticism from a wide range of actors, including many on the African continent (Taylor 2009). Despite the fact that China suspended arms exports to Sudan for a period of time and re-called an arms shipment to Zimbabwe in 2008 (Holslag 2008: 10, Reuters 2008), China's international reputation had been tarnished, as some questioned whether it was acting responsibly. In defence terms, Chinese officials argued that it was not Africa's largest source of weapons and that the US, EU member states and others remain equally culpable for SALW proliferation, both historically – during the Cold War – and in the contemporary period.[13] Indeed, while Chinese military support for the regimes in Sudan and Zimbabwe is much discussed in the West, direct and indirect arms transfers to countries of concern by the US, Russia, the United Kingdom (UK), France and other big arms exporters, sometimes do not attract the same level of criticism, which Beijing labels as geopolitical hypocrisy.

Clearly, there is a need for establishing avenues for discussion and dialogue to agree upon what constitutes responsible arms transfers to establish a normative framework that guides future transfers of SALW. The architecture of the EU-China Strategic Dialogue already includes provisions for expert-level dialogue on non-proliferation and conventional arms exports (Brodsgaard, Lim 2009: 4): it is these avenues that need to be utilized as entry points, so as to clearly identify which areas of agreement can be progressively built upon. Furthermore, the Council of the EU's (2006: 10) SALW Action Plan explicitly stresses the need to 'seek consensus' with exporting countries over what constitutes appropriate criteria on exports. Linked to this, current efforts within the UN towards an international Arms Trade Treaty (ATT) provides a crucial opportunity for heightened debate about transnational responsibilities, including the possibility of cooperating to adopt common high standards based on international law to control the spread of conventional arms. The EU has explicitly voiced its support for an ATT, while China remains much more cautious.

One cannot ignore the fact that there exist some substantial obstacles to Africa-China-EU cooperation. EU-China relations themselves make discussing responsible arms transfers difficult for two reasons. Firstly, EU member states' criticism of China's arms exports to regimes with poor human rights records during periods of violent unrest, has led to a defensive retort from China, making the entire discussion very sensitive. Secondly, and of equal importance, is the fact that the EU has an arms embargo on China itself. Despite discrepancies between member states, the EU officially maintains that the Chinese government's failure to better protect human rights means that the embargo will not be lifted. Chinese officials and members of the policy community perceive the embargo to be deeply unfair, claiming that its continuation is entirely geopolitical. The motivations and interests behind maintaining or lifting the embargo are in fact complex and

---

13   For a full discussion of this debate see Le Billon, Spiegel (2009) and Taylor (2010: 113–33).

multi-layered. This means that a resolution of the issue seems far off, which is problematic, as the thorny issue is of a higher priority to Beijing than holding discussions on responsible arms exports or finding ways to cooperate with the EU in Africa.

Conclusion

In fact, meaningful progress on closer Africa-China-EU cooperation in any area already appears to be some way off. In 2008, the European Commission reached out to Beijing and African capitals in order to initiate a trilateral dialogue on a broad range of issues related to development in Africa. As to date, little progress has been made. This may stem from the fact that some African governments are weary of being sidelined by cooperation among exogenous powers, especially if China were to start mirroring European conditionalities on assistance. Others may also want to maintain the benefits of playing external powers off one another to maximize their gains. Beijing itself may be suspicious as to what the EU's intentions are behind pursuing closer cooperation and may perceive this proposition to be an obstacle in terms of meeting the mantra of South-South cooperation. Whatever the causes to the current impasse, it appears that at least for now, the context within which Africa-China-EU relations operate in, is not yet conducive to high-level engagement.

More specifically to SALW, is the fact that China's commitments made in the 2006 *Beijing Action Plan* were never implemented, while SALW are not even referred to in the 2009 *Sharm El Sheik Action Plan*. This raises the question whether the Chinese government is willing to redouble its commitment to the control of SALW. Linked to this, a question mark remains over whether African governments themselves perceive SALW control as a priority for assistance: their demand for assistance is key to keeping SALW on the agenda, and their reluctance to push for it in within the avenues of dialogue with China suggests that it is not an important issue within the wider agenda of China-Africa relations. Despite the fact that some countries appear keen to push forward efforts against SALW proliferation, one cannot ignore the politics of international engagement driving African governments (each with varied and individual considerations) in defining their positions on engagement with China or even the EU on such issues. Given this, more must be done by the wide spectrum of interested actors to keep SALW on the agenda of decision-makers, not just in China and Europe but also in Africa. These actors include African civil society and political leaders who have in the past spent considerable efforts in bringing to the world's attention the devastating effects SALW proliferation has had in certain unstable regions of Africa. As China emerges as a source, not only of weapons but also of assistance, these actors need to re-evaluate and re-focus their energies in identifying problems and pointing to solutions that better reflect the new realities of China's growing impact on African peace and security.

There are clearly obstacles to closer cooperation. However, these do not render the opportunities meaningless and should not dissuade those who pursue it. There are undoubtedly peace and security issues which need addressing and which are in the shared interests of African, EU and Chinese actors. The case of Somali piracy, where various external actors, including the EU and China are cooperating, illustrates this potential. Furthermore, an observable, albeit cautious, change in Beijing's policy to deepen cooperative engagement has been noted. Such change may in turn present opportunities for the EU to engage with China on how – given their mutual interests – they can work together. SALW might just be one such area. They link many of Africa's security challenges together and in principle there is a foundation, based on the commitments both external actors have made, for jointly supporting on-the-ground initiatives in Africa.

In fact, it could be argued that successful agreements and the consequent implementation of such initiatives by the EU, China and African states, could be used as an entry point to wider cooperation. Instead of broad dialogue on an extensive set of issues held between high-level officials, a more effective strategy of driving cooperation would be to encourage the relevant in-country officials and practitioners to identify specific small-scale practical projects, where joint support will have a measurable benefit. Success at this level may serve to drive further discussions on how to broaden cooperation on other security issues in Africa – indeed, it is these very issues that drive the demand for SALW in the first place. China is increasingly showing interest in peacekeeping and post-conflict reconstruction, both areas in which the EU is also engaged in. Demonstrating the success of cooperation on the ground may prove pivotal to generating interest in further cooperation in Brussels, Beijing and African capitals. In an increasingly globalized, interdependent and mutlipolar world, such cooperation will be instrumental to safeguarding its peaceful progression.

Bibliography

Book References

HIIK. 2006. *Conflict Barometre 2006*. University of Heidelberg: Heidelberg Institute for International Conflict Research (HIIK).

IANSA, Oxfam and Saferworld. 2007. *Africa's Missing Billions: International Arms Flows and the Cost of Armed Conflict*. London: Saferworld.

Li, W. 2008. *Beijing Summit and the Third Ministerial Conference of the Forum on China-Africa Cooperation – Appraisals and Prospects*. Shanghai: Shanghai Institutes for International Studies.

Muggah, R. and Batchelor, P. 2002. *Development Held Hostage: Assessing the Effects of Small Arms on Human Development*. New York: United Nations Development Programme.

Raine, S. 2009. *China's African Challenges*. London: Routledge.

Small Arms Survey. 2003. *Small Arms Survey 2003: Development Denied.* Cambridge: Cambridge University Press.
Small Arms Survey. 2009. *Small Arms Survey 2009: Shadows of War.* Cambridge: Cambridge University Press.
Taylor, I. 2009. *China's New Role in Africa.* Boulder: Lynne Rienner.

Journal Articles

Alden, C. and Alves, A.C. 2009. China and Africa's natural resources: the challenges and implications for development and governance. *SAIIA Occasional Paper*, 41, 1–28.
Aning, K. and Lecoutre, D. 2008. China's ventures in Africa. *African Security Review*, 17(1), 40–50.
Bates, G. and Huang, C. 2009. China's expanding role in peacekeeping: prospects and policy implications. *SIPRI Policy Paper*, 25, 1–52.
Bates, G., Huang, C. and Morrison, S.J. 2007. Assessing China's growing influence in Africa. *China Security*, 3(3), 3–21.
He, W. 2007. The balancing act of China's Africa policy. *China Security*, 3(3), 23–40.
Holslag, J. 2008. China's next security strategy for Africa. *BICCS Asia Paper*, 3(6), 1–13.
Le Billon, P. and Spiegel, S.J. 2009. China's weapons trade: from ships of shame to the ethics of global resistance. *International Affairs*, 85(2), 323–46.
Shi, Y. 2008. China's peaceful development, harmonious world and international responsibility: achievements and challenges. *SIIS Global Review*, Spring 2008, 19–28.
Teitt, S. 2009. Strengthening China's role in protecting populations from mass atrocity crimes. *Paper Presented to International Studies Association 2009 Conference*. New York: Marriott Marquis.
Yu, J. and Wang, Z. 2008. China-Africa strategic partnership ushered in a new era. *China-Europe-Africa Cooperation: Chances and Challenges – Proceedings of the Sixth Shanghai Workshop on Global Governance*, 14–15 March 2008, Shanghai Institutes for International Studies/Friedrich-Ebert-Stiftung, 77–105.

Websites

2000. *Forum on China-Africa Cooperation 2000: Beijing Declaration.* [Online]. Available at: http://www.fmprc.gov.cn/zflt/eng/zyzl/hywj/t157833.htm [accessed: 3 February 2010].
2003. *Forum on China-Africa Cooperation Addis Ababa Action Plan 2004–2006.* [Online]. Available at: http://china.org.cn/english/features/focac/185197.htm [accessed: 3 February 2010].

2006. *Forum on China-Africa Cooperation Beijing Action Plan 2007–2009*. [Online]. Available at: http://www.fmprc.gov.cn/zflt/eng/zyzl/hywj/t280369. htm [accessed: 3 February 2010].

2009. *Forum on China-Africa Cooperation Sharm El Sheik Action Plan 2010–2012*. [Online]. Available at: http://bw.china-Embassy.org/eng/xwdt/t628555. htm [accessed: 3 February 2010].

AllAfrica.com. 2009. *Liberia: China again! Turns over US$5.5M barracks*. [Online]. Available at: http://allafrica.com/stories/200904300911.html [accessed: 9 July 2010].

BBC News. 2007. *Scores die in Ethiopia oil attack*. [Online]. Available at: http://news.bbc.co.uk/1/hi/world/africa/6588055.stm [accessed: 10 June 2010].

BBC News. 2008. *China hostages killed in Sudan*. [Online]. Available at: http://news.bbc.co.uk/1/hi/world/africa/7694106.stm [accessed: 10 June 2010].

BBC News. 2009. *Kenyans rearming for 2012 poll*. [Online]. Available at: http://news.bbc.co.uk/1/hi/8293745.stm [accessed: 5 March 2010].

Burgis, T. 2009. *China seeks big stake in Nigeria oil*. [Online]. Available at: http://www.ft.com/cms/s/0/9d714f96-ac60-11de-a754-00144feabdc0. html?catid=4&SID=google [accessed: 10 March 2010].

CRI. 2010. *China, Ethiopia vows to build closer military ties*. [Online]. Available at: http://www.eastafricaforum.net/2010/06/29/china-ethiopia-vow-to-build-closer-military-ties/ [accessed: 15 March 2010].

Foreign Policy. 2010. *Money can buy love*. [Online]. Available at: http://www. foreignpolicy.com/articles/2010/06/21/money_can_buy_love [accessed: 15 July 2010].

Hu, J. 2009b. *Hu Jintao delivers an important speech in Dar es Salaam, 16 February 2009*. [Online]. Available at: http://www.fmprc.gov.cn/eng/wjdt/wshd/t537784.htm [accessed: 15 March 2010].

International Alert, Saferworld and The University of Bradford. 2006. *Implementation of the PoA in Africa*. [Online]. Available at: http://www.saferworld.org.uk/downloads/pubdocs/BtB-Africa-briefing-jun06.pdf [accessed on: 10 July 2010].

Kendo, O. 2008. *China has proved it is not a friend to count on*. [Online]. Available at: http://www.afrika.no/Detailed/16063.html [accessed: 23 March 2010].

Large, D. 2008. *China's role in the mediation and resolution of conflict in Africa*. [Online]. Available at: http://www.hdcentre.org/files/Dan%20Large%20China%20in%20Africa%20WEB.pdf [accessed: 17 March 2010].

PLA Daily. 2009. *"Peace Angel 2009" kicks off*. [Online]. Available at: http://english.pladaily.com.cn/site2/special-reports/2009-06/23/content_1830057. htm [accessed: 15 March 2010].

Reuters. 2007. *ICBC to buy Standard Bank stake*. [Online]. Available at: http://www.reuters.com/article/idUSSHA11075020071025 [accessed: 15 July 2010].

Reuters. 2008. *China recalls Zimbabwe arms amid election crisis*. [Online]. Available at: http://www.reuters.com/article/idUSL24880687 [accessed: 15 July 2010].

Reuters. 2009a. *Oxfam: Somalia biggest challenge for aid workers.* [Online]. Available at: http://af.reuters.com/article/topNews/idAFJOE5940DB2009100 5?pageNumber=2&virtualBrandChannel=0 [accessed: 16 March 2010].

Reuters. 2009b. *Fact-box: International efforts at military reform in Congo.* [Online]. Available at: http://af.reuters.com/article/drcNews/idAFLDE5BM0UF2009122 3?pageNumber=2&virtualBrandChannel=0 [accessed: 16 March 2010].

Tuju, R. 2006. *Address to Ministerial summit on armed violence and development in Geneva.* [Online]. Available at: http://www.mfa.go.ke/statement%20by%20 the%20Minister.htm [accessed: 12 March 2010].

United Nations Development Programme. 2005. *UNDP Human Development Report 2005.* [Online]. Available at: http://hdr.undp.org/en/media/HDR05_ complete.pdf [accessed: 5 March 2010].

UNREC. 2010. *UNREC focus: special Kinshasa Convention.* [Online]. Available at: http://www.unrec.org/index/index.php?option=com_content&view=article &id=183&Itemid=133&lang=en [accessed on: 10 July 2010].

Wang, W. 2010. *China and Africa envision new security cooperation.* [Online]. Available at: http://www.china.org.cn/opinion/2010-06/25/content_20350297. htm [accessed: 12 July 2010].

Xinhua News Agency. 2010. *China, Zimbabwe pledge to enhance military relations.* [Online]. Available at: http://news.xinhuanet.com/english2010/ china/2010-06/13/c_13349173.htm [accessed: 15 March 2010].

Command Papers

Council Common Position 2008/944/CFSP of 8 December 2008 Defining Common Rules Governing Control of Exports of Military Technology and Equipment. 2008. Brussels: Council of the European Union.

EU Strategy to Combat Illicit Accumulation and Trafficking of SALW and Their Ammunition. 2006. 5319(2006). Brussels: Council of the European Union.

European Union Strategy for Africa: Towards a Euro-African Pact to Accelerate Africa's Development. 2005. COM 489(2005), Brussels: European Commission.

National Report of the People's Republic of China on the Implementation of the United Nations Programme of Action. 2008. Beijing: Ministry of Foreign Affairs of the People's Republic of China.

National Report of the People's Republic of China on the Implementation of the United Nations Programme of Action. 2010. Beijing: Ministry of Foreign Affairs of the People's Republic of China.

UN Protocol Against the Illicit Manufacturing of and Trafficking in Firearms, Their Parts and Components and Ammunition, Supplementing the UN Convention Against Transnational Organized Crime. 2001. A/55/383/Add.2. New York: United Nations.

United Nations Office of the Secretary-General. 2008. *Small Arms: Report of the Secretary-General.* S/2008/258. New York: United Nations.

White Paper on Arms Control 2005. 2005. Beijing: Information Office of China's State Council.

Newspapers

2009. China-Africa trade up 45% in 2008 to US$107 billion. *China Daily*, 11 February.

PART III

Chapter 6

The EU's Perceptions and Interests towards China's Rising Influence on Human Rights in Africa

Ian Taylor

Introduction

In the European Union's (EU) promotion of 'good governance', one commentary has averred that 'The EU tends to export to third countries the EU model of political and economic development based upon economic liberalization and the rules of [the] free market, democratic norms and practices, and human rights protection' (Panebianco, Rossi 2004: 6). Commitments to promote democratic principles, the rule of law and human rights are explicitly set out in the Treaty of the European Union (Articles 6 and 11). Such principles are based on the European experience, which is then extrapolated and exported as *universal*. Whether this is appropriate to Africa is vitally important in discussing any putative 'clash' between the EU and China over 'human rights'.

In August 2006, the European Commission launched a new *Communiqué* on *Governance in the European Consensus on Development – Towards a harmonized approach within the European Union*. In paragraph 13 of this document, it is reaffirmed that 'development is a central goal by itself, and that sustainable development includes good governance, human rights and political, economic, social and environmental aspects' (European Commission 2006). Among the common values avowed by the declaration was the following: 'EU partnership and dialogue with third countries will promote common values of: respect for human rights, fundamental freedoms, peace, democracy, good governance, gender equality, the rule of law, solidarity and justice' (European Commission 2006).

The European Union Delegation to the African Union further underlined this, stating that 'The support that the EU has brought to New Partnership for African Development (NEPAD) since its conception is largely based on [c]ommitment to core values, especially democracy, human rights, good governance and the rule of law' (EU Delegation to the African Union 2002). Indeed,

> The EU strongly supports the political values at the heart of New Economic Partnership for African Development (NEPAD), because they correspond with the 'essential elements' of the EU's external cooperation policy regulated by

the Maastricht Treaty and completed by the Lomé/Cotonou principles, the Mediterranean process and the Agreement with South Africa. These are good governance, strengthening democratic practices, respect for human rights and the rule of law (Grannell 2002: 18).

Because the EU's own conception of 'good governance' (and its concomitant human rights) is technocratic and apolitical, the personalization of political power – either at low or high social levels – which stakes out well-defined roles within most African polities, is barely understood by the EU's own officers, even in the field. When and where the EU speaks regarding 'human rights', this is in an individualistic or technical sense and misses the *political* dimensions. Indeed, the EU's own prescriptions for designing 'good governance' structures draws upon the international financial institutions' 'broadly agreed best international practices of economic management' (IMF 1997).

The turn to 'good governance' by the EU can be related to both the dominance of technocratic neo-liberal thinking and a refusal to acknowledge that European policies have not worked in Africa to promote development. Certainly, the refusal by Brussels to acknowledge that policies have not worked is central to the emergence of the 'good governance' discourse within the EU's development rhetoric. Instead of questioning their own prescriptions, European elites have sought to advance 'good governance' as a necessary precondition for reforms to finally work, deftly ignoring the elephants in the room – gross levels of subsidization to Europe's farmers and the effective blocking of much of Africa's export potential by EU policies and the reality of neo-patrimonial rule (cheerily supported by key EU states such as France and the United Kingdom).

The turn to 'good governance' itself reflects the conviction amongst major global institutions that neo-liberalism is the only way forward and that the origins of the problems linked to good governance has emerged not from the content of various assistance programmes, but rather from their implementation and wider institutional setting in the borrowing states. As Weaver notes regarding the World Bank, 'governance and anti-corruption issues ran head-first into the economic, technocratic, and apolitical features of the Bank's "intellectual culture"' (Weaver 2008). After all, there existed 'the dominance of neo-classically trained economists within the Bank [mainly] recruited from academia with little or no experience in government and with little interest in or appreciation of non-economic factors affecting development' (Weaver 2008).

The above accounts for the often distinct naivety that the EU operates from in their dealings with large parts of the continent, with regard to human rights. As Claude Ake notes:

> One of the most amazing things about the literature on development in Africa is how readily it assumes that everyone is interested in development and that when [African] leaders proclaim their commitment to development and fashion their impressive development plans and negotiate with international organizations for

development assistance, they are ready for development and for getting on with it (Ake 1991: 319).

This is a major problem for the EU in crafting coherent and long-term developmental relationships, in terms of the EU's stated foreign policy goals, although short-term commercial exchanges of mutual benefit to African elites and European corporations are evidently possible. Further complicating this milieu is the importance of China's rise in Africa, a subject we now turn to.

The China Variable

Taking into consideration all the above, the entry of the Chinese into Africa may make the EU's governance projects irrelevant. Chinese economic and political activities in Africa are growing at exponential rates and this expansion of Chinese involvement in Africa is arguably the most momentous development on the continent since the end of the Cold War (Taylor 2006, 2009). The People's Republic of China (PRC) is now Africa's second most important trading partner, behind the United States but ahead of France and the United Kingdom. In parallel to the increase in China's economic activity in Africa, have come accusations that China is a new 'colonizing' power, exploiting Africa's natural resources, flooding the continent with low-priced manufactured products whilst turning a blind eye to Africa's autocrats. Senior EU politicians have enunciated this view: for instance, Karin Kortmann, Parliamentary State Secretary in the German Development Ministry, declared in November 2006 that 'Our African partners really have to watch out that they will not be facing a new process of colonization' in their relations with China (The Guardian 2006).

There is an explicit concern that China's perceived stance is threatening Western interests.[1] For instance, while major donor countries and institutions have embraced the notion that good governance and respect for human rights are an integral part of any foreign policy toward Africa, the sense that '[China's] diplomacy and economic outreach in Africa are not contingent upon this fundamental requirement [and therefore] may undermine important development and diplomatic goals in Africa' (Bartholomew 2005: 79) has grown, particularly after 2005, the so-called 'Year of Africa'. In 2006, one British newspaper went so far as to state that 'a year on from Live 8, China has trounced all hope of change in Africa by doing deals with its kleptocrats', adding that 'China will deal with anyone, and pariah states are a gap in the market'; indeed, it went further, predicting serious implications for British foreign policy: 'The Department for International Development is now trying to encourage good governance by cutting back aid to countries that persecute opposition leaders and supporters. The latest approach makes sense. But, sadly, the game is up: China makes it irrelevant' (*The Times* 2006). In a nutshell, the criticisms from Europe have

---

1   Interview with a Western diplomat, Asmara, Eritrea, 29 June 2006.

been that Beijing will do business with any government, regardless of its human rights or democratic record, and that it thereby undermines attempts to advance constitutional rights and champion broader issues of good governance on the continent. Both these criticisms and the arguable contradictions, fluctuations and limitations of Beijing's stances on non-interference and the definition of human rights will be discussed in this chapter. However, it is apposite that we first turn to what constitutes the Chinese government's own understanding of human rights.

Chinese Conceptions of Human Rights

According to Wan Ming (2001: 1), 'Few issues in the relations between China and the West invoke as much passion as human rights'. Although the concept of human rights is often central to criticisms of China's relations with Africa, its definition is a point of contention between Beijing and the West – one that has moved down the bilateral agenda ever since then United States (US) President Bill Clinton delinked human rights and Most-Favoured Nations trade status in May 1994. Subsequently, 'although Western criticism of China's human rights remained, it gradually became ritualized and marginalized on Western diplomatic agendas in China' (Wan Ming 2005: 288). Why and when the topic was resurrected with regard to Sino-African ties is in itself an interesting question that undoubtedly relates to anxieties regarding how China's rise may affect Western interests.

Negative focus is usually placed on China's transgressions of the norms adopted by the United Nations (UN). However, it would be erroneous to regard what Chinese sources call China's human rights outlook, which is grounded in native tradition, as one-dimensional – and thus, by inference, inimical to the international human rights regime. As Albert Chen (2000: 2) points out:

> When we turn to the Chinese tradition, we can, as in the case of the West, find [...] elements that have affinities with, or can contribute to, the modern conception of human rights as well as elements that contradict that conception. The former elements include the Confucian principle of benevolence as the basic norm governing relations between human beings [and] the idea of the equality of all human beings in terms of the capacity for moral cultivation and growth.

Traditionally, the dominant Chinese discourse on rights has focused on the obligations and responsibilities of citizens in building a rich and strong society. This emphasis has underpinned most official Chinese positions since 1949 and dominates Beijing policy-makers' thinking on the subject today. Very briefly summarized, China's discourse on human rights is characterized by a communitarian emphasis on solidarity and duty toward others, which coincides with the Confucian concern for promoting harmony. The perception within China by the leadership that the country is unstable also leads to Beijing's prioritization of social stability. This discourse is informed by pragmatic nationalism, with a strong emphasis on developmentalism.

If one accepts the Chinese discourse on human rights and the centrality of development, then one might argue that China has made considerable progress over the past few decades:

> It would be churlish of Western commentators to underestimate the enormous achievement, in the context of China's recent history, [that] is represented by the current economic development and material improvement in the day-to-day life of the Chinese population, albeit largely urban. [...] It has lifted over 150 million people out of poverty in less than a decade. By way of corroboration, according to figures from UNICEF, the UN, and UNESCO, China does better than India, a country with a similar population level, in infant mortality, life expectancy, and primary school enrolment. There are many more statistics indicating that although China is a lower-middle-income country, it outperforms a number of other countries in its class in relation to the basic economic, social and cultural indicators (Lee 2007: 448).

Indeed, as Daniel Burstein and Arne de Keijzer (1999: 136) point out, 'To the Chinese, the human rights to food, clothing, shelter, economic development, and security [...] are paramount over traditional Western-style individual political liberties. Judged by this standard, China in the [p]ast twenty years is a leader, not a laggard, in promoting the human rights of its people'.

Peerenboom (2005) notes that the rule of law, good governance, and the codification of most rights (including civil and political rights) correlate to relatively high-levels of wealth. Thus, a comparison of China to the developed world unsurprisingly reveals that the former has more departures from the rule of law, weaker state institutions, more corruption and fewer individual freedoms than their Western counterparts. Peerenboom offers a variety of explanations for his view that the comparison is unfair and that China is held to higher (or even double) standards than other lower-middle-income countries. Among these are that the Western-dominated international human rights community is biased toward democracies that promote liberal, civil and political rights, holding non-democratic countries to the same standards despite their differing needs and values. China is also singled out because of its potential threat to Western domination; Beijing's growing economic and geopolitical muscle is seen to pose a normative challenge to the liberal human rights regime insofar as China's elites could deploy it to defend and advance rights-based policies and ideals that clash with those of the West, predicated as they are on secular liberalism.

Ostensibly, it is in an ideological clash with the liberal West that China finds itself on the defensive. With its strong emphasis on social stability, Beijing sees the notion that states must guarantee freedom and liberty for individuals as an abstraction at best and a danger at worst. A 2005 commentary in *Xinhua* on human rights put it thus:

> Human rights [are] enjoyed by the collective in addition to [the individual]. The individuals' interests are upheld via the realization of collective interests. So China attaches importance to collective human rights as well as to individuals' human rights. This is in contrast to Western countries, where much emphasis is put on individuals' human rights while collective human rights are neglected (Xinhua News Agency 2005).

This has become the position that Chinese officials generally take when discussing China's non-interference stance in Africa.[2] For instance, Foreign Minister Li Zhaoxing, when 'asked about China's investment in nations with records of human rights abuses – notably Sudan and the Central African Republic – replied: "Do you know what the meaning of human rights is? The basic meaning of human rights is survival – and development"' (Associated Press 2007).

Importantly, China adheres to the Five Principles of Peaceful Coexistence. Though these principles originally prescribed relations only between China and India, by the 1970s they extended to relations with all states. It should be noted that a paper on China's *Africa Policy* released by the Ministry of Foreign Affairs in 2006, expressly states that 'China stands ready to develop friendly relations and cooperation with all countries on the basis of the Five Principles of Peaceful Coexistence' (Ministry of Foreign Affairs of the People's Republic of China 2006: 3). Non-interference and the importance of sovereignty – central to the Five Principles – are explicitly connected to the issue of human rights: 'Human rights are something covered by the sovereignty of a country. A country's sovereignty is the foremost collective human right. [...] And sovereignty is the guarantor of human rights'. Historical perspective underpins the statement, quoted in *Xinhua* that:

> In the humiliating old days, China was bullied by foreign powers. Its sovereignty was trampled on, and [so were] the Chinese people's human rights. So the Chinese people know very well that sovereignty is a precondition to their enjoying human rights. In sum, there would be no human rights to speak of in the absence of sovereignty (Xinhua News Agency 2005).

How remembrance of the past informs contemporary China's ideas of sovereignty and human rights is important to consider (Scott 2007).

We should point out that the West has shown only recent interest in China's human rights record (Nathan 1994). As China opened up to the global economy in the 1980s, Beijing began to involve itself in various international regimes *vis-à-vis* human rights:

> Perceived as undergoing a much-applauded modernization programme with social as well as economic ramifications, Beijing was throughout the 1980s given favourable treatment by the Western media who saw/hoped that China was

---

2　Interview with a Chinese diplomat, Abuja, Nigeria, 5 September 2007.

being remade as a Chinese imitation of the West's self-image. Western policy-makers replicated this wishful aspiration, and [...] complaints over China's *laogai* (forced labour) system, public executions and lack of democracy were eerily absent (Taylor 1998: 446).

The West appeared unconcerned that Beijing's contribution to human rights progress was mostly rhetorical. Chinese praise for the Universal Declaration of Human Rights as 'the first international instrument that systematically sets forth the specific contents regarding respect for and [the] protection of fundamental human rights' – despite China's transgressions thereof – underscores this point (Xinhua News Agency quoted in Zhang Yongjin 1998: 188).

It was after Tiananmen Square that human rights came to the fore of China's international relations and that Africa's place in Beijing's foreign policy was reconsidered following a decade of neglect (Cooper 1994, Taylor 2006). Beijing was shocked by the level of Western criticism regarding Tiananmen and sought to counter it by attentively courting the developing world.[3] Anti-imperialist rhetoric was dusted off and employed in combination with an emphasis on state sovereignty and the advancement of different definitions of human rights and democracy. Beijing profoundly resented critiques of its human rights record and perceived attempts by outsiders to interfere in China's affairs, which it linked to ulterior motives to halt China's modernization programme, revealing deep-seated collective memories of colonial interference in China, in the nineteenth century, as well as a xenophobia that is arguably integral to Chinese political culture.

At the time of the Tiananmen Incident, Deng Xiaoping commented, 'I am Chinese and familiar with the history of foreign aggression against China. When I heard [...] Western countries [...] have decided to impose sanctions on China, my immediate association was [of] 1900, when the allied forces of eight foreign powers invaded China' (Deng 1994: 344). According to Ming Wan (2005: 291), 'In discussions with Chinese diplomats and officials [...] I sense a strong indignation [...] and an equally strong conviction that the [...] human rights pressure was simply an excuse for keeping China weakened and subordinated, a humiliating situation that Chinese patriots should not allow to happen [again]'. Indeed, the comment made by Deng Xiaoping in September 1989 that 'there are many people in the world who hope [China] will develop, but there are also many who are out to get us' (Deng 1994: 309) is typical. Such depths of feeling influence Beijing's foreign policy: they are often expressed in the context of Sino-African relations, usually with respect to China's subjugation and Africa's colonial experience, and to assert the common history of China and Africa.

In sum, there remain two key elements to the PRC's foreign policy stance regarding human rights. The first involves the importance of the right to pursue economic prosperity. On a visit to China in April 1993, the Zambian Foreign

---

3 Interview with Wang Xuexian, China's Ambassador to South Africa, Stellenbosch, 13 February 1998.

Minister concurred with Beijing's assessment that for 'developing countries, the most basic human rights are the rights to subsistence and to development' (Xinhua News Agency 1993). He Wenping, director of the African Studies Section at the Chinese Academy of Social Sciences (CASS), has likewise averred that Chinese policy-makers do not believe 'human rights should stand above sovereignty. [...] We have a different view on this, and African countries share our view' (Mooney 2005: 2). A Chinese commentary argues that such a position is in line with the UN's own:

> The Universal Declaration of Human Rights is the first international document ever to put forward the principle of respecting and guaranteeing the most fundamental of human rights, reflecting the importance attached by the international community to the promotion of human rights and basic freedom. China's human rights outlook is in keeping with the basic principles of the Universal Declaration of Human Rights (Xinhua News Agency 2005).

Indeed, Beijing's focus on economic and developmental rights does gel with some of the Declaration's articles, notably Article 25, which asserts that 'everyone has the right to a standard of living adequate for the health and well-being of himself and of his family, including food, clothing, housing and medical care and necessary social services'. This fits comfortably with a focus on developmentalism. Yet, it effectively deems other articles of the Declaration secondary; examples include Article 18, which states that 'everyone has the right to freedom of thought, conscience, and religion'; Article 19, whereby 'everyone has the right to freedom of opinion and expression'; and Article 20, which claims that 'everyone has the right to freedom of peaceful assembly and association'. It is a question of emphasis on economic as opposed to political rights; Beijing is little different from any other government in upholding some aspects of the Declaration while overlooking others.

As clear as Beijing's position on the Declaration is, it insists that China's human rights regime is a work in progress.[4] A statement issued at the time of the PRC's signing of the International Convention on Civil and Political Rights is worth quoting at length:

> The Chinese government believes that the principle of the universality of human rights must be respected, but the specific conditions of each country must also be taken into consideration in observing this principle. In such a large developing country with a population of 1.2 billion [as] China, it is essential to protect and promote the right to subsistence and the right to [the] development of its people. Over the past five decades, especially the past [20] years and more, since the introduction of reform and opening up, China has largely succeeded in meeting the basic needs of its people and improving their living standards significantly.

---

4   Interview with a Chinese diplomat, Addis Ababa, Ethiopia, 15 May 2007.

It has thus ensured its people greater enjoyment of their economic, social, and cultural rights. China, which is a socialist country under the rule of law, attaches equal importance to the [people's] civil and political rights. It opposes any encroachment upon the citizens' lawful rights. Since 1978, the legislative body of China has made more than 300 laws and law-related decisions. As a result, China has a fairly complete set of laws for the protection of human rights. These progresses [*sic*] and achievements that China has obtained have laid a solid foundation for China's signature and accession to more international legal instruments on human rights (Ministry of Foreign Affairs of the People's Republic of China 2000).

The second element of the PRC's philosophy of human rights concerns the principle of non-interference in others' domestic affairs and the norm of state sovereignty. In Chinese diplomacy, as we have seen, sovereignty often trumps other norms – a fact that leads some critics to complain that China invokes sovereignty and non-interference selectively.[5] As far back as 1973, analysts like Jerome Cohen were denouncing as hypocritical 'the PRC's enthusiastic participation in UN condemnations of the South African and Rhodesian governments for abuses against their respective peoples despite [its] earlier protests that UN condemnation of the PRC's conduct in Tibet constituted intervention in China's domestic affairs' (1973: 489). The PRC has also been accused of reserving the implicit right to condemn countries for any perceived ill-treatment of ethnic Chinese (particularly in Southeast Asia), in effect adhering to a race-based policy on so-called interference in other countries' affairs (Barabantseva 2005, Sautman 1997). Meanwhile, Beijing has made a point of blaming liberal democracy for many of Africa's woes, going directly against the view of the Western mainstream that it is a lack of democracy that partly accounts for Africa's maldevelopment.[6] During the high-water mark of the democratic swell in Africa in the late 1980s and early 1990s, when a number of African autocrats were being peacefully removed via the ballot box, Chinese commentaries dismissed the electoral process as an 'obsession' and a 'temptation' (Xinhua News Agency 1992). Later, as the wave began to ebb, Chinese sources dubbed Africa's experiment with democratization a 'disaster' (Xinhua News Agency 1994), arguing that 'multiparty politics fuelled social turmoil, ethnic conflicts and civil wars' (Beijing Review 1996). Recently, Beijing has sought to downplay the importance of liberal democracy: 'For a starving man, which should he choose, bread or ballot, if he is supposed to choose only one? The ballot is of course important. But he must feed himself with bread before he can cast a ballot' (Xinhua News Agency 2005). And on 14 January 2008, following post-election violence in Kenya, the *People's Daily* announced that:

---

5   Interview with a Western diplomat, Asmara, Eritrea, 29 June 2006.
6   Interview with a Chinese diplomat, Abuja, Nigeria, 5 September 2007.

Transplanted Western democracy [can]not take hold in Africa. The African people have been living on the continent for generations; have forged special links among different ethnic groups; and have cultivated a unique African culture long before falling victim to Western colonialism. [...] The post-election crisis in Kenya is a product of democracy bequeathed by Western hegemony and a manifestation of values clashing when democracy is transplanted onto disagreeable land.

Opinions of this sort are welcomed by various African leaders for reasons linked to their states' modalities of governance. Although it is debatable whether stability generally 'comes first in [a] country's development' [*sic*] (as the *People's Daily* put it), in the African context, 'stability' usually means prioritizing elite interests, which has long proven problematic.

However, it is important to point out that the debate over the PRC's policies on human rights in Africa does not simply involve Beijing versus Europe. A number of African leaders interested in the continent's welfare take positions that are arguably contrary to those of the Chinese government, expressing concern for the possible 'danger that China will serve to help rollback initiatives such as NEPAD, even if unintentionally', out of adherence to its stated principles.[7]

The EU's Misperception of China's Evolving Human Rights Stance in Africa

From Beijing's perspective, China and Africa 'support each other in international affairs, especially on major issues such as human rights, [to] safeguard the legitimate rights of developing countries' (Embassy of the People's Republic of China in the Republic of Zimbabwe 2000). The *Beijing Declaration of the Forum on China-Africa Cooperation*, in late 2006, makes it official:

> Countries that vary from one another in social system, stages of development, historical and cultural background and values, have the right to choose their own approaches and models in promoting and protecting human rights in their own countries. [...] Moreover, the politicization of human rights and the imposition of human rights conditionalities on economic assistance should be vigorously opposed, as they constitute a violation of human rights (as quoted in Xinhua News Agency 2006).

There is arguably some convergence between Chinese attitudes toward human rights and liberal democracy, and those of the African elites. Many African leaders simply do not share the West's concerns.[8] They look at the economic and political

---

7   Interview with an African Union official, Addis Ababa, Ethiopia, 15 May 2007.
8   Interview with a Ugandan academic, Mbarara, Uganda, 2 November 2006.

inroads China has made into Africa very differently from Western critics who call China the 'Patron of African Misgovernment' (New York Times 2007).

However, while it is true that China's leaders and many of Africa's Presidents share attitudes toward human rights and governance, the latter do not necessarily put economic rights over political rights or value national development the way the former do. National development for a broad-based productive economy is far less a concern to elites within most African political systems, than is control of resources for their advantage and that of their clientelistic networks. In fact, development might stimulate opposition. As Bertrand Badie explains:

> On the one hand, economic development is a goal that every head of state must pursue. [...] On the other hand, an overly active policy of development risks producing several negative results: it would valorize the competence of the technocratic elite relative to that of the fragile political elite, break up social spaces and favour the constitution of a civil society capable of counterbalancing the political system, and, indeed, neutralize neo-patrimonial strategies (Badie 2000: 19).

Beijing's 'politics of development' are continually hidebound by the real possibility that 'China's economic and political support could offer African politicians increasing leeway in misusing public funds or manipulating institutions to preserve their own power' (Lewis 2006: 2, Lewis 1996).

It is important to remember that the PRC's policy of non-interference in others' domestic affairs is not specific to Africa. It is in fact long-standing, rooted in humiliations China endured in the nineteenth century, to emerge as a mainstay of Beijing's foreign policy[9] – as Article 54 of China's first plenary session of the Chinese People's Political Consultative Conference makes explicit: 'The principle of the foreign policy of the People's Republic of China is protection of the independence, freedom, integrity of territory and sovereignty of the country'. This principle underpins Beijing's interpretations of human rights and democracy in Africa or elsewhere. The emphasis on collective development, rather than individual civil and political liberty, as the paramount human right has to be understood. As David Shinn (2006: 1) points out, 'If the West fails to take these different perceptions into account, it will never deal effectively with the challenges posed by China in Africa'.

In this regard, much of the criticism heaped on China for its Africa policies *vis-à-vis* human rights and governance by Brussels is rather misplaced; such policies are not particular to Africa. The problems start when the philosophies behind them converge with those of African leaders themselves, particularly the heads of neo-patrimonial regimes and 'quasi states' (Jackson 1993) who are more than happy to

---

9   Interview with Shu Zhan, Chinese Ambassador to Eritrea, Asmara, Eritrea, 29 June 2006.

have China as an ally.[10] It could be persuasively argued that the Chinese are, like all others, simply acting in a pragmatic and self-interested manner, according to their own understandings of particular concepts. Although justifiable disquiet surrounds those aspects of Chinese engagement in Africa that may undermine political and economic reform, much of Africa's predicament is complex, so erecting a scapegoat to blame makes little sense – beyond masking ulterior anxieties regarding China's African sojourn.[11] Here, we may level the charge of hypocrisy against the West, as do Daniel Burstein and Arne de Keijzer:

> While the human rights situation in China is not good by American standards, it is not unlike that in Indonesia, India, or Saudi Arabia, for instance. Yet in most of these cases, the United States is able to have normal and even close relationships that are not overwhelmed by the human rights agenda (Burstein, de Keijzer 1999: 137).

A 2006 editorial takes the point further:

> European and North American leaders in general, and French politicians in particular, tend to give their African counterparts lessons on democracy, respect for human rights, and governmental transparency – even if such lessons are also exercises in Western hypocrisy. France, for instance, maintains privileged relations with the corrupt regimes of oil-rich Gabon, ruled since 1968 by Omar Bongo and of Congo-Brazzaville (Republic of the Congo). And the United States has been wooing African dictators such as Teodoro Obiang Nguema and José Eduardo dos Santos, who rule oil-rich, poverty-ridden Equatorial Guinea and Angola, respectively, both since 1979 (Godoy 2006).

Indeed, it is important to observe with Peerenboom (2007), that many critiques of China's human rights record are shaped by an interest in containing China's development and influence. Conversely, notes Zheng Yongnian (1999: 105), the Chinese suspect that certain 'forces do not like to see a strong China with a rapid[ly] growing economy. Because they perceive China as their potential rival, they will use all possible means, including the Taiwan, Tibet and human rights issues, to contain China's development'.

By focusing narrowly on Beijing's approach to human rights in Africa to the neglect of other features of the relationship, international critics implicitly delegitimize China and, by extension, the actions of 'the Chinese', whether at home or abroad.[12] This is not to say that Beijing is or should be above criticism but

---

10   Interview with a Ugandan academic, Mbarara, Uganda, 2 November 2006.

11   Interview with Robin Sherborne, editor of *Insight,* Windhoek, Namibia, 14 August 2006.

12   Interview with Henning Melber, Namibian political economist, Windhoek, Namibia, 14 August 2006.

only that context is required in order to avoid exoticizing, if not the demonizing of China, when discussing its engagements in Africa.

Before critiquing those aspects of Chinese involvement in Sub-Saharan Africa that impact upon governance and human rights, analysts need to understand both the Chinese human rights discourse and the nature of most African states. That said, there is a certain illogic to Beijing's position that needs reflection. Let us accept that different conceptions of human rights as well as different interpretations of the Universal Declaration exist. As we have seen, Beijing privileges rights to food, clothing, shelter and economic development and has been quite active in asserting that its primary mission is to develop the productive forces of society, underlining the slogan that development is the absolute principle. From the perspective of Chinese policy-makers, the liberal conception of human rights advocated by the West poses a potential threat to the stability essential to development.[13] That is certainly the message communicated by China's official Africa policies.

Yet what if Sino-African diplomacy not only clashes with the advancement of 'universal' (Western) norms regarding human rights but actually manages to undermine the very development that is ostensibly so essential to Beijing's own definition of rights? What if Beijing's diplomacy in Africa helps to consolidate governments that actively obstruct development insofar as it threatens elite control? The non-interference policy implicitly grants that Beijing will not interfere in the domestic affairs of the countries it assists. Yet, if sovereignty is the guarantor of human rights, as the Chinese declare, on the one hand, and a means to effectively undermine development on the other, then there is a clear contradiction at the heart of the Chinese discourse on human rights. Surely in such cases Beijing is complicit not only in autocratic attempts to sabotage the nascent human rights movement (one now supported by a number of African states) but also in problematizing its own concept of human rights as measured by development, as well as its own interpretation of the linkage between human rights and sovereignty. As evidenced in Zimbabwe and elsewhere, support for abusive regimes can indirectly destabilize development plans; in lending such support, Beijing directly contradicts its own pronouncements on the meaning of human rights.

It is clear, for instance, that Mugabe's government not only tramples on the civil and political rights the West ostensibly holds dear, but also subverts Zimbabweans' economic and social rights which China claims to prize. In such cases, to reiterate, the PRC resorts to a fundamentalist bottom line whereby sovereignty itself is the basis of human rights; it is up to each sovereign state to establish its own conception of the rights of its people – what they are in any given context and how they should be realized – without interference from outside forces. However, the reification of states and the attendant amalgamation of sovereignty and rights into a single principle of non-interference make little real sense in a milieu dominated by quasi states and neo-patrimonial regimes; as one African informant put it, "'Non-

---

13   Interview with a Chinese diplomat, Addis Ababa, Ethiopia, 15 May 2007.

interference" is an implicit green light to autocrats'.[14] Furthermore, if Chinese actors, adhering to the principle of non-interference, actually make things worse for some in Africa, then the other great shibboleth of Chinese human rights rhetoric – that basic socio-economic rights are more important for the poor than abstract political rights – rings hollow.

Of course, the Chinese government can then reinvoke sovereignty by arguing that African states are free to deal with China or not, as they so desire,[15] but if Beijing's leaders genuinely believe that they will not repeat the crimes and misdemeanors of European colonizers in Africa, then engaging without damaging remains a big challenge: 'China isn't the first outside industrial power to behave badly in Africa. But it should not be proud of following the West's sorry historical example' (New York Times 2007).

That said, we should remember that China is changing, and so are its conceptions of human rights and sovereignty. China's official policies toward Africa are therefore likewise developing and maturing.[16] One of the reasons Beijing finds itself in such compromising positions with pariah regimes like Zimbabwe's and Sudan's is that, as relative latecomers to Africa, Chinese actors go where more established actors and corporations cannot or will not go. In other words, they sometimes end up in places impulsively, before the political environment is settled.[17]

Yet we should also note that relations with a regime such as Mugabe's are not typical of Sino-African diplomacy.[18] There is a realization among Beijing's policy-makers that attempts to separate politics and business do not generally succeed, particularly in many of the African countries with which China engages. This shift in attitude and the attendant evolution of Beijing's foreign policies, however pragmatic, means the status quo on non-interference in domestic human rights affairs is unlikely to continue, particularly if and when Chinese interests are endangered. Like all investors in Africa, the Chinese recognize that success requires security and stability, as well as economic rationality. Wherever human rights abuses destabilize a polity, Chinese interests will be threatened.[19] By the same token, Beijing's focus on development is central: it sees a stable international order based on economic and political cooperation as key to a supportive environment in which to develop China.[20] Given that it is eager to be seen in turn as an unthreatening, responsible power, Beijing is concerned about the way China is perceived abroad: government officials and business leaders alike recognize that

---

14   Interview with an African Union official, Addis Ababa, Ethiopia, 15 May 2007.

15   Interview with Shu Zhan, Chinese Ambassador to Eritrea, Asmara, Eritrea, 29 June 2006.

16   Interview with He Wenping, CASS, Beijing, China, 18 September 2007.

17   Interview with a British diplomat, Addis Ababa, Ethiopia, 15 May 2007.

18   Interview with a Chinese diplomat, Abuja, Nigeria, 5 September 2007.

19   Interview with a British diplomat, Addis Ababa, Ethiopia, 15 May 2007.

20   Interview with Shu Zhan, Chinese Ambassador to Eritrea, Asmara, Eritrea, 29 June 2006.

a bad national image is damaging to broad Chinese interests and power (Lampton 2008: 23). Thus Chinese policy-makers are, in the future, likely to think twice about any action that might undermine a stable environment or undercut Beijing's attempt to cast itself as a responsible player on the world stage.

Conclusion

It is true that at the moment there appears to be some divergence between the EU and Chinese policy aims regarding governance and that this at times suggests a convergence between Beijing and certain types of African leaders. However, this can only ever be temporary in nature if China wishes to have a long running and stable relationship with Africa. China is like all other actors in Africa – it needs stability and security in order for its investments to flourish and for its connections with the continent to be coherent. EU member states have had to learn the hard way that propping up dictators willy-nilly is not sustainable nor desirable (even if this continues) and China will likewise learn this as its relations unfold. As Obiorah notes:

> After an initial phase of snapping up resource extraction concessions, it is almost conceivable that China will be compelled by instability and conflict in Africa to realize that its long-term economic interests are best served by promoting peace in Africa and that this is most likely to come about by encouraging representative government in Africa rather than supporting dictators (Obiorah 2007: 40).

This has started to happen:

> China's changing calculation of its economic and political interests has partly driven this shift. With its increased investments in pariah countries over the past decade, China has had to devise a more sophisticated approach to protecting its assets and its citizens abroad. It no longer sees providing uncritical and unconditional support to unpopular, and in some cases, fragile regimes as the most effective strategy (Kleine-Ahlbrandt, Small 2008: 38–9).

Thus, whilst in the current period there sometimes appears to be divergence, there can ultimately only be growing convergence with EU policy aims – maybe not with regard to democracy, but certainly with regard to governance and security and by implication, a greater connection to the downside of supporting regimes that undermine development and China's own notions of human rights.

Furthermore, China's integration into the global economy and the concomitant responsibilities that have come with this greater incorporation necessitate structural and systemic reforms in Beijing, particularly through increasing membership of multilateral bodies. In the long-term, these could conceivably have an impression on Beijing in the development of a regime that incorporates increased respect for the rule of law and a better safeguarding for universal human rights. For instance, Beijing's key commitments pertaining to its membership of the World Trade Organization (WTO) comprises responsibilities to advance the transparency, consistency and standardization of China's legal system. And it is more than obvious that over the past 20 years or so, Beijing has signed up to and ratified a growing number of international instruments pertaining to human rights and labour as it embeds itself in various multilateral regimes. The task for EU policy-makers is to encourage such developments, not perpetually criticize Beijing:

> The Western countries should accept that they are not any longer in a position to prevent the rise of China and other actors of global change. The objective should be to design a strategy toward China that does not only constrain competition, but develop common commitments on how to deal together on pressing global challenges (Gu, Humphrey, Messner 2007: 288).

Finally, the Chinese have actually been quite explicit in their support for NEPAD. At the second Forum on China-Africa Cooperation, Beijing agreed to: 'strengthen cooperation with Africa on priority sectors identified under the NEPAD' (Xinhua News Agency 2003). Setting the governance strictures to one side, NEPAD is fundamentally a neo-liberal project aimed at opening up African markets and developing liberalized economies. Just as China has, since 1978, pursued the capitalist path to development, so too now Beijing is *de facto* encouraging Africa to likewise accept and advance the precepts of liberalized capitalism. This is in the EU's interests, given its explicitly capitalist agenda.

Bibliography

Book References

Badie, B. 2000. *The Imported State: The Westernization of the Political Order*. Stanford, CA: Stanford University Press.
Burstein, D. and De Keijzer, A. 1999. *Big Dragon: Future of China – What It Means for Business, the Economy and the Global Order*. New York: Touchstone.
Deng, X. 1994. *Selected Works 1982–1992: Volume 3*. Beijing: Foreign Languages Press.
Jackson, R. 1993. *Quasi-States: Sovereignty, International Relations and the Third World*. Cambridge: Cambridge University Press.
Lampton, D. 2008. *The Three Faces of Chinese Power: Might, Money, and Minds*. Berkeley: University of California Press.
Scott, D. 2007. *China Stands Up: The PRC and the International System*. London: Routledge.
Taylor, I. 2006. *China and Africa: Engagement and Compromise*. London: Routledge.

Taylor, I. 2009. *China's New Role in Africa*. Boulder: Lynne Rienner.
Wan, M. 2001. *Human Rights in Chinese Foreign Relations: Defining and Defending National Interests*. Philadelphia: University of Pennsylvania Press.
Weaver, C. 2008. *Hypocrisy Trap: the World Bank and the Poverty of Reform*. Princeton: Princeton University Press.
Zhang, Y. 1998. *China in International Society Since 1949: Alienation and Beyond*. Oxford: St. Martin's Press.

Book Chapters

Ake, C. 1991. How politics underdevelops Africa, in *The Challenge of African Economic Recovery and Development*, edited by A. Adedeji, O. Teriba and P. Bugembe. London: Frank Cass, 316–29.
Obiorah, N. 2007. Who's afraid of China in Africa?, in *African Perspectives on China in Africa*, edited by F. Manji and S. Marks. Cape Town: Fahamu, 35–56.
Wan, M. 2005. Democracy and human rights in Chinese foreign policy, in *China Rising: Power and Motivation in Chinese Foreign Policy*, edited by Y. Deng and F. Wang. Lanham: Rowman and Littlefield Publishers, 279–304.

Journal Articles

Barabantseva, E. 2005. Transnationalizing Chineseness: overseas Chinese policies of the PRC's central government. *ASIEN: Journal for Politics, Economy and Culture*, 96, 7–28.
Bartholomew, C. 2005. Statement of Ms. Carolyn Bartholomew, Commissioner, US-China Economic and Security Review Commission, *Hearing Before the Subcommittee on Africa, Global Human Rights and International Operations of the Committee on International Relations*, House of Representatives, One Hundred Ninth Congress, First Session, Serial Number 109–74. Washington, D.C.: Government Printer, 17–21.
Chen, A. 2000. Chinese cultural tradition and modern human rights. *Perspectives*, 1(5), 1–12.
Cohen, J. 1973. China and intervention: theory and practice. *University of Pennsylvania Law Review*, 121(3), 471–505.
Cooper, J. 1994. Peking's post-Tiananmen foreign policy: the human rights factor. *Issues and Studies*, 30(10), 65–78.
Grannell, F. 2002. The European Union and the New Partnership for Africa's Development (NEPAD). *The Courier ACP-EU*, 194, 28–29.
Gu, J. Humphrey, J. and Messner, D. 2008. Global governance and developing countries: the implications of the rise of China. *World Development*, 36(2), 274–92.
Kleine-Ahlbrandt, S. and Small, A. 2008. China's new dictatorship diplomacy: is Beijing parting with pariahs?. *Foreign Affairs*, 87(1), 23–37.

Lee, K. 2007. China and the International Covenant on Civil and Political Rights: prospects and challenges. *Chinese Journal of International Law*, 6(2), 445–74.

Lewis, P. 1996. Economic reform and political transition in Africa: the quest for a politics of development. *World Politics*, 49(1), 92–129.

Lewis, P. 2006. China in Africa. *Saisphere*, Winter, 1–5.

Mooney, P. 2005. China's African safari. *YaleGlobal*, 3 January, 1–3.

Nathan, A. 1994. Human rights in Chinese foreign policy. *China Quarterly*, 139, 622–43.

Panebianco, S. and Rossi, R. 2005. EU attempts to export norms of good governance to the Mediterranean and the Western Balkans. *Paper to the Fifth Pan-European international relations conference: constructing world orders*, The Hague, 9–11 September 2004.

Peerenboom, R. 2005. Assessing human rights in China: why the double standard?. *Cornell International Law Journal*, 38(1), 71–172.

Sautman, B. 1997. Racial nationalism and China's external behaviour. *World Affairs*, 160(2), 78–96.

Shinn, D. 2006. The China factor in African ethics. *Policy Innovations*, 21 December 2006.

Taylor, I. 1998. China's foreign policy towards Africa in the 1990s. *Journal of Modern African Studies*, 36(3), 443–60.

Command Papers

China's Africa Policy. 2006. Beijing: Ministry of Foreign Affairs of the People's Republic of China.

Good Governance: the IMF's Role. 1997. Washington, D.C.: International Monetary Fund.

Governance in the European Consensus on Development – Towards a Harmonized Approach within the European Union. 2006. COM (2006)421, Brussels: European Commission.

NEPAD and the African Union (Newsletter). 2002. Addis Ababa: The EU Delegation to the African Union.

The Beijing Declaration of the Forum on China-Africa Co-operation. 2000. Harare: Embassy of the People's Republic of China in the Republic of Zimbabwe.

The Signing of the International Convention on Civil and Political Rights by the Chinese Government. 2000. Beijing: Ministry of Foreign Affairs of the People's Republic of China.

Newspapers

1992. Democracy's dangers. *Xinhua News Agencies*, 1 July.

1993. Zambian visitor praises China. *Xinhua News Agency*, 10 April.

1994. Disastrous experiment in democracy leads to re-think. *Xinhua News Agency*, 22 December.

1996. Lessons learned in Africa. *Beijing Review*, 29 July–4 August, 4.

2003. China to strengthen cooperation with Africa on NEPAD priorities. *Xinhua News Agency*, 17 December.

2005. Human rights can be manifested differently. *Xinhua News Agency*, 12 December.

2006. Beijing Declaration on the Forum on China-Africa Cooperation. *Xinhua News Agency*, 19 October.

2006. Is China Africa's new imperialist power?. *The Guardian*, 16 November, 5.

2007. Patron of African misgovernment. *New York Times*, 19 February.

2008. Stability comes first in country's development. *People's Daily*, 14 January.

Godoy, J. 2006. Africa: China reaches into Europe's resource-rich 'backyard'. *Inter Press Service*, 15 November.

Nguema, R.A. and Doland, A. 2007. China courts Africa with aid, projects. *Associated Press*, 8 January.

Rozenberg, G. 2006. Africa is not going to rock to Bono's tune. *The Times*, 4 July.

Chapter 7

China, Sovereignty and the Protection of Civilians in Armed Conflict in Africa: The Emergence of a 'Third Paradigm' of International Intervention?

Sara van Hoeymissen

Introduction

Conflicts in Africa currently involve over 70 percent of the military personnel deployed worldwide under United Nations (UN) auspices (Centre on International Cooperation 2009). Since 1999, these UN forces have increasingly been tasked with protecting civilians. Current-day conflicts often take a particularly heavy toll on civilians, who may get caught up in the violence and are sometimes even directly targeted by armed groups. Civilians in conflicts also die as a result of disease and malnutrition, frequently caused by displacement (Human Security Centre 2005). According to a traditional Westphalian understanding of the principles that guide international relations, the protection of civilians in armed domestic conflicts is a matter under the jurisdiction of the sovereign state where the violence occurs. However, in the post-Cold War era, the security and welfare of civilians in conflict situations have increasingly evolved into matters of international concern. Since the end of the 1990s, a broad array of issues related to the protection of civilians have entered the agenda of the UN Security Council (UNSC), ranging from addressing the particular needs of women, children and internally displaced persons (IDPs), to ending the proliferation of small arms and ensuring the safety and access of humanitarian personnel (Bellamy, Williams 2009: 13–14). The protection of civilians 'under imminent threat of physical danger' has also increasingly become part of the mandate of UN peacekeeping or peace enforcement forces (Holt, Berman 2006). Internationally, there is growing acceptance that states must be held accountable for how they provide security to their citizens and promote their welfare. The seminal work of the UN Secretary-General's Special Representative on IDPs, Francis Deng, and researchers from the Brookings Institute working on the concept of 'sovereignty as responsibility' in the mid-1990s, proposed to recognize these state obligations as a necessary condition of sovereignty (Deng et al. 1996).

This chapter looks at China's position on and contribution to international efforts to protect civilians in armed conflicts in Africa. On paper, there is a sharp contradiction between concepts such as 'sovereignty as responsibility' or 'civilian protection' and the principles that underpin China-Africa relations. Respect for sovereignty and non-interference in domestic affairs have figured as cornerstones of China's rhetoric in its relations with Africa since the 1960s (Straus 2009). However, China's Africa policy is not disengaged from its wider foreign policy. It has been noted that China's position on humanitarian intervention is less rigid than generally assumed. Chinese views on multilateral humanitarian intervention have evolved over the course of time, despite China's continued rhetorical insistence on the need to respect sovereignty. For example, Allen Carlson's exchanges with foreign policy elites in China around the turn of the millennium revealed that many among them were adopting a more flexible understanding of sovereignty and were cautiously accepting that multilateral intervention was legitimate as a last resort in major humanitarian crises (Carlson 2004: 18–19, 23–5).

Nowadays, Chinese scholars openly contemplate the possibility of change in China's non-intervention policy. In 2009, Chinese international relations scholar Pang Zhongying suggested that China is gradually moving towards a 'third paradigm' of international intervention. In Pang's view, such a paradigm would be different from both China's traditional paradigm of non-interference and Western paradigms of intervention. Pang points out that in the past decade the non-interference principle has come under discussion in some regions of the world, where it used to be unquestioned. In Africa for example, the African Union (AU) and the Economic Community of West African States (ECOWAS) have qualified their members' sovereignty in cases of grave humanitarian crises. Chinese analysts have been paying close attention to the development of new norms and views with regard to sovereignty and intervention in Africa (Luo 2003: 49, Pang 2009: 248–9, Yuan 2008: 61). Pang asserts that following the AU's lead, which attaches great importance to non-interference but has nonetheless pledged to adopt a stance of 'non-indifference' in case of grave human rights abuses, China needs to add new content to the old principles of non-interference (Pang 2009: 248–50) and 're-assess the question of intervention in some circumstances, for example, at least, in cases of major humanitarian crises' (Pang 2009: 249). This chapter will try to assess whether we are witnessing signs of the acceptance of such a 'new paradigm' in China's stance on intervention, in the particular case of civilian protection in Africa.

An often noted characteristic of China's foreign policy and political culture in general is that it pragmatically combines rhetorical commitment to long-standing principles in practice (Pye 1988, Zhao, Pollack 2004). China's adherence to a traditional concept of sovereignty as seen in its rhetoric on Africa, does not necessarily mean intransigence on actual cases of civilian protection in Africa. It is therefore important to look beyond the principles and to identify the understandings of national interests and strategic calculations that inform Chinese deliberations in practice. This is particularly important with regard to China's current, fast evolving relations with Africa. As Dan Large (2009: 611) points out, in the past decade these have gone from being 'thick' in ideological rhetoric and 'thin' in actual content, to being much more substantial in terms of economic and political interests. A key aim of this chapter is therefore to assess what impact China's evolving interests in Africa is having on its stance on civilian protection issues.

While the first section of this chapter touches briefly on China's position on the civilian protection in thematic debates on the topic, the major part of this study is concerned with the protection of civilians as part of the everyday deliberations in the UNSC and UN peacekeeping operations. It analyses China's stance on two ongoing cases of international efforts to provide protection to civilians against the backdrop of conflict in Africa, namely Eastern Congo and Sudan's Darfur region. The analysis reveals that China's direct involvement in both cases of civilian protection is fairly limited. With regard to the Democratic Republic of Congo (DRC), China emerges as a low-profile participant in a multilateral process that is increasingly focused on civilian protection. Nonetheless, China has also shown itself sympathetic to Congolese concerns about national sovereignty and provides assistance in having these concerns voiced in the UNSC. China's position on Darfur attracted a lot of international attention and went through a remarkable evolution towards greater acceptance of, and contribution to, international involvement in civilian protection. The two case studies show that in spite of its sovereignty concerns, China can be persuaded to play a non-obstructionist and even constructive role. In the final section, the chapter uses three variables defined by Thomas Weiss and Don Hubert to identify some of the factors that have induced China to engage with international efforts to address human security crises. The chapter ends by questioning whether, at least in practice, we are witnessing signs of the emergence of a 'new paradigm' in China's stance on civilian protection efforts, as described by Pang Zhongying.

Human Security and Civilian Protection: Chinese Views and Concerns

A conceptual precursor to the idea of civilian protection was that of human security, which first received mention in the United Nations Development Programme's (UNDP) 1994 Human Development Report. The report argued that security studies had for too long maintained a narrow focus on territories and national interests and needed to be expanded in order to include the security concerns of ordinary people (United Nations Development Programme 1994: 22). In China, the concept of human security failed to gain much recognition. Chinese analysts contend that it is up to states to judge their domestic human security situation and provide safety to their citizens (Chu 2002: 9, Li 2007: 5). This state-centric approach to human security falls in line with China's discourse on human rights in general, which places strong emphasis on sovereignty and the right to non-interference in domestic affairs. China's ruling elites view sovereignty as 'the only premise and guarantee of human rights within each nation' (Chu 2001).

China's insistence on the primacy of the state in providing human security does not mean that it sees no role for the international community as far as the protection of civilians in conflict-affected countries is concerned. In the first ever thematic debate held at the UNSC on the issue of civilian protection in September 1999, China has already recognized that it was legitimate for the international community to be concerned with the suffering of civilian caught up in armed conflicts (United Nations Security Council 1999). However, China maintains that any external assistance to ease such suffering should respect the will and sovereignty of the host country. China maintains that 'no arbitrary intervention should be imposed on the government concerned over its objection' (United Nations Security Council 2007). China therefore prefers humanitarian aid over other, more intrusive forms of international intervention.

In 2005, China joined the global endorsement of the principle of the 'responsibility to protect' at the World Summit (United Nations General Assembly 2005: paragraph 135). This endorsement marked an important breakthrough as China signalled its willingness to consider humanitarian intervention under specific circumstances of grave human suffering. According to the World Summit Outcome Document, governments have a responsibility to protect their populations from genocide, war crimes, ethnic cleansing and crimes against humanity. Should national authorities be 'manifestly failing' in their responsibilities, the international community declared itself 'prepared' to take timely and decisive collective action through the UNSC. Two aspects of the World Summit consensus are frequently stressed by China, pointing to some of the reservations and concerns that China still has about the responsibility to protect (Teitt 2008: 8–9). The first is that the primary responsibility for civilian protection lies with states, not with the international community. Past precedents reveal that when there is no longer a functioning government in a state, China is more accepting of multinational intervention. The collapse of central authority in states such as Liberia and Somalia in the early 1990s, and the resulting failure of the state to protect its citizens, enabled China to agree to international intervention in those countries (Vesel 2003: 23, Wheeler 2000: 186). However, as China's former Ambassador to the UN, Wang Guangya explained:

> [T]here are cases where you can say that the country is a failed country. But wherever there is a government, I think the best way to do it is by giving good advice wherever you can, tough way or soft way, to let the government pick up its main responsibility (Traub 2006).

The second element is that any multilateral intervention under the responsibility to protect requires the endorsement of the UNSC. China insists on UNSC approval of any international measures that invoke the use of force in peace and security crises (Fravel 1996, Reilly, Gill 2000). The use of force for the protection of civilians is no exception to this (United Nations Security Council 1999). In practice, the requirement of a UNSC mandate means that as a permanent UNSC member, China can expect to have a potentially decisive say on all proposed measures regarding humanitarian intervention.

China's willingness to discuss civilian protection on a case by case basis opens the door to exercising the pragmatism that has often been identified as a key characteristic of its diplomacy. The following section leaves the realm of concepts and thematic debates to turn to the world of diplomatic practice. Two recent cases of conflict in which civilian protection has come to the forefront will be analysed, namely Eastern Congo and Sudan's Darfur region. The aim is to assess China's current-day diplomacy on civilian protection in Africa and the interests and concerns that shape it.

From Eastern Congo to Darfur

Eastern Congo

The United Nations Organization Mission in the Democratic Republic of Congo (MONUC) started off as a traditional peacekeeping operation but gradually acquired a very assertive mandate concerning the protection of civilians (Holt, Berkman 2006: 91). In spite of its misgivings about civilian protection, China acted as a relatively cooperative partner in the multilateral process that turned MONUC into a civilian protection mission. The following section will discuss the motivations behind China's cooperative stance and the concerns that China nonetheless raised when the UN made the protection of the citizens of a sovereign member state, into one of its main objectives.

MONUC was established by the UNSC in November 1999, to monitor the implementation of the *Lusaka Ceasefire Agreement*. This Agreement intended to bring a halt to the second Congolese war, which had involved the Congolese government, a number of other African countries and various armed groups. MONUC possessed some of the characteristics that China considers crucial for a peacekeeping mission to be acceptable and effective. Most importantly, the force was deployed with the consent of the Congolese government, which was a signatory to the *Lusaka Agreement*. As a result, China strongly supported MONUC's deployment (Taylor 2008: 147). The fact that the Congolese government's authority was highly tenuous in certain parts of the country and that some rebel movements had not signed up to the *Lusaka Agreement*, did not dampen China's support of MONUC. As Ian Taylor points out, this indicates that China's insistence on host nation consent, as a condition for the deployment of a UN peacekeeping force, only pertains to the consent of 'the state that is a party' – and not necessarily to that of all parties involved – in that conflict (2008: 147).

The implementation of the *Lusaka Agreement* made little progress throughout the year 2000. The critical humanitarian situation that endured on the ground induced the UNSC to expand MONUC's mandate with the insertion of Chapter VII: 'authority to protect civilians'. In February 2000, China joined the other UNSC members in passing resolution 1291, which turned MONUC into only the second UN mission ever to benefit from a civilian protection mandate

(Marks 2007). The signing of the *Pretoria Accord* in July 2002 and an agreement on the formation of an interim national government later that year, eventually officially ended the Congolese war. However, fighting persisted in the Kivu provinces and the Ituri district in the East. In addition to the 2.8 million IDPs already present in the country by the end of 2002, an additional 600,000 Congolese were displaced over the course of 2003, primarily due to continued instability in the East (Tull 2005: 14–15). The UNSC reviewed and strengthened MONUC's civilian protection mandate and capacity on several occasions from 2003 onwards. Civilian protection was thus gradually turned into a core task for MONUC. The line between peacekeeping and peacemaking or peace enforcement became increasingly blurred (Holt, Berkman 2006: 157, 178, Mansson 2005, Tull 2009: 224). China has been sending engineers and medical personnel to MONUC since February 2003. Its participation in MONUC was its first major deployment as part of a UN peacekeeping operation in Africa and more than doubled the number of Chinese peacekeepers taking part in UN missions at the time (Kim 2006: 297–8). Participation in MONUC thus provided China with a way to show its willingness to contribute to conflict resolution in Africa and its commitment to UN peacekeeping (Staehle 2006: 57–8). While providing valuable services to MONUC and to the local population (Gill, Huang 2009: 25), the medical staff, engineers and military observers that China sends to MONUC are by nature not significantly engaged in civilian protection duties.

Remarkably, China voted in favour of each resolution that strengthened MONUC's civilian protection mandate. However, in the UNSC, China's representatives seldom dwelled on civilian protection matters in their statements on the DRC. From the start, China generally supported the UN's initiatives in as far as they enjoyed the support of the Congolese authorities (Staehle 2006: 42). Occasionally, China echoed Kinshasa's objections on the impact that some of the UN's initiatives had on Congo's sovereignty (International Crisis Group 2005: 4). With regard to civilian protection for example, China initially expressed reservations about proposals to strengthen MONUC's mandate to prevent and respond to widespread sexual violence against women in Congo in 2007. The UN estimated that in 2006, 27,000 women were raped in Southern Kivu alone (Gettleman 2007). Apart from rebel forces, the *Forces Armées de la République Démocratique du Congo* (FARDC), the country's regular armed forces, which have integrated thousands of former combatants, were implicated in the abuses. China only agreed to the sensitive new provisions in the MONUC mandate when it was assured that the Congolese government was not opposed to them.[1] As with other civilian protection issues, China maintains that the protection of women is the primary responsibility of national governments and that external assistance should respect the will of the country in question (United Nations Security Council 2008).

---

1 Interview with a Western diplomat, Brussels, June 2009.

Over the course of 2009, differences emerged about the future of MONUC as Joseph Kabila's government began to push emphatically for the UN to devise an exit strategy for MONUC. Kinshasa argued that since the DRC had entered a new phase, MONUC's continued presence would constitute a violation of its sovereignty. At the UN, however, there was concern about a rise in human rights violations in Eastern Congo during military operations by the FARDC against the Democratic Forces for the Liberation of Rwanda (FDLR). Experts attribute many of these human rights abuses, which included random killings of civilians, to poorly trained and weakly disciplined Congolese army forces (IRIN 2010). In December, the UNSC expressed its 'extreme concern' at the 'deteriorating' humanitarian situation in the DRC (United Nations Security Council 2009). UN Under-Secretary-General for Humanitarian Affairs, John Holmes, warned that violence could get out of control if all peacekeepers were pulled out (Associated Press 2010). China demanded that the Congolese government's sovereignty concerns be taken into consideration but supported intensive diplomatic efforts by the UNSC to broker a compromise. In May 2010, the UNSC eventually decided unanimously to replace MONUC with the smaller United Nations Organization Stabilization Mission in the DRC (MONUSCO), on 1 July 2010. The tasks to be included in the stabilization mission's mandate and the order of priority to be given to them, emerged as a topic of contention during the last-minute discussions among Council members.[2] China echoed the views of the Congolese authorities that the stabilization mission should devote more attention to peace consolidation than to civilian protection. A compromise was eventually worked out: MONUSCO's mandate still lists civilian protection as the Mission's first task but emphasizes the need for MONUSCO to work closely with the Congolese government and support its efforts.

Darfur

At no occasion in the history of China-Africa relations has China's stance on civilian protection been scrutinized so closely as with regard to the conflict in Western Sudan's Darfur region. This conflict flared up at the beginning of 2003, when Darfur rebel forces attacked government military installations in frustration at their region's political and economic marginalization and neglect. The attacks sparked a government-sponsored counter-insurgency campaign, led by the Janjaweed, which involved mass killings, abductions, sexual violence and scotched earth tactics. The violence triggered a stream of IDPs and refugees. In April 2004, a ceasefire was brokered between the Sudanese government and the main rebel groups. With the consent of the Sudanese government, the AU sent forces to Darfur to monitor the implementation of this agreement.

When the UNSC held its first major discussion on Darfur in mid-2004, it quickly became apparent that China was not in favour of allowing tough UN action in the

---

2   Telephone interview with a Western diplomat, Leuven, July 2010.

region. China had built up significant interests in Sudan. China National Petroleum Corporation (CNPC) had been investing in the country's oil industry since the mid-1990s. By 2004, Sudan had become a top energy investment destination for China and the supplier of 4.7 percent of China's oil (Large 2008b: 285). China was also an important supplier of military equipment and technology to Sudan, ranging from jet fighters and military weapons to small arms (Large 2007, Shinn 2008: 170–72). During 2004 and 2005, China threatened to use its veto so as to water down proposed UNSC resolutions which sought to impose sanctions against Sudan or contained an explicit threat of sanctions. China's actions had a significant impact on the UNSC's initial response to the Darfur crisis. For example, the UNSC's first resolution on Darfur (resolution 1556, 30 July 2004) invoked Chapter VII of the UN Charter to set a 30-day deadline for the Sudanese government to disarm the Janjaweed militias. However, the resolution only vaguely threatened 'measures as provided for in Article 41 of the UN Charter' in case Sudan did not comply (Nabati 2004).

The resolution also imposed an arms embargo on the Darfur region but this applied only to non-governmental entities. When the deadline of resolution 1556 expired, the UN Secretary-General reported that '[s]topping attacks against civilians and ensuring their protection is the responsibility of the government of the Sudan. The government has not met this obligation fully, despite the commitments it has made and its obligations under resolution 1556(2004)' (United Nations Secretary-General 2004). During the discussions among the members of the UNSC in September 2004, China was alarmed by the United States (US)-drafted proposals calling for a resolution which threatened to impose economic sanctions on Sudan, should Khartoum continue in failing to meet its obligations in terms of disarmament and the provision of security. China only agreed to abstain on resolution 1564 after the threat of automatic imposition of sanctions was removed from the draft (Voice of America 2004, Wang 2004).

In 2006, China's position on Darfur eventually started shifting. China continued to oppose sanctions, stating that they would 'victimize civilian populations' (S/ PV. 5423 2006), but it gradually changed its mind on the role the international community should play in Darfur, in particular with regard to peacekeeping. Initially, China had strongly supported an exclusive peacekeeping role for the AU Mission in Darfur, which operated with the consent of the Sudanese government. However, logistical and capacity constraints rendered that force – which was the first AU mission with explicit permission to engage in civilian protection (Badescu, Bergholm 2009: 297–8) – incapable of providing effective protection to civilians and humanitarian organizations (Kagwanja, Mutahi 2007: 7). In March 2006, the AU agreed to a takeover by the UN of its weak and overstretched operation. This development made it more difficult for China to advocate letting the AU deal primarily with Darfur. In August 2006, China abstained in the vote on resolution 1706, which authorized the expansion of the UN Mission in Southern Sudan to Darfur. The resolution invoked Chapter VII of the UN chapter to authorize the peacekeeping force to use 'all necessary means' to 'protect civilians under threat of physical violence'. The resolution was the first to refer to the 2005 World Summit's 'responsibility to protect' with regard to a particular country. However, rather than stating this as an obligation for the international community to intervene in a state that had failed to protect its citizens, the resolution 'invited the consent' of the Sudanese government for the UN deployment in Darfur. China was among the countries that had insisted on this addition, which turned the resolution into what UN staff dubbed 'Chapter VI and a half' (Cohen 2008: 20).

The prospect of the Sudanese government consenting to UN deployment in Darfur appeared dim as Khartoum invoked sovereignty and security concerns so as to refuse UN involvement in Darfur. China stated that 'as a sovereign state and also as an equal partner in the international efforts to address the issue [Darfur], they [Sudan] have the right and are entitled to have reservations' (Srinivasan 2008: 71). However, in a remarkable development, China began persuading the Sudanese government into taking a more accommodating stance. Active diplomacy by China's Ambassador to the UN Wang Guangya, its Special Envoy for Africa Liu Guijin, Assistant Foreign Minister Zhai Jun and even President Hu Jintao played a significant role in gaining Sudan's eventual acceptance of a UN peacekeeping force in June 2007 (Large 2008a: 100–2, Holslag 2008: 78–81). Resolution 1769, the first on Sudan that China has voted in favour of, eventually established the United Nations-African Union Hybrid Operation, in Darfur (UNAMID), set up in July 2007. A primary objective of UNAMID was the protection of aid workers and civilians, for which it was authorized to use force under Chapter VII of the UN Charter. Even though Sudan announced its approval of resolution 1769 in August 2007, the full deployment of UNAMID was obstructed by a lack of key military equipment and continuing intransigence on the part of Khartoum. China accepted Sudan's explanation that 'technical difficulties' were causing the delays (Raine 2009: 263) but tried to assist in clearing remaining obstacles through diplomacy (International Crisis Group 2009: 21, Ministry of Foreign Affairs of the People's Republic of China 2008). China has been participating in UNAMID since November 2007, providing mostly military engineers.

China has at times walked a tightrope between maintaining good ties with Sudan and meeting the expectations of the international community. For example, China has consistently opposed sanctions but has also pointed out Khartoum's responsibility in avoiding sanctions and refusal to tackle problems – moves that have antagonized the international community (Baldauf et al. 2008). In March 2009, Sudan reacted to the International Criminal Court's (ICC) issuance of an arrest warrant against President Omar al-Bashir by expelling a dozen leading aid agencies from the country. China resisted international pressure on the Sudanese government to reverse its decision and joined AU and Arab League calls for a suspension of the arrest warrant. However, Beijing also expressed 'serious concern' about the expulsion of the aid workers and called on the Sudanese government to show restraint in order to prevent the humanitarian situation from worsening (Varner 2009).

Notwithstanding their insistence on respecting Sudan's sovereignty, Chinese leaders and diplomats have on several occasions stepped out of a state-focused discourse and dwelled on the plight of civilians in Darfur, in their statements and actions (Large 2009: 619–20). For example, during his visit to Sudan in February 2007, Hu Jintao included the need to improve the 'living conditions of the people' in the four key principles he proposed for addressing the Darfur crisis. A few months later, Assistant Minister of Foreign Affairs, Zhai Jun, visited three refugee camps in Darfur. Occasionally, Chinese statements on Darfur utilized concepts such as sovereignty as responsibility and even the responsibility to protect (Gill, Huang, Morrison 2008: 14). For example, Hu Jintao is reported to have told Sudanese President Bashir that 'Darfur is a part of Sudan and you have to resolve this problem' (Large 2008a: 93). In 2008, Liu Guijin stated that 'the Sudanese government should make greater efforts' to improve the humanitarian and security situation 'because Darfur is Sudan's Darfur' (Ministry of Foreign Affairs of the People's Republic of China 2008). Nonetheless, China generally believed the humanitarian situation in Darfur not to be as serious as often portrayed by the West (Wang 2008: 54). Upon his return from Sudan in 2007, Zhai Jun described the situation in Darfur as 'basically stable' and the refugee camps as 'well managed with sound health conditions' (Zhai 2007).

What factors informed the remarkable evolution in China's stance on Darfur from the end of 2007 onwards? Rising international criticism of China's close ties with Sudan was an important aspect underlying the policy shift. For a country that takes great pains to foster an image of a responsible power, the damage that Darfur was causing was worrisome (Large 2008b: 289–90). China's permanent membership of the UNSC turned out to be a double-edged sword in this regard: while it provided China with considerable influence over the actions of the UNSC, it also turned the international spotlight on China. International campaigns that renamed the 2008 Beijing Olympics, 'Genocide Olympics' and called for a boycott of the Games were particularly alarming for China. As Darfur became an issue in China's bilateral relationships with the US and the European Union (EU), the Chinese government had to decide to what extent it could continue to allow its limited energy interests to affect its international reputation (Tunsjø 2010: 35).

Concerns about its standing among African countries also played an important part, especially after it became clear that these had turned in favour of greater UN involvement in Darfur. China risked being perceived as the country that was thwarting the proposals of key African actors such as the AU on the way forward in Darfur. A deeper lying reason for the policy shift was growing Chinese concern about the security of its economic interests and citizens in Sudan. China's close association with the central government in the eyes of the rebel groups rendered its presence on the ground vulnerable (Large 2009: 618, Wu 2010: 63–4). Attacks by Darfur rebel groups on Chinese oil installations in 2006 and 2007 revealed that sound ties with the central government in Khartoum did not guarantee security for Chinese operations on the ground in other parts of Sudan (International Crisis Group 2008: 26). There was a growing fear in China that instability in Darfur could spread elsewhere, most notably to Southern Sudan, where China had its most substantial interests (Wu 2010: 64). After Chad severed diplomatic relations with Taiwan in August 2006, China started paying closer attention to the regional dimensions and implications of the Darfur conflict. Concerns were raised that spreading instability could threaten China's budding interests and investments in Chad (Large 2008b: 289–90, Holslag 2008: 75).

Exploring China's Position

Do the two case studies above point to the emergence of a 'third paradigm' of interference in China's stance on major human security crises? In the framework of research conducted by the International Commission on Intervention and State Sovereignty (ICISS), Thomas Weiss and Don Hubert identified three simple variables that define a country's willingness to participate in multilateral humanitarian interventions. They are: geographic proximity and cultural affinity, national interest understandings and domestic political culture (Weiss and Hubert 2001: 209–12). The following section centres on these variables and attempts to define the paradigm of intervention that characterizes China's stance on civilian protection in practice. What emerges is a paradigm that is largely reactive in nature and does not involve active participation in international civilian protection efforts. However, it does not impede China from engaging with international efforts to address human security crises if its core interests are not at stake or if it considers it in its long-term interest to do so.

Geographical Proximity and Cultural Affinity

Weiss and Hubert pose that what happens nearby, or to a state with shared affinities, is usually more likely to generate political will in favour of intervention. Interestingly, for China, the correlation between geographical proximity and acceptance of intervention appears to be reverse: there is more room for policy flexibility with regard to areas that do not directly neighbour China and where China's vital national interests are less at stake. China is far more worried about the consequences of international intervention in Burma or North Korea than in distant African states such as the DRC or Somalia (Li, Zheng 2009). However, China strongly emphasizes its shared affinities with African countries in its *Africa Policy* discourse and has a long-standing policy of paying attention to the wishes of African countries on African peace and security issues. Apart from the important factor of acceptance by the host nation, the opinions of African regional organizations and key regional players influence China's stance on the acceptability of intervention in a certain crisis (International Crisis Group 2009: 23–5). The case study on Darfur in this chapter revealed that the AU's desire to see greater UN involvement in Darfur had an important impact on China's position on the desirability of a UN peacekeeping force for Darfur. China's openness to a UN presence in Darfur towards the end of 2006 marked a shift of its stance towards the AU's standing and away from that of the Sudanese government, which at the time continued to oppose UN involvement, as a measure to protect its sovereignty.

Understandings of National Interests

Changing perceptions of national interests and strategic calculations are important factors determining a country's stance on any given humanitarian intervention. According to Weiss and Hubert, 'the reality of the 1990s has been that humanitarian motives alone rarely suffice to sustain an intervention' (2001: 211). The political and economic relations that China has carefully built with incumbent African governments in recent years, suggest that China has a stake in the preservation of the political status quo in its African partner countries. This dovetails with an approach to human security issues that emphasizes sovereignty and non-interference. China remains suspicious about humanitarian initiatives advocated by Western countries. In China's view, in a world marked by power politics, humanitarian interventions inevitably become politicized (Chen, Song 2008: 22, Large 2009: 612). Humanitarian agendas are therefore often believed to be aimed at achieving a regime change favourable to Western interests. Such fears of hidden regime change motives were particularly acute with regard to Darfur, given China's interests in Sudan (He 2010: 161).

In the long run, as China deepens its economic engagement in Africa, its assessment of the costs and risks associated with conflict may change. In a market entry phase, conflicts can present opportunities as competitors shy away from chaos and instability. Nowadays, however, China's investments in many countries and sectors are moving into a consolidation phase, whereby concerns about long-term stability and the safety of China's citizens in Africa come more to the forefront (Alden 2007: 90, Large 2009: 625–6, Pang 2009: 249). As the analysis previously demonstrated, concerns about tensions between the centre and the periphery in Sudan and the spreading of instability from Darfur to other regions, were a factor that helped to shape China's change of policy. In the DRC, violence in the East was brought a lot closer to home for China in 2008, when rebel leader Laurent Nkunda voiced strong objections against the massive mining-for-infrastructure deal that China had signed, in 2007, with the Congolese government. While Mr Nkunda was probably using the mining deal as an attempt to boost his standing with Western powers and among Congolese wary of China's engagement, diplomatic tours to the region by Liu Guijin and Zhai Jun suggested that China was nonetheless alarmed by his statements (International Crisis Group 2009: 16). Chinese mining companies also expressed concerns that continuing instability in Kivu could slow down Chinese investments in Congo as a whole (Jansson et al. 2009: 35–6).

A final factor that has come to the forefront in the case studies, which has induced greater openness from the Chinese with regard to international interventions based on humanitarian grounds, is the desire to project a cooperative or positive international image. There is a broad range of literature describing how reputational concerns drive Chinese participation in multilateral cooperation and adherence to international norms (Carlson 2006, Foot 2001, Johnston, Swaine 1999, Rabinovitch 2008). China likes to be seen as a responsible member of the global society. With regard to grave humanitarian crises, Beijing is careful to avoid being cast as the country that is obstructing international efforts to relieve human suffering. This was already the case in the first half of the 1990s, when China agreed to a UN intervention in Somalia that was highly humanitarian in nature (Yin 2007: 25). The case studies reveal that reputational concerns continue to influence China's participation in humanitarian initiatives until today. China's participation in MONUC provided a way to show its commitment to African causes and to UN peacekeeping missions. On Darfur, the link between China's national image and its Darfur policy became a particularly prominent topic of much debate in China from 2007 onwards. Analysts advocated strategies such as working more closely with the UN, propagating China's views more actively and entering into a dialogue with Western countries on sensitive issues to improve China's image (Jiang, Luo 2008a, Li 2008, Luo 2007, Wu 2010). As shown above, from 2007 onwards, China became much more active and vocal on Darfur, making a conscious effort to contribute to international diplomatic efforts to resolve the crisis and to voice its views, which were at times mildly critical of the Sudanese government.

China's Domestic Political Culture

According to Weiss and Hubert, a country's domestic political culture is shaped by its history, by its general public and political elite's views about its place in the contemporary world. China's historical experience at the hands of foreign powers and its current-day social and political situation as a large multi-ethnic one-Party state, are among the factors that continue to shape its emphasis on sovereignty in debates concerning humanitarian intervention (Chu 2002, Evans 2004: 275, Zhang 2000: 122). In Weiss and Hubert's view, China's political culture against intervention is 'so deeply ingrained that it would take more than a generation to change' (2001: 215). Indeed, while significant changes have occurred in China's acceptance of the legitimacy of humanitarian intervention, important obstacles remain. As Zhang Yongjin points out, a fundamental reason for China's insistence on sovereignty in contemporary normative debates is its fear of endorsing new arguments for legitimate statehood. Any global normative shift towards the premise that for states to be legitimate, they should provide human security and human rights to their citizens is perceived by China as a potential threat to its national unity and to the legitimacy of its claims of sovereignty over Tibet or Taiwan (2008: 140–1). China refutes any notion that human rights are more important than sovereignty or that sovereignty is conditional upon a state's provision of the protection of fundamental human rights. The actions of sovereign states are thus considered *a priori* and by definition legitimate. This means that even in cases of extreme human security crises like Darfur or Eastern Congo, China's approach will almost inevitably be reactive in nature (Large 2009: 625).

The 'responsibility to protect' entails that the international community reserves the right to assess states' capacity and willingness to protect its citizens. This remains deeply problematic for China, which maintains that 'prudence is called for in judging a government's ability and will to protect its citizens' (Ministry of Foreign Affairs of the People's Republic of China 2005). China itself consistently shies away from identifying state actors as facilitators or perpetrators of human rights abuses and from condemning human rights violations by those who are supposed to guarantee the protection of such rights. For example, in those areas of civilian protection where the Congolese authorities and armed forces have been accused of direct involvement in human rights abuses, China has called on the UN to proceed with caution and not to act without the support of the Congolese authorities. For example, in 2009, China's Ambassador to the UN insisted that 'in addressing issues related to sexual violence', the UN should 'distinguish the acts committed by governments and rebel groups' and seek prior consent from the authorities before taking any initiatives (Liu 2009). In Sudan, as one analyst explains, 'in many instances the armed forces and security institutions of the state have become indistinguishable from the Janjaweed' (Haggar 2007: 119). In their analyses of Darfur, Chinese officials and scholars do not focus on the agency of individuals or entities, or on the political dynamics driving the conflict. Instead, they refer to some structural 'root causes', such as environmental degradation and underdevelopment (He 2008: 53–4, Jiang, Luo 2008b, Li 2007, Liu, Li 2008, Xu 2008). In line with this interpretation of the nature of the Darfur conflict, development assistance has been part of the solution that China has advocated for Darfur from an early stage onwards. By February 2008, China had not only delivered RMB80 million worth of humanitarian assistance to Darfur but also RMB50 million worth of development projects (Large 2009: 612–13). China also states that its investments in Sudan are helpful for solving the Darfur crisis, as they bring development and therefore stability to Sudan (Large 2009: 612–13). This representation of the benefits that economic relations with Sudan bring for the resolution of the Darfur conflict, overlooks the processes of suppression and exploitation that characterize relations between the centre and the peripheral regions in Sudan. These processes are in fact a major cause of the conflicts that have beset the country (De Waal 2007: 4–11).

Conclusion

Different Chinese responses to multilateral efforts to provide protection to civilians in conflict have been highlighted in this study. With regard to the DRC, few core interests were at stake for China, who therefore acted as a quiet participant in a multilateral process that increasingly focused on civilian protection. Nonetheless, China also showed deep sympathy for the Congolese authorities' desire to safeguard and re-establish their sovereignty. China occasionally provided assistance in having Congolese sovereignty concerns considered within the UNSC framework. China's Darfur policy went through a remarkable evolution. International condemnation and a re-assessment of its long-term interests forced China to leave its comfort zone, in order to agree to use its influence in Khartoum to clear obstacles for international civilian protection efforts. Equally remarkable in their statements on Darfur, Chinese diplomats have occasionally explicitly linked sovereignty and responsibility in a mildly prescriptive manner.

This chapter started with the question whether we are seeing signs of the emergence of a 'third paradigm of international intervention' in China's stance on civilian protection issues. On the one hand, China supports humanitarian assistance and is even emerging as an important humanitarian aid donor. It accepts the legitimacy of humanitarian interventions under grave circumstances and is open to incorporating civil protection tasks in peacekeeping mandates on a case by case basis. Chinese analysts are also tuned into debates on the African continent, about the need to substitute the non-interference principle with 'non-indifference' in cases of grave human rights violations. A number of caveats remain, however. Most importantly, China's insistence on the primary responsibility of governments in dealing with human security issues and on host nation consent for international intervention is problematic in cases where governments are directly involved in human rights violations. In situations when protectors become perpetrators, China shies away from identifying the threats emanating from state actors and argues against the right of the international community to judge a government's will to protect.

All in all, China's stance remains largely passive and reactive in nature. China's more active contributions to the international civilian protection efforts, discussed in this chapter, occurred mostly in response to concerns about its image or about its long-term economic and political interests in those concerned regions. In this regard, China is realizing that situations that constitute a threat to the security of ordinary Africans, may also endanger the security of its own interests and citizens in Africa. However, there is as yet little sign of China developing a novel paradigm of interference that would enable it to respond to international human security crises in a more active or proactive manner. The new norms concerning sovereignty and humanitarian intervention that are being debated and developed in Africa still find little reflection in the discourses and practices that underpin China's relations with the continent.

Fundamental concerns about newly developing norms that redefine the relationship between human rights protection and legitimate statehood, will continue to instill great caution in China's political elites. However, this chapter also shows that a cautious China does not need to be considered as an insurmountable obstacle and can, in fact, play a constructive role. China's increasing interests and leverage in Africa will probably result only in more calls for Chinese interventions, when necessary, as a constructive partner in situations of humanitarian crises.

Bibliography

Book References

Alden, C. 2007. *China in Africa*. London: Zed Books.

Chu, S. 2002. *China and Human Security*. Vancouver: Northeast Asia Cooperation Project.

Deng, F., Kimaro, S., Lyons, T., Rothchild, D. and Zartman, I.W. 1996. *Sovereignty as Responsibility: Conflict Management in Africa*. Washington, D.C.: Brookings Institute Press.

Gill, B. and Huang, C. 2009. *China's Expanding Peacekeeping Role: Prospects and Policy Implications*. Solna: SIPRI.

Holt, V.K. and Berkman, T.C. 2006. *The Impossible Mandate?: Military Preparedness, The Responsibility to Protect and Modern Peace Operations*. Washington, D.C.: The Henry L. Stimson Centre.

Human Security Centre. 2005. *Human Security Report 2005: War and Peace in the 21st Century*. New York and Oxford: Oxford University Press.

Jansson, J., Burke, C. and Jiang, W. 2009. *Chinese Companies in the Extractive Industries of Gabon and the DRC: Perceptions of Transparency*. Stellenbosch: Centre for Chinese Studies.

Liu, H. and Li, X. 2008. *Quanqiu shiyexia de Da'erfu'er wenti yanjiu (Darfur Issue Under the Global Perspective)*. Beijing: World Knowledge Press.

Pye, L.W. 1988. *The Mandarin and the Cadre: China's Political Cultures (Michigan Monographs in Chinese Studies 58)*. University of Michigan Centre for Chinese Studies: Ann Arbor.

Raine, S. 2009. *China's African Challenges*. Abingdon: Routledge for the International Institute for Strategic Studies.

Teitt, S. 2008. *China and the Responsibility to Protect*. Brisbane: Asia-Pacific Centre for the Responsibility to Protect.

Tull, D.M. 2005. *The Reconfiguration of Political Order in Africa: A Case Study of North Kivu (DR Congo)*. Hamburg: Institute of African Affairs.

United Nations Development Programme. 1994. *Human Development Report 1994: New Dimensions of Human Security*. New York: Oxford University Press.

Weiss, T.G. and Hubert, D. 2001. *The Responsibility to Protect: Research, Background, Bibliography*. Ottawa: IDRC.

Wheeler, N.J. 2000. *Saving Strangers: Humanitarian Intervention in International Society*. Oxford: Oxford University Press.

Yin, H. 2007. *China's Changing Policy on UN Peacekeeping Operations*. Stockholm: Institute for Security and Development Policy.

Zhao, S. and Pollack, J. 2004. *Chinese Foreign Policy: Pragmatism and Strategic Behavior*. Armonk: ME Sharpe.

Book Chapters

De Waal, A. 2007. Sudan: the turbulent state, in *War in Darfur and the Search for Peace*, edited by A. de Waal. London: Justice Africa, 1–38.

Haggar, A. 2007. The origins and organization of the Janjawiid in Darfur, in *War in Darfur and the Search for Peace*, edited by A. de Waal. London: Justice Africa, 113–39.

He, W. 2010. The Darfur issue: a new test for China's Africa policy, in *The Rise of China and India in Africa*, edited by F. Cheru and C.I. Obi. London and New York: Zed Books, 155–66.

Johnston, A.I. and Swaine, M.D. 1999. China and arms control institutions, in *China Joins the World: Progress and Prospects*, edited by M. Oksenberg and E. Economy. New York: Council on Foreign Relations Press, 90–135.

Kim, S.S. 2006. Chinese foreign policy faces globalization challenges, in *New Directions in the Study of China's Foreign Policy*, edited by A.I. Johnston and R.S. Ross. Stanford: Stanford University Press, 276–306.

Large, D. 2008b. From non-interference to constructive engagement? China's evolving relations with Sudan, in *China Returns to Africa: A Rising Power and a Continent Embrace*, edited by C. Alden et al. London: C. Hurst and Co. Publishers Ltd., 275–94.

Shinn, D. 2008. Military and security relations: China, Africa and the rest of the world, in *China Into Africa: Trade, Aid and Influence*, edited by R. Rotberg. Washington, D.C.: Brookings Institute Press, 155–96.

Srinivasan, S. 2008. A marriage less convenient: China, Sudan and Darfur, in *Crouching Tiger, Hidden Dragon? Africa and China*, edited by S. Naidu and K. Ampiah. Cape Town: University of KwaZulu Natal Press, 55–85.

Zhang, Y. 2000. China: whither the world order after Kosovo?, in *Kosovo and the Challenge of Humanitarian Intervention: Selective Indignation, Collective Action, and International Citizenship*, edited by A. Schnabel and R. Thakur. Tokyo: United Nations University Press, 117–27.

Zhang, Y. 2008. Anticipating China's future diplomacy: history, theory and social practice, in *China's New Diplomacy*, edited by P. Kerr et al. New York: Palgrave Macmillan, 131–49.

Journal Articles

Badescu, C.G. and Bergholm, L. 2009. The responsibility to protect and the conflict in Darfur: the big let-down. *Security Dialogue*, 40(3), 287–309.

Bellamy, A.J. and Williams, P.D. 2009. Protecting civilians in uncivil wars. *Asia Pacific Centre for the Responsibility to Protect Program on the Protection of Civilians Working Paper*, 1, 1–45.

Carlson, A. 2004. Helping to keep the peace (albeit reluctantly): China's recent stance on sovereignty and multilateral intervention. *Pacific Affairs*, 77(1), 9–27.

Chen, X. and Song, L. 2008. Guoji rendaozhuyi weiji guanli: zhidu anpai yu xianshi kunjing (Management of international humanitarian crises: institutional arrangement and practical difficulty). *Guoji Luntan (International Forum)*, 10(3), 20–24.

Chu, S. 2001. China, Asia and issues of sovereignty and intervention. *Pugwash Occasional Papers*, 2(1).

Cohen, R. 2008. Humanitarian imperatives are transforming sovereignty. *ILSA Quarterly*, 16(3), 14–23.

Evans, P.M. 2004. Human security and East Asia: in the beginning. *Journal of East Asian Studies*, 4(2), 263–84.

Foot, R. 2001. Chinese power and the idea of a responsible state. *The China Journal*, 45, 1–19.

Fravel, M.T. 1996. China's attitude toward UN peacekeeping operations since 1989. *Asian Survey*, 36(11), 1102–1121.

He, W. 2008. Guanyu Sudan Da'erfu'er wenti (On Sudan's Darfur problem). *Shishi Baogao (Current Report)*, 6, 53–57.

Holslag, J. 2008. China's diplomatic manoeuvring on the question of Darfur. *Journal of Contemporary China*, 17(54), 71–84.

International Crisis Group. 2005. A Congo action plan. *Africa Briefing (International Crisis Group)*, 34.

International Crisis Group. 2008. Preventing implosion in Sudan. *African Briefing (International Crisis Group)*, 50.

International Crisis Group. 2009. China's growing role in UN Peacekeeping. *Asia Report (International Crisis Group)*, 166.

Jiang, H. and Luo, J. 2008a. Da'erfu'er weiji de hejie jincheng yu Zhongguo guojia xingxiang suzao (Settlement of Darfur crisis and the build-up of China's national image). *Wayjiao Pinglun (Foreign Affairs Review)*, 103, 44–50.

Kagwanja, P. and Mutahi, P. 2007. Protection of civilians in African peacekeeping missions: the case of the African Union mission in Sudan, Darfur. *ISS Occasional Paper*, 139, 1–20.

Large, D. 2007. Arms, oil and Darfur: the evolution of relations between China and Sudan. *Small Arms Survey Sudan Issue Brief*, 7, 1–12.

Large, D. 2008a. China and the contradictions of 'non-interference' in Sudan. *Review of African Political Economy*, 35(115), 93–106.

Large, D. 2009. China's Sudan engagement: changing Northern and Southern political trajectories in peace and war. *China Quarterly*, 199, 610–26.

Li, A. 2007. China and Africa: policy and challenges. *China Security*, 3(3), 69–93.

Li, A. 2008. Wei Zhongguo zheng ming: Zhongguo de feizhou zhanlüe yu guojia xingxiang (In defence of China: China's African strategy and state image). *Shijie Zhengzhi (World Economics and Politics)*, 4, 6–15.

Li, H. and Zheng, Y. 2009. Re-interpreting China's non-intervention policy towards Myanmar: leverage, interest and intervention. *Journal of Contemporary China*, 18(61), 617–37.

Luo, J. 2003. Dui feizhou zizhu weihe xingdong de sikao (Thoughts on Africa's independent peacekeeping). *Xiya Feizhou (West Asia and Africa)*, 3, 45–50.

Luo, J. 2007. Zhongguo dui feizhou waijiao shiye zhong de guojia xingxiang suzao (The crafting of national image in China's foreign policies toward Africa). *Xiandai Guoji Guanxi (Contemporary International Relations)*, 7, 48–53.

Mansson, K. 2005. Use of force and civilian protection: peace operations in the Congo. *International Peacekeeping*, 12(4), 503–19.

Marks, S.J. 2007. The pitfalls of action and inaction: civilian protection in MONUC's peacekeeping operations. *Africa Security Review*, 16(6), 1–14.

Nabati, M. 2004. The UN responds to the crisis in Darfur: Security Council resolution 1556. *ASIL Insights*.

Pang, Z. 2009. China's non-intervention question. *Global Responsibility to Protect*, 1(2), 237–52.

Rabinovitch, S. 2008. The rise of an image-conscious China. *China Security*, 4(3), 33–47.

Reilly, J. and Gill, B. 2000. Sovereignty, peacekeeping and intervention: the view from Beijing. *Survival*, 42(3), 41–60.

Strauss, J. 2009. The past in the present: historical and rhetorical lineages in China's relations with Africa. *China Quarterly*, 199, 777–95.

Tull, D.M. 2009. Peacekeeping in the Democratic Republic of Congo: waging peace and fighting war. *International Peacekeeping*, 16(2), 215–30.

Tunsjø, Ø. 2010. Hedging against oil dependency: new perspectives on China's energy security policy. *International Relations*, 24(1), 25–45.

Vesel, D. 2003. The lonely pragmatist: humanitarian intervention in an imperfect world. *BYU Journal of Public Law*, 18(1), 1–58.

Wang, J. 2008. Zhong mei zai chuli Da'erfu'er wenti shang de chongtu hezuo (China-US cooperation and conflict on the Darfur issue). *Meiguo Wenti Yanjiu (Fudan American Review)*, 1, 43–70.

Wu, F. 2010. China's energy diplomacy and international responsibility: a case study of Darfur. *Alabo Shijie Yanjiu (Arab World Studies)*, 3, 59–66.

Xu, W. 2008. The origin of the Darfur crisis and some suggestions for its solution. *Paper Presented to the Symposium on Chinese-Sudanese Relations*, London, 26 July 2007.

Yuan, W. 2008. Shilun Zhongguo zai feizhou neibu chongtu chuli zhong de zuoyong – Cong 'baohu de zeren' lilun tan qi (On China's role in dealing with Africa's internal conflicts – assessment from the theory of 'Responsibility to Protect'). *Xiya Feizhou (West Asia and Africa)*, 10, 58–62.

Websites

Associated Press. 2010. *Congo wants peacekeepers out*. [Online]. Available at: http://www.stuff.co.nz/world/africa/3682229/Congo-wants-peacekeepers-out [accessed: 2 July 2010].

Baldauf, S., Ford, P. and Winter, L. 2008. *China speaks out on Darfur crisis.* [Online]. Available at: http://www.csmonitor.com/World/Asia-Pacific/2008/0225/p01s03-woap.html [accessed: 27 January 2010].

IRIN. 2010. *Analysis: fighting for peace in the Kivus.* [Online]. Available at: http://www.irinnews.org/Report.aspx?ReportId=88193 [accessed: 16 July 2010].

Liu, Z. 2009. *Statement at the Security Council by Ambassador Liu Zhenmin, Deputy Permanent Representative of China to the United Nations, on women and peace and security.* [Online]. Available at: http://www.china-un.org/eng/chinaandun/securitycouncil/thematicissues/women_ps/t577493.htm [accessed: 11 January 2010].

Ministry of Foreign Affairs of the People's Republic of China. 2008. *The Chinese Government's Special Representative on the Darfur issue holds a briefing to Chinese and foreign journalists.* [Online]. Available at: http://www.fmprc.gov.cn/eng/zxxx/t414377.htm [accessed: 15 January 2010].

Traub, J. 2006. *The world according to China.* [Online]. Available at: http://www.nytimes.com/2006/09/03/magazine/03ambassador.html [accessed: 15 January 2010].

Varner, B. 2009. *China advises Sudan not to let Darfur crisis worsen.* [Online]. Available at: http://www.bloomberg.com/apps/news?pid=newsarchive&sid=a FiV2P17gsiY [accessed: 27 January 2010].

Zhai, J. 2007. *Assistant Foreign Minister Zhai Jun holds a briefing for Chinese and foreign journalists on the Darfur issue of Sudan.* [Online]. Available at: http://za.china-Embassy.org/eng/zt/darfur/t329292.htm [accessed: 10 January 2010].

Newspaper

Gettleman, J. 2007. Rape epidemic raises trauma of Congo war. *New York Times*, 7 October.

Command Papers

Report to the Secretary-General. 2004. S/2004/703, New York: United Nations Secretary-General.

United Nations Security Council Meeting Provisional Report. 1999. S/PV.4046, New York: United Nations.

United Nations Security Council Meeting Provisional Report. 2006. S/PV.5423, New York: United Nations.

United Nations Security Council Meeting Provisional Report. 2007. S/PV.5703, New York: United Nations.

United Nations Security Council Meeting Provisional Report. 2008. S/PV.5916, New York: United Nations.

United Nations Security Council Resolution. 2009. S/RES/1906, New York: United Nations.

World Summit Outcome. 2005. A/RES/60/1, New York: United Nations.

Chapter 8
Limited Sovereignty: Chinese Peacekeeping Operations in Africa[1]

Jianxiang Bi

If names are not rectified, then language will not be appropriate, and if language is not appropriate, affairs will not be successfully carried out... (名不正 言不，言不事不成…) (Confucius 1979).

Introduction

Africa has become a focal point of Chinese foreign policy, with the ultimate goal of shifting the centre of gravity for a new international order. Inspired by President Hu Jintao's self-fulfilling ideal of building a harmonious world, an end of the utopian paradise and a means to project power across the globe, China presents itself as a driving force for good, vigorously championing the universal desire for peace in Africa. The ethical aspiration for being good and 'doing good', as opposed to coercion and exploitation and the practice of power politics, marks perhaps the most divisive way of managing this underdeveloped and often forgotten continent to maximize its share of power, constructed in the increasingly multipolar system, thereby capturing long-overdue attention (Taylor 2006, Alden 2008, Rotberg 2008, Foreign Ministry of the People's Republic of China 2007). As a catalyst, this sophisticated foreign policy focus has quietly falsified Beijing's perceptions and agendas far beyond its traditional thinking of sovereignty and goodwill, now a distant memory, which used to define its intimate relations with its African partners. The resulting deconstruction of the mindsets and practices for 'doing good', as a metaphor illustrates the painstaking efforts made by China to strive to develop the image of a responsible caregiver, not a ruthless power seeker, at least in this particular region. This Confucian rectification-centred image would, as expected, persuade the world community to use a non-coercive way to solve security and development issues, justifying its pursuit of ideals, influence and interests, which would in turn lead to the common good.

Today, as was the case yesterday, Beijing seems inextricably bound to Africa, with the increasing demands of natural resources for sustainable development at home, of secured access to regional markets for Chinese products, and of political capital for countering the great powers in the areas vital to its national interest

---

1   The author wishes to thank Benjamin Barton, Jing Men and Peter von Staden for their constructive comments on an earlier draft of this chapter.

(Wen 2009, Woods 2008). Opting for the pro-active approach to Africa or acting altruistically to meet these urgent needs reflects its belief in the 'adjustment to the world', as a policy mechanism to balance order and disorder through trade for the fulfilment of moral and power aspirations (Weber 1963). This conventional wisdom has shaped its Africa strategy for exploring the ideational, economic and political potentials of, if not the dominance over, the continent. Doing so, it has more than alerted the curiosities of the great powers.

As a peace builder, Beijing offers its African partners a variety of support for regional development, which they desperately need, but it remains extremely reluctant to impose the established value systems, such as democratic governance, human rights and social responsibility on them, as it is unwilling to raise the sensitive questions of how and to what extent its partners and their weak institutions tackle the frustrating human security issues. This *laissez-faire* approach mirrors its policy of mutual respect and non-intervention in the domestic affairs of the recipient countries, the backbone of Chinese diplomacy. As Beijing's soul mate, African partners appreciate the distinct Chinese way of dealing with their controversial value systems and of maximizing weak state institutions as an alternative to pushing for strong political structures for problem-solving. The asymmetric systems and institutions appear not to work elsewhere, but fortunately they do function in Africa (de Waal 2009). This non-coercive choice acts as an arbitrary decision devoted to facilitating their cooperation on security and development.

China's obsession with Africa coincides with rising political instability on the domestic front of its major partners, as well as in the region, which inevitably tests its skills of political leadership, conflict management and public relations. As far as regional peace is concerned, Beijing appears to understand that its long-standing arbitrary mindset and sovereignty has restrained its policy flexibility making itself an undesirable partner for the world community. The preoccupation with this negative image ironically produces policy mechanisms and agendas reactive in character: the political arrangements of peacekeeping operations must be based on the traditional principles of consent, neutrality and the non-use of force, except in cases of self-defence, which would promise peace, not war. However, critical questions remain unanswered: does China's sovereignty ideal matter given the political anarchy in Africa? If it needs to reset its strategy, what channels exist for the Middle Kingdom to find the space for a reform of its policies, without its objective for peace being compromised as a result? Does Beijing's practice of peacekeeping validate its ideal of 'being good' and 'doing good', in order to attain the privileged status of being considered as a responsible power in Africa?

This chapter argues that limited sovereignty and peacekeeping operations, as a mutually constructed tool of conflict resolution for humanitarian crises in Africa, give new meaning to the representation of China's harmony-centred ideals that allows all the parties to maximize their shared interests for peace. In other words, the contextual interplay leads Beijing to revisit its cultural ideals and the African strategic environment in a great effort to justify itself as a force for the common good of order and peace. Firstly, this chapter deconstructs China's decades-long perceptions of sovereignty as a strategy for peace in Africa, highlighting the moral dilemmas inherent in its available security and development choices. Secondly, it focuses on limited sovereignty as a condition for peace, within the context of the Chinese and international practices, to display the policy utilities for peace, not war. Thirdly, the chapter tests the Chinese peacekeeping operations in Africa, so as to recapture and ascertain the meaning of 'doing good' for the world.

Deconstructing Sovereignty as a Strategy for Peace

The transversal struggle of peacekeeping casts doubt over the Chinese principle of sovereignty, the paradox of state jurisdiction and moral responsibility, which reflects deep fissures in the very foundation of international security. The lessons learned from interaction with the great powers and the desire to survive in the enduring environment of power politics, creates and instantiates the enduring identities of foreign policy, which in China's case, culminated in the codification of the five principles of peaceful coexistence – sovereignty, territorial integrity, non-aggression, non-interference and mutual benefit – as the fundamental basis to its foreign policy. These are the same principles that lie at the heart of international law and of the United Nations (UN) Charter. In defending its absolute sovereign rights against the stronger powers, its territorial boundaries are seen as the inviolable state jurisdiction in law and in practice, thus forbidding any form of intervention. With the ideological responsibility to support the communist revolutions that cut across state boundaries, on the other hand, China faithfully exported Mao Zedong's radical thoughts around the world, to encourage subjected groupings to fight for their freedom but this conflicting behaviour violated its ideal of sovereignty, or at least made it problematic. Despite the twists and turns in foreign policy, to Beijing, moral and ideological influences did not need to respect the borders of the strong or the weak.

As a result of globalization, the spread of technology and the de-territorialized ethics of peace enforcement and coercive protection, reorganized political activities have been progressively transgressing the sovereign limits of the mutually exclusive and exhaustive oppositions – inside and outside (Ashley 1988, Walker 1993). Against the backdrop of this trend for sustainable peace, Beijing actively sought an articulate way to sanction its professed image of a peace-maker in Africa, but its inability to establish the synergy between its ideals and its behaviour raises more questions than answers to its theory and practice of sovereignty. To make matters worse, the literature on China and Africa relations ignores the anomalies of sovereignty and its direct implication for peacekeeping, thus pointing to a poorly developed theoretical insight (Lynch 2009, Glaser, Medeiros 2007, Large 2009, Alden, Hughes 2009). Furthermore, research on peacekeeping missions is too descriptive to display any critical reflections on the Chinese ideal of moral responsibility and any potential implications of this uncritical mindset for Beijing's Africa policy (Gill, Huang 2009, Asia Report 2009).

Offensive realists believe that status quo powers are rarely found in world politics, since the system has created powerful incentives for the states to seek a window of opportunity to gain power at the expense of their rivals, and to take advantage of the situation when the benefits outweigh the costs (Mearsheimer 2001). For this school of thought, whatever the motives, China by nature is not a status quo power since it tends to maximize its influence that matches its status in Africa and in the world. It is alarming, but the prediction fails to explain under what conditions China will become a revisionist state *vis-à-vis* the great powers in Africa without falsifying its ideal of respect for sovereignty.

The neo-liberals, on the other hand, see that norm-based cooperation among states facilitates the achievement of common interests through adjusting their behaviour to the anticipated preferences of others. International politics, in essence, is more normatively regulated than the offensive realists contend (Keohane 1984). Contrary to their ideals and perceptions, the norms of international institutions and international relations are indicative of power politics. It is undeniable that China and the emerging powers alike are in a weak position to deal with the Western-dominated financial institutions, such as the International Monetary Fund (IMF) and the World Bank, which often force them to accept unequal terms of reference regarding domestic political, economic and financial policies. This power politics calls the autonomy and the authority of the state within its borders into question. In the case of Africa, China is an attractive partner for the powerful African Union (AU), due to its global vision constantly overshadowing regional development agendas, despite the claim that it does not intervene in the internal affairs of AU member states. However, its increasing ability to influence the economic sector in the region eventually becomes a political and security issue. The anomalies of the unequal relations indeed frustrate neo-liberals, unable to provide convincing explanations about interests and power.

In different ways, the constructivists contend that ideas defined as world views, principled beliefs and causal beliefs matter most and shape the behaviour of the state (Goldstein, Keohane 1993). For them, the value system persists throughout space and time, but their hypothesis of causal connections fails to elucidate how the Chinese value system affects the internal and external sovereignty of African countries, or the extent to which African political culture influences Beijing's policy towards regional powers for economic or political development. Their ideational power in relation to Chinese behaviour in Africa remains a puzzle.

The idea and practice of sovereignty are problematic, as humanitarian crises and the moral responsibility of the great powers and of international institutions mutually nurture the new norm of peace enforcement and coercive protection, beyond the *de facto* and *de jure* borders. With this humanitarian nature, the urgent need to deconstruct sovereignty is to balance, if not reverse, the competence, independence and legal equality of the state (Krasner 1999, Derrida 1978). The deconstruction of causality provides a means to intervene in the field of sovereignty it criticizes, thus producing the problem-solving ground of humanitarian protection it proposes. In peacekeeping operations, what started 'as an ethical parade' ironically and evidently ends 'as a glorification of power' pure and simple (Hoffmann 1981: 27).

For Beijing, deconstruction is the reconstruction of its tradition. The Chinese were culturally superior. This strong sense of superiority, along with the structure of the Chinese world order, based on three interlocking rankings of the Sinic, Inner Asian and Outer Zones, systematically undermined state boundaries, reflecting their righteous responsibility of taking care of both the weak and the world, for the common good of human beings (Fairbank 1973, Lewis 1969, Allan 2007). Whether this identity was regarded as a dogma or as a guide to action, the moral regime revolved around China in theory under the universal pre-eminence of the Son of Heaven, with the mystical mandate and power to ensure world order and peace. The ideal pattern as a principled stand, suggests that Heaven, the highest lord of the Zhou dynasty, was the spirit and its power affected the passage of time and space. With the divine authority over all-under-Heaven, China was the world, thereby de-territorializing political life of other states. China's hegemony served as the irrefutable moral responsibility to preserve social harmony by the application of knowledge, discipline, and if necessary, physical force.

As a criterion of theorizing moral responsibility, a metaphor beyond space, time and geography legitimized the use of coercive action, the '*parabellum* strategic cultural outlook' for order and harmony (Johnston 1995). This peace-centred responsibility, coercive in nature, implies great efforts to neutralize conflict for the common interests of the community. The key point is that China advocates the ideal of mutually adjusted harmony and order, rather than zero-sum games. There is no doubt that war is hell, but force remains a possible policy option, inseparably complementary for upholding harmony and order, which are viewed as the moral fundamentals, not as an antithesis, contradiction or dichotomy of harmony and order. The structure constituted by China, the neighbours, and the world community gives inter-subjective meanings to their political action and their way of international socialization.

China's highly selective peacekeeping missions in Africa serve as an effective means not only to communicate with the world, but also to enhance the new version of harmony: 'peace and development as its responsibility and destiny' (Xu 2009: 2). Though scholars, analysts and policy-makers alike have different views about the Chinese desire for peace during these missions, the Confucian ideals of humanity and his critical spirit aimed at going beyond them, offer persuasive explanations about logical connections between moral responsibility and Chinese behaviour in the international community. As the book *Great Learning* indicates, the way of harmony and order is based on the framework of 'self-cultivation, take care of your family, manage the state affairs, and world peace', a framework that is designed to overcome the gap of responsibility or conflict among individuals, the family and the state for order, as a result of the division of power and labour (Zhu 1992: 6). Obviously, Confucius does not deny self-interest, since people have different value systems and behave selfishly. With the common interests in mind, the exercise of proper self-control over individual, family and state behaviour, generates moral orientations highlighting the concrete description of the desirable and the undesirable. Self-transcendence is thus rewarded.

At the individual level, self-cultivation through education leads to personal self-realization or the attainment of the highest virtues of benevolence, essential to moral leadership and family welfare. As the head of the family, the responsibility of the father is to take care of every family member so as to maintain family harmony and order, which would offer an intellectual response to the burning political, social and economic issues the state must oblige to during that time. The Chinese state, as Max Weber contends, is a 'family state', in which everyone knows where he or she stands. This understanding of the state contributes to social and political order. Thus, 'when the family is regulated, the state will be in order; and when the state is in order, there will be peace throughout the world' (Zhu 1992: 7). Yet, the inner and outer realms of harmony and order rest on the management of coercive means, if necessary, to bring order; in Confucius' words, the state uses force only when there is no alternative, since force is 'perfectly beautiful but not perfectly good' (Confucius 1979: 71). When confronted with disorder, one must defend harmony and restore order by using force but with care and caution. The Confucian ideal of universal kindness is later defined by Fang Zhongyan as the duty of elite scholar-officials and, by extension, China – 'Before the rest of the world starts worrying, the scholar worries; after the rest of the world rejoices, he rejoices' (de Bary, Bloom 1999: 56). Promoting love, care and governance, transcends state boundaries, thus outlaying China's sacred responsibility.

The Confucian ideal of moral responsibility as a guide shapes the Hu Administration's harmony-centred foreign policy, in the hope of building a soft image in the world community. In achieving this strategic objective, China expresses interests in shouldering some financial and human burden of African crisis management, including peacekeeping missions to protect the victims of conflict, inter-state or intra-state. For Beijing, this mutually constructed model of peacebuilding lies in or at least echoes its traditional ideal of moral responsibility devoted to balancing norms and rules on the one hand, and material interests and power on the other. The peacekeeping operations in China's hands become a coercive means to foster harmony and peace beyond space and time.

Moral responsibility, as the identity-defining core of the Mandate of Heaven, constructed throughout history, categorically denies the legitimacy of state jurisdiction, with the goal of projecting soft influence across the globe. In the name of 'doing universal good', Beijing remains confident that its way of managing order and stability, in contrast to that of the West, provides a natural synergy for peace and development in Africa (Ramo 2009). Surely, this is a healthy escape from the dilemma of interests and principles. At this juxtaposition, Beijing quietly deconstructs its orthodox rhetoric of sovereignty as a testimonial that its new mandate is to 'build a harmonious world', if not directly to deal with humanitarian crises, such as genocide, ethnic cleansing and natural disasters in Africa, which perhaps can never purely be considered as a domestic matter. In Beijing's eyes, the term humanitarian intervention remains negative and indicative of coercion, as the rewards from the West appear as a distant promise or in a state of ambiguous motion. On the other hand, the neutrality of peacekeeping offers enough room for China to define its UN-led missions of using military force for humanitarian purposes, as an option for building an unbiased and responsible image in the region, thereby championing a new international order of harmony and balance that propels Beijing decisively forward, beyond state boundaries.

Limited Sovereignty as a Condition for Peace

China's peacekeeping operations in Africa, as a form of representation, are an arbitrary choice designed to promote and legitimize limited sovereignty, the policy practice used in response to moral responsibility, which rationalizes conflict resolution in acceptable terms. In search of comprehensive political settlements, the practice of limited sovereignty allows the state to deliberately compromise its sovereign rights within limited space and time, over the crises it faces. This policy choice, though unorthodox, matches the reality of regional security and the Chinese desires to be credited as a peace-maker, the image that Beijing values most and has been fighting for over the past years. The construction and justification of limited sovereignty for 'doing good', further demonstrates China's attempts to position itself as a global player with a broad spectrum of ethical, civilian and military capabilities which, in the end, helps to ensure a peaceful environment for its economic development. Thus, the aspirations to 'do good', go hand in hand with being a force for 'doing good', endorsing China's rapid rise as a responsible power in the community.

The traditional policy practice of sovereignty, in contrast, was a by-product of its painful modern history, especially in relation to the devastating wars Beijing was forced to fight. The fear of inferiority *vis-à-vis* superior forces, and the discourse on power politics and war, put Beijing in 'a permanent social relationship – the ineradicable basis of all relations and institutions of power', which compelled China not only to seek regime survival, but also to face emerging challenges in the world (Foucault 2003: 49). As a rational choice, Beijing aggressively pursued an absolute sovereignty policy of non-intervention in domestic affairs, in the hope of neutralizing foreign influence over domestic issues and regulating state relations on an equal footing. Therefore, China was willing, if necessary, to use force or coercive means to defend its territorial integrity or to enhance order and stability at home, which constitute the absolute rights of the sovereign state (Johnston 1998). This hyper-sovereignty value has dominated Beijing's approaches to international politics, but this policy also reflected the fact that the Chinese economy was independent of both the international market and the great powers, or in other words, that Beijing thoroughly and completely enjoyed its economic sovereignty. The time frame, the strategic environments and the interpretation of the past events were fundamental to the constitution of absolute sovereignty, which prevailed during Mao's era.

What is imperative is that economic reform, introduced in 1978, increasingly de-territorialized political life and undermined China's conception of sovereignty, thus asking of Beijing to reassess the security environments it faces in order to develop a new set of values shaping its relations with the great powers and the developing countries. As a driving force for deconstruction and construction, the globalization of production and markets makes China part of this 'complex interdependence' (Keohane, Nye 1977). With the resulting free flow of goods, services, technology and capital, in conjunction with China's emergence as a world factory, sovereignty has been losing its previously held privileged status as the supremacy and independence of a state, in relation to other states in the international system. The established principles, such as 'the organization of authority within a given state and its effective control', 'authority and independence based on mutual recognition', and 'territorial integrity and formal judicial autonomy' have become limited, not absolute (Krasner 2001, Jackson 2007).

The motives behind this new norm of international politics are invariably mixed. Whatever the notions, China surely does not accept limited sovereignty as its official discourse vocabulary because the term might weaken the legitimate rights enjoyed by the state and, worse, allow interference in its domestic affairs by the great powers, seeking regime change or value-based conflict resolution. As a result of the security concerns, it prefers to use the vague term of 'sovereignty' in its official discourse, while proactively engaging the international community in the direction of its harmonious world for maximizing its discourse power. The overt textual interplay suggests that interest and power behind the scene have led Beijing to introduce a new approach to international order and peace.

The quiet revolution in motion prompts China's gradual acceptance of limited sovereignty as a recognized norm of conflict resolution in public, but the idea itself does not necessarily imply a complete break from the past practice of sovereignty. The clash is especially evident when push comes to shove over sovereignty in China or in Africa, since Beijing has a very limited capability to manage the structure of power politics, which still works to the great powers' advantage. The other end of the spectrum is that limited sovereignty does help China enjoy its policy flexibility to rationalize expectations and outcomes, especially in the case of maritime security, Hong Kong and the border issue with Russia.

Maritime sovereignty dominates China's development and security agendas prominently. As a response to these multifaceted environments, Beijing started to adopt a flexible policy toward the territorial disputes over the Spratly Islands and the Diaoyu Islands, where all the claimants insist on their absolute sovereignty (Zhong 2004, Li 2005). In defending its sovereign rights, China develops a variety of evidence to convince its counterparts and the world community that the islands are an integral part of China – whether imperial and later Communist. When faced with potential conflict situation, which might derail its rise, Beijing under Deng Xiaoping then tried to separate territorial sovereignty from economic interests, calling for 'a joint exploitation' as the preventive measure, rather than settling the territorial problems once and for all. At the same time, the Chinese Navy increased its power projection capabilities in the regions as deterrence against any possible escalation of the disputes. This limited sovereignty proposal, though unsuccessful, is to defuse the risk of conflict, but also to bring benefits to all parties in the short-run. This tradition continues. As the Hu Administration has signalled, the joint exploitation serves as a policy option for appealing to its South China Sea neighbours, as well as Japan.

The return of Hong Kong to China by the United Kingdom (UK) in July 1997, for example, highlights China's innovative handling of delicate sovereignty issues. The proposed and later implemented policy of 'One Country, Two Systems' is to seek the strategic balance between sovereignty and Hong Kong's economic freedom and state personality, as much as possible, under the name of 'Hong Kong China' (Deng 2000). Nonetheless, Hong Kong's membership to the World Trade Organization (WTO), World Health Organization (WHO), Asian Development Bank (ADB) and Asia-Pacific Economic Cooperation (APEC) has violated Beijing's domestic sovereignty as a primary agent of state authority and control. At the same time, the international legal recognition of Hong Kong as a WTO, ADB, WHO and APEC member illustrates China's determination to preserve this former British colony as a symbol of economic independence, thereby guaranteeing its stability and prosperity at least for 50 years. As the case demonstrates, Beijing intentionally grants Hong Kong a unique hybrid polity, with significant state authority and personality, contrary to its sovereign ideals.

Territorial integrity is China's primary concern about the long-standing border disputes with Russia, which overshadowed their bilateral relations during the Cold War. The negotiation on the return of the Bear Island to Beijing, occupied by the Soviet Red Army in 1927 as a response to the forced deportations of the Soviet Siberian railway employees by the Manchurian warlord, once again indicates China's willingness to pursue a more pragmatic policy for solving the border dispute, which ended up dividing the island into two equal parts, with the upstream side (170 square kilometres) being ceded to China and with the rest (170 square kilometres) belonging to Russia. For the liberals in both capitals, the case is a typical example of rationalizing national interests in the new millennium. Conversely, these die-hard Chinese and Russian nationalists refuse to accept this deal again in the name of national interests. It is clear that Beijing and Moscow are the winners, after having stabilized the frustrated borders at the expense of China's sovereignty – central to its relations with its neighbours and the great powers.

In pursuit of political and economic interests, Beijing tries to justify and later theorize this peaceful approach to conflict resolution for its rise. The term 'peaceful' however appears problematic and polarizes liberal and die-hard realist scholars and officials. For Zheng Bijian, a former Vice President of the Party School in Beijing, it includes three key components: China must staunchly advance economic and political reforms as an institutional guarantee of its peaceful rise; it must boldly draw on the fruits of human civilization while enhancing Chinese civilization to ensure cultural support for its peaceful rise; and it must harmonize the interests across sectors and regions for ensuring a social environment for peaceful rise (quoted in Glaser, Medeiros 2007: 294). The structure of the peaceful rise suggests that the textual interplay of interests, cultures and environments constitutes the policy orientation, which in the end challenges the traditional mindset of sovereignty. In spite of the efforts, Zheng's concept remains vague about the geographic scope and the potential implications for international security and, worse, the theory itself ignores the role of coercion in reinforcing international order, a primary responsibility of the great powers, when and where necessary.

For the People's Liberation Army (PLA), the term 'peaceful' refers not only to the economic and military capabilities designed to enhance development and defence potentials for national interests in Taiwan, the South China Sea and the traditional territories, but also to the vast areas beyond the legal borders now defined as the 'strategic frontier', the resilient space most relevant to the national strategic, political and economic interests (Xu 2009). The rapid expansion of Chinese economic interests around the globe forces China to adopt new measures for cultivating intimate relations with its business partners, while playing a leading role in securing regional order. In other words, sovereignty is both absolute and unlimited depending on how to characterize the national interests that become an inseparable part and extension of the traditional borders. In making them explicit and prominent, the PLA scholars define peaceful development under 'rich nation, strong army' *vis-à-vis* peaceful rise. In Hu's words, the objective of development is to 'optimise the integration of "rich nation and strong army" in the process of systematically building a moderately prosperous society' (quoted in Liu 2007: 59). As a responsible power, China urgently needs the counterforce capabilities best suited to safeguarding peace in the places where Beijing has strategic interests. The PLA unmistakably recognizes the importance of peaceful development, but there is remarkably little policy debate on the mechanisms and even less about the ethical implications of the ongoing peacekeeping operations in Africa, for Chinese security.

Of particular importance to both is the painstaking efforts to undermine the idea of sovereignty in order to bring 'limited' back into the definition. In this respect, international practice has endorsed, rather than rejected, the Chinese concept of limited sovereignty as a way of conflict resolution. The norm of the responsibility to protect (R2P), sanctioned by the UN General Assembly in 2005, demonstrates the consensus around the protection of the weak but also abandons the simplifying and unchanging logic of sovereignty, which has dominated international relations almost at all times and places since the start of the Westphalian era. The synergy of domestic and international responsibilities as sovereignty has become the recognized rule of international security. Given its own policy practice, Beijing quickly backs the idea of R2P that was later reaffirmed by the non-binding 2006 Security Council Resolution 1674 and accepts its responsibility to conduct the UN sanctioned missions in the states that are unable to protect their own citizens, and where it also has strategic interests (Bellamy 2008).

The Chinese concept and practice of sovereignty have been constructed from the absolute to the limited reflecting the changes in the perceptions of responsibility and power, but the sovereignty issues, related to Tibet, Taiwan and human rights, remain absolute, not limited (Carlson 2006). With China's rise, Beijing has been showing growing concerns about what happens in African countries – such as, civil war, humanitarian crises and natural disasters, assessing the potential impact of its relations with these countries on its image and seeking peaceful solutions matching its political ideals and interests, local environments and diplomacy-centred international norms. Whatever the concerns, the stability-oriented, rather than democracy-centred choice remains the most critical fault line of Chinese foreign policy. The sharp contrast of the language preference and the policy practice is at the heart of sovereignty, but China's active involvement in the peacekeeping missions in Africa, with the aim of building a harmonious world, increasingly falsifies its ambiguous principle of sovereignty.

Limited sovereignty, however defined, is a mutually constitutive norm of world politics. In fostering peace, China and the international community face tough challenges ahead, because humanitarian intervention as well as conflict resolution is often triggered by internal conflict – war-induced partition or partition-induced war. The most frustrating issue for sovereign states and international organizations is whether minority people have legitimate rights to use force against their legitimate government or whether the legitimate government has rights to use force to ensure order and stability at home. Sitting on the fence, the international community, especially the great powers, is unwilling to draw a clear-cut boundary between them in order to protect the weak. This sensitive issue in fact neutralizes collective efforts to take preventive measures for de-escalating conflict.

The Chinese practice of limited sovereignty as flexibility in application, constructs a rational approach to conflict resolution, for regional peace or at least the status quo in the era of global interdependence. Though it lacks conceptual clarity and masks political vulnerability in space and time, the policy rationale shows that with a deep concern of moral responsibility for 'doing good' in an altruistic sense, Beijing endeavours to earn the status of an ethical power in relation to Washington, the coercion-centred superpower, by combining moral consideration to its strategic interests for creating a situation good for all parties. Thus, limited sovereignty is now at the forefront of Chinese foreign policy, characterizing the peacekeeping operations as the cornerstone of R2P, which often requires the use of force as a last-resort adjunct of other, peaceful, diplomatic and humanitarian measures. As the ideational and policy mandate of building a harmonious world grows in profile across the globe, it is hard for Beijing, as a responsible power, to back off from UN sanctioned peacekeeping missions designed to ensure peace and stability.

Peacekeeping as a Means of Limited Sovereignty for Peace

China's peacekeeping missions in Africa are aimed at winning the hearts and minds of local people, which serves primarily as the launch pad of its charm-offensive foreign policy, but its Africa policy appears to perplex the world. As a result of the fact that China favours limited sovereignty in both normative theory and policy practice, there is as yet no coherent or officially sanctioned policy of limited sovereignty. The mindset of non-interference in domestic affairs still represents the political and psychological barrier that Beijing must overcome in order to recognize the 'protection of the weak' above state sovereignty in Africa. On a deeper policy level, bringing ethics and moral responsibility into the political and legal equation will certainly frustrate decision-makers, since it is not about the capability issue, but the national humiliation these African states face – and which Beijing shares with them – as a result of their value systems that markedly differ from those of the great powers and, above all, as a consequence of the economic interests it has in Africa. Inaction will, on the other hand, invite harsh criticisms of China's moral responsibility as a great power thus risking the regime losing face in public. The image of 'doing good' which China fights for, might inevitably result in being bound by self-interests and by immoral definitions of 'doing good', that are undeniably self-defeating.

This political-moral impasse compels Beijing to rethink its peacekeeping operations in Africa. Violence is a means that the state relies on to construct itself as the legitimate authority but it is also the condition from which the citizens of that state must be protected (Campbell, Dillon 1993). When faced with delicate issues at the UN, China prefers to abstain rather than vote at the Security Council on resolutions as a form of avoidance and, at times, it acts as a vigorous defender of sovereignty against power politics. On the ground, China as the 'impartial balancer' is involved in peacekeeping missions in African countries vital to its political and economic interests. This conflicting behaviour implies that under pressure, Beijing is willing to assume its moral responsibility to protect the weak in terms of genocide and other brutal acts against mankind, while respecting the integrity of a sovereign state. The protection of the weak, though reluctant, is now deemed as the sacred duty of a great power. As Confucian ethics and Hu's ideal of a harmonious world advocate, a bad ruler must be punished with the permission of Heaven, which has the judicial and moral obligation to protect the weak and to enforce such protection.

China's harmony-centred practice of limited sovereignty in Africa favours the consent of the host state and UN authorization. As early as the 1980s, Beijing for the first time cast its vote on extending the mandate of the UN peacekeeping force in Cyprus, in contrast to the interpretation of this peacekeeping mission being a crude tool for aggression. Later, it sent military observers to the UN Transition Assistance Group monitoring the elections in Namibia, formally starting a new chapter of participation in UN peacekeeping missions. In August 2009, China became the fourteenth largest contributor of personnel to UN peacekeeping missions. Yet Beijing's peacekeeping policy remains inconsistent, again, as a result of sovereignty. On the one hand, the PLA calls for a high-calibre peacekeeping contingency and for the development of financial and technological support for the missions because peacekeeping itself provides the PLA with a training ground for managing contemporary military operations, but also a platform for demonstrating its military muscle. On the other hand, China's position on peacekeeping is largely decided on a case-by-case basis and its final decision normally echoes its moral concerns, such as, the extent to which the crisis violates its value-centred definitions of security and whether the missions are fully designed to sustain unbiased peace in favour of the legitimate government.

By design, the structure of the Chinese peacekeeping units highlights the moral priority for 'doing good'. Three-quarters of Chinese peacekeepers deployed in Sudan, the Democratic Republic of Congo, Liberia, Cote d'Ivoire and Western Sahara, for instance, are engineers and medical doctors, not combat soldiers. Their primary function is to provide logistical support to the UN peacekeeping operations, rather than to engage in peacemaking. With the tradition of developing sustainable civil-military relations, that is, helping local people repair roads, rebuild bridges and schools, and provide medical services, the military engineers and medical doctors fit into the missions perfectly and accrue the image of China as a responsible power in the region. Meanwhile, the Chinese naval fleet patrolling the Gulf of Aden follows the identical strategy of avoiding direct conflict – firing warning shells to deter the armed pirates. This strategy itself has become problematic (Yao 2009). In the spring of 2010, for instance, the Somali pirates hijacked a Chinese cargo ship, but the Chinese naval fleet was unable to rescue the crew, partly because it was concerned about the possible escalation of conflict making China a prime target for pirates, and perhaps even terrorists. It also partly lacked the real time technologies to pinpoint the location of the ship, the knowledge and capability of managing such a high-profile case in a multilateral environment. Except in case of self-defence, the use of force by the heavily armed destroyers is seen to put Chinese national interests at risk.

On the other hand, China attempts to avoid biting off more than it can chew or sending combat troops to these peacekeeping missions. The direct involvement in conflict contradicts the priority of Chinese foreign policy, but also raises issues about the capability of the PLA *vis-à-vis* local rebels and pirates. With its self-imposed military modernization agenda, the PLA has been trained and perhaps will continue to be trained for fighting modern conventional war, though it pays growing attention to asymmetric warfare (Peng 2002). If the combat troops are sent to critical areas, where they will be expected to fight and win the battles, the soldiers must have solid experience in combat and peacekeeping operations, functional language skills of communication with local people, expertise on coordination with counterpart units and sound legal knowledge of dealing with captured insurgents. The frustration in China is that the PLA does not have any combat experience at all. One of the dangerous bottlenecks for these missions concerns the rapid deployment of power projection capabilities, such as heavy helicopters and air transport, for combat and support contingency requirements. Worse still, most of the soldiers are totally illiterate in local languages and unable to communicate with local people during combat missions.

For Beijing, higher expectations on the part of its peacekeeping partners and the international community might engender its involvement in operations, as it does not have the range of experiences that missions require. As an agent under the UN authority and as a source of standby force, the PLA can undertake less sophisticated peacekeeping operations. One of the best examples is the Chinese missions in the DRC, where the peacekeepers help build an image of goodwill devoting resources to the community-building projects, such as schools and roads (Zhang 2008). Another prominent case is the Darfur region, where China demonstrates its firm response to international concerns and expectations. Though Beijing insists on its policy of non-interference in domestic affairs, it uses its gentle diplomacy, 'influence without interference' to convince, if not force the parties to support the deployment of a UN sanctioned peacekeeping force in Darfur, to the detriment of the Sudanese government. Following the pattern of 'One Country, Two Systems', moreover, China has developed working relations with and invested in Southern Sudan, which lead to the opening a new consulate in Juba, on 1 September 2008 (Large 2009, Deng 2002).

The potential implication of the Sudanese case for China is that the provision of the January 2005 Comprehensive Peace Agreement (CPA) between the National Congress Party (NCP) and Sudan People's Liberation Movement (SPLM), which granted the Southern Sudanese the right to self-determination – a simple solution to civil war thus being partition. The referendum in Sudan noticeably created a moral and policy dilemma for the Chinese: with the Southern Sudanese choosing to vote yes, the problem now for Beijing is how to cope with the soft separation movements at home in light of its official R2P policy. With the aim of fighting against separatism at home, the Chinese soft approach to the Darfur issue might inflame ethnic separation movements in Tibet and Xinjiang, where Beijing seems primarily to care about ethnic separatism, not poverty and corruption that nurture it (Zhou 2010).

The 'doing good' strategy illustrates China's efforts to avoid getting involved in internal conflict and the lesson learned from the United States' (US) biased approach of managing regional conflict – by supporting one fraction against another. For Beijing, military force alone does not and will not settle conflict and the prejudiced involvement in conflict increases political and economic costs, given that China has a variety of interests in Africa. Fearful of being labelled a neo-colonialist, Beijing favours the soft issues often associated with its image of being 'a good guy', thus justifying its decision to forcefully impose good behaviour on the Chinese peacekeeping units, corporations, and people working in Africa, where they ferociously compete for economic interests and business potentials (Alden, Hughes 2009: 572). Without an institution equivalent to the US Peace Corps and the United Kingdom Voluntary Services Overseas, 'doing good' rests on the shoulders of the peacekeepers and the Ministry of Foreign Affairs.

The key to operational mechanisms is limited sovereignty associated with the civic duty and responsibility devoted to building peace and, in turn, to promoting the positive image of China across Africa. With the purpose of appealing to local people, China focuses on the goodwill, not sovereignty-related aspect of its operations for defusing conflict. Therefore, each new operation is an opportunity for Beijing to achieve its consistency and coherence in integrating its policy instruments. However, the selection of peacekeeping operations rests on its ideals and interests, rather than on purely principled grounds, such as conformity with the UN Charter or humanitarian needs. This pattern, with its emphasis on limited risk and cost, training values, traditional connections and moral concerns, is imperative to operations. More significantly, the missions in the DRC and Sudan make it hard for other countries to argue that China pursues a policy of neo-colonialism in Africa. The high-profile cases could, in turn, improve its image as a guardian of R2P that people mostly need in case of severe breaches of human security and rights.

Conclusion

Domestic politics and international security mutually construct the Chinese concept and practice of limited sovereignty. As a grand strategy, the deconstruction of sovereignty symbolizes the cultural ideals, the urgent policy needs and the economic interests, which remain as essential elements of China's peacekeeping and defence of the weak against the strong in Africa. Central to these low-key Chinese peacekeeping operations is goodwill and balance, but the political discourse on the missions unambiguously pays special attention to the consent of the host country and to the UN's authorization. In spite of its new approach to sovereignty, Beijing still faces policy challenges which might reshape its African agenda.

Firstly, Beijing is unwilling to make moral responsibility a core of its foreign policy, despite it being detrimental for any aspiration towards great power status. This reluctance highlights that the Chinese ideals are policy, not principle oriented. In other words, the critical barrier for building a harmonious world in Africa is not the ideal of moral responsibility, but the interests which determine the Chinese development policy without interfering in governance issues or changing local political structures. Development is the priority shared by China and its African partners, with the unusual complementary association – Africa is rich in natural resources and political capital, whereas Beijing has economic and financial power. However, China does a poor job in telling the world that its distinct form of harmony as a serious, desirable and viable model helps promote the development of infrastructure, regulatory frameworks and civil society vital to peace and prosperity in Africa. There is no solid evidence to show that the Chinese model includes these critical criteria for measuring peace and prosperity. Put simply, the idea and practice of limited sovereignty serve as a means to ensure limited regional peace for maximizing the interests that all the partners fight for.

Secondly, the dilemma of the Chinese peacekeeping operations in Africa is the asymmetry of sovereignty and the R2P: the states concerned enjoy international recognition, but are unable to provide security and welfare for their own citizens. In tackling this asymmetry, the frustrating issue is the value system, which dictates the policy options; and the impact would be devastating, as there is no consensus among the great and regional powers on this issue. It is ideal to build the political structure based on freedom, equality and the rule of law leading to perpetual peace in the region. Although this policy would make all the parties happy, it is unable to secure long-term peace. These moral and legal issues require China and the world to rethink the balance of interest, not power, as a means to conflict resolution.

Thirdly, peacekeeping operations have become the business of developing countries, given that the developed countries are hesitant to send peacekeepers on the ground, but continue to command and provide financial support for the missions. The central issue here is whether China is willing to take the lead in and to make a long-term commitment to, these operations, without any hope that the missions will result in meaningful peace. As long as Beijing wants to behave as a responsible power in Africa and continues to have special interests over there, the regional peacekeeping problem is perhaps, after all, China's problem.

Bibliography

Book Reference

Alden, C. 2008. *China Returns to Africa: A Superpower and a Continent Embrace.* London: C. Hurst and Co. Publishers Ltd.
Campbell, D. and Dillon, M. 1993. *The Political Subject of Violence.* Manchester: University of Manchester Press.
Confucius. 1979. *The Analects.* London: Penguin Books.
De Bary, W.M.T. and Bloom, I. 1999. *Sources of Chinese Tradition: from Earliest Times to 1600.* New York: Columbia University Press.
Derrida, J. 1978. *Writing and Difference.* London: Routledge.
Fairbank, J.K. 1973. *The Chinese World Order: Traditional China's Foreign Relations.* Harvard: Harvard University Press.
Foucault, M. 2003. *Society Must Be Defended.* London: Penguin Books.
Goldstein, J. and Keohane, R. 1993. *Ideas and Foreign Policy: Beliefs, Institutions, and Political Change.* Ithaca: Cornell University Press.
Hoffmann, S. 1981. *Duties Beyond Borders: on the Limits and Possibilities of Ethical International Politics.* Syracuse: Syracuse University Press.
Jackson, R. 2007. *Sovereignty: Evolution of an Idea.* Cambridge: Polity Press.
Johnston, A.I. 1995. *Cultural Realism: Strategic Culture and Grand Strategy in Chinese History.* Princeton: Princeton University Press.
Keohane, R. 1984. *After Hegemony: Cooperation and Discord in the World Political Economy.* Princeton: Princeton University Press.
Keohane, R. and Nye, J. 1977. *Power and Interdependence: World Politics in Transition.* Princeton: Princeton University Press.
Krasner, S. 1999. *Sovereignty: Organized Hypocrisy.* Princeton: Princeton University Press.

Krasner, S. 2001. *Problematic Sovereignty: Contested Rules and Political Possibilities*. New York: Columbia University Press.

Liu, M. 2007. *Rich Nation, Strong Army*. Beijing: People's Armed Police Press.

Mearsheimer, J. 2001. *The Tragedy of Great Power Politics*. New York: W.W. Norton.

Peng, G. 2002. *The Science of Military Strategy*. Beijing: Military Science Press.

Ramo, J.C. 2009. *The Age of the Unthinkable: Why the New World Disorder Constantly Surprises Us and What We Can Do About It*. New York: Hachette Book Group.

Taylor, I. 2006. *China and Africa: Engagement and Compromise*. New York: Routledge.

Walker, R. 1993. *Inside/Outside: International Relations as Political Theory*. Cambridge: Cambridge University Press.

Weber, M. 1963. *The Religion of China*. New York: Macmillan.

Xu, C. 2009. *The Chinese Army for the Multiple Military Missions*. Washington, D.C.: the Centre of Strategic and International Studies.

Zhu, X. 1992. *Commentaries on the Four Books*. Hainan: Hainan Press.

Book Chapters

Carlson, A. 2006. More than just saying no: China's evolving approach to sovereignty and intervention since Tiananmen, in *New Directions in the Study of China's Foreign Policy*, edited by A.I. Johnston and R. Ross. Stanford: Stanford University Press, 217–41.

Deng, F. 2002. Self-determination and national identity crisis: the case of Sudan in *The Self-Determination of People*, edited by W. Danspeckgruber. London: Lynne Rienner Publishers, 253–86.

Journal Articles

Alden, C. and Hughes, C. 2009. Harmony and discord in China's Africa strategy: some implications for foreign policy. *The China Quarterly*, 199(9), 563–84.

Allan, S. 2007. Erlitou and the formation of Chinese civilization: toward a new paradigm. *The Journal of Asian Studies*, 66(2), 461–96.

Ashley, R. 1988. Untying the sovereign state: a double reading of the anarchy problematique. *Millennium*, 17(2), 227–62.

Bellamy, A. 2008. The responsibility to protect and the problem of military intervention. *International Affairs*, 84(4), 615–39.

De Waal, A. 2009. Mission without end? Peacekeeping in the African political marketplace. *International Affairs*, 85(1), 99–113.

Glaser, B. and Medeiros, E. 2007. The changing ecology of foreign policy-making in China: the ascension and demise of the theory of peaceful rise. *The China Quarterly*, 190(6), 291–310.

International Crisis Group. 2009. China's growing role in UN peacekeeping. *Asia Report*, 17 April 2009.

Large, D. 2009. China's Sudan engagement: changing Northern and Southern political trajectories in peace and war. *The China Quarterly*, 199(9), 610–26.

Lewis, J. 1969. The Chinese world order. *The American Political Science Review*, 63(2), 549–51.

Lynch, D. 2009. Chinese thinking on the future of international relations: realism as the Ti, rationalism as the Yong. *The China Quarterly*, 197(3), 87–107.

Woods, N. 2008. Whose aid? whose influence? China, emerging donors and the silent revolution in development assistance. *International Affairs*, 84(6), 1205–21.

Websites

Li, Z. 2005. *President Hu's visit to three ASEAN countries*. [Online]. Available at: http://news.xinhuanet.com/world/2005-04/28/content_2891208.htm [accessed: 12 November 2009].

Ministry of Foreign Affairs of the People's Republic of China. 2007. *Forum on China-Africa Cooperation: Beijing Action Plan, 2007–2009*. [Online]. Available at: www.fmprc.gov.cn/zflt/eng/wjjh/hywj [accessed: 2 November 2009].

Zhong, Y. 2004. *On sovereignty over the Diaoyu Island*. [Online]. Available at: http://news.xinhuanet.com/ziliao/2004-03/261/content_1386025.htm [accessed: 12 November 2009].

Newspaper

Wen, J. 2009. Building a new China-Africa strategic partnership. *People's Daily*, 9 November.

Xu, G. 2009. The peaceful rise must give priority to strategic frontiers. *PLA Daily*, 31 October.

Yao, Y. 2009. Escorting secrets: the special report on the Chinese navy fighting pirates. *Nangfang Zhoume (Southern Weekend)*, 26 March.

Zhang, G. 2008. Sacred missions: Chinese peacekeepers enjoying good reputation in Africa. *PLA Daily*, 5 November.

Zhou, S. 2010. The Central Committee of the CCP held the meeting on Xinjiang. *Xinhua News Agency*, 20 May.

PART IV

Chapter 9

How China is Influencing Africa's Development

Martyn Davies

Introduction

The global financial crisis has accelerated China's investment into Africa, a region that is becoming increasingly important to Chinese firms that are beginning to venture out into the global economy. In the first half of 2009, during the lowest ebb of the global economic crisis, investment from China had increased an impressive 81 percent, when compared to the same period the previous year, accounting for US$523 million. The sizeable values of concessional loan finance that is deployed in Africa, by Chinese policy banks, excludes this Foreign Direct Investment (FDI) figure.

Despite a historically close political relationship, a number of 'China Inc.'s' investments on the continent have failed and more will undoubtedly fail in the future. The ability of Chinese firms to adapt to local African market conditions and operate in sometimes challenging political and economic environments will determine whether Chinese investment in Africa is truly long-term-strategic, rather than merely short-term mercantilist, characterized and enabled by elite political support.

This chapter considers what impact China's engagement in Africa is having on the development of the continent. In response, three questions are posed: does China's concessional finance model offer a new mode of developmental finance for Africa's extractive industries? Will China's investment in infrastructure on the continent assist regional integration of African economies? What contribution will China have on industrialization efforts in Africa? Having addressed these questions, this chapter will put forward an opinion on the impact that China will have on the long-term developmental prospects of Africa.

The New Growth Coupling between China and Africa

According to the International Monetary Fund (IMF), Africa's Gross Domestic Product (GDP) grew at 5.2 percent in 2008. This is robust by any standard and was largely achievable due to buoyant commodity prices and strong demand from the

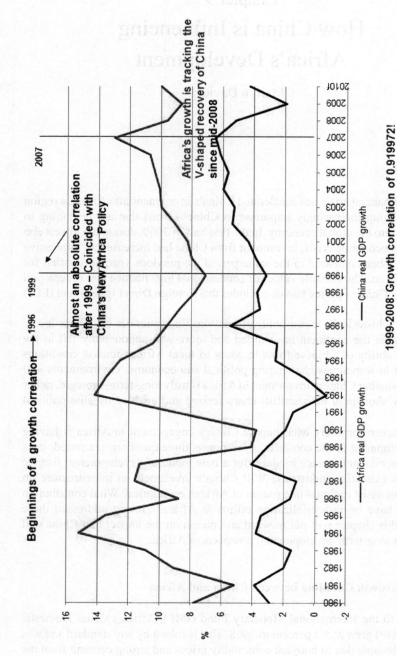

Figure 9.1   The new growth coupling between Africa and China

Source: IMF, EIU and Frontier Advisory analysis.

Chinese economy. In recent years, China's demand for resources has underwritten African growth.

From the other perspective, for China to continue to achieve high rates of GDP growth in the future, its manufacturing economy requires key commodities and energy imports. Considering China's growing investment presence and influence on the continent, Africa will increasingly be the supplier of these resources. The Chinese roll-out of infrastructure in Africa is partly designed to facilitate this process – to alleviate the supply side transportation constraints.

Thus China's growth prospects will increasingly become more dependent upon the abilities of African economies to supply raw materials. This is the new coupling, where China and Africa's growth trajectories become intertwined, as shown in Figure 9.1.

Does China's Concessional Finance Model Offer a New Mode of Developmental Finance for Africa's Extractive Industries?

The bulk of Chinese capital deployed in Africa is being channelled through China's policy banks. A capital risk model is being constructed that is calculated differently to traditional (Western) investors. It is more answerable to political stakeholders pursuing a defined national interest than it is to private shareholders. The state-owned structure of Chinese policy banks allows for an approach where capital is invested in a manner that is arguably more suited to the long-term development needs of developing economies and does not chase a short-term return on investment.

The sharp end of 'China Inc.'s' move into Africa over the past decade is China Export-Import (EXIM) Bank. Established in 1994, with the function of acting as China's official export agency, looking after trade and investment guarantees; providing aid administration and acting as the policy bank that deals with foreign aid coming into China, the Bank is instrumental in providing credit lines to 'strategic' sectors such as infrastructure (roads, power plants, oil and gas pipelines, telecommunications and water projects) and investment loans targeting the energy, mining and industrial sectors. The Bank's main source of finance is the bond market (Wang 2007).

The Chinese government published its foreign policy White Paper on Africa in January 2006, setting out the terms of its engagement with Africa. The policy 'encourages and supports Chinese enterprises' investment and business in Africa, and will continue to provide preferential loans and buyers credit to this end' (Ministry of Foreign Affairs of the People's Republic of China 2006). The concessional finance model as implemented by China EXIM Bank underwrites this policy and provides capital for the market entry of Chinese state-owned enterprises (SOEs) into African economies. They are receiving large sums of finance from China EXIM Bank, the sole provider of the government's concessional loans, to establish an entry position in the recipient African economy and be viewed as 'first movers' in China's 'Go-Global' strategy.

The Chinese government's strategy in Africa is starting to mimic the approach adopted in the domestic market itself, one that channels sizeable amounts of capital through state-owned (policy) banks targeting key sectors. At the Forum On China-Africa Cooperation (FOCAC) IV summit held in Sharm El Sheikh, in November 2009, the People's Republic of China (PRC) committed to spend US$10 billion in concessional loan finance to Africa over the course of the next three years.[1]

Despite the large amount of interest and uptake by African governments of China EXIM Bank's commodities-for-infrastructure concessional finance deals, the financing model employed is coming under a great deal of scrutiny and suspicion by external stakeholders. Do China's concessional package-deal projects undermine the debt sustainability efforts in highly indebted poor African countries or does the concessional structure offer a new model of development capital in Africa?

It has been stated that the Bank's policy loans are influenced by the PRC government and do not 'operate in full compliance with market rules' (Institute of Economic and Research Management 2003: 129). Key countries in Africa that have been recipients of China EXIM Bank's concessional financing include Angola, Equatorial Guinea, Congo Brazzaville, Ethiopia, Guinea, Nigeria, Sudan and Zimbabwe – countries that have questionable governance regimes and some of which may not qualify for funding from traditional developmental finance institutions. In June 2007, at the World Economic Forum's Africa meeting, held in Cape Town, China EXIM Bank's Chief Executive Officer (CEO), Li Ruogu (2007), stated that as much as 40 percent of the bank's loan book is now held in Africa – such is the political commitment of the PRC to its commercial drive in Africa.

Besides extending concessional funding, the Bank finances export buyer's credits and overseas construction and investment projects. Funding goes to Chinese corporate behemoths that dominate strategic sectors in the Chinese economy itself and many are destined – at least intended as such by the PRC government's national planning agency, the National Development Reform Council – for Fortune 500 status. Client firms include the national oil corporations, the Chinese National Offshore Oil Company (CNOOC), the Chinese National Petroleum Corporation (CNPC), Sinopec, telecom players Huawei Technologies,

---

1   On the 9 November 2009, at the Sharm El Sheikh FOCAC meeting, Premier Wen Jiabao set out eight commitments that the PRC would fulfill over a three-year period. The third commitment stated that, 'China will help Africa build up financing capacity. China would provide US$10 billion in concessional loans to African countries, and support Chinese financial institutions in setting up a special loan of one billion dollars for small- and medium-sized African businesses. For the heavily indebted countries and least developed countries in Africa having diplomatic relations with China, China would cancel their debts associated with interest-free government loans due to mature by the end of 2009' (Wen 2009).

Zhongxing Telecom (ZTE) and construction and engineering firms China Harbour, China State Construction Engineering Corporation (CSCEC) and the China National Electronics Import-Export Corporation (CEIEC).

In principle, concessional loans are used for procuring equipment, materials, technology and services, with no less than 50 percent of the contract's procurement coming from China. The loan is denominated in Chinese Renminbi (RMB) and has a maximum maturity of 20 years. A grace period of three to seven years may be granted to the borrower, during which the borrower will only repay interest payments and not the principal. The interest rate is subsidized and underwritten by Chinese government finances. To subsidize its concessional lending, China EXIM Bank's loan programme to foreign states also taps into funding from the Ministry of Commerce's aid budget.

Aid as Part of the Package

In November 2006, at the FOCAC summit in Beijing, President Hu Jintao promised to 'double aid to Africa by 2009' (Ministry of Foreign Affairs of the People's Republic of China 2006). Due to the inclusion of aid commitments by China into the large financial loan packages as disbursed by China EXIM Bank in Africa, it is impossible to accurately calculate the value of these aid disbursements. Aid pronouncements are clearly included to sweeten the deal for recipient governments.

China's interpretation of what the term 'aid' encompasses can be perceived as corresponding to the Organization for Economic Cooperation and Develop (OECD)'s Development Assistance Committee (DAC) definition,[2] as applied by traditional donors. However, despite some broad correlations between these interpretations, China's foreign aid policy has a wider, more ambiguous scope. It can be argued that the PRC government, in particular, the Ministry of Commerce, is itself in the process of defining what constitutes 'aid'. There is, at present, apparently no official definition of aid within Chinese government circles.

Under the November 2006 FOCAC commitments, foreign aid disbursements to Africa in the political, economic, social and cultural spheres are growing rapidly. The monitoring of these commitments and their implementation, as well as delivery to Africa is proving difficult for Chinese government authorities and state-aligned think-tanks to track – not to mention African institutions themselves. Many of these Chinese aid projects in Africa have not succeeded and are currently undergoing a review by the Chinese government with a view towards providing more impact and sustainability for its aid projects.

---

2   According to the DAC definition, grants or loans that are extended to developing countries constitute Overseas Development Assistance (ODA) when they are undertaken by government or government bodies, with the promotion of economic development and welfare as their main objectives, at concessional financial terms. For more information, see www.oecd.org/dac/.

China's So-Called 'Angola Model'

China EXIM Bank's financing arrangement, that ties a commodity off-take agreement with the provision of infrastructure in the contracting African country, is commonly referred to as the 'Angola Model'. The Bank's first such major deal was concluded with Angola's Ministry of Finance in March 2004, when the first US$2 billion financing package was agreed to. This funding has been sponsoring construction of Angolan infrastructure in the areas of energy, water, health, education, fisheries, road, rail and airport public work projects (Campos, Vines 2007).

In May 2007, an extension to the original loan was negotiated to the value of US$500 million from China EXIM Bank, to add to existing infrastructure spending. In September 2007, a further oil-backed loan of US$2 billion was signed between Angola and the Bank to finance an additional 100 projects that were prioritized by Angola's Council of Ministers in November 2007 (Campos, Vines 2007).

The total US$4.5 billion loan disbursed is providing Angola with the reconstruction of vital infrastructure whilst guaranteeing a minimum daily supply of oil to China's national oil corporation, Sinopec – in a joint-venture arrangement with Angola's Sonangol.

This agreement was not just developmentally oriented, but also politically significant for Luanda, considering Angola's difficulties in recent years in securing capital from Western-aligned international financial institutions, such as the Paris Club and the IMF, due to their concerns over financial governance and political accountability. Kose Pedro de Morais, of Angola's Ministry of Finance, states that 'The fact that we secured a loan from China EXIM Bank has set a new benchmark with which new loans are now being aligned'. Other lenders to Angola, including international commercial banks, are now lending to Angola on more favourable terms to compete with China EXIM Bank's loan structure.

Rising oil prices in recent years have emboldened the Angolan government to eschew 'traditional' sources of finance, when the prospect of financing from Beijing emerged (Corkin 2007). Other African governments, fatigued by the continuing, but apparently developmentally ineffective aid disbursements from traditional actors, are starting to lean towards China's concessional finance model – that is transactional rather than contributory.

Sustainability of the Deals

It is argued that China EXIM Bank's unique long-term financing structure is more suited to Africa's extractive industries. While the extractive industries are the mainstay of the continent's economy, the resources are both difficult to extract and require lengthy lead times to commercialize. Most African recipient economies of China EXIM Bank's concessional loans are, however, endowed with rich oil reserves. It is in these economies, where the concessional deals are tied to an off-take agreement, that this model seems to be functioning best, as led by the Angolan example.

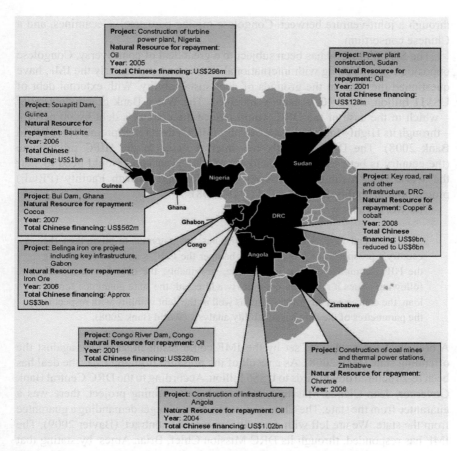

Figure 9.2   Selected Chinese concessional finance deals in Africa

Source: Frontier Advisory analysis.

Given the recent dramatic drop in commodity prices following the onset of the financial crisis, the question over the sustainability of this sovereign-backed debt arises. The question became especially pertinent in the case of China's EXIM Bank's deal with the Democratic Republic of Congo (DRC) (Jansson 2009).

Undoubtedly, one of the most well-known deals struck between China and an African country, during 2008, was the barter deal signed in April between the DRC government and the Chinese companies – China Railway Engineering Corporation (CREC) and Sinohydro. The deal agreed that a Sino-Congolese joint-venture named Sicomines would provide the DRC with China EXIM Bank financed infrastructure in exchange for copper and cobalt mining concessions. Mining of these deposits is due to begin in 2013. In return, Chinese firms will build US$6 billion worth of infrastructure. Another US$3 billion will be invested in mining infrastructure through a joint-venture between Congolese mining parastatal, Gécamines, and a Chinese consortium.

The Sicomines deal has been subject to a great deal of controversy. Congolese opposition groups along with international institutions, particularly the IMF, have questioned the deal on the grounds of debt sustainability. With external debt of US$11 billion, the DRC is heavily indebted. The World Bank grants debt relief – which in the case of the DRC would reduce the country's debt by 90 percent – through its Highly Indebted Poor Country (HIPC) debt relief programme (World Bank 2008). The DRC currently has interim status in the HIPC programme (the country is between decision and completion point) and would need to start the World Bank's three-year Poverty Reduction and Growth Facility (PRGF) programme to qualify for debt relief (IMF 2008).

The World Bank writes that,

> [t]his financial agreement, although [it] has the potential to strengthen the country's prospects for growth, could hamper the DRC's chances of reaching the HIPC completion point to alleviate, sustainably, the debt burden, if the following issues it raises are not quickly addressed: the state guarantee for the loan, the concessionality of the loan, as well as the debt viability with respect to the parametres of the debt sustainability analysis (World Bank 2008).

A breech of the guidelines set by the IMF could result in sanctions against the offending state (IMF 2008). As a result of the pressure from the IMF, the deal has been re-structured downwards to US$6 billion. According to the DRC Central Bank Governor, Jean-Claude Masangu, 'Concerning the mining project, there was a guarantee from the state. The Chinese partners are no longer demanding a guarantee from the state. We are left with a purely commercial contract' (Bavier 2009). The IMF has responded, through its DRC Mission Chief, Brian Ames, by stating that 'When the IMF services confirm that the revised agreement is compatible with the viability of the debt, the Congolese authorities will be in measure to solicit financial assurances for (a new IMF) programme from the lenders of the Paris Club' (IMF 2008). Within the Sino-Congolese contract, Chinese infrastructure projects are already being built – to the value of US$750 million in 2009.

Will China's Infrastructure Projects on the Continent Facilitate African Integration?

A significant development in Africa over the past decade has been the trend that Chinese construction firms building infrastructure on the continent. The market entries of large Chinese state-owned or state-aligned construction enterprises have largely been covered by the Chinese government, through financing provided by the China EXIM Bank, the *de facto* project financing arm of 'China Inc.' in Africa. Although relatively few in number, in relation to the overall project funding on the continent, the Bank's new commodities-for-infrastructure financing model is rapidly gaining in appeal to cash-strapped African governments that are willing to exchange commodity resources for the building of infrastructure. Will China's infrastructure projects on the continent assist the regional integration process of African economies?

Africa's Wanting Infrastructure

According to the World Bank, China's investment commitments to building infrastructure in Sub-Saharan Africa was more than US$7 billion in 2006 – China's declared 'Year of Africa'. In the following year, the country committed a further US$4.5 billion (Foster 2008). While China's investment in African infrastructure is often described as being purely extractive in nature, it is important to note that as China's investment in Africa both broadens geographically and deepens in terms of financial commitment, China itself will increasingly have a vested interest in Africa's long-term developmental success.

While Africa's GDP performance has been robust in recent years, a major constraint on sustainable development has been the poor state of the continent's infrastructure. The inability of economies to integrate themselves with neighbouring countries in order to promote wider markets, continues to be a serious obstacle to trade and to the development of all sectors in Africa – both primary and secondary. The logistical challenges constrain the ability to transport products within the region and ultimately frustrate the formation of value chains for production. It is estimated that Africa requires at least US$40 billion *per annum* to fund and maintain its existing core infrastructure capacity (Sandrey, Edinger 2009). This undoubtedly has a detrimental impact on the competitiveness of African economies (Edinger 2009). A recent report by the Infrastructure Consortium for Africa (ICA) states that 'In most African countries, particularly the lower-income countries, infrastructure emerges as a major constraint on doing business, depressing firm productivity by about 40 percent' (Cropley 2009).

Costs of transportation are higher in Africa than other developing economies. According to the United Nations Conference on Trade and Development (UNCTAD), freight costs, on average, account for 5.4 percent of imports in the global economy – in Africa, this figure is up to five times higher (Hanouz, Lawrence 2009). In addition, the energy infrastructure deficit is estimated to have resulted in up to six percent in yearly industrial production losses (Edinger, Herman 2009). Deficient infrastructure has thus stifled trade, both regionally and internationally, and further isolates Africa from the global economy. Currently, Africa accounts for less than three percent of both exports and imports in world trade (Hanouz, Lawrence 2009). Added to this, intra-regional trade in Africa is only nine percent of overall African trade – the lowest of any region in the global economy (Edinger, Herman 2009).

China's Financing of African Infrastructure

According to the World Bank, in 2007, China contributed US$4.5 billion towards infrastructure projects in Africa. This is a major increase from the US$1 billion contributed annually from 2001–2003, but marks a decrease when compared to the US$7 billion peak in 2006 (World Bank 2008). China's financing commitments have intersected largely with China's foreign policy objectives on the continent, channelled mostly through China's EXIM Bank.

In terms of the power sector, 'research into Chinese policy bank financing in Africa reveals that great focus is placed on hydropower projects, with approximately US$5.3 billion being invested in this sector' (Sandrey, Edinger 2009). For example, China EXIM Bank has financed the construction of the large-scale Bui Dam project in Ghana. The project, valued at US$660 million, is to provide 400MW of power to be distributed nationally and to neighbouring countries. It is estimated that almost two-thirds of African states have received financing from China – mostly through China EXIM Bank – for thermal and hydropower projects in Africa (Sandrey, Edinger 2009). The World Bank states that Chinese funded projects will generate a power capacity of more than 6,000 MW – over a third of Africa's existing hydropower generating capacity (Foster et al. 2008).

In the rail sector, Chinese financing commitments in Africa are reportedly standing at no less than US$4 billion for both the rehabilitation of old lines and the construction of new lines, with a number of large deals having been announced in Nigeria, Gabon and Mauritania (Foster et al. 2008). After having been put on hold during a period of governmental transition, an agreement was signed in October 2009, to construct a railway line from Abuja to Kaduna. This project is valued at US$850 million and is to be constructed over a three-year period. China's largest planned rail project in Africa, to date, is the rehabilitation of over 3,200km of rail in the DRC – an infrastructure development commitment that forms part of the commodity-for-infrastructure deal being implemented by a consortium of Chinese firms (Foster et al. 2008).

In the realm of ICT, China EXIM Bank is providing finance for the supply of equipment hardware from leading firms such as ZTE and Huawei Technologies. The World Bank estimates that Chinese telecom firms have supplied over US$3.2 billion worth of telecoms equipment to Africa – with particular reference to Ethiopia, Ghana, South Africa and Sudan (World Bank 2008).

Furthermore, it is estimated that project finance for the rehabilitation and construction of roads stands at approximately US$550 million, with this number set to increase as projects progress from their planning stages. In this respect, the DRC deserves particular mention, once again, as it is reported that over 7,000km of road rehabilitation and construction is to be carried out by Chinese contractor companies (Centre for Chinese Studies 2008–2009).

A key facilitator and contributor to these infrastructure projects has been China EXIM Bank. The Bank has, according to the IMF, financed more than the combined total foreign investment in the African power sector between 2001 and

2006, via Official Development Assistance (ODA) and Private Participation in Infrastructure (PPI).

Given the desperate state of Africa's infrastructure, the continent needs to embrace China as a new large-scale infrastructure financier, specifically in light of the global recession and withdrawal of capital out of emerging markets and Africa. For China, its involvement in Africa's construction and infrastructure sectors has proved most effective in building relations with African governments, increasing influence and expanding or facilitating transportation access within and between African economies.

Senegalese President Abdoulaye Wade stated that, 'With direct aid, credit lines and reasonable contracts, China has helped African nations build infrastructure projects in record time – bridges, roads, schools, hospitals, dams, legislative buildings, stadiums and airports. In many African nations, including Senegal, improvements in infrastructure have played important roles in stimulating economic growth' (Wade 2008). It is, however, claimed by many international observers that infrastructure projects funded by Chinese financial institutions in Africa are tied to the extraction of natural resources. These assertions do not take into account the fact that Chinese financiers largely sponsor projects that are proposed by the recipient governments themselves. Decisions on the choice of infrastructure project are thus taken in African capitals and not in Beijing.

Chinese financing could make a potentially significant contribution towards economic diversification in African countries, in that infrastructure development would promote and attract further investment in all related sectors of the economy. This is particularly relevant to the extractive industries which contribute toward the bulk of most Sub-Saharan African economies' GDPs.

Additionally, local benefits developed through production can be supported via access to enabling infrastructure. Both local productivity and international investment will be enhanced as the cost of doing business and other transaction costs decrease, through the greater capacity that would be generated as a result of increased infrastructure provision.

Criticism is common of Chinese firms that often operate as 'insulated actors' in recipient African economies. Construction firms that utilize only Chinese labour for their contracts do so in the interests of rapid completion of their projects. The desire to deliver the infrastructure on time often takes precedence over the inclusion of the local community – projects which have delivery dates often determined by governments seeking the political kudos from their completion.

China and Regional African Infrastructure Coordination?

'China has a plan for Africa but Africa does not have a plan for China'. This comment, pertaining to China-Africa relations, has been repeated at numerous conferences in recent years. Beijing is often criticized for not engaging Africa at a more multilateral level – coordinating its infrastructure investment activities at a regional rather than a national level. Nevertheless, is this criticism fair?

With respect to African integration, a conference hosted by the Development Bank of Southern Africa, in 2008, found that:

> As China's role in the provision of infrastructure has broadened throughout Africa, it has become clear that the continent needs to coordinate a regional response to the potential advantages China could bring in this regard in the future [...]. While the potential benefits from China's engagement on the continent, specifically in the provision of infrastructure, was great, it could only be harnessed once African governments realized these benefits and the advantages that regional actions could bring to their country, as well as its neighbours.

The lack of adequate cross-border infrastructure within African regions undoubtedly hampers attempts to promote intra-regional trade and economic cooperation. Regional efforts to alleviate these bottlenecks and inefficiencies are beginning, but a great deal of work has to be done to improve regional coordination which is weak and aggravated by under-resourced institutions within African countries, at the multilateral level, that in many cases have had little interaction with Chinese policy-makers or financial actors.

An organization such as the New Economic Partnership for Africa's Development's (NEPAD) Business Foundation (NBF) – a private sector body spun out from the NEPAD Secretariat – is working to prioritize and coordinate infrastructure development around key development corridors, but its efforts are largely only applicable to the Southern African region. The NEPAD Secretariat and NBF have engaged with the Chinese government at the November 2006 FOCAC summit, but this is not the case for the mandate to negotiate project investment on behalf of African governments, or other private sector stakeholders.

It could be argued that the sheer geographic enormity and great diversity of Africa will most often prevent common African positions from being found – especially in relation to infrastructure, where its economic benefits are largely localized. The bureaucratic processes involved in seeking common regional positions amongst states that have – despite geographic proximity – greatly varying interests, has also discouraged Chinese commercial actors in Africa from engaging multilateral institutions rather than at a bilateral level.

Will China Assist African Industrialization?

The trend of China's 'counter-cyclical' investment abroad is becoming increasingly apparent in Africa. It extends beyond the sizeable concessional deals signed between Chinese policy banks and African governments, and that of Chinese companies' investments into Africa's resource and infrastructure sectors.

China's 'Go-Global' strategy, announced in 2002, to encourage Chinese firms to establish an international investment presence, is gaining momentum following the onset of the global crisis. The state-inspired policy formulated by the Ministry of Commerce (MOFCOM) includes the encouragement of Chinese enterprises to establish offshore operations in designated Chinese Special Economic Zones (SEZs), in the global economy. This strategy forms an integral part of the PRC's Eleventh Five Year Plan (2006–2010). According to MOFCOM, manufacturing accounts for just eight percent (or US$9.52 billion) of its total outbound FDI stock of US$118 billion, by the end of 2007 (Davies 2009). This figure is likely to rise as Chinese firms seek to offset the protectionist sentiment that has arisen as a result of the global economic crisis.

The SEZs, which are being set up in countries as diverse as Cambodia, Egypt, Mauritius, Nigeria, Pakistan, Russia, Tanzania, Thailand and Zambia, are intended to promote China's foreign commercial interests and create safe-havens for Chinese capital (Davies 2008). The zones are thus expected to assist Chinese companies in securing new markets on the African continent through investment in clustered industrial zones. While these may begin to serve as catalysts for broader industrial activity in their host economies, the broader impact of China's rapidly rising exports of manufactured products to African economies may be to undermine the already weak manufacturing sectors of African states. The general lack of success in adding downstream profit-making industries in African economies may be further exacerbated with the increase of imports from China.

In addition to the economic rationale, a political motivation exists. The establishment of these SEZs will ultimately result in job creation for local citizens and will therefore serve to offset criticism that trade with China erodes the industrial base of its Africa trading partner, and also help to defy the myth that Chinese firms only seek to invest in the extractive industries, especially in Africa. What are the strategies behind the establishment of Chinese SEZs in Africa and what contribution will they have toward industrialization efforts on the continent?

Clustering for Competitiveness

The share of manufacturing value-added in the GDPs of African economies is very low when compared to other emerging market peer economies (Kaplinsky 2008). Many Asian economies' industrial success over the past four decades originates from the creation of manufacturing and export processing zones, with incentives provided to investors to set up industrial clusters. Other economies, not least in Africa, implemented import substituting industrialization policies, which served to restrict economic openness and result in protectionist tendencies.

According to Porter (1998), the global economy is characterized by these clusters – critical masses in one place of linked industries and institutions. They are 'geographic concentrations of interconnected companies and institutions around particular sectors'. The trend of clustering contributes to competitiveness in three ways: it increases the productivity of companies that are located in or around the cluster; promotes the direction and pace of innovation; and leads to the creation of new businesses within the cluster.

Porter (1998: 78) states that clusters regularly 'extend downstream to channels and customers and laterally to manufacturers of complementary products and to companies in industries related by skills, technologies or common inputs'. Clustering is most often underdeveloped or absent in poor or developing countries. These economies are unable to compete beyond supplying non-beneficiated raw resources. Porter (1998: 78) states that to move beyond this lowly state of economic development, the nurturing of well-functioning clusters is essential.

Following the political change, and the dramatic shift in economic policy that took place in China in the late 1970s, the country's leadership thereafter created dedicated geographical zones on the East coast that served as experiments for market liberalization, in order to attract Chinese diaspora and foreign capital. These zones increased in number as Chinese reform efforts gained economic traction.

Four SEZs were introduced two years after the party's Eleventh Central Party Committee in December 1978. The conference recognized the need for the country to implement economic reform, promoting a market-led policy to encourage higher levels of foreign capital, trade, technology and growth in an economy that had, until then, been insular and based on the premise of self-sufficiency. The state acted as the primary funding agency of the SEZs in their initial growth stages.

The new 'Open-Door policy' and the SEZs were mechanisms to open the country's economy, gradually, to the rest of the world. SEZs in Shenzhen, Zhuhai and Shantou in Guangdong Province, in Fujian Province and in Xiamen – including Xiamen Island and Gulangyu Islet – were announced in 1980. A fifth zone in Hainan Province was created in 1988, after the passage of a resolution to establish Hainan Province and the Hainan SEZ. As one of the largest of the zones, this SEZ included six cities and 13 counties with a total population of 7.4 million.

Similar attempts of launching dedicated zones to attract capital investment on the African continent have, however, enjoyed considerably less success. Apart from Mauritius, Africa has generally failed to achieve tangible gains from the establishment of these liberalized investment zones (Jauch 2009).

Chinese Clusters in Africa

China could potentially be a catalyst for the promotion of industrial activity in selected African economies where Chinese-funded SEZs are established. The SEZ investment proposal originated at the FOCAC summit, in Beijing, in November 2006. Under the Beijing Action Plan, it was stated that 'China is ready to encourage, in the next three years, well-established Chinese companies to set up three to five overseas economic and trade cooperation zones in African countries where conditions permit'. This commitment was to be fulfilled before the following FOCAC summit hosted by the Egyptian government in November 2009.

In Beijing's eyes, the zones are expected to improve the investment climate and thus attract foreign private investment into dedicated investment clusters. The terms of these zones are being negotiated between Beijing and targeted African governments that are willing to offer the requested policy concessions, in order to receive committed Chinese investment. These could potentially include investment incentives such as tax breaks, customs duty waivers, discounted land and other such services.

The zones are becoming more attractive to African states which seek to promote the clustering effect in their economies and to move away from simple resource extraction. A sizeable capital injection from Chinese financiers or investors could provide a good base to expand beyond the zone. The emergence of a Chinese funded cluster zone could contribute to backward (to the country's hinterland) and forward (to export markets) linkages in the economy. Most importantly, the zones are seen as facilitators to creating employment opportunities and generating greater foreign exchange reserves through more diversified sources of income (Sandrey, Edinger 2009).

To date, positive interest in the establishment of such zones has been shown by both Chinese anchor investor companies and recipient African states. Six official zones have been announced thus far by the PRC government, but progress remains at an early stage in the development of these zones and their operational success remains to be seen (TradeInvestNigeria 2007).

China's Special Economic Zones in Africa

It is expected that these proposed SEZs will focus on value-added industries and provide liberalized investment environments for investors. Furthermore, the zones will not exclusively provide for Chinese investors but seek to attract capital from other domestic or foreign investors.

A number of African economies are more familiar with the establishment of Export Processing Zones (EPZs) and attracting capital into these zones. Kenya, Egypt and Mauritius are probably the most proactive economies on the continent in establishing such zones (Edinger 2008).

The first zone, announced in February 2007 during President Hu Jintao's tour of Africa, is located in Chambishi – the heart of Zambia's Copperbelt region. Characterized as a Multi Facility Economic Zone (MFEZ), its main objective is to catalyze 'industrial and economic development in the manufacturing sector for the purpose of enhancing both domestic and export-orientated business' and will 'operate on the principal of value-addition' (Zambian Development Agency 2009). The anchor investment is a copper smelter project with a project value of US$250–US$300 million, to be built by the China Nonferrous Metal Mining Group (Zambia Development Agency 2009).

Total investment in the zone is expected to reach between US$800 million and US$1 billion. By early 2009, it was reported that more than ten Chinese firms had established operations in the zone, creating over 3,500 local jobs. Contracts across a number of industries including mining, smelting and chemical engineering have been inked and more than US$300 million in contracts are expected to be reached for local procurement. Altogether, more than 50 Chinese businesses are expected to invest in the zone over the medium-term, with between 6,000 and 7,500 job

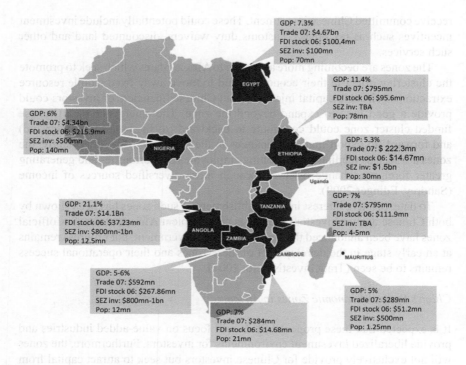

GDP: 7.3%
Trade 07: $4.67bn
FDI stock 06: $100.4mn
SEZ inv: $100mn
Pop: 70mn

GDP: 11.4%
Trade 07: $795mn
FDI stock 06: $95.6mn
SEZ inv: TBA
Pop: 78mn

GDP: 6%
Trade 07: $4.34bn
FDI stock 06: $215.9mn
SEZ inv: $500mn
Pop: 140mn

GDP: 5.3%
Trade 07: $ 222.3mn
FDI stock 06: $14.67mn
SEZ inv: $1.5bn
Pop: 30mn

GDP: 21.1%
Trade 07: $14.1Bn
FDI stock 06: $37.23mn
SEZ inv: $800mn-1bn
Pop: 12.5mn

GDP: 7%
Trade 07: $795mn
FDI stock 06: $111.9mn
SEZ inv: TBA
Pop: 4-5mn

GDP: 5-6%
Trade 07: $592mn
FDI stock 06: $267.86mn
SEZ inv: $800mn-1bn
Pop: 12mn

GDP: 5%
Trade 07: $289mn
FDI stock 06: $51.2mn
SEZ inv: $500mn
Pop: 1.25mn

GDP: 7%
Trade 07: $284mn
FDI stock 06: $14.68mn
Pop: 21mn

Figure 9.3   China's special economic zones in Africa
Source: Frontier Advisory analysis.

opportunities directly created and up to 15,000 indirectly created in the Zambian economy.

International commentators have, however, expressed caution against Chinese investment in Africa due to the common usage of large numbers of expatriate Chinese labour utilized on construction projects and exclusive Chinese procurement practices. Concern has also been expressed over the Zambian government offering special tax concessions to Chinese investor firms, which may possibly erode the country's fiscal revenue base if not monitored cautiously and effectively.

The second SEZ, in Mauritius, was announced in mid-2007. Located near Port Louis, in the Indian Ocean Rim region, construction of the zone was due to commence in October 2007. Called the Mauritius Tianli Economic and Trade Cooperation Zone, the zone is subject to an investment of US$500 million by the Shanxi Tianli Enterprise Group over the next five years. The zone will focus on the service industry, servicing Chinese enterprises operating and investing in mainland Africa.

Mauritius provides a strategic destination for Chinese investment in that it is an offshore financial centre with attractive investment laws; its economy is well integrated into the economies of South Asia; the country is a member of the Southern African Development Community (SADC) and the Common Market for Eastern and Southern Africa (COMESA) and thus enjoys preferential market access into the African region; and Mauritius has a sizeable ethnic Chinese community that is active in trading with the Chinese economy. The zone is expected to earn about US$200 million in export earnings *per annum*, once fully operational.

The third 'official' zone is intended to be located in Egypt. Most foreign investment in Egypt already takes place under the laws which define incentives around SEZs, promoting both public and privately managed investment zones. In early 2007, Chinese investment in Egypt's SEZ, near the Suez Canal, was announced and twinned with the very successful cluster development in the northeast Chinese city of Tianjin. Tianjin Economic and Technological Development Area Suez International Cooperation Company is the major shareholder of the Egypt-Teda zone initiative – a Sino-Egyptian joint-venture overseeing the development of the zone. The first phase of the zone is expected to be completed by 2011, with an initial capital investment of US$100 million. This phase is forecast to create 10,000 jobs, mainly for local workers. Construction of the entire zone is expected to be completed in 2018, with an estimated investment of US$2.5 billion made by the PRC into this zone – focused on automotive components, electronics, logistics, clothing and textiles sectors (Chinese Stock Information 2009). The zone is strategically positioned to expand market access into the Middle East and North Africa (MENA) region and Sub-Saharan Africa. It also provides, to an extent, market access into the European Union (EU), as well as to the United States (US) market.

Added to the above is the Lekki Free Trade Zone, due to be established in Nigeria. This zone is to be developed in three phases and seeks to attract more than US$5 billion in investments. The Vice President of the Chinese anchor investor in the zone – Guangdong Xinguang International Group – Sun Jianxiong, stated that Nigeria was chosen to host one of the official SEZs due to its large domestic market and accessibility to West African and European marketplaces (Rotberg 2008: 148).

Other potential Chinese-invested zones are being mooted in Angola, Ethiopia, Mozambique, Tanzania and Uganda. The zones in Mauritius, Egypt and Nigeria are partially supported by the China-Africa Development Fund (CADFund), which is assisting both with zone construction, infrastructure roll-outs and providing support for Chinese companies looking to expand into these zones. While these developments are still at an early stage, there could be potential benefits to the industrial development of these economies through the Chinese invested SEZs.

Conclusion

In most cases, Africa has welcomed Chinese investment, especially with regard to Chinese investment in its 'strategic assets', and there has been little apparent political resistance shown on the continent towards China's economic interest. Whilst debate and political opposition to Chinese investment have been increasing with the pace of 'China Inc.' moving abroad, no such political resistance from African governments has been forthcoming. The political obstruction – however real or perceived – of Chinese SOE acquisitions in Western economies is likely to further encourage these firms to seek out investments in Africa, centred largely on commodities.

Yet beyond the impressive growth of Chinese investment in Africa, the question remains as to whether the politically conceived investment drive will prove sustainable. China's current government is clearly intent on expanding and deepening its investment commitment to the continent using the state-owned vehicles that it has at its disposal. Spearheaded financially by China EXIM Bank and by the Chinese development banks, with leading SOE firms in tow, it is apparent that commercial intent reinforces Beijing's political rhetoric. A review of China's foreign policy approach toward Africa may be in store when China's new government is installed after the seventeenth Chinese Communist Party congress due in March 2013. Over the medium-term, China's commercial presence in Africa will continue to gain in strength and this has been reinforced by Beijing's financial commitments to the continent, as outlined at the FOCAC summit in Sharm El Sheikh.

The challenge for 'China Inc.', however, will be less political and more operational. A gap is becoming apparent between the vision held towards Africa by Chinese politicians and Chinese firms that are serving to act upon and implement the 'Going-Global' policy. The operational environment in most African states is challenging and not conducive to promoting private sector growth. The operational difficulties facing Chinese firms are no different from other foreign firms and their ability to manage and overcome challenges and investment risk in Africa is not yet proven.

Inter-cultural challenges are also an obstacle facing Chinese firms operating in Africa. Chinese firms are used to dealing with tough and competitive conditions, but are far less adept at these early stages of their internationalization at understanding local cultural circumstances. African societies also have a relatively low understanding of China and the Chinese. It is imperative that African organizations and governments build their knowledge, networks and experience in dealing with Chinese commercial institutions.

It is difficult to say that we, as Africans, have even begun to comprehend the long-term strategic implications of China's growing commercial presence in Africa. A shift in Africa's economic relations is occurring – away from traditional economies, toward the East and China. This force has not been created by the current crisis that is inflicting Western economies, but it has definitely accelerated this process. The developmental impact of this shift in Africa will become clearer as the depth of China's commercial penetration becomes greater.

Bibliography

Book References

Institute of Economic and Resource Management. 2003. *A Report on the Development of China's Market Economy*. Beijing: China Foreign Economic Relations and Trade Publishing House.

Book Chapters

Davies, M.J. 2008. Special economic zones: China's developmental model comes to Africa, in *China into Africa: Trade, Aid and Influence*, edited by R. Rotberg. Washington, D.C.: Brookings Institute Press, 137–54.
Hanouz, M.D. and Lawrence, R. 2009. Enhancing trade in Africa: lessons from the enabling trade index, in *The Africa Competitiveness Report 2009*. Davos: World Economic Forum.

Journal Articles

Campos, I. and Vines, A. 2008. A pragmatic partnership. *CSIS Working Paper*, 1–16.
Centre for Chinese Studies, Stellenbosch University. 2008–2009. *Field research carried out in the DRC, through 2008 and 2009*.
Davies, K. 2009. While global FDI falls, China's outward FDI doubles. *Columbia FDI Perspectives*, 5, 1–3.
Jauch, H. 2002. Export processing zones and the quest for sustainable development: a Southern African perspective. *Environment and Urbanization*, 14(1), 101–13.
Kaplinsky, R. 2008. What does the rise of China do for industrialization in Sub-Saharan Africa?. *Review of African Political Economy*, 35(115), 7–22.
Li, R. 2007. A proper understanding of debt sustainability of developing countries. *World Economics and Politics*, 4, 63–73.
Porter, M.E. 1998. Clusters and the new economics of competition. *Harvard Business Review*, November-December Issue, 77–90.
Wang, J. 2009. What drives China's growing role in Africa?. *IMF Working Paper – African Department*, 1–30.

Websites

Bavier, J. 2009. *Congo to downsize Chinese deal in debt relief bid.* [Online]. Available at: http://www.reuters.com/article/idUSLI37257520090818 [accessed: 31 July 2010].

China Stock Information. 2009. *Sino-Egyptian economic zone to be completed in 2018.* [Online]. Available at: http://www.chinesestock.org/show.aspx?id=40372&cid=13 [accessed: 16 September 2010].

Cropley, E. 2009. *Africa needs US$93 bln/yr for infrastructure.* [Online]. Available at: http://www.alertnet.org/thenews/newsdesk/LB294340.htm [accessed: 31 July 2010].

Edinger, H. 2009. *Inadequate infrastructure restrains development.* [Online]. Available at: http://www.frontieradvisory.com/inadequate-infrastructure-restrains-development/#more-700 [accessed: 31 July 2010].

Foster, V., Butterfield, W., Chen, C. and Pushak, N. 2008. *Building Bridges – China's growing role as infrastructure financier for Sub-Saharan Africa.* [Online]. Available at: http://siteresources.worldbank.org/INTAFRICA/Resources/Building_Bridges_Master_Version_Wo-Embg_with_cover.pdf [accessed: 31 July 2010].

International Monetary Fund. 2008. *The poverty reduction and growth facility (PRGF).* [Online]. Available at: from http://www.imf.org/external/np/exr/facts/prgf.htm [accessed: 1 December 2008].

Jansson, J. 2009. *DRC: Chinese investment in Katanga.* [Online]. Available at: http://www.pambazuka.org/en/category/africa_china/63573 [accessed: 31 July 2010].

Sandrey, R. and Edinger, H. 2009. *South Africa's trading environment and FTA prospects with China.* [Online]. Available at: http://www.pambazuka.org/en/category/africa_china/57384 [accessed: 31 July 2010].

TradeInvestNigeria. 2007. *Ogun free trade zone ready to go.* [Online]. Available at: http://www.tradeinvestnigeria.com/news/799305.htm [accessed: 29 September 2010].

Wen, J. 2009. *Speech by H.E. Wen Jiabao at the opening ceremony of the fourth ministerial conference of the forum on China-Africa cooperation.* [Online]. Available at: http://www.focac.org/eng/dsjbzjhy/zyjh/t627391.htm [accessed: 31 July 2010].

World Bank. 2008. *Democratic Republic of Congo economic report: fall 2008.* [Online]. Available at: http://siteresources.worldbank.org/CONGODEMOCRATICEXTN/Resources/DRC_Fall_Econ_Report_08.pdf?resourceurlname=DRC_Fall_Econ_Report_08.pdf [accessed: 31 July 2010].

Zambia Development Agency. 2009. *Chinese investment in Zambia.* [Online]. Available at: http://www.zda.org.zm/246-chinese-investments-zambia [accessed: 31 July 2010].

Newspapers

Corking, L. 2007. Angola flexes newfound muscle. *BusinessDay*, 23 March.

Command Papers

China's Africa Policy. 2006. Beijing: Ministry of Foreign Affairs of the People's Republic of China.
Heavily Indebted Poor Countries (HIPC) Initiative and Multilateral Debt Relief Initiative (MDRI) – Status of Implementation. 2008. Washington, D.C.: International Development Association and International Monetary Fund.

Chapter 10

China's Aid to Africa:
A Challenge to the EU?

Xinghui Zhang

Introduction

Since the 1990s, China's influence has been continuously increasing in the world to the point where China is described as an 'emerging' actor and the European Union (EU) a 'traditional' one on the African continent (Herman, Davies 2009: 3). China's aid to Africa – based on the principle of mutual benefit – has gained such popularity that Joseph Kabila, the Democratic Republic of Congo's (DRC) President has labelled the Chinese deals as 'exemplary cooperation' (The Economist 2008: 10). However, with the wild spread of China's influence combined to the 48 African heads of state gathered in Beijing for the Forum on China-Africa Cooperation (FOCAC) summit in November 2006, much concern was shown by this 'traditional' actor. Some Europeans believe that China broke into Europe's 'backyard'; others believe that China has launched a form of neo-colonialism in Africa. One EU official, working for the Director General for Development at the European Commission, proclaimed that 'the rapid emergence of China as a dynamic actor in Africa with different approaches from Europe and the strong reaction to this phenomenon affects the EU-Africa and EU-China partnerships' (Wissenbach 2009: 1).

This chapter will therefore tackle the issue of development aid in Africa. In order to provide the correct setting and background to the debate, the first section will focus on the history of China's development aid policy to Africa, which will be divided into four sections covering Mao Zedong and Deng Xiaoping's respective leaderships, the post-Tiananmen phase and developments from 2005 onwards. The second section will cover the contentious topic of the quantitative evaluation of China's development aid. This should lead onto the final section which analyses whether China's aid to Africa – as discussed in this chapter – represents a threat to the EU's development strategy and political interests in Africa. In this section, despite the growing presence of China in the field of African economic development, the following point will be raised that China's development aid strategy does not represent a threat to the EU's and this for three principle reasons, which are explained in further depth.

The Evolution of China's Aid Policy to Africa

China's aid policy has fluctuated in conjunction with its developing Africa policy, and shifts in China's Africa policy are closely interlinked with its domestic development strategies, as well as international events. Like other countries, China uses foreign aid as a tool to serve its foreign policy goals and domestic demands. In short, China's foreign aid is not only a part of its foreign policy but also an extension of its internal affairs.

Since the People's Republic of China (PRC) was founded in 1949, its foreign policy and foreign aid have experienced a variety of adjustments and changes. Its continuity, however, is preserved due to the 'Five Principles of Peaceful Coexistence' introduced by the late Chinese Premier Zhou Enlai in 1954 and its subsequent impact on Chinese foreign policy: mutual respect for sovereignty and territorial integrity; mutual non-aggression; non-interference; equality and mutual benefit; peaceful coexistence (People's Daily 2010). On the basis of these principles, China has strived to develop cooperative relationships with all members of the international community over the past five decades, in which time, Chinese aid policy has experienced about four different phases.

The Ideology/Politics Phase (1949–1978)

This phase – which started with the founding of PRC in 1949 – ran from the 1950s to the 1970s. This was a time when China's policy was dominated by thoughts and ideas emanating from the 'Extreme Left'. In domestic policy, class struggle was the overriding priority; in foreign affairs, China's top leader announced the 'Leaning to One Side' policy, in order to embrace the Socialist Camp which was led by the Soviet Union (Hu 2008). This policy lasted for approximately ten years.

As to the Chinese policy towards Africa, it mainly unfolded along two mainstreams. One was concentrated on supporting African people in their struggle for national independence and the other focused on uniting African countries in the struggle against colonialism and imperialism. Aid policy was thus subject to China's general Africa policy and it was used as an important tool to reach China's diplomatic goals on the continent. This strategy is reflected in the 'Five Principles on China's Relations with African and Arab Countries', put forward by Zhou Enlai during his tour to 13 African and Asian countries, between December 1963 and February 1964. The first principle reads that, 'China supports the Arab and African peoples in their struggle to oppose imperialism and old and new colonialism and to win and safeguard national independence' (The Ministry of Foreign Affairs of the People's Republic of China 2000).

In addition, the eight principles for the allocation of foreign aid were also put forward during the Premier's tour (The Ministry of Foreign Affairs of the People's Republic of China 2000). These eight principles expressed China's sincere desire in seeking to conduct economic and cultural cooperation with the newly-emerging countries in Asia, Africa and Latin America. These relations would be founded on equality, mutual benefit and respect for the sovereignty of the host nation. Loans would be unconditional, interest-free and easily rescheduled. Projects would use high-quality materials, produce quick results and boost self-reliance. In the wake of the tour, China committed a total of nearly US$120 million in aid to Congo-Brazzaville, Ghana, Kenya, Mali and Tanzania (Brautigam 2009: 32).

However, problematic cases arose concerning the allocation of aid to those who recognized Beijing as 'China' instead of Taipei and those who supported China's attempts to regain its permanent seat at United Nations (UN) Security Council. In such cases, ideological affinity seemed less important because the Taiwan issue was related to the PRC's territorial integrity, which was taken as China's core national interests; and the seat in the UN Security Council was seen as the symbol of China's position as a great power on the international stage. As countries switched support away from Taipei, they were rewarded with aid programmes. By 1971, China had won diplomatic recognition from 26 African countries, enough for it to regain its seat at the UN.

During this period, the Tanzania-Zambia railway was a model for Chinese assistance to African countries. China, in turn, sought and gained support from African countries in the international arena, namely support for China's seat at the UN Security Council. This support is still often referred to by Chinese leaders. President Hu Jintao, in his opening speech at the 2006 FOCAC summit, stated that 'We in China will not forget Africa's full support for restoring the lawful rights of the People's Republic of China in the United Nations' (Hu 2006).

The Reform Focus Phase (1979–1988)

The second phase started with a move away from ideology to a focus on economic reform in China, where two big events happened in 1976: the end of the Cultural Revolution and the demise of Chairman Mao Zedong. It was Mao's passing away that paved the way for reformers to transform China from a planned economy into a market-economy. In 1979, Deng Xiaoping announced that China would open up to the outside world and pursued a policy of building up a market-economy using Chinese socialist characteristics.

The Cultural Revolution (1966–1976) was a catastrophe for China, resulting in nation-wide chaos and economic disarray, which negatively impacted on China's Gross Domestic Product (GDP). This also meant a decrease in Chinese aid to African countries. On the other hand, in order to speed up domestic economic development, the Chinese government not only put aside its ideological divergences with developed capitalist countries but also opened its door to them, by offering favourable conditions to attract foreign investment or by establishing joint-ventures in collaboration with them. To this point, Japan acted as a vastly important economic support for China. From 1979 to 1984, Japan provided 330 billion yen (US$1.4 billion) in official development assistance to China (Park 1993: 54).[1]

Yet after the Chinese reformers worked out how foreign aid would fit into their new domestic and foreign goals, they moved again to engage with Africa. Chinese Premier Zhao Ziyang travelled to Africa in December 1982 to promote 'South-South cooperation' and to announce that China was adding a new principle to its foreign aid: 'diversity in form' (Brautigam 2008: 10). The new principle marked a significant reform and its impact is still being felt today.

Nevertheless, aid to Africa was dwarfed by other economic ties. For example, in 1978, China and Japan signed a general 'counter-trade' agreement whereby China agreed to buy US$10 billion in capital goods from Japan, from 1978 to 1985, and pay for them by exporting the equivalent value of oil (Morino 1991: 90). Deng Xiaoping also proposed the same counter-trade to Western firms: 'importing plant and equipment from the West for the development of China's oil and coal industries, and then paying for these imports with the resulting output from the plants' (Park 1993: 53). This early investment set the stage for the production of sufficient energy capacity, thus helping in lifting a significant constraint on China's economic development.

After working out new policies to reconcile aid with the country's new commitment to its own economic development, Chinese leaders recommitted to its development aid programme. In 1984, China announced aid commitments to Africa that surpassed those of Japan, Norway, Sweden and the United Kingdom (Brautigam 2008: 11). Although it was assumed by many that China had only recently 'returned' to Africa, it showed that China, in fact, was quite active throughout the 1980s.

The Transition Phase (1989–2004)

In 1989, communism collapsed in Eastern Europe, which simultaneously caused significant social and political turmoil in China. Even after the Tiananmen Square Incident, the West, led by the United States (US), launched a campaign laying economic sanctions and a military embargo upon China. Therefore, good relations with developed countries, formed since the Open-Door policy, deteriorated rapidly. Under such circumstances, Taiwan believed that there was an opportunity to take advantage of reinvigorating its 'dollar diplomacy' in order to win international recognition. By the end of 1990, three African countries, Guinea-Bissau, Liberia and Lesotho, had re-established diplomatic relations with Taiwan. Over almost the next two decades, some African countries made the switch back to Taipei. The rivalry with Taiwan sparked something of a bidding war, with escalating amounts of aid offered from both sides.

---

1   In this instance, the yen is converted into dollars at the medium rate utilized in January 1984.

Meanwhile, China's bid to join the World Trade Organization (WTO) marked another big event which forced the Chinese government to undertake reforms, so as to conform with WTO legislation. Among them, reforms of the state-owned banks were prominent. The three 'policy banks' (China Development Bank, China Export Import Bank and China Agricultural Bank) were established, enabling the state to intervene in areas where the market-led activity was less prominent, with the aim of promoting its targeted aid programmes in Africa.

The Partnership Phase (2005–present)

In this phase, the Chinese government made efforts to construct partnerships with different African states. Surrounding this core mission, the channels by which Chinese aid is distributed in Africa have pluralized. In 2005, President Hu Jintao presented a 'five point pledge' which marked a new era in China's aid to foreign countries and three new instruments were added to the existing basket of assistance tools: concessional loans with interest subsidized by the Chinese government; government-supported joint-ventures and equity stakes in productive projects; grants, primarily for countries suffering from economic difficulties or crises (Hu 2005).

2006 marked the fiftieth anniversary of the inauguration of diplomatic relations between China and African countries. This was a historic year for China-Africa relations in terms of political achievements. In January 2006, China adopted its *Africa Policy* by which 'the Chinese government wishes to present to the world the objectives of China's policy towards Africa and the measures to achieve them [thus] bringing the mutually beneficial cooperation to a new stage' (Ministry of Foreign Affairs of the People's Republic of China 2006). The policy outlines the principles that guide China's African engagements and details the different areas for cooperation.

In November 2006, China hosted the third FOCAC summit meeting. This high-level meeting marked the adoption of a declaration which proclaimed 'the establishment of a new type of strategic partnership between China and Africa featuring political equality and mutual trust, economic win-win cooperation and cultural exchanges'. An Action Plan for 2007–2009 was adopted which included measures to be taken by the two sides. China, in President Hu Jintao's opening speech, made a number of pledges reiterated in the Action Plan (Hu 2006).

The 2006 FOCAC summit was a manifestation of the increased cooperation between China and Africa. Chinese President Hu and Premier Wen have also, in recent years, made visits to Africa signing mutually beneficial deals where China gains access to raw materials against investments in infrastructure and other types of economic assistance. The framework for China's aid today still closely reflects these policy shifts.

Estimates of Chinese Aid to Africa

China's development-oriented activities in Africa are attracting more and more attention. Especially in recent years, China has bolstered its diplomatic presence and garnered international goodwill through its financing of infrastructure and natural resource development projects, assistance in the development of such projects and provision of large sources of economic investments in Africa.

However, with the amounts of China's African aid progressively increasing, many in the West, including European countries, began complaining about the lack of data transparency and urged the Chinese government to publicize more information concerning its distribution of aid. Yet, of late, it has become apparent that China's lack of transparency on aid distribution is slowly changing. For instance, in 2006 Premier Wen Jiabao provided, for the first time, a figure in a statement in which he stated that China – from 1949 to present – has spent RMB44.4 billion (approximately US$5.6 billion) assisting African countries (Davies 2007: 47). This was viewed as a major improvement by some experts, whilst others questioned the validity of the figures.

A Big Gap between Figures

It is a fact that there exists a big gap between the official Chinese aid figures and the foreign estimates as they have, to large extent, different understandings of development aid. Under the aegis of the Organization for Economic Co-operation and Development (OECD), there is a Development Assistance Committee (DAC) which is tasked to define 'official development assistance (ODA)' in a manner that would allow for reliable international comparison (Riddell 2007: 17–21).

According to the definition provided by the DAC, ODA would be defined as funds and technical assistance given on strictly limited concessional terms with a grant element of at least 25 percent, provided by official agencies which have a clear development or anti-poverty purpose in developing countries that fall below a threshold income level.

China has no clear criteria for how aid is calculated, or at least no public criteria. The Chinese government is currently looking into what could be defined as aid. Chinese scholars provide the following explanation that aid is loosely defined and carried out within the framework of South-South cooperation, meaning that it is only one part of the picture concerning China's developmental agenda overseas (Davies 2007: 51).

Many forms of Chinese foreign assistance share only a few characteristics with traditional development assistance as provided by major aid donors and have often been overlooked in the literature on global foreign aid. Although they do not often fit into the OECD's narrow definition of development assistance, many of China's economic activities in developing countries are supported by the Chinese government and provides benefits to recipient countries. Furthermore, many Chinese economic investments abroad can be counted as aid rather than foreign direct investment

(FDI) because they are secured by official bilateral agreements, do not impose real financial risks upon the Chinese companies involved, or do not result in Chinese ownership of foreign assets (Lum et al. 2009).

In 2007, global net ODA provided for Africa amounted to US$38.7 billion, representing 37 percent of total aid (Africaneconomicoutlook.org 2010). Chinese aid flows were equal to about 20 percent of the value of China's trade flows in the early 1990s. That ratio declined to 3–4 percent in 2004–2005, even though China had stepped up its ODA to Africa since the first FOCAC summit, which was held in 2000. Indeed, in dollar terms, annual ODA flows from China to Africa increased from about US$310 million in 1989–1992 to an estimated US$1–1.5 billion in 2004–2005 (Africaneconomicoutlook.org 2010). However, according to multiple reports found in different IMF quarterly magazines,[2] there are major difficulties in estimating Chinese aid disbursements because of a lack of official time series and problems in valuing Chinese technical assistance and in-kind aid. Moreover, the IMF reported that incomplete data complicates any comparison to the terms on which China provides debt relief to the terms incorporated into the Heavily Indebted Poor Countries Initiative (HIPC) (OECD 2009).

However, it is interesting to note that an estimate of the percentage of China's ODA in relation to its Gross National Income (GNI) in 2005 – based on figures recently provided by Wang (2007) – demonstrates that China spends 0.65 percent of its GNI on ODA. This is much more than many European countries and the US.

Brautigam's research shows that the Chinese aggregate budget figures for external assistance expenditures are published annually in the *China Statistical Yearbook*. Yet the Chinese do not use the same criteria as the OECD. For example, the Chinese have used its foreign investment to support joint-ventures between Chinese firms and firms located in developing countries. China also includes military aid in its expenditures for general foreign aid. These additional figures would probably not qualify as ODA in terms of the OECD's definition (Brautigam 2009: 166).

China's Total African Aid

How much of this aid went to Africa? Brautigam's research also provided forceful findings on this. She divided Chinese aid into three areas: the Ministry of Finance's external assistance expenditure, China Export-Import (EXIM) Bank's concessional loans and debt relief. Between 1986 and 1995, annual reviews of China's engagement with Africa – prepared by Chinese officials – reported a varying percentage of Chinese aid to Africa, from a low of 37 percent to a high of 75 percent, with no clear trend (Brautigam 2009: 169).

In 2003, the Chinese Minister of Foreign Affairs, Li Zhaoxing, stated that the provision of development aid to Africa, between 2000 and 2003, absorbed an average

---

2   For more information, see http://www.imf.org/external/pubs/ft/fandd/2010/06/index. htm.

of 44 percent of China's total aid distribution (Li 2003). Chinese officials told Brautigam that less than a third of China's aid is now allocated to Africa and that China's total 2006 distribution of development aid amounted to US$300 million. A 30 percent increase would raise the Ministry of Finance's official foreign assistance expenditures, for 2006, to approximately US$309 million. 50 percent of China EXIM Bank's concessional loans go to Africa. Furthermore, it is essential to recall that China cancelled US$3 billion in debt for Africa, between 2001 and 2008 (Brautigam 2009: 169).

Indeed, there are some other estimates which deserve to be mentioned. Jerker Hellström's report, released in May 2009, argued that China has strategically aligned its ODA with its outward FDI policy to support Chinese enterprises investing in Africa. In the meantime, China's ODA is believed to represent more than twice that of China's FDI flows to the continent and this has also increased in conjunction with China's trade relations on the continent (Hellström 2009). With regard to Chinese FDI, available data is insecure and in parts contradictory. The World Bank estimates that cumulated Chinese investment in Africa has exceeded the US$1 billion level in 2006. According to the Chinese government, Chinese FDI in Africa amounted to US$6.27 billion in 2005 (Schmitt 2007).

China has established approximately 800 aid projects, covering nearly every African country. Between 1960 and 1989, China provided an estimated cumulative sum of US$4.7 billion worth of aid to Africa, accounting for nearly a half of China's total aid flows worldwide for this period (Hellström 2009: 16). By May 2006, China's contribution to assistance in Africa had reached US$5.7 billion. In other words, this equated to more than twice the amount of its outward FDI in Africa, representing a total of US$2.6 billion by the end of 2006 (OECD 2008). In 2006 alone, China's ODA and debt relief to Africa combined equalled to US$2.3 billion, according to another estimate (Wang 2007).

At the FOCAC summit, in November 2006, President Hu Jintao announced eight policy measures to boost cooperation with Africa, including a pledge to double aid to Africa by 2009 and to set up a US$5 billion development fund (van der Merwe 2008). In May 2007, China hosted the annual African Development Bank conference in Shanghai, where it made an additional US$20 billion pledge for infrastructure development in Africa over the next three years (Gill et al. 2007).

Chinese Aid to Africa: No Threat to the EU

Regarding China's aid to Africa, it is obvious that its donations are rising, its ranges are widening and its modalities are diversifying. China's assistance to Africa is aimed at helping African countries develop their economies and improve their standards of living on the principles of mutual benefit and win-win cooperation. Some Europeans, however, have different views. They see Chinese activities in Africa as 'neo-colonialist'. For example, *The Guardian* warned that Chinese aid to Africa may do more harm than good (*The Guardian* 2007). Inexplicably, some Members of the European Parliament also threw stones at China, arguing that China's engagement in Africa 'seems confined to resource-rich countries, bypassing a large number of other African nations' (Gomes 2009).

These opinions already led to certain erroneous or partly erroneous conclusions which have pushed many Europeans to believe that China's involvements in Africa represent a challenge to the EU. Why is this so? The reasons may be numerous, but the following three explanations help provide a better understanding of the foundations behind European fears.

Aid for Resources

In her *Report on China's Policy and its Effects on Africa*, the Member of European Parliament, Ana Maria Gomes (2009) stated:

> What are the strategic drivers for China's 'go out' policy in Africa? First and foremost, oil. Some 30 percent of China's crude oil imports now come from Africa and oil accounts for 50 percent of Africa's exports to China. China is also looking for other natural resources (uranium, copper, cobalt, ore and timber).

These remarks, to some extent, typically represent European criticisms of China's African aid policy. It is undeniable that China's activities in Africa are more and more oriented towards natural resources, but it is unfair that only on this basis do many draw the conclusion that China's aid is strictly focused on resources. In this case, certain facts have been neglected. Firstly, China provides aid to every single country in Sub-Saharan Africa. Even relatively wealthy South Africa and Mauritius are recipients of China's aid (Gomes 2009: 9).

For example, Mali is not a resource-rich country, however, China dispatched medical teams and provided treatment for local people free of charge during a lengthy time span. In 2009, China paid for all the expenses in the building of the Number Two Bridge across the Niger River. The local inhabitants happily claimed, 'This is our bridge built by the Chinese'. Amadou Toumany Toure, the Malian President, then exclaimed that he 'felt embarrassed when [he] met your President Hu Jintao, because he gave us everything we wanted, but we had nothing to give him back'.[3]

Secondly, in the past three decades, the Chinese economy has boomed at an annual growth rate of over eight percent, its social development has vastly improved and hundreds of millions of Chinese have been alleviated from poverty. Although these are China's achievements, they also incarnate China's contributions to world development because China features as one integral part, amongst others, of the world in this global age. For instance, *the Voice of America* reported that Chinese automakers sold 13.6 million units in 2009, an increase of 46 percent over the

---

3   Quote taken from the author's meeting with the Malian President.

previous year. In the US, industry figures highlight that only 10.4 million vehicles were sold last year, a 21 percent drop in comparison to 2008. Surging sales have helped China overtake the US as the world's largest automobile market (Voice of America 2010). As the largest car producer and consumer in the world, it is natural that China needs more oil.

Thirdly, European countries are traditional donors due to their colonial connections. However, after the Cold War, European countries withdrew from Africa, for a time, because Africa's strategic significance weakened which permitted China's entry. For example, in Angola, in 1975, civil war broke out which ended in 2002. During this ever-lasting 30 year conflict, Western companies, including European ones, gradually left the Angolan market. Under such circumstances, China stepped up and provided loans to assist the Angolan government in rebuilding the country only if Angola was willing to accept the terms of this concessional loan. Thereafter, this transaction was entitled the 'Angola Model', which was widely introduced into China's other African aid practices.

Loans Creating a New Debt Crisis

In recent years, China has accelerated its loans transfer, such as zero-interest and concessional loans, to African countries, which has worried many in Europe because of the possibility of inducing new debt upon Africa. Headlines such as 'China loans create "new wave of Africa debt"', and 'EU will not cover Chinese loans to Africa', began to appear in the newspapers (Beattie, Callan 2006, Almeida 2007). During Portugal's EU Presidency, in 2007, the Secretary of State for Foreign Affairs, João Cravinho stated that, 'Europe has tried to end Africa's debt in the past and will not do the same with Chinese debt. [...] We hope China takes that into account' (The Ministry of Foreign Affairs of the People's Republic of China 2007). Is it possible for Chinese loans to create a new debt crisis in Africa?

The answer remains highly unlikely. Firstly, China is still a developing country. Although its loans to Africa are rising, China is still an aid recipient. This dual identity, of being simultaneously a donor and a recipient, limits China's capacity to issue loans to Africa. The criticism surrounding China and African debt sustainability indicate that Europeans still do not understand the volume of Chinese assistance – it is still relatively small. For large construction projects, stadiums, conference centres, hospitals, schools and roads, China provides grant assistance or interest-free loans which will not increase the burden on African countries. Therefore, whether a new debt crisis takes place in Africa will not depend so much on China.

Secondly, the evidence indicating the rise of new debt in Africa's poorest countries is not robust and neither is the causal link between the increase of loans emanating from all non-traditional lenders (Russia, India, Korea and Brazil, for example) and the increase in new debt burdens for Africa's poorest countries (Reisen, Ndoye 2008). An OECD study highlighted that the available information suggests that Chinese loans are well matched to the country's ability to repay.

In Angola and Sudan, Chinese investment and the higher prices stimulated by China's demand for raw materials has considerably improved debt-distress indicators in both countries (Davies 2007: 91–2).

Thirdly, China does not expect repayment from African countries – if the accord constitutes a government to government loan or if governments are facing difficulties with their repayments. This standpoint was confirmed by David Dollar, the World Bank Country Director for China, who outlined that China has a long history of debt forgiveness: 'a historian would say that every time a country could not pay back, a loan would be forgiven' (Davies 2007: 92). China has provided debt relief to 31 African countries to the amount of RMB10.9 billion (approximately US$1.38 billion) and has made further pledges of cancelling interest free and low interest governmental loans, owed by HIPCs and the Least Developed Countries (LDCs) in Africa (Davies 2007: 92).

'No Political Strings Attached Policy' – Harming the Environment and Human Rights

China's *Africa Policy*, released in 2006, pointed out that China will 'respect African countries' independent choice of the road of development' and provide assistance 'with no political strings attached' (The Ministry of Foreign Affairs of the People's Republic of China 2006), which gave birth to the so-called 'no political strings attached policy'. In substance, the 'no political strings attached policy' is synonymous with non-interference, one of the Five Principles of Coexistence, which constitutes one of the fundamental policy pillars of China's development assistance.

However, from the EU's perspective, this 'no political strings attached policy' may be the most controversial and fiercely criticized policy. Some advocated that this policy supported dictators and worsened human rights situations. Some suggested that this policy damaged the recipient country's environmental surroundings. In 2006, the European Investment Bank (EIB) President, Philippe Maystadt, complained to the *Financial Times* that Chinese banks had snatched projects from under its nose by offering weaker conditions in terms of social and environmental standards. He said, rather bluntly, 'they don't bother about social or human rights conditions' (Beattie, Parker 2006).

Certain Europeans conceive such misperceptions on the 'no political strings attached policy', or non-interference policy, primarily because they do not have a deep and thorough comprehension of Chinese foreign policy culture and history. Firstly, China once suffered from Western interference when it was semi-colonized. Owing to this historical experience, China designed the non-interference policy after the founding of PRC in 1949. African countries shared similar sufferings with regards to external interference, therefore China is careful not to tread over African sovereignty in the name of development aid.

Secondly, sovereignty is the last frontier of dignity, for which China and African countries have long fought to preserve. However, European countries often ignore this fact. When dealing with African countries, from time to time, China pays more attention to mutual respect and dignity – a feature that African countries value highly. Every time an African leader visits China, regardless of the country of origin, China receives the leader with warm praise and with the necessary protocol. Even for leaders of small nations visiting China, the overall assessment is that China will never attempt to belittle its African partners (Ding 2008).

Thirdly, China's own development experience is another factor which helps explain China's policy. China's ability to develop according to its own national context has been the key to its economic success. China has also managed to lift hundreds of millions of people out of poverty, a fact which is highly praised by the international community. Similarly, China fully respects African countries, and '[is] fully confident that Africans have the ability to develop their own economy' (Davies 2007: 78).

China's 'no political strings attached policy' does not necessarily imply that China will remain inert in the face of Africa's environmental and human rights issues. Domestically, China is making efforts to prioritize environmental issues on its agenda, which would inevitably benefit Africa, via the flows of Chinese development aid. For example, because of the backlashes – such as those in Zambia, where protests have been held against poor working conditions, mining explosions and accidents on Chinese project sites – the Chinese authority were encouraged to implement urgent improvements. The government has also asked companies to take social and environmental responsibility, a change from the original 'Go-Global' strategy, when companies were encouraged to invest abroad and little attention was paid to such responsibilities. The FOCAC Action Plan (2007–2009) includes a commitment to prioritize the protection of the local environment and to promote sustainable social and economic development in Africa. China's State Council has issued nine principles for enterprises seeking to invest overseas, which stipulate that companies must abide by local laws and bid for contracts on the basis of transparency and equality, protect the labour rights of local employees and the environment (Zhou 2006). In 2007, China EXIM Bank, which finances most of the grand-scale Chinese infrastructure projects in Africa, made public its environmental policy as adopted in 2004. Although it includes strict principles, these are not elaborated in much detail (Davies 2007: 81–3).

Concerning China's engagements in Sudan and Zimbabwe, many Europeans have ignored the adaptations and changes applied in China's approach. In early 2007, Hu Jintao sent a strong message to Sudanese president Omar al-Bashir, urging him to accept the UN proposal to send a hybrid UN-African Union peacekeeping force to Darfur. Meanwhile, China appointed a special envoy to Sudan. All these activities were welcomed by the international community. 'Beijing is shifting in Sudan from being an obvious part of the problem to a significant part of the solution' (Evans, Steinberg 2007). As to Zimbabwe, a change is also apparent. China has indicated that it will follow the lead of African organizations such as the

African Union or the Southern African Development Community on Zimbabwe (Brautigam 2009: 291).

Both the EU and China are outsiders in terms of African political affairs. How should the Chinese policy be evaluated? The final say should belong to Africans. Just like the Ethiopian Prime Minister Meles Zenawi once said, 'I think it would be wrong for people in the West to assume that they can buy good governance in Africa. Good governance can only come from inside; it cannot be imposed from outside' (Wallis 2007).

Conclusion

It is clear that both the EU and China have the goodwill to cooperate with African countries in promoting social, cultural, political and economic development in Africa. From this viewpoint, China and the EU have a common goal. In order to reach this goal, both must constantly explore the means – such as holding summits, or high-level meetings with African countries, or releasing policy papers to outline the EU and China's principles of engagement with Africa. Henceforth, the EU and China should continue such efforts.

Both the EU and China should also view African countries as equal partners. From this perspective, China has some positive experiences from which the EU can learn from. For the last 50 years, China has pursued the development of diplomatic relations with African countries under the guidance of the 'Five Principles of Peaceful Coexistence'. When providing aid, China sticks to the 'no political strings attached policy', that places China and African countries equally as 'brothers', or 'partners', instead of the unequal 'donor-recipient' relationship.

The EU's aid policy toward Africa has been through different periods and experiences. The *Rome Treaty* (1957) mainly prescribed that the EU and Africa unfold mutually beneficial cooperation on the basis of trade, which approximately equates to China's current cooperation with Africa. Only in 1995, almost 40 years later, did the EU begin applying political conditions to the aid that it provided to Africa, when the Fourth Lomé Convention was under re-evaluation by the European Commission (Jiang 1995). This experience demonstrates that the EU's African aid policy has also witnessed changes and reform. Therefore, it is safe to assume that China's Africa policy will also be updated and upgraded incrementally.

Finally, Chinese African aid does not represent a challenge to the EU. The understandings of the allocation of development aid to Africa should therefore be pluralized and diversified.

Bibliography

Book References

Brautigam, D. 2008. *China's African Aid: Transatlantic Challenges*. Washington, D.C.: German Marshall Fund.
Brautigam, D. 2009. *The Dragon's Gift: the Real Story of China in Africa*. Oxford and New York: Oxford University Press.
Davies, P. 2007. *China and the End of Poverty in Africa – Towards Mutual Benefit?*. Sundbyberg: Diakonia.
Riddell, R. 2007. *Does Foreign Aid Really Work?*. Oxford: Oxford University Press.

Journal Articles

Gill, B., Huang, C.H. and Morrison, S.J. 2007. Assessing China's growing influence in Africa. *China Security*, 3(3), 3–21.
Hu, N. 2008. Chances for Sino-American accommodation after the founding of the PRC. *US-China Foreign Language*, 6(7), 1–4.
Lum, T., Fischer, H., Gomez-Granger, J. and Leland, A. 2009. China's foreign aid activities in Africa, Latin America, and Southeast Asia. *US Congressional Research Service Report R40361*, 1–25.
Morino, T. 1991. China-Japan trade and investment relations. *Proceedings of the Academy of Political Science*, 38(2), 87–94.
Park, J.H. 1993. Impact of China's open-door policy on Pacific Rim trade and investment. *Business Economics*, October Issue.
Reisen, H. and Ndoye, S. 2008. Prudent versus imprudent lending to Africa: from debt relief to emerging lenders. *OECD Development Centre Discussion Paper*, 268, 1–56.
Wang, J.Y. 2009. What drives China's growing role in Africa?. *IMF Working Paper – African Department*, 1–30.

Website

African Economic Outlook. 2010. *Growth of aid to Africa*. [Outline]. Available at: http://www.africaneconomicoutlook.org/en/outlook/external-financial-flows-to-africa/official-development-assistance-oda/growth-of-aid-to-africa/ [accessed: 10 January 2010].
Ding, X.W. 2008. *The secrets of Chinese African policy: giving Africans dignity*. [Online]. Available at: http://finance.sina.com.cn/economist/jingjiguancha/20080131/13244477872.shtml [accessed: 2 February 2010].
Gomes, A.M. 2009. *Report on China's policy and its effects on Africa*. [Online]. Available at: http://www.europarl.europa.eu/meetdocs/2004_2009/documents/pr/697/697015/697015en.pdf [accessed: 30 January 2010].

Hellström, J. 2009. *China's emerging role in Africa*. [Online]. Available at: http://www.foi.se/upload/Kinaiafrika.pdfwww.foi.se/asia [accessed: 2 January 2010].

Herman, H. and Davies, M.J. 2009. *The EU and China: prospects for partnerships in democracy building in Africa*. [Online]. Available at: http://www.idea.int/resources/analysis/upload/Herman_paper4.pdf [accessed: 2 January 2010].

Hu, J. 2006. *Full text of President Hu's speech at the China-Africa summit*. [Online]. Available at: http://www.dawodu.com/china1.htm [accessed: 5 January 2010].

Jiang, J.F. 1995. *European Union's external aid to Africa*. [Online]. Available at: http://idof.3mt.com.cn/article/frame.aspx?turl=http%3a//ido.3mt.com.cn/pc/200512/20051212291531.shtm&rurl=&title=%u6B27%u76DF%u5BF9%u975E%u6D32%u7684%u63F4%u52A9%u7B80%u8FF0%20---%20ido.3mt.com.cn [accessed: 18 January 2010].

Ministry of Foreign Affairs of the People's Republic of China. 2000. *Premier Zhou Enlai's three tours of Asian and African countries*. [Online]. Available at: http://www.fmprc.gov.cn/eng/ziliao/3602/3604/t18001.htm [accessed: 5 January 2010].

OECD. 2008. *China 2008*. [Online]. Available at: http://www.oecdchina.org/OECDpdf/China_flyer_cn_mod02.pdf [accessed: 25 January 2010].

People's Daily. 2010. *Five principles of peaceful coexistence*. [Online]. Available at: http://english.people.com.cn/92824/92845/92870/6441502.html [accessed: 2 January 2010].

Schmitt, G. 2007. *Is Africa turning East? China's new engagement in Africa and its implications on the macro-economic situation, the business environment and the private sector in Africa*. [Online]. Available at: http://www.businessenvironment.org/dyn/be/docs/160/Schmitt.pdf [accessed: 2 January 2010].

The Voice of America. 2010. *China overtakes US as world's biggest auto market*. [Online]. Available at: http://www1.voanews.com/english/news/economy-and-business/China-Overtakes-US-as-Worlds-Biggest-Auto-Market-81181722.html [accessed: 11 January 2010].

Van der Merwe, S. 2008. *Reflections on 10 years of bilateral relations between South Africa and the PRC*. [Online]. Available at: http://www.dfa.gov.za/docs/speeches/2008/merwe0821.html [accessed: 28 January 2010].

Wissenbach, U. 2009. *The EU's response to China's Africa safari: can triangulation match needs?*. [Online]. Available at: http://asiandrivers.open.ac.uk/the%20EUs%20response%20to%20china%20africa%20safari.pdf [accessed: 2 January 2010].

Newspapers

2008. Special report: China's quest for resources. *The Economist*, 15–21 March, 10.

Almeida, H. 2007. EU will not cover Chinese loans to Africa. *Reuters*, 30 July.

Beattie, A. and Callan, E. 2006. China loans create 'new wave of African debt'. *Financial Times*, 7 December.

Beattie, A. and Parker, G. 2006. EIB accuses Chinese banks of undercutting Africa loans. *Financial Times*, 29 November.

Evans, G. and Steinberg, D. 2007. Signs of transition. *The Guardian*, 11 June.

McGreal, C. 2007. Chinese aid to Africa may do more harm than good. *The Guardian*, 8 February.

Wallis, W. 2007. Ethiopia looks East to slip reins of Western orthodoxy. *Financial Times*, 6 February.

Zhou, S. 2006. China as Africa's 'Angel in White'. *Asian Times*, 3 November.

Command Papers

China's Africa Policy. 2006. Beijing: Ministry of Foreign Affairs of the People's Republic of China.

Development Co-operation Report 2009. 2009. Paris: Organization of Economic Cooperation and Development.

Hu, J. 2005. *Promote Universal Development to Achieve Common Prosperity*. New York: High-Level Meeting on Financing for Development at the Sixtieth Session of the United Nations.

Li, Z. 2003. *Report by H.E. Mr Li Zhaoxing, Minister of Foreign Affairs of the People's Republic of China, to the Second Ministerial Conference of the China-Africa Cooperation Forum*. Beijing: Ministry of Foreign Affairs of the People's Republic of China.

PART V

PART V

Chapter 11
The EU and China: Friends or Foes for Sustainable Regional Infrastructure Development and Resource Extraction in Africa?

Eric Kehinde Ogunleye[1]

> We should begin on the basis of consensus to establish, in a gradual, but progressive way, a cooperative three way agenda with both our African and Chinese partners in a number of areas where synergies and mutual benefits can be maximized (European Commission 2008).

Introduction

While Europe is an established political and economic player in Africa, China is a recent major economic force in the continent. China's activities in Africa range from economic and technical cooperation (ETC), trade, investment and infrastructure development to resource development and extraction. Physical infrastructure development remains the most important engagement through which Chinese presence could be felt in Africa. By 2006, Chinese infrastructure finance had reached US$7 billion (Foster et al. 2008). These involve wide-ranging projects that include roads, railways, bridges, airports, power, water and Information and Communication Technologies (ICT). Another important area where Chinese presence is being largely felt in Africa is in the natural resource sector. Engagements in this sector take the form of mineral and oil resource development and extraction. For instance, the World Bank-Public Private Infrastructure Advisory Facility (PPIAF) Database revealed that confirmed Chinese investment in African resource activities amount to over US$10.5 billion between 2001 and 2007. Africa is becoming increasingly important in satisfying the Chinese need for mineral and energy security, with exports to China rising from US$3 billion in 2001 to US$22 billion in 2006.

Several benefits are discernible from these engagements. They include: filling a large existing gap in African infrastructure development; improving the

---

1   The findings, interpretations and conclusions expressed in this chapter are entirely personal to the author and do not necessarily represent the views of the African Centre for Economic Transformation, its President, management and funders.

investment climate and easing the process of doing business; providing cheap and effective finance for African countries, especially those with dire need for post-war reconstruction; welfare gains in the form of job creation; creation of additional fiscal revenue, improving debt sustainability and creating more fiscal space for net mineral and oil exporting countries, thus relaxing traditional constraints on economic growth. On the flip side, however, are less desired challenges and risks emanating from these engagements. These include: poor environmental and working conditions; lack of transparent engagements in some countries; concerns by civil society and the international community about China's indifference to situations in countries with troubling records of transparency, with claims that they covertly collude with them in violating human rights; and possible aggravation of the Dutch disease and resource curse problems (ACET 2009).

There is a recent and ongoing debate on the expanding role of China in Africa. This debate is multidimensional, ranging from China's motive and strategy of engagements, sectors of engagements, human rights dimension of engagements, safety standards, adherence to labour laws and regulations, rapid resource depletion, nature and mode of infrastructure development. The list is long and keeps growing. While it is believed by some that these debates were initiated and fuelled by the West, because it is losing its grip on Africa to China, others believe that these views are valid and rooted in the experiences of China's engagements in the region. These debates have generated concern about the activities of both European countries and China in Africa. Despite these debates, it is noteworthy that African development has been identified as a key priority by both China and Europe in their current engagements in the continent. However, important questions remain: are European countries, on the one hand, and China, on the other, partners or competitors in Africa? Should they be friends or foes in their engagements in Africa? Is there room for cooperation, partnership and friendship, especially in infrastructure development and sustainable resource extraction in Africa?

This chapter answers in the affirmative and provides trilateral settings for cooperation, partnership and friendship between European Union (EU) member states, China and Africa from an African perspective, emphasizing that this is an important precondition for Africa to maximize the potential benefits presented by current European and Chinese engagements on the continent, while mitigating the risks and challenges posed by their activities in areas of infrastructure development and resource extraction. The findings in this chapter present very useful information for African policy-makers in developing national, subregional and regional strategies and policies in their engagements of EU member states and China, for maximum and sustained impact. Given the objectives of this chapter, the focus is on the potential trilateral areas of friendship and cooperation between the EU, China and African countries in regional infrastructure development and sustainable resource development and extraction. The chapter is organized in the following manner: the first section focuses on the sources of competition and conflict between EU member states and China in Africa; real and potential areas of friendship and cooperation between EU member states and China are articulated in the second section; the following part provides a role for African countries in the proposed relationship, and the final thoughts are laid out in the conclusion.

Sources of Competition and Conflict between the EU and China in Africa

One of the bases of Western fears and concerns are:

> the fact that everyone can clearly see through its [Western countries] inconsistencies, such as the colonial legacy which contradicts claims of democratization in Africa, its notable Cold War protection and support of corrupt dictators and, even worse, its stark failure to come up with any real economic success story in Africa, despite decades of policies devised by its technocrats (Gaye 2008).

While this position may not be true in its entirety, the notion here is that while European countries have been very active in Africa for a long time, the negative aspects of their colonial policies and legacies still linger in the minds of Africans. These include policies such as the style of governance employed in the colonies (divide and rule), ethnicity, infrastructure development policies which focused on linking resource extractive locations to the ports to ease exports, absence of substantial local capacity-building and direct and indirect support for violent change of government. This breeds mistrust and explains the opposition expressed by African countries in the face of the EU's free market policy approach during the 2007 EU-Africa summit in Lisbon. This source opines that Europe is trying to cover up their failures by painting China black in its African engagements and by criticizing its activities in the realm of infrastructure development and resource extraction on the continent. However, this need not be the case, nor should there be any comparisons between Europe's colonial history in Africa and current Chinese engagements in the continent.

Another source of conflict is the fact that the presence of the EU and China in Africa is motivated by the same need: energy supply security; political alliance; sustained market for manufactures; and their conviction that Africa is vital in realizing these goals. To illustrate with the case of oil and gas,[2] Europe consumed over 15 million barrels of oil per day (mbpd) in 2005, with a projected increase to 16 mbpd by 2020 and stagnation at this level thereafter. The region is currently the world's biggest importer of oil and gas with imports accounting for about 50 percent of its total oil requirements. Similarly, China became a net oil importer in 1993, consuming about 8 mbpd, and by 2030, estimates indicate that it will reach 16 mbpd. The country currently imports about 50 percent of its oil requirements with a projected rise to 80 percent by 2030 (Wong 2008). Similar trends are observed in oil and gas consumption with a respective growth of 1.5 percent and 5.5 percent

---

2   This is also the case for minerals.

Table 11.1 **Relative share of Africa's construction market between European countries and China**

Contractor Nationality	Market Share (%)						Growth Rate between 2000 and 2005
	2000	2001	2002	2003	2004	2005	
Europe	51.75	46.61	44.45	46.49	49.91	49.33	-4.68
UK	1.69	2.53	1.37	1.77	2.84	5.04	198.22
Germany	9.81	8.93	6.46	6.38	5.01	6.12	-37.61
France	25.20	20.89	18.97	20.47	24.70	23.96	-5.74
Italy	5.12	6.69	7.53	6.95	9.06	7.02	37.11
Netherlands	1.70	0.18	1.30	0.89	0.01	0.05	-97.06
Others	8.01	7.38	8.82	10.02	8.29	7.14	-10.86
China	7.07	7.42	9.91	11.79	14.75	21.36	202.12
Total	58.2	54.03	54.36	58.28	64.66	70.69	-

Source: Adapted from Chen et al. (2007).

for Europe and China between 2005 and 2030. Given the ongoing tension in the Middle East, Africa increasingly remains the most important and viable source for satisfying the energy needs of both Europe and China. For instance, Africa's share in total Chinese oil imports has risen tremendously. The aggressive efforts of both Europe and China in securing sustainable energy supply from Africa have been a major source of competition and conflict between them. Little wonder, therefore, that the current engagements of these diverse actors in Africa have been christened the 'new scramble for Africa'.

China appears to be overtaking European firms in Africa, especially in the construction industry, by leveraging on its global competitive advantage in the infrastructure sector. This advantage emanates from China's high supply of low-cost skilled labour, hands-on management style, high degree of organization and access to relatively cheap capital (CCS 2007). China also possesses the largest construction market globally (Burke, Corkin 2006, Chen et al. 2007). Indeed, the recent large-scale entry into the African market has led to the loss of market-share of long-standing European, Brazilian and South African construction firms in the industry. Comparing the relative share of European and Chinese construction firms in Africa, it is clear that while Europe experienced a decline in share between 2000 and 2005, China's share increased by over 200 percent over the same period (see Table 11.1). The realization of this brews rivalry between them.

The recent global economic crisis has further aggravated the conflict between China and the West, with the country increasingly challenging the primacy of the dollar and euro, and using the opportunity to assert its global influence by providing the bulk of loans to developing countries. A recent example is that of Jamaica where its traditional allies, the United States (US) and the United Kingdom (UK) were so preoccupied with their own financial problems that they could not help the country. China came to the rescue by providing loan packages totalling US$138 million in March 2009, making China Jamaica's biggest financial partner (Cha 2009). This and several other overseas aid and assistance programmes provided to developing countries by China are leading to growing talk that a new 'Beijing Consensus' might soon replace the long-dominant 'Washington Consensus'. The 'Beijing Consensus', a complete abstraction from the *status quo*, is defined as the 'promotion of economies in which public ownership remains dominant; gradual reform is preferred to "shock therapy"; the country is open to foreign trade but remains largely self-reliant; and large-scale market reform takes place first, followed later by political and cultural change' (Cha 2009). China is pushing for a new world or Asian reserve currency to replace the dollar and euro, with strong support from several developing countries. Within five months, China signed US$95 billion in currency swap agreements with six countries that now hold part of their reserves in Renminbi (RMB). In addition, the People's Republic of China's (PRC) government now allows companies in Southern China to pay foreign contractors in RMB instead of dollars or euros (Cha 2009).

Areas for Cooperation

Two major economic growth and development challenges facing Sub-Saharan African (SSA) countries today are infrastructure deficiency and natural resource mismanagement resulting from unsustainable extraction and the less than equitable use of the accruing revenues, which ideally should be used to benefit and promote the well-being of all its citizens, especially at the grassroots level. Behind this failure is the interplay between political and economic factors at the national and international levels (Custers, Matthysen 2009). As highlighted earlier, the competition for African natural resources between EU member states and China, added to European fears of losing grounds in Africa – as they perceive themselves being gradually pushed out of their traditional markets by China – remain major sources of conflict between them.

However, this need not result in conflict. Rather, what African countries need from the engagements of these two important global players is cooperation and synergy, especially in infrastructure development and sustainable resource extraction. African countries should be active and not passive in the process of making sure, clear and known what they really want out of the engagements with these partners. They should set the stage by making specific demands from these partners of what they expect from them as players in the socio-economic landscape of their countries. Only Africans can decide what is best for them. Moreover, the competition between the EU and China should be seen as an avenue for African countries to negotiate better deals and outcomes from both parties. To achieve this, cooperation should be emphasized as opposed to conflict in solving the greatest development and transformation challenges faced in the region. Several areas of such cooperation could be identified. However, for our present purpose we will concentrate on just two, namely, infrastructure development and sustainable resource extraction.

Infrastructure Development

African countries urgently need both national and regional infrastructure development to help bridge the infrastructure gap, facilitate intra-regional trade, tourism, development and to promote improved welfare standards and poverty reduction. Such infrastructural needs are wide-ranging and include energy, roads, railways, bridges, buildings, ICT and water. In what follows, we provide descriptions of specific areas of cooperation and friendship between EU countries and China in ensuring not just national infrastructure development, but more importantly regional infrastructure development.

Energy   Improving energy, especially power supplies that will ensure reliable energy and electricity supply in Africa, is a very important area of cooperation between the EU, China and African countries. It is noteworthy that both the EU and China are individually progressing with their investments and funding of energy projects in the region. As mentioned earlier, the European Development Fund (EDF) prioritizes energy supply and China's infrastructure commitments in Africa are heavily concentrated on energy, as the sector receives the highest financing commitments. The EU has established an EU-African Infrastructure Trust Fund aimed at financing infrastructure projects in Africa with a high concentration devoted to energy. In fact, between 2007 and 2009, energy projects formed almost 70 percent of the Fund's total approved grant operations (EIB 2010). However, synergy between both partners will promote access, coverage and guarantee sustainability. Such cooperation will also ensure initiating projects that might be too expensive for them to undertake individually. A very important energy source that can be exploited to achieve this objective is gas flaring in Nigeria. Gas flaring is both an environmentally unfriendly practice and a waste of important energy and economic resource in a region that is energy-starved and desperately needs to boost its power output. In addition to its environmental and social costs, gas flaring was estimated to represent an annual economic loss of over US$2.5 billion in 2004 (FOEI 2004). China and EU member states are called upon to pool their resources, expertise and common interests in African infrastructure development together to initiate projects that will convert this large economic waste to energy and power generation for Western African countries. Similar potential energy sources in other African regions should be identified and similarly harnessed towards the same end. One proposal that can be undertaken to ensure the success of this cooperation is for each party (the EU and China) to specialize in specific aspects of the project. For instance, China could concentrate on building the structures given its global competitive advantage in construction, while the EU could focus on the power generation aspect given its wide experience in energy infrastructure development in the region. In this case, each member in this trilateral relationship would gain: China and EU would still be able to make the needed profits in this project, given their co-funding of the project and Africa would also gain, with improved power supply and access to infrastructure, that would have been impossible in the absence of financial and technical synergy between China and the EU.

Furthermore, African countries are very rich in renewable energy resources such as hydro and geothermal resources. It is interesting to note that China is currently active in the development of hydropower in Africa. The Merowe in Sudan, Lower Kafue Gorge in Zambia, Tekeze and Amerti-Neshe in Ethiopia, Mphanda Nkuwa in Mozambique, Mambila in Nigeria, Bui in Ghana and Imbolou in Congo represent just a few of the Chinese dam-funded projects in Africa. Similarly, some of the energy projects funded by EU member states include the Benin-Togo Power Rehabilitation, the construction of transmission lines between Zambia and Namibia, the construction of a power transmission line between Ethiopia and Kenya, the construction of transmission lines and high-voltage substations between the Côte d'Ivoire and Ghana, the construction of a hydroelectric plant on the Ruzizi River and the power interconnection from the Côte d'Ivoire to Guinea (EIB 2010). If further developed, the Akosombo dam in Ghana and, the Kanji and Shiroro dams in Nigeria have the potential to generate electricity for almost all of Western Africa.

In addition, there are several other dams and rivers in these and other African countries that could be developed to serve as additional sources of power generation on the continent. Attention should be focused on uncompleted power projects across Africa with the capacity for continent-wide power generation potential. Another useful area of synergy in energy generation is bio-mass and solar energy. There are several Chinese-made atomistic solar energy devices in use in African countries. Given the high solar energy potentials of African countries, cooperation between EU member states and China is solicited in developing this potential and converting it into impressive power generation facilities for the continent. To ensure success in this proposed synergy, it is recommended that there should be a division of labour between these partners. China should specialize in hydropower generations given its wide engagements in this activity and further help develop African solar power given its technical expertise, while the EU should focus on transmission and distribution given its extensive abilities in this area. Such a division of labour will help promote synergy and avoid conflicts of interest.

Roads, Railways, Bridges and Buildings   As highlighted earlier, China is a very strong force in building roads, bridges, stadiums, airports and public buildings in Africa (Foster et al. 2008). This is a great complement to the efforts of European countries that have a long history of providing assistance in building infrastructure for roads in Africa. However, one important observation about China's role in building roads, bridges and other buildings in Africa is quality. It appears that when the quality of Chinese projects is compared to those of European countries, there seem to be some quality differences. European construction firms such as Julius Berger are noted for the quality of their construction work.

There are two areas of cooperation here. Firsly, China should learn from European countries' policy on infrastructure development by insisting on quality construction production. The fact remains that Chinese construction firms are amply capable of delivering quality works as demonstrated by the quality of road infrastructure in China. Some Chinese construction firms do sometimes shift the blame on African countries with the claim that the quality of roads and buildings provided are based on the demands of the countries for low quality roads. Many African countries are said to prefer quantity over quality, but the same countries are often found engaging European construction firms to benefit from a higher quality of service. China should learn from the methods and techniques used by European construction firms, by increasing its cooperation with EU member states in this sector. Information sharing on strategies for managing the political economy of persuading government authorities on the importance of quality projects is an excellent area for cooperation between China and the EU. China should seek – and the EU should be willing to share – information on how to develop such a strategy.

Secondly, there is a need for coordinating the construction of roads, bridges and building efforts of both EU member states and China in Africa. While each of these development partners may pursue with their individualistic and country-specific building projects, they are encouraged to cooperate in undertaking regional and subregional road and railway development projects that would further enhance regional development and integration. Specifically, we are proposing cooperation in developing subregional ring roads and railways in Central, Eastern, Southern and Western Africa, with each of the ring roads linking up with the closest one in such a way that the whole continent is thus interlinked. This is a huge project that promises to be very expensive. However, financial and technical synergy between China and the EU will help deliver this. Such intra-regional roads and railways would greatly improve intra-African trade, tourism, integration and development. Given the EU's focus on regional infrastructure networks and China's own country-specific projects, one possible area for cooperation is to avoid conflict by maintaining this set-up. In this way, the country-specific and regional specialization will complement each other and promote rapid infrastructure development across the continent. In a similar vein, cooperation could be maintained by ensuring that the EU continues to focus on the construction of roads and bridges, while China concentrates on the construction of railways. Thus, through this division of labour, relative comparative advantage will be harnessed, creating complementarity that would promote rapid infrastructure development in Africa.

Another area for cooperation is for the EU member states to learn from China the ways and means of providing relatively cheap infrastructure development for African countries, without compromising quality. China is noted for providing relatively cheap infrastructure compared to the EU member states. It is imperative for the EU to cooperate with China in understanding how this is done. Such knowledge will help release additional scarce resources for increased infrastructure development across African countries. Again, cooperation on information sharing between the two actors is important. EU and Chinese construction firms in Africa should begin by pooling human and capital resources and expertise together to make cooperation possible. If there is both financial and technical synergy in executing projects, there would then be no hesitation on the part of both actors to share information.

Information and Communication Technology   An important area of cooperation is to establish regional ICT assembly plants and development centres in Africa. Cheap labour and a less inhibitive tax system were deemed to be the notable factors behind China's success in attracting Foreign Direct Investment (FDI) and cheap mass production for exports. All of these factors are also available in most African countries. It is recommended that the EU and China cooperate together in establishing ultra-modern ICT incubation centres, which will harness labour abundance and favourable tax policies in African countries. One possible argument against this proposed project is that African countries lack skilled labour for such large-scale technical production. This need not be a constraint. There are several similar privately-organized projects going on across several African countries. A typical example is the computer village in Lagos, Nigeria. In this village, there are African workers engaged in the most intricate ICT works that range from assembly to servicing. This suggests that the required basic skills are not only available but can be further cultivated given the ingenuity of Africans. All the major telecommunication firms in China and EU countries are called upon to pool financial and technical expertise together, in order to establish these institutions for the purpose of developing local capacities in Africa.

Water   It is interesting to note that the EU member states recognize the importance of water as a welfare-improving and poverty reducing tool in Africa. In contrast, the assessment of Chinese water infrastructure development in Africa reveals that the sector attracts the least investment and assistance despite its strategic importance for poverty reduction and meeting the Millennium Development Goals (MDGs) (ACET 2009). For instance, between 2001 and 2007, China committed a total of about US$320 million to water infrastructure development in Africa, representing a mere two percent of total infrastructure commitments (Foster et al. 2008). It appears that China is not so much interested in water projects in Africa, perhaps because this sector is not profitable. However, profit should not be the motive in this instance. Rather, the welfare effect of providing clean water for Africans should override any profit-making motive. Cooperation is required between the EU and China in developing water infrastructure in African countries. China should learn from the EU about adding social benefits to its profit-making motives. China is called upon to team up with the EU member states in developing clean water projects at local, national and regional levels. Expertise on the construction of water reservoirs remains China's strengths and this added-value could complement the EU's proficiency with regard to water technology.

Sustainable Resource Development and Extraction

Natural resource exploitation and energy or mineral security are at the core of the EU and China's engagements in Africa. While there are no direct concerns at stake in this respect, the way and manner they deal with this is very important for the future of African countries, whose present and future generations depend on these resources. The idea that China is aggressively seeking exclusive access to oil, gas and mineral supplies in Africa without consideration for the sustainability of these exhaustible resources, has become a cause for concern (ACET 2009). Africa may be sacrificing potentially higher future revenues from its natural resources at current lower rates, due to the bartering techniques employed by the Chinese when engaging its African partners. Thus, there are concerns that the acclaimed 'win-win' rhetoric in China's relationship with natural resource producing countries might not be mutually reinforcing given the wide belief that China is deriving greater benefits. Africa may be mortgaging its natural resources in exchange for cheap loans and other forms of assistance from China, thus jeopardizing long-term economic prosperity and development prospects (Rocha 2008). Within the present framework of resource exploitation, very little provisions are being made towards the future exhaustion of these resources. The real determinant of sustainable growth, namely consumption, is being given very little attention. This concern is prevalent in most net natural resource exporting African countries (Ampiah, Naidu 2008).

It is noteworthy that the EU has a well-defined sustainable development strategy for natural resource extraction in Africa. For instance, the EU's 2006 renewed *EU Sustainable Development Strategy* thus states:

> Sustainable development means that the needs of the present generation should be met without compromising the ability of future generations to meet their own needs. It is an overarching objective of the European Union set out in the Treaty, governing all the Union's policies and activities. It is about safeguarding the earth's capacity to support life in all its diversity and is based on the principles of democracy, gender equality, solidarity, the rule of law and respect for fundamental rights, including freedom and equal opportunities for all. It aims at the continuous improvement of the quality of life and well-being on earth for present and future generations (Council of the European Union 2006: 2).

While this is highly commendable, some European multinationals such as Shell and Agip are still guilty of prioritizing short-term revenues instead of prioritizing sustainable resource extraction in African countries. EU member states are also being accused of unacceptable practices with respect to natural resources in the Economic Partnership Agreement (EPA) negotiations, relegating them to the status of merchandise, rather than that of a public good that needs to be protected. This approach does not take into consideration the overall consequence of the lives and livelihoods of Africa's forest-dependent communities that are threatened and the risks posed by climate change, which can be mitigated by the presence of natural resources, especially forests (FOEI 2008). This following section provides perceived areas of cooperation between the EU and China in ensuring sustainable natural resource extraction in Africa in oil and gas, minerals and timber logging.

Mining (Oil, Gas and Minerals)   The terms of engagement of Chinese firms in oil and gas activities in most African countries are opaque with noticeable, widespread reluctance on the part of both the Chinese and African government officials to clarify the terms of engagement (CCS 2007). In most cases, the exact structure and value of most deals are undisclosed (Campos, Vines 2008). On the other hand, most EU oil processing multinationals are promoting transparency in the African oil and gas sector, by supporting global transparency initiatives such as the Extractive Industry Transparency Initiative (EITI), Equator Principles and the International Council on Mining and Metals (ICMM) Framework for sustainable development both at the global and national levels. Chinese oil and gas firms must show cooperation on this vital issue. The Chinese firms should learn and cooperate with EU multinationals in becoming a party to these transparency initiatives in the extractive industries. A possible explanation for the lack of transparency of Chinese firms in the African extractive industries is that China's state-owned extractive firms present in Africa are in the early formative stages toward becoming multinationals and are thus relatively unsophisticated in their strategies when entering African markets (Davies 2007). This is where China needs to learn from long-standing EU multinationals. Though not always faultless, they are more sophisticated in terms of transparency and corporate social responsibility toward their host communities.

Cooperation is also required between EU countries and China in improving the working conditions in the African mining sector. Chinese firms operating in the mining sectors are sometimes accused of poor working conditions and in the laxity of their safety rules. For instance, there were sporadic mining accidents in Chambishi and Kabwe (in Zambia) and Equatorial Guinea, all blamed on lax safety and poor working conditions (Baah, Jauch 2009). Again, EU multinationals are relatively more developed than their Chinese counterparts in applying international best practices in safety rules and working conditions, which include compliance with international mining and environmental standards. There is a need for knowledge sharing, for improving working conditions and compliance with internationally accepted best practices concerning environmental standards.

The willingness of Chinese firms to take risks in developing the African mining sectors is commendable. Such actions are noticeable in countries like Equatorial Guinea, Gabon, Sudan and Angola where China is engaging in offshore and deepwater oil and gas investment (ACET 2009). These investments have improved the economic prospects of existing net oil and minerals exporters, while increasing the potentials of prospective net resource exporting African countries. In contrast, EU firms appear to be risk averse. Unlike China, that is making new inroads into the natural resource sector in Africa, European firms appear to be complacent with their established areas of operation, without much emphasis on expanding to potential resource abundant African countries. This is a good platform for EU firms to cooperate with and to learn from Chinese firms. While immediate profit-making motive is a major driver of most investments, EU investors are encouraged to also consider the long-term sustainable development of natural resource potentials in African countries that have yet to develop, especially in countries that have not yet attained the status of net exporters of such resources. For projects that may seem extremely risky and expensive, synergy through joint-ventures should be formed between EU and Chinese investors, in order to help bring such projects to life. This will help pool together the expertise and resources of both parties for the ultimate benefit of African countries.

More importantly, there is a need for cooperation between EU countries and China in guaranteeing sustainability of resource extraction in African countries for the benefit of both the current and future generations of Africans. To this end, trilateral cooperation is required among EU member states, China and African countries in establishing an Oil and Minerals Sustainability Fund that will help cushion the shocks from market price volatility and cater for the needs of both the present and future generations of Africans, who jointly own the resources. Issues of equitable distribution of the revenues from resource extraction for poverty reduction and for the general welfare of all should be incorporated into the use of the Fund. Transparent and accountable management of the natural resource revenues should become the benchmark for the terms of engagements in all natural resource transactions. A percentage of this fund should be set aside for capacity-building in all the natural resource sectors of African countries, with a focus on professional training and retraining. In addition, wanton resource extractions that do not respect the long-term sustainability focus should be strongly discouraged. This implies that sustainability issues should be built into all natural resource extraction contracts in African countries, and applied to all European and Chinese firms.

The issues of health, safety, the environment and human rights are cross-cutting and very important in relation to investment and development assistance aimed at the promotion of sustainable resource development and extraction, or regional infrastructure development. Presently, these issues are not well addressed in China's *Africa Policy*. This presents another important area of cooperation. There is a contrast between Western European countries and the US, on the one hand, and China, on the other, when dealing with these issues. While Western countries have a long record of health, safety, environmental and human rights standards, China does not. China should learn from these countries. Ofodile (2009) provides a brief review of how China can integrate human rights into its Africa policy, by learning from the US' experience. European countries have a rich and close historical background in Africa, though they sometimes falter. China should be willing and ready to learn from their good examples. This will help improve the development impact of the Chinese presence in Africa and thus benefit African nations more generally. It has been acknowledged that China poses challenges for the existing development assistance regime, especially on standard-setting by both the private sector actors and multilateral institutions on the one hand (Woods 2008), and European countries – that have industry codes of conduct for their transnational companies that set the standards of engagement – on the other. While European countries are implored to further improve the application of these codes in their engagement in African countries, China should also learn from these codes so as to contribute, not just to the economic, but also to the social development of African countries.

The Role of Africa

A very pertinent question to ask at this juncture is what role African governments and policy-makers play in this scenario? What specific actions should African policy-makers take to help promote the proposed trilateral EU-Sino-African relationship? In what follows, we attempt to outline specific actions for African governments and policy-makers so as to make the best of this relationship.

African governments should establish an African counterpart for the China-Africa Development Fund that may be called the African-China Development Bank. The aim of this Fund is to help big, medium and small African enterprises cope with the competitive challenges emanating from Chinese firms making inroads into the African continent and to help promote African enterprises that are interested in investing in China. Such fund should be used to hone the skills and capacity of African investors and may be concentrated on the most problematic and challenging sectors. The premise behind this Fund is that without it, most African firms would lose their competitive edge to Chinese investors in Africa, given that most of these Chinese firms are state-owned and enjoy generous domestic government support. It is important to stress that while establishing the Fund, stiff institutional mechanisms should be put in place which would prevent the Fund from being hijacked, looted or embezzled. The institutional mechanism should be strengthened to ensure effective supervision, transparency and accountability. The African Union (AU) and the African Development Bank (AfDB) should design the modalities and assume the responsibilities for such a process.

African governments should also foster a continental or regional policy for engaging China. While it is true that African countries are not homogenous in terms of the nature of their needs or expectations of China, several common areas of interest exist across these countries. In addition, the smaller African countries are also limited in the extent to which they can negotiate alone with China in order to get the best out of their bilateral relationship. While a continental approach to engaging China could be complex to manage, a regional approach would be much more manageable and should be considered at the levels of the Economic Community Of Western African States (ECOWAS), the East African Community

(EAC) and the South African Development Community (SADC). The beauty of using such a subregional approach is that most economies in these groupings already have potential convergence across economic interests and variables. African countries should explore the areas of common interests such as regional infrastructure development, natural resource exploitation and development, technology transfer, labour regulations and environmental issues. Again, the AU and AfDB should champion the process for actualizing this.

Capacity development is also imperative for making African-Chinese engagements mutually beneficial. In this respect, African governments should seek Africans at home and in the Diaspora that possess Chinese language and negotiation skills to deal with the diverse facets of China's engagements in Africa. This will ensure that the current difficulties concerning the language barrier are overcome and thus ensure that the best is obtained from the sector- and activity-specific engagements. The recommendation here is that African governments should set up a technocratic group composed of experts in the domains of Chinese language and negotiation skills, Chinese culture and economic environment and, of course, African culture and economic environment, in order to expand the efforts of African governments in constructively engaging China. This group should be hosted either by the AU or AfDB and should be a reference point for all African governments in their dealings with China.

It is also imperative for African governments to develop their own home-grown development strategy where interactions with China can present a significant and homogenous added-value across the continent. This will abstract from the current trend where China largely takes the final decision of where and when to engage in Africa. China and other development partners should not be the ones driving and crafting development policies for the continent through their choice of engagement. Rather, African governments should take the driver's seat and not let others become the masters of its destiny. Thus, the current system of scholarship allocation, where China decides the attribution of scholarships to African students and in which discipline these scholarships are to be distributed, should be altered. African governments should have a development strategy that identifies, for instance, the professionals requirements needed in specific disciplines. This should provide the basis for engaging China with regards to scholarships, educational exchanges and funding.

Conclusion

Friendship and cooperation between EU member states, China and Africa are of utmost importance to all parties in the relationship (Davies 2008). Such cooperation should be wide ranging. Although this chapter was focused on infrastructure development and natural resource development and extraction, due to its limited scope and space, such trilateral cooperation should be cross-cutting. Other important areas of cooperation that demand attention include sustainable logging, aid disbursement, human rights and the implications of China's non-interference policy.

Engagements of both EU member states and China in Africa are aimed at one and the same ends: bolstering diplomatic presence; accumulating international goodwill; and ensuring supplies of energy and mineral resources. It is also interesting to note that both parties claim to be committed to the economic and social development of Africa. This can be best illustrated with China's pledge at the Forum on China-Africa Cooperation (FOCAC) summit in Egypt where China, among others, promised African countries US$10 billion worth of soft loans, US$1 billion in loans for small and medium-sized enterprises, more debt write-offs, 100 new clean energy projects and a gradual lowering of customs duties on 95 percent of imported products from African countries.[3] This is a great complement to the efforts of European countries in these areas. The fusion of the wide experiences of EU member states in such engagements and China's special development model, provides an excellent opportunity for the sustainable transformation of African economies. This provides room for synergy, complementarity and mutual win-win situations.

However, in doing so, there is a need for a very methodical and systematic approach. Firstly, African countries should not watch helplessly while their future is being determined. They need to play an active role in the process. African countries should realize the power they hold in this respect. In fact, the current competition between the EU and China in Africa should provide African countries with a higher bargaining power and greater opportunities to negotiate better terms of engagements. They should, therefore set the stage by first having a full grasp of what they *really* want out of the relationship with both partners. This chapter provides background information for African countries on the specific projects that require support from both the EU and China in order to guarantee African countries a veritable added-value in the development of the aforementioned projects. Secondly, trilateral cooperation should embrace all stakeholders, involving government, national and regional institutions and Non-Government Organizations (NGOs). This will guarantee that the interests of all stakeholders are catered for, while none is unduly sidelined. Thirdly, the activities of all parties should be well coordinated to ensure there is no duplication of efforts. Fourthly, there is a need for dedication and strong commitment from all parties involved to make the cooperation happen. Fifthly, EU member states should lead by example, by fulfilling their promises. This can be done through the self-assessment of the consistency of their policies and by sticking to their promises made to African countries, especially with respect to development aid commitments.

In effect, African countries suffer from their weak capacities in monitoring infrastructure projects and developing sustainable natural resource development and extraction policies. The EU and China should cooperate with African countries

3   For details, see http://bw.china-Embassy.org/eng/xwdt/t628555.htm.

in developing such capacities and strengthening existing ones. They should also be willing and ready to apply internationally acceptable standards in their respective operational sectors. It is interesting to note that the European Commission has already taken steps along this line with the launch of a Communication for setting up trilateral dialogue and cooperation between the EU, Africa and China, in October 2008. This provides an excellent platform for realizing the targets in ensuring regional infrastructure, and resource and extraction development in African countries, as mentioned in the quotation that commenced this chapter. The trilateral relationship should be gradual and incremental in scope. The starting point should be to build upon the bilateral relationship structures that exist between African and EU member states on the one hand, and Africa and China, on the other.

Bibliography

Book References

ACET. 2009. *Looking East: A Guide to Engaging China for Africa's Policymakers.* Accra: African Centre for Economic Transformation.
Baah, A.Y. and Jauch, H. 2009. *Chinese Investments in Africa: A Labour Perspective.* Windhoek: African Labour Research Network.
Burke, C. and Corkin, L. 2006. *China's Interest and Activity in Africa's Construction and Infrastructure Sectors.* South Africa: Centre for Chinese Studies, University of Stellenbosch.
CCS. 2007. *China's Engagements of Africa: Preliminary Scoping of African Case Studies, Angola, Ethiopia, Gabon, Uganda, South Africa, Zambia.* South Africa: Centre for Chinese Studies, University of Stellenbosch.
Custers, R. and Matthysen, K. 2009. *Africa's Natural Resources in a Global Context.* Antwerp: International Peace Information Service.
FOEI. 2004. *Gas Flaring in Nigeria.* Amsterdam: Friends of the Earth International.
FOEI. 2008. *Forests in a Changing Climate: Will Forests' Role in Regulating the Global Climate be Hindered by Climate Change?.* Amsterdam: Friends of the Earth International.
Wong, L. 2008. *The Impact of Asian National Oil Companies in Nigeria or 'Things Fall Apart'.* London: Chatham House.

Book Chapter

Rocha, J. 2008. China and African natural resources: development opportunity or deepening the resource curse?, in *New Impulses from the South: China's Engagement of Africa*, edited by H. Edinger et al. University of Stellenbosch: Centre for Chinese Studies, 54–65.

Journal Articles

Chen, C., Chiu, P.C., Orr, R.J. and Goldstein, A. 2007. An empirical analysis of Chinese construction firms' entry into Africa. *Chinese Research Institute of Construction Management International Symposium on Advancement of Construction Management and Real Estate*, Sydney, Australia, 8–13 August.

Ofodile, U. 2009. Trade, aid and human rights: China's Africa policy in perspective. *Journal of International Commercial Law and Technology*, 4(2), 86–99.

Websites

Cha, A.E. 2009. *China uses global crisis to assert its influence.* [Online]. Available at: http://www.washingtonpost.com/wp-dyn/content/article/2009/04/22/AR2009042203823.html [accessed: 18 September 2009].

Council of the European Union. 2006. *Renewed EU sustainable development strategy as adopted by the European Council on 15/16 June 2006.* [Online]. Available at: http://register.consilium.europa.eu/pdf/en/06/st10/st10917.en06.pdf [accessed: 17 November 2009].

Davies, M. 2007. *My China: China's PR battle in Africa.* [Online]. Available at: http://www.ccs.org.za/downloads/My%20China%20-%20Business%20Day%20-%203 1052007.pdf [accessed: 12 August 2009].

Davies, P. 2008. *Think piece on aid and development cooperation post-Accra and beyond – steps towards a development dialogue for the twenty-first century: the example of EU, China and Africa.* [Online]. Available at: http://www.eurodad.org/uploadedFiles/Whats_New/News/Post%20Accra%20China-Africa%20think%20piece%20January%202009.pdf [accessed: 17 November 2009].

Foster, V., Butterfield, W., Chen, C. and Pushak, N. 2008. *Building Bridges: China's growing role as infrastructure financier for Sub-Saharan Africa.* [Online]. Available at: http://siteresources.worldbank.org/INTAFRICA/Resources/Building_Bridges_Master_Version_wo-Embg_with_cover.pdf [accessed: 17 November 2009].

Newspaper

Gaye, A. 2008. China in Africa: why the West is worried. *New African*, March.

Command Paper

EU-Africa Infrastructure Trust Fund 2009 Annual Report. 2010. Luxembourg: European Investment Bank.

Chapter 12
The EU, China and Africa: Working for Functional Cooperation?

Uwe Wissenbach

Introduction

When African leaders flocked to Beijing in November 2006 to seal a strategic partnership with China, this came as a surprise to the European Union (EU), the United States (US) and other countries. They had failed to anticipate China's rapid emergence as a dynamic actor in Africa.[1] The summit came on the heels of alarm in the Western business community about Chinese oil for infrastructure deals in Africa. Not surprisingly, the initial reactions were a mixture of hostility, panic and self-righteousness. China found itself caught in a dilemma – it did not want to spoil its relations with its most important global partners, but it insisted that it had the better approach to Africa – equality, mutual respect and non-interference in domestic affairs. Much of the initial criticism proved to be lopsided, ill-informed and ill-intentioned, while China's often stereotyped and clumsy reaction to it, made things worse.

I argue that China's emergence in Africa is a 'normal' phenomenon, albeit with potentially deep and lasting impacts, consistent with China's emergence as a truly global economic power. In fact, China's influence in Africa grew with its Gross Domestic Product (GDP), trade and overseas investment figures, not as a deliberate strategy to diminish Western influence, which was what some African leaders tried to use the new partner for. Developing countries see China increasingly as a role model (but rarely as an attractive political system) and development partner, or – more soberly – as a key business partner presenting healthy competition for traditional Western partners.

The EU was the first global player who tried to come to terms with the 'new kid on the block' having realized that in many areas, China, the EU and

---

1 In fact China had presented its *Africa Policy* in January 2006 in a government White Paper ahead of the summit. That summit was linked to the third ministerial meeting of a cooperation process – the Forum on China Africa Cooperation (FOCAC) – that had been launched in 2000. It had not been widely noticed then. It also seems that the FOCAC initiative was taken by African politicians to seize the opportunities provided by a long-time ally developing into a global economic player. See Li (2008), Shelton, Paruk (2008), Bach (2008), Adebajo, Fakier (2009).

Africa's interests overlap and that the opportunities provided by China could complement its own Africa initiatives, whereas differences could be addressed through dialogue. Thus, the EU proposed a multilateral cooperative approach (European Commission 2008). However, the initial criticism had created distrust in China and in Africa and some African leaders, riding high on the commodity boom, were no longer hesitant about sharing their years' worth of frustration with the former colonial powers (Wade 2008) and fuelled an imagined strategic competition between China and the EU for Africa's riches. The old ghost of a scramble for Africa's resources was called back by African leaders themselves rather than by Western companies.[2] China's Africa safari revealed as much the divisions among Africans as the diversity of agendas of outside powers.

The current global crisis has spelt a reversal of fortunes for Africa after a decade of growth and hope (South Centre 2010).[3] The crisis is also demonstrating that China has a key role to play in the global economic recovery, re-balancing and governance (G20). It is likely that China will reinforce its recent quest for new markets for its surplus production and capital, to diversify away from the crisis-hit US and EU markets. China's engagement in Africa is therefore likely to expand and become more diversified. This may well lead to an acceptance that the initial criticism of China's mercantilism has been 'much ado about nothing'. Rather, China may have given Africa what it needs.

However, as it emerges, China has to deal with diverse opportunities and problems, demands from its African partners, difficult negotiations including with non-governmental actors and more multilateral cooperation, while Africa needs more intra-African cooperation to deal with external partners in a consistent manner. Each country needs to strategically use new opportunities and deal with new challenges. The traditional donors and trading partners of Africa have to make room, reform their own policies and come to an arrangement with Africans and Chinese about future policy (Grimm et al. 2009). Investors who believe, like China, in the growth potential of Africa will have to hone their strategies. China's relations with Africa have distinctive features, and specific and deep impacts, including in the manner with which traditional 'donors' interact with Africa. It is part of the challenge that emerging powers – above all China – present for the hitherto Western-dominated world economy and world politics. In the sections below, I attempt a current-day assessment of China-Africa myths in this context and then briefly assess the EU's reaction to it. In the conclusion, I make some proposals on how to come to terms with this new phenomenon through functional multilateralism.

---

2   Nigerian President Obasanjo's controversial Asian oil deals are a good example of that (Vines 2009).

3   Kaplinsky, Morris (2009) argue that the commodity super-cycle is likely to continue.

China's New Partnership with Africa – a Reality Check

China was largely conceived as a monolithic, strategic and powerful actor, while Africans were lumped together in the role of the victim (Cooper Ramos 2004). Emboldened by Western criticism of China, African leaders hoped to forge a political alliance with China to promote fairer globalization through enhanced South-South cooperation. Many saw China as a dynamic saviour and an alternative to the declining West (Gaye 2006, Wade 2008, le Pere 2007, Shelton 2007, Habib 2008). Yet this could not be further from the truth.

Western criticism often ignored Africa's voices or selectively chose from those Africans who formulated 'grassroots' criticism of China. Journalists went in search of stories that fitted their editors' preconceptions often picking up statements from single individuals or rumours to 'analyse' China's African 'safari'.[4] Many media reports focused on the wrong culprits – the Chinese – instead of corrupt movers and shakers in African countries (Vines 2009). Most Western media and analysts were essentially patronizing Africa.[5]

Again, contrary to widespread criticism, China's military cooperation (military attachés, joint manoeuvres, arms sales) with Africa seems not to have increased in recent years as opposed to economic cooperation and China's privileged military partner seems to be democratic South Africa, not pariah regimes (Marks 2009).

Politically, in international fora, there is a rapprochement between Chinese and African positions on issues such as human rights (Gowan, Brantner 2008) in line with the politico-ideological Bandung bond, to challenge the dominance of Western policies and defend developing countries' interests on the basis of solidarity. In fora where rhetoric and diplomatic statements are less important than actual negotiations (WTO, UNFCCC, G20) such an alliance is much less obvious. South Africa and China have found themselves at odds about textile imports in a similar way to the EU and China, when China opted for the primacy of WTO rules and competition over Third World solidarity (van der Westhuizen 2007).

This indicates that China had to struggle to come to terms with the African realities as much as Africa had to search its soul to come to terms with the Asian giant (Gaye 2006). The situation in African countries varies enormously depending on political culture, governance capacity, geographic location, economic and social structure, resilience and capacity to adapt to globalization and historical relations with external partners (Oyejide 2009, Vines 2009, Andrews-Speed 2006,

---

4   Mawdsley's (2008) review of English newspaper reports is interesting in this regard.

5   As Manji (2008) puts it eloquently: 'Open any newspaper and you would get the impression that the African continent, and much of the rest of the world, is in the process of being "devoured" by China. Phrases such as the "new scramble for Africa" and "voracious", "ravenous", or "insatiable" "appetite for natural resources" are typical descriptors used to characterize China's engagement with Africa. In contrast, the operations of Western capital for the same activities are described with anodyne phrases such as "development", "investment" and "employment generation"'.

Asche 2008, Kragelund 2009). This diversity has made it difficult for Africa to formulate a coherent strategy in the Forum on China-Africa Cooperation (FOCAC). It is also a challenge for the United Nations (UN) agencies and Western policy-makers, as the widespread stereotypes of crisis, coups and hunger and the almost exclusive focus on the Millennium Development Goals (MDGs), do not capture Africa's diverse realities and growth potential.

China-Africa Cooperation Principles

The Chinese principles for cooperation with Africa – non-interference, mutual respect and equality – have hardly changed since 1949. These principles were reaffirmed in the recently revised Chinese Communist Party (CCP) Constitution (Zhou 2008). There were some pragmatic adaptations in the margins (le Pere 2008: 32), but how relevant are the Chinese principles in today's Africa and how relevant are they in an anti-Western discourse when China has largely subscribed to the Western economic model and traditional pattern of exchange with Africa?

China's principles are often misunderstood by Africans and Western observers alike.[6] In Africa, China's interest is simply assumed to be largely identical with that of other developing countries and informed by anti-imperialist thinking. Africa pins high hopes on China's support for a reform of the international system, yet also started to realize that China's interests diverge from their own (Adebajo, Fakier 2009, Gaye 2006). The often high expectations in Africa that China will lead the challenge to the West contrasts with the dominant view among China watchers that China is a status-quo power drawing huge benefits from the international system. China's harmonious world concept is clearly aimed at rejecting claims that China may attempt to challenge established powers (He 2007, Yuan 2007, Wissenbach 2007, Godement 2006, Men 2007). China pursued its reforms and opening-up policy clearly focusing on trade and investment relations with the rich industrialized countries and on joining the Western dominated international institutions. In effect, economic and aid exchanges with Africa diminished in the first two decades of China's reform policy. These economic dynamics are also reflected in the evolution of China's foreign aid policy from a one-way solidarity based approach to a commercial win-win strategy (Brautigam 2008, Zhou 2008).

China's emphasis on non-interference, and its status as a developing country and South-South cooperation, remains a pillar of China's foreign policy and serves to maintain affinity with – and win diplomatic support from developing countries (Pang 2009: 245), underpinning this relationship that is widely based on the economic interaction described below. However, the rhetoric of solidarity and non-interference is obviously at odds with economic interdependence and competition on the one hand and changes in the African agenda – notably on non-interference – on the other hand (Murithi 2009). Yet, the solidarity card is paying

---

6   As well as by Chinese provincial officials and private companies.

dividends as long as Western criticism allows African leaders to use it. The more criticism of China, the more valuable this card becomes while hindering African attempts to impose its norms on China.

The emphasis on these principles is an expression of China's non-negotiable core national interest (Taiwan, Tibet). The principles themselves are not specifically Chinese, they are part of the UN Charter and accepted by all nations – but they serve as a convenient rallying cry to oppose Western conditionality. Yet conditionality in Africa is not China's core problem: it is territorial integrity and the protection of its political system (including the human rights question) – thus China fears the precedent of principled intervention especially without a UNSC mandate. The underlying problem is therefore in many respects very different from the conflict situations in some African countries. The African Union (AU) has gone beyond the principle of non-intervention when adopting its Charter and the African Peer Review Mechanism (APRM). The AU's policy interventions in cases of anti-constitutional transfer of power or genocide was applied already in the Comoros, Darfur, Somalia and Madagascar cases (Article 4h of the AU Charter).

Finally, the non-interference doctrine may simply provide convenient cover for China's lack of power, capacity and willingness to influence other countries. China avoids getting entangled if it is not in its national interest. It is a pragmatic choice not to create moral obligations for itself, perhaps because China could observe how difficult it has been for Western powers to stick to moral principles.

I argue that beyond the rhetoric on the core principles, the importance of good governance[7] is actually becoming clearer to the Chinese government, as China is engaging more and more in the international field and investing abroad, including in countries which are fragile and where the legal frameworks are unreliable.[8] The sovereignty of governments in producer countries can act as an obstacle to the sustainable exploitation of resources, thus increasing business and political costs for investors. Taylor (2007: 22–3) argues that the national sovereignty of quasi-states may be an appropriate terrain for China's access to resources, but in the long run, the absence of state rules and power create a dangerous vacuum for all actors in Africa, including China. Vines's (2009) study on Nigeria illustrates this point. Consequently, Chinese scholars have started to discuss the principle of non-intervention (Pang, Chen, Huang 2009). Thus, the core principles are important diplomatically, but it would be wrong to assume that China's Africa

---

7   While Chinese officials reject the term as ideologically biased, they often share the substance. Central Bank Governor Zhou for instance used the term 'soft infrastructure' in a speech at the Annual Meeting of the African Development Bank (AfDB), in May 2007, to describe the issues subsumed by good governance, short of references to a particular political system (authors' notes of the speech).

8   The emphasis on a legal framework is relevant in the Chinese context as China's own progress towards the rule of law has so far focused on legislation relating to the economy and business (Delmas-Marty 2005). It is thus important for Chinese companies.

Policy is principally aimed at forging an anti-Western alliance in the developing world (similar to the Cold War period with China's Third World theory).

To find the key rationale for China's Africa policy we need to look at the economic drivers.

The Economic Drivers of China's Africa Policy

China's economic approach and impact on Africa is merely a part of a bigger picture grounded in the intrinsic dynamics of its development path and its emergence as a major economy and manufacturing hub. In order to sustain its economic growth and population size, high GDP growth rates and the outward orientation of its economy, China needs resources and export markets on a massive scale (Godement 2006). The lion's share of China's business in Africa is with resource-rich countries. An expectation to the contrary would have been surprising considering the structural opportunities and constraints for business in Africa, which remains centred on its resources wealth and its needs for affordable consumer goods, infrastructure and capital. There is thus a high degree of complementarity between China and many African countries. Africa's leaders have recognized, however, that this is not a desirable development path and pin high hopes on Chinese investment contributing to an industrial take-off based on China's own example (AUC 2006, Oyejide 2009: 503).

China's integration into the global economy has led to a steep rise in the demand of commodities and a sustained drop in the prices of manufactured goods. These are structural phenomena (South Centre 2010). Both factors have strong – but diverse – direct and indirect impacts on African countries. It is crucial to disaggregate the trade and investment figures by country in order to understand these diverse impacts on individual countries. Oyejide (2009) thus find that only a limited number of African countries (those with oil and minerals) have maintained a favourable trade balance with China. For Chinese companies, economic engagement remains dependent on the real business opportunities in Africa and whether they can make profits. Falling commodity prices in 2008–2009 have already led to a partial disengagement by some of the smaller or private Chinese operators (which are more risk-averse and short-term because informally financed)[9] while state-backed companies go bargain hunting based on cheap capital made available by Chinese banks who can thus invest China's excessive foreign exchange reserves (Herbst, Mills 2009).

The positive impact of demand for energy, minerals and timber for countries endowed with these resources contrasts with a negative impact in those countries which have to import these commodities at higher prices (South Centre 2010). The competitiveness of Chinese consumer goods is – as in Europe – a mixed blessing. Consumers benefit while local industries are often unable to compete. The industrialization process of African countries is thus widely believed by African analysts to be under threat (Kaplinsky 2008), with the exception of Mauritius

---

9   Congo Miners suffer as boom turns to bust, *The Financial Times*, 9 March 2009.

Table 12.1   Rankings for total two-way trade

Ranking	2006	2007	2008
1	Angola	Angola	Angola
2	South Africa	South Africa	South Africa
3	Sudan	Sudan	Sudan
4	Egypt	Egypt	Nigeria
5	Nigeria	Nigeria	Egypt
6	Congo-Brazzaville	Algeria	Congo-Brazzaville
7	Equatorial Guinea	Congo-Brazzaville	Libya
8	Libya	Morocco	Algeria
9	Algeria	Libya	Morocco
10	Morocco	Benin	Equatorial Guinea
Top five as a % of overall	56%	58%	61%
Top ten as a % of overall	78%	78%	79%

Notes: Table 12.1 shows that, despite huge growth in the aggregate level of two-way trade, there has been considerable stability in the top ten trading partners since 2006. The top five countries accounted for 61 percent of total two-way trade in 2008, with the top ten accounting for 79 percent.

Source: China's Ministry of Commerce.

(Ancharaz 2009), while China takes the long-term view that Africa may emulate Asia and become a dynamic growth market (Li 2007).

China's cooperation with Africa, as with other world regions, has indeed mainly focused on trade, investment and a quest for resources for China's industrial growth in particular.[10] It is characteristic that China bundles these vectors of engagement in similar ways as Western countries during the colonial period (Kaplinsky, Morris 2009: 561). This bundling is precisely what created a stir in the development community, as it tends to run counter to decades of efforts to untie aid and move away from colonial-style engagement. Looking at trade in particular (currently one of the few measurable impact indicators, as long-term development impacts of China's cooperation with Africa will only be measurable in a decade), we can see that China-Africa economic relations are dominated by familiar patterns of resource exports against the import of manufactured goods (Broadman 2006). While some policy-makers have resuscitated the old theory of dependency which explains Africa's predicament by external factors and terms of trade, such an approach does not cover the diversity of actors or impacts and the increased policy space many African countries have in fact gained through the

___

10   A number of patterns of interaction were informed by China's earlier engagement with its Asian neighbourhood (Eichengreen 2007).

Table 12.2   Ranking of African exporters to China

Ranking	2006	2007	2008
1	Angola	Angola	Angola
2	South Africa	South Africa	South Africa
3	Congo-Brazzaville	Sudan	Sudan
4	Equatorial Guinea	Congo-Brazzaville	Congo-Brazzaville
5	Sudan	Equatorial Guinea	Libya
6	Libya	Libya	Equatorial Guinea
7	Gabon	Algeria	Gabon
8	Mauritania	Gabon	Democratic Republic of Congo
9	Democratic Republic of Congo	Mauritania	Mauritania
10	Morocco	Nigeria	Algeria
Top five as a % of overall	77%	78%	79%
Top ten as a % of overall	90%	91%	93%

Notes: Table 12.2 shows trading partners ranked by the largest exporters to China between 2006 and 2008. This table shows that in 2008, 79 percent of all exports from Africa came from just five oil and mineral exporting countries. In the same year, 93 percent of exports came from ten countries with little movement within the top ten. These countries tend to have a favourable trade balance with China, while most other African countries tend to import more from China than they export. South Africa is also virtually the only African country which has substantial investment in China.

Source: China's Ministry of Commerce.

emergence of alternative trade, investment and development partners in the last decade of growth.

Africa's share of China's global trade is around 3 percent on a par with the small share Africa has in other major economies' trade. For many Chinese companies investing in Africa, the continent is a stepping stone for a wider global presence, a market in which there is far less competition than in the West or back home, and which is not a strategic market *per se*. Economic cooperation with Africa is thus a sub-strategy in a global pattern of change driven by China's rise in the global economy. Some, such as infrastructure construction exports to Africa, are even a by-product of overcapacity in China. Still, this shift in the global economy sparked by China's integration into the global economy provides other developing countries with long-term opportunities and experiences (as well as competitive pressure for change) that African countries need to analyse and use strategically for their own development (Dollar 2008, Ravalion 2008, Asche 2008, Berger, Wissenbach 2007).

Studies show that as a newcomer to Africa's resources market, China has been obliged to invest into hornets' nests such as Sudan, Angola, Zimbabwe and the DRC to fill the voids left by Western businesses or donors for various reasons.[11] The perceived or real hostility of Western countries to allow Chinese investment in strategic sectors (such as the thwarted attempt by the Chinese National Off-shore Oil Company (CNOOC) to take over Unocal in 2005) has contributed to Chinese companies searching for easier entry points. The easiest entry points were provided through Western sanctions. Chinese companies – and the government – have taken risks that they assumed would be in the interest of the company, the state and sometimes both. China has had to learn to deal with resource nationalism. This can be a costly and frustrating experience rather than a win-win situation notably in countries where the legal framework is weak and politics unpredictable such as Nigeria (Vines 2009). Whether a buyer of resources comes from Europe or China does not make a difference if market conditions are applied (which is more or less what resource rich African countries do). The net effect is enhanced bargaining power and potential income for African resource countries. For China, this is costly because the import dependence – notably for energy and rare minerals or metals that are concentrated in a few countries – is high.

China is not necessarily the most attractive foreign partner for African governments or companies in terms of technology and management. China has to bargain hard with, or pay over the top to, resource-rich countries for access to make up for these comparative disadvantages. Thus China needs to bring in its comparative advantages such as abundant capital, diplomacy and infrastructure delivery capacity. This explains the strategic bundling of three vectors of interaction (aid, trade, investment) which China needs to access new resources, while established industrialized clients can rely more easily on markets and established connections but suffer from a lack of price competitiveness for low and medium range technology or services (Vines 2009: 56).

But cost and risk assessments differ from shareholder interest-driven Western companies.[12] One risk factor – antagonizing Western governments – only started to play a role with the momentum of the 'genocide Olympics' campaign. Otherwise,

---

11 Alden, Rothmann (2006), le Pere (2007), Fandrych (2007), Corkins (2008) describe how cooperation with Angola is based on a package of preferential credits, investment, trade, technical support and development of infrastructure. Grioñ (2007), Vines (2009) give a detailed account of the China-Angola relationship including its risks. Ali (2007) gives a detailed overview of the political economy underpinning Sudan-China relations, which by many critics are reduced to the Darfur issue and Srinivasan (2008) examines Sudan's relations with China and the West. Curtis (2008) in her review of the Democratic Republic of Congo (DRC), rejects the dichotomy of the partnership-predator paradigm. Guenther (2008) analyses China's impacts on the resource curse in Sub-Saharan Africa with the DRC as an example.

12 Chinese companies want to make a profit in Africa regardless of development, ethical or image considerations, but a few big players with global ambitions are more conscious of branding, image and Corporate Social Responsibility (CSR) as shown by their membership to the UN Global Compact.

finger pointing at China's 'unscrupulous' practices was simply countered by African and Chinese criticism of Western double standards, with Western companies and governments accused of long-established records of corruption and collusion with unsavoury regimes that have not been erased by recent efforts to promote good governance in Africa (Li 2007). While rhetorically this has been China's easiest defence line, criticism from civil society in Africa, kidnappings of or attacks on Chinese citizens in Africa or demonstrations and strikes show that many in Africa are no longer ready to tolerate corruption and collusion with dictators by whoever, including otherwise welcome fellow developing countries (Adebajo, Fakier 2009: 4).

China's government initially assumed that business deals sealed during high-level visits, solidarity rhetoric and modest development assistance were sufficient to build an Africa policy almost from scratch (Berger, Wissenbach 2007). China neglected to analyse local political dynamics, state-society relations and social conditions inside countries, mainly because of little available knowledge and research capacity (with the constraint that most published research has the patriotic duty to provide arguments to back up the party line in particular in the face of foreign criticism).

On the other hand deals made by African leaders with their Chinese counterparts are often not properly implemented by the line ministries and bureaucracy as political control is even less far-reaching than in China. This adds to the complexity of defining an African response, generally ill-informed about China's ways, while the Chinese seem to expect higher administrative capacity (similar to their own) from their African counterparts.

Infrastructure Investment and Trade versus Development Aid

China's increasing importance as an economic and political partner has provided new opportunities for Africa and dynamic alternatives to the West, but has it created a really new option for Africa's development?

Ravalion (2008) and Dollar (2008) both argue that some of China's domestic experience is relevant in African contexts. Chinese analysts mostly assume that China's experience as a developing country is automatically more appropriate (Li 2007). The rejection by African governments and civil society organizations of how Western aid is delivered paved the way for China's bundling strategy. Paradoxically, it was the Western economic doctrine itself which was providing the rationale for the shift away from Official Development Aid (ODA) towards trade and Foreign Direct Investment (FDI), liberalism instead of government planning (Kiely 2007), at the same time as it was informing a new EU development policy approach (European Union 2006).

Western criticism of China's Africa policy undermining the Organization for Economic Cooperation and Development's (OECD) aid consensus, failed to understand that China-Africa business was not aid and that Africans were looking precisely for alternatives to Western ODA for several reasons:

1. ODA is not sufficient to develop an economy
2. business partners are on the same level, donors and aid recipients are not
3. the impact of business and infrastructure on economic growth and employment is more immediate, visible and politically appealing for a leader fighting an election than that of ODA
4. financial volumes involved are higher and flow faster
5. there are more possibilities of rent-seeking or political returns
6. there is a strong psychological comfort zone in South-South cooperation that overrides differences between developing countries on issues of substance
7. ODA pledges have more often than not been broken.

Chinese government funding that could be called aid in the OECD Development Assistance Committee (DAC) sense is usually relatively small (in particular as a percentage of China's Gross Domestic Product) and concentrated on social sectors: agriculture, technical assistance and training in China (Brautigam 2008).

The specific nature of Chinese cooperation is most obvious in the infrastructure area (Centre for Chinese Studies 2006, Foster et al. 2008, Besada 2006). Chinese packages allow countries which are short of capital to finance large infrastructure investments quickly to kick-start the economy or to start re-building countries emerging from conflict. Vines (2009) shows that this approach worked for mutual benefit in Angola while it failed in Nigeria. The Chinese engagement allows African countries to choose from different offers of capital and to reject overly intrusive alternatives (IMF conditionalities in Angola (Fandrych 2007, Corkins 2008)), or slow-processing ODA from traditional donors (Curtis 2008, Guenther 2008). The project financing comes from more or less preferential loans by the cash-rich Chinese banks and are based on a business philosophy focusing on economic growth rather than an all-encompassing sector-wide sustainable development approach.[13] In most cases, Chinese banks' primary objective is to help Chinese state-owned enterprises (SOEs) do business abroad, not to have African countries achieve the MDGs. Of course, the bank assumes that business and building infrastructure are good for economic growth and will eventually yield development benefits and therefore portrays China-Africa relations as a development partnership (Li 2007). This is in line with evolving international thinking on development through growth, but the wider developmental impacts on debt sustainability, social and environmental impacts (Dahle, Muyakwa 2008) and the MDGs tend to be little assessed before concrete projects are undertaken.

---

13 The China Development Bank (CDB) was a major policy tool in China's domestic strategy. That the CDB is now turning towards Africa and managing the China-Africa Development Fund is an indication that China's domestic development serves as a blueprint for its overseas development policy.

The consequences are that there is a lot of criticism of Chinese 'aid' internationally and locally, where this is actually business which cannot be benchmarked against aid standards. The uncritical treatment of these volumes of finance as aid have led some to believe that China is suddenly a huge 'donor' where it is in reality an investor with mainly commercial objectives (Berger, Berkovsky 2009). Yet, investment is believed to lead to growth, job creation and development.

The new development paradigm for many African countries therefore involves continued aid from the EU and other traditional donors as well as business, investment and aid packages from China. The AU is urging African countries to strategize the various partnerships and make them complementary.

Africa's governments have to reform their administration dealing with foreign partners and make the switch from management of foreign aid to managing foreign aid, investment, business and trade to create synergies between the various partners and opportunities. Some African countries have simply tried to play off China against former colonial powers, but the impact of the economic crisis on African growth rates has shown the limits of this approach. What is needed is a better understanding of the various policies and a sober analysis of opportunities and risks involved. Then, functional multilateral frameworks could allow bringing in everyone's views on an equal basis and aiming at common results (specific partnerships on infrastructure, energy, resources management for instance). Africans have to use their regional and continental frameworks to devise strategies in cooperation with all partners to be effective. The real challenge is for African businesses not to get trampled to death by fighting elephants.

The EU's Reaction to China's New Partnership with Africa: Competition and Cooperation

The Evolving European Policy towards Africa

In its Africa and development policy reviews since 2005, the EU refocused on ownership at continental (AU), regional (Regional Economic Cooperation) and national levels in Africa and started to review 'conditionality'.[14] This review – culminating in the second EU-Africa summit agreements – can be explained by the failure of the earlier conditional approaches to yield desired development outcomes, the success of the transformation of the Central and Eastern European

---

14 In the early years of EC-Africa cooperation (Yaoundé and Lomé Conventions) the EC strictly respected sovereignty and non-interference principles in its trade and aid agreements because of the sensitive relations it held with these countries after decolonization. Not all of its member states did of course. The pendulum seems to swing back to this earlier policy (Linklater 2005, Bach 2008).

countries and the enlargement of the EU to non-colonial powers (Mayall 2005, Bach 2008).

The EU was not able to fundamentally solve some of its structural impediments to a more coherent approach to Africa, such as the diversity of budgetary instruments used to finance the various partnership initiatives and the deficits in policy coherence (trade, investment).[15] However, the summit and joint strategy undoubtedly transformed the hitherto neglected post-colonial donor-recipient relationship into a new forward-looking foreign policy and development partnership (Grimm 2008). At the Lisbon summit, the EU negotiated a new, more balanced partnership (Africa-EU Strategic Partnership 2007) which incidentally challenges the lopsided FOCAC structure, which is almost entirely managed by China and produces little information on implementation (Adebajo, Fakier 2009: 3, Shelton, Paruk 2008). The EU thus re-asserted its traditional strengths in its partnership with Africa and brought up to date older policies that were no longer adequate in the changed geopolitical environment. The EU also took a bet on making the AU its main political interlocutor.

The EU now offers political and financial incentives for good governance.[16] This marks a change from both the unconditional support to African dictators in return for strategic benefits during the Cold War and the overly prescriptive approach of the 'Washington Consensus'. This is in part due to the confidence in the vitality of African democracy and good governance trends (as embodied in the AU Charter, the APRM and democratic developments in many countries); partly it is also due to the realization that change cannot be imposed from the outside. The EU shows a certain confidence in African efforts (through the AU in particular) to build democratic states even if this will be a long, drawn-out process. It is encouraging that Africans themselves have created and are enforcing democratic benchmarks which over time will put dictators and coup leaders on the defensive. Interference from former colonial powers has the opposite effect, as solidarity among Africans may very well outweigh the criticism of a non-democratic regime in their midst. Zimbabwe seems to be a case in point. So far, there is hardly any evidence that China has intentionally contributed in a measurable way to bad governance. Dictators and corruption have been there for some time. There is equally scarce measurable evidence that Western ODA has actually led to major improvements of good governance. Indeed, imposing

---

15   Despite the drive for aid effectiveness, where Europe plays the leading global role, its aid is still fragmented, spread over too many instruments that are locked in outdated approaches because of internal disagreements, like with the division of Africa into EC budget instruments and the EDF, and between several Directorates-General DEV, RELEX, TRADE (Bach 2008, Grimm 2009).

16   A key factor in the EU for this agenda is societal pressure to use taxpayers' money transparently in ways to fight poverty, confront dictators and human suffering, promote social and human rights agendas, and root out corruption – a pressure that does not exist in China.

change works less well if alternatives exist (Schwersensky 2007). With the AU Charter and the APRM, Africa has created a counter-platform to conditionality. This platform is, institutionally, still in its infancy but it is taken seriously by the EU.

On some crucial issues, however, such as the Economic Partnership Agreements (EPAs), the EU failed to enlist African support from the outset (Draper 2007) and resistance is strong (South Centre 2010). It is interesting that civil society and African government mobilization against the EPAs has been so vocal while discussions of most African countries' trade deficits with China and limited market access by China for African goods has been confined to a small number of African specialists (Kaplinsky, Morris 2008), trade unions (van der Westhuizen 2007) or foreign observers. It is plausible that such discussions are going on between the FOCAC partners but they are shielded from public view (Adebajo, Fakier 2009). The lack of Chinese civil society organizations, independent media and public opinion interested in African development issues also deprives critics of a powerful pressure instrument. African governments have certainly realized that it is more effective to negotiate with China behind closed doors than on the public marketplace.

Europe's new Africa rhetoric is in some points not dissimilar to that of China's *Africa Policy*: equality, solidarity, common objectives and ownership (Ministry of Foreign Affairs of the People's Republic of China 2006, Africa-EU strategic partnership 2007). The enhanced strategic position of Africa as a new potential growth pole in the global economy, due to its resources wealth or consumer potential, the need for Africa's support on global challenges and Africa's new Chinese and other international partners have influenced this evolution away from the framing of Africa as a humanitarian challenge. Europe's influence in Africa had been decreasing, partly for lack of business and political interest, partly because emerging powers such as China offered attractive alternatives to African leaders who did not have many serious choices before (Wissenbach 2007b). Yet, during the financial crisis, African governments have realized that ODA is still relevant, in particular as an 'automatic' stabilizer for public expenditure.

Moving towards an EU Partnership with Africa and China?

When examining the EU's reaction to China's Africa policies, it is crucial to recall that the EU also has a strategic partnership with China which is one of its major trading partners and a key interlocutor for dealing with global challenges (Fox, Godement 2009). The EU-China strategic partnership is a good example of a constantly widening and deepening cooperation, characterized by regulated but intense competition and a constant balancing of interests with each side strictly preserving normative differences (Godement 2006, Wissenbach 2007a, Wissenbach 2009). A possible confrontation over Africa could have affected this balance in the EU-China partnership which may explain why the European Commission has proposed a cooperative platform in which it would like to see Africa's interests at the core. The EU proposed to engage in a process in which China is considered as a partner with legitimate interests in Africa, identifying common interests between the EU, Africa and China and pursuing those through dialogue and cooperation, while also addressing differences through dialogue (European Commission 2008, Berger 2008, Grimm 2008b).

Between Africa, the EU and China, common objectives exist such as fighting poverty, promoting economic growth and achieving the MDGs. Chinese and European soldiers participate in UN peacekeeping missions. The EU, China and the AU all have a role to play at the G20 so as to deal with the economic crisis and its impacts on Africa since the Toronto summit added development to the G20 agenda. Both the EU and China are urging the international community to respect their commitments to Africa for different reasons – on the one hand because the EU is by far the largest donor of ODA to Africa, and on the other because China, by seeking to gain political credit from its African partners, is demanding that Western countries fulfil their pledges. Yet, besides this cooperative agenda, competition for Africa's resources and markets may have negative consequences for multilateralism and for global governance.

The EU – in line with its strategic commitment to effective multilateralism – proposed a cooperative model that takes account of the triangular global value chains, sustainable development and business experiences (Wissenbach 2009). The AU, the EU and China could cooperate functionally in certain areas of concern to deal with specific issues. That would not exclude competition and differences in other areas or in normative approaches. Functional multilateral cooperation regimes can be created despite value differences and competitive relationships on the basis of shared and jointly defined interests to address sustainable management of forest resources, provision of renewable energy, fighting desertification or building continental infrastructure. They do not require new institutional frameworks or a normative consensus. They require an African strategy notably through regional and continental institutions, and political will to work with different partners for sustainable development. Cooperation could enhance identification of best practice or innovation and promote African interests. Global goods such as security, development and the environment require functionally structured cooperation. The EU and China are more likely to engage on a cooperative platform (with elements of competition) proposed by Africa, than on a confrontational one (about resources or political influence in Africa). This requires equal footing between the partners, not moralizing. China's own way of responding to complexity and interdependence point to the need for pragmatism, functional cooperation and bargaining, not ideology or hedging strategies to deal with development challenges.

Africa's efforts to create its normative framework for engagement with outside partners should be the starting point for both China and the EU to build up their cooperation. This is about the socialization of African values and behaviour as laid down in the AU Charter. Appropriate behaviour by outsiders can thus be directed by Africans themselves. As the AU Charter is catering for elements of both the EU's and China's normative preferences (for example democracy, human rights, rule of law, good governance, responsibility to protect versus sovereignty, self-determination), it should be the normative framework of choice for functional cooperation. The AfDB and regional development banks could lend themselves as an African financial framework to help implement policy.

The EU therefore cautiously welcomed China as an important partner for Africa and in Africa (European Commission 2008) that prompted debate on the continent and in China, and thus provided a new impetus to discussions on aid effectiveness in Accra.[17] The current evolution is still open and a number of assumptions and challenges need to be critically examined to chart the course for a constructive policy that would maximize development outcomes for Africa (Grimm 2008b, Berger 2008).

The European Commission took a diplomatically balanced approach after a report by the European Parliament[18] had antagonized Chinese diplomats, despite the Chinese Ambassador having been invited to a preparatory hearing. The EP report took up the usual criticism of China in terms of human rights and good governance. The European Commission chose to focus on shared interests and proposed that Africa lead trilateral cooperation with China while making some concrete suggestions in which areas the EU would stand ready to engage: either by supporting the African Security Architecture, promoting regional infrastructure development, improving the sustainable management of natural resources starting with the timber trade, and – based on a Chinese suggestion – rural development.

While these are politically sensitive areas, the proposals were pragmatic and constructive based on an analysis of what Africa, the EU and China were already doing in these areas and where interests could coincide.[19] The EU reaffirmed its commitment to its norms, but recognized that asking China to change its norms as a precondition for cooperation would equate to entering into an era of ideological rivalry rather than multilateral cooperation, where in reality it was important to identify overlapping interests to address Africa's development. As a result, China was invited to be part of the solution, while the EP – who also had been invited to the hearing – portrayed China as part of the problem.

The EU also reaffirmed its confidence in Africans to be the masters of their own destiny, by putting an offer of trilateral cooperation on the table, rather than trying to impose it. The EU thus recognized the potential of China's contributions to Africa's development which is ultimately also in Europe's interest. The EU also recognized the downsides of China's engagement in Africa, but rather than simply standing by and criticizing, the EU suggested concrete partnerships to address problems and find common solutions – solutions which are not imposed by the EU, but rather worked out in partnership. This is the only way to make

---

17   The Accra Agenda for Action adopted in September 2008 by the High-level Forum for Aid Effectiveness contains a reference to trilateral cooperation in Article 19.

18   See   http://www.europarl.europa.eu/meetdocs/2004_2009/documents/pr/697/69 7015/697015en.pdf.

19   See Commission Staff Working Document annexed to European Commission (2008): http://ec.europa.eu/development/icenter/repository/SWP_COM_2008_0654_annexes_en.pdf.

multilateralism effective, as leadership cannot be imposed from one side on its terms. Leadership can be won by starting and managing processes and suggesting solutions agreeable to all. Trilateral cooperation with China would not compromise the EU's principles for its development and African policies in the same way as it would not ask China to abandon theirs. Rather, both the EU and China will have to continuously adjust their policies to new African realities.

Through its dialogue with China on Africa launched in 2006, and through bilateral contacts between EU member states with China's special representative for Africa, the EU was aware that China was trying to find a viable compromise to one of the thornier problems that had become emblematic for China critics: the crisis in Darfur. The EU recognized that it did not see China as the cause of the problem but as part of the international solution. Nevertheless, the EU would have liked China to have a more critical and differentiated policy towards the regime in Khartoum. In return, China debriefed the EU on China's initiatives to find a solution to the establishment of the hybrid UN/AU peacekeeping mission.

For the AU, there is no contradiction between working with partners, such as the EU and China simultaneously, who may have a different focus. Yet, the step of trying to bring different partners together around concrete African initiatives (as advocated by the EU) has not yet been made, not least given the difficulties to create a consensus among African countries on how to work with different partners. And this may well be the key difficulty ahead: will the AU be strong enough to rationalize, structure and strategize African international partnerships or will it be undermined by bilateral initiatives and competition among African countries for foreign funds? In the FOCAC case, Chinese diplomats have rejected AU initiatives to rebalance the secretariat process for two reasons: firstly, because of those AU members that recognize Taiwan and secondly – although rather bluntly – because of the lack of African consensus existent at the AU. Thus China seems to play the bilateral card against the multilateral one.

Conclusion: towards Functional Multilateral Cooperation?

China's *Africa Policy* is now more widely accepted as the EU's policy paper has shown, but it is not necessarily well understood. China has provided more development opportunities for many countries and strengthened African bargaining positions with other external partners but it has also put considerable strain on African industry and society. China has also been confronted with a number of challenges, that both the government and the business actors were ill-prepared for. One such challenge concerned the political risk of concluding high-level business deals, which are non-transparent or where the bureaucracy has not been involved, and the complexity of the political environment with opposition and civil society groups not necessarily sharing government enthusiasm. And finally, there is the political fall-out of dealing with dictatorial regimes, both in Africa and in the international community. In Africa, China's rhetoric, lack of accountability and transparency, and the confusion surrounding the mixing of business practices with solidarity or aid created an expectation gap. China remains a small donor (Manji 2008), but a big financier, investor and trading partner entailing conflicts of interest, as Africa is ill-prepared for hard-nosed competition.

Paradoxically, while China's economic interaction with Africa starts resembling the traditional North-South pattern, politically the references to South-South cooperation principles – as a framework for FOCAC – abound. One can observe a rapprochement of the global South and a clear tendency to challenge Western agendas (in particular the development agendas such as aid effectiveness, good governance and the dominance of OECD standards (Brautigam 2008, Davies 2007, Dahle, Muyakwa 2008)) – and in the UN Human Rights Council (Gowan, Branter 2008). The challenge to the West in the hardcore areas of trade and finance is much more muted given the huge disparities of trade interests between China and most other developing countries, its hard-nosed approach to the textile industry in Africa, the high concentration on a few resource-rich countries and the negative impact of Chinese exports of cheap manufactures on fledgling industries in Africa (Kaplinsky, Morris 2008, Besada 2006).

There is thus a lingering tension between China's political discourse and market-driven economic patterns of interaction which play out in the increasingly dense complexity of the China-Africa-EU relationship. This is not a question of good or bad, right or wrong, predator or saviour, market or mercantilism, democracy or authoritarianism, which have unfortunately dominated the debate about China and Africa. Rather, it is a problem of managing complexity, interdependence, competition and cooperation which is not adequately described by the outdated categories of the twentieth century (great power rivalry, dependency theory) and which is not uniquely an Africa-China problem. This is the normality of international relations in the era of globalization – competition and cooperation. China need not shy away from working with others in order to address these challenges by accepting the fact that different approaches are not just problematic, but they can actually constitute an advantage.

We need functional solutions, in a period of transition where many global institutions no longer perform adequately. Functional multilateralism with a variable geometry can provide effective solutions in Africa despite value differences and competition in bilateral relationships on the basis of shared and jointly defined interests to address particular development challenges. They do not require new institutional frameworks or a normative consensus. They do require that stakeholders respect each other as equals when addressing a particular task while leaving more fundamental differences to bilateral relationships. They only need a limited set of objectives and rules whilst 'membership' can be restricted to the most relevant parties: that can be a particular peacekeeping operation, a regional infrastructure initiative or cooperation on forest management or rural development, but should be linked to existing ones aimed at increasing legitimacy (AU, UN).

In engaging China, Africa and the EU need to take a more balanced view that not only focuses on China's alleged or real strengths, but also accounts for its weaknesses and strategic constraints. China's lack of transparency in aid for Africa and its insistence on non-interference are also designed to hide its weaknesses. Furthermore, it is unlikely that Africans accept a new dependency on China. However, China's Africa policy provides a political and psychological boost to Africa's emancipation and development by reducing dependence on and intellectual domination by the West. Different approaches increase Africa's choices – there is no need for conformism of African partners with either European or Chinese templates, but there is a need for dialogue and cooperation around these different approaches based on a collective African strategy on external relations, in an attempt to create a different, pragmatic approach to development after the failure of the 'Washington Consensus'.

Interdependence between the different state and non-state actors, domestic and external policies, political and commercial activities or mutual reactions form a complex web of opportunities and challenges that cannot be captured by simple power games such as the EU against China or by rigid normative templates – synergies need to be found in order to create win-win-win situations. Thus while the clamour about China in Africa was 'much ado about nothing', China's emergence as a partner for Africa spells a new era for Africa's development and perhaps a last chance for Africa's inclusion into the world economy. The EU's merit is that it has recognized this and proposed a constructive platform to work together with Africa and China. Now, it is Africa's turn to lead.

Bibliography

Book References

Alden, C. and Rothman, A. 2006. *China and Africa Special Report: Terms of Endearment from Marxism to Materials*. Shanghai: CLSA Asia-Pacific Markets.

Brautigam, D. 2008. *China's African Aid: Transatlantic Challenges*. Washington, D.C.: German Marshall Fund.

Broadman, H. 2006. *Africa's Silk Road. China's and India's New Economic Frontier*. Washington, D.C.: World Bank.

Cooper Ramos, J. 2004. *The Beijing Consensus*. London: The Foreign Policy Centre.

Davies, P. 2007. *China and the End of Poverty in Africa – towards Mutual Benefit?*. Sundbyberg: Diakonia.

Fox, J. and Godement, F. 2009. *A Power Audit of EU-China Relations*. London: ECFR.

Gaye, A. 2006. *Chine-Afrique: Le Dragon et l'Autruche*. Paris: L'Harmattan.

Gowan, R. and Brantner, F. 2008. *A Global Force for Human Rights? An Audit of European Power at the UN*. London: ECFR.

Kaplinsky, R. 2008. *Africa's Cooperation with New and Emerging Development Partners: Options for Africa's Development*. Report prepared for The Office of Special Advisor on Africa. New York: United Nations.

Le Pere, G. 2007. *China in Africa – Mercantilist Predator, or Partner in Development?*. Midrand: IGD.

Li, W. 2008. *Beijing Summit and the Third Ministerial Conference of the Forum on China-Africa Cooperation – Appraisal and Prospects*. Shanghai: Shanghai Institute for International Studies.

Ravallion, M. 2008. *Are There Lessons for Africa from China's Success against Poverty?*. World Bank Policy Research Working Paper 4463. Washington, D.C.: World Bank.

Shelton, G. and Paruk, F. 2008. *The Forum on China-Africa Cooperation: A Strategic Opportunity*. Monograph 156. Pretoria: Institute for Security Studies December 2008.

Vines, A., Wong, L., Weimer, M., and Campos, I. 2009. *Thirst for African Oil. Asian National Oil Companies in Nigeria and Angola*. London: Chatham House.

Book Chapters

Ali, A. 2007. The political economy of relations between Sudan and China, in *China in Africa – Mercantilist Predator, or Partner in Development?*, edited by G. Le Pere. Midrand: IGD, 172–85.

Andrews-Speed, P. 2006. China's energy policy and its contribution to international stability, in *Facing China's Rise: Guidelines for an EU Strategy*, edited by M. Zaborowski. Paris: Chaillot Paper No. 94, 71–82.

Bach, D. 2008. The European Union and China in Africa, in *Crouching Tiger, Hidden Dragon? Africa and China*, edited by A. Kweku and S. Naidu. Cape Town: University of KwaZulu Natal Press, 278–93.

Corkins, L. 2008. All's fair in loans and war: the development of China-Angola relations, in *Crouching Tiger, Hidden Dragon? Africa and China*, edited by A. Kweku and S. Naidu. Cape Town: University of KwaZulu Natal Press, 108–23.

Curtis, D. 2008. Partner or predator in the heart of Africa? Chinese engagement with the DRC, in *Crouching Tiger, Hidden Dragon? Africa and China*, edited by A. Kweku and S. Naidu. Cape Town: University of KwaZulu Natal Press, 86–107.

Delmas-Marty, M. 2005. La construction d'un etat de droit en Chine dans le contexte de la mondialisation, in *La Chine et la Démocratie*, edited by M. Delmas-Marty et P.E. Will. Paris: Seuil, 551–76.

Godement, F. 2006. Neither hegemon nor soft power: China's rise at the gates of the West, in *Facing China's Rise: Guidelines for an EU Strategy*, edited by M. Zaborowski. Paris: Chaillot Paper Number 94, 51–70.

Grimm, S. 2008. The European Union's Africa policy, in *Chinese and European Perspectives on Development Cooperation in Africa: Values, Objectives and Modalities*, edited by W. Jung, D. Messner and G. Yang. Beijing: KAS Schriftenreihe China, 84, 14–22.

Grioñ, E.M. 2007. The political economy of commercial relations: China's engagement in Angola, in *China in Africa – Mercantilist Predator, or Partner in Development?*, edited by G. Le Pere. Midrand: IGD, 141–59.

Habib, A. 2008. Western hegemony, Asian ascendancy and the new scramble for Africa, in *Crouching Tiger, Hidden Dragon? Africa and China*, edited by A. Kweku and S. Naidu. Cape Town: University of KwaZulu Natal Press, 259–77.

Le Pere, G. 2008. The geo-strategic dimensions of the Sino-Africa relationship, in *Crouching Tiger, Hidden Dragon? Africa and China*, edited by A. Kweku and S. Naidu. Cape Town: University of KwaZulu Natal Press, 20–38.

Linklater, A. 2005. A European civilizing process?, in *International Relations and the European Union*, edited by C. Hill and M. Smith. Oxford: Oxford University Press, 367–87.

Mayall, J. 2005. The shadow of empire: the EU and the former colonial world, in *International Relations and the European Union*, edited by C. Hill and M. Smith. Oxford: Oxford University Press, 292–316.

Schwersensky, S. 2007. Harare's 'look East' policy now focuses on China, in *China in Africa – Mercantilist Predator, or Partner in Development?*, edited by G. Le Pere. Midrand: IGD, 186–200.

Shelton, G. 2007. China and Africa: advancing South-South co-operation, in *China in Africa – Mercantilist Predator, or Partner in Development?*, edited by G. Le Pere. Midrand: IGD, 99–122.

Srinivasan, S. 2008. A marriage less convenient: China, Sudan and Darfur, in *Crouching Tiger, Hidden Dragon? Africa and China*, edited by A. Kweku and S. Naidu. Cape Town: University of KwaZulu Natal Press, 55–85.

Taylor, I. 2007. Unpacking China's resource diplomacy in Africa, in *China in Africa*, edited by H. Melber. Uppsala: Nordiska Afrikainstitutet, 10–25.

Van der Westhuizen, C. 2007. The clothing and textile industries in Sub-Saharan Africa: an overview with policy recommendations, in *China in Africa – Mercantilist Predator, or Partner in Development?*, edited by G. Le Pere. Midrand: IGD.

Journal Articles

Adebajo, A. and Fakier, Y. 2009. Taming the dragon? Defining Africa's interests at the Forum on China-Africa Co-operation (FOCAC). *CCR and IGD Policy Brief*, 2, 1–50.

Ancharaz, V. 2009. David V. Goliath: Mauritius facing up to China. *The European Journal of Development Research*, 21(4), 622–43.

Asche, H. 2008. Contours of China's 'Africa mode' and who may benefit. *China Aktuell*, 3, 165–81.

Berger, B. and Berkofsky, A. 2009. Chinese outward investments. Agencies, motives and decision-making. *CASCC Briefing Paper*.

Berger, B. and Wissenbach, U. 2007. EU-China-Africa trilateral development cooperation. Common challenges and new directions. *DIE Discussion Paper*, 21, 1–34.

Besada, H. 2006. Foreign investment in Africa: challenges and benefits. *South African Journal of International Affairs*, 13(1), 159–68.

Centre for Chinese Studies (CCS), Stellenbosch University. 2006. *China's interest and activities in Africa's construction and infrastructure sectors*, report prepared for the Department for International Development (DFID) China.

Dahle Huse, M. and Muyakwa, S.L. 2008. *China in Africa: lending, policy space and governance*, Report prepared for the Norwegian Campaign for Debt Cancellation, Norwegian Council for Africa.

Dollar, D. 2008. Lessons from China for Africa. *World Bank Policy Research Working Paper 4531*. Washington, D.C.: World Bank.

Eichengreen, B., Rhee, Y. and Tong, H. 2007. China and the exports of other Asian countries. *Review of World Economics*, 143(2), 201–26.

Fandrych, S. 2007. China in Angola – nachhaltiger wiederaufbau, kalkulierte wahlkampfhilfe oder globale interessenpolitik? (sustainable reconstruction, calculated electoral support or global interest policy?). *IPG*, 2, 62–74.

Foster, V., Butterfield, W., Chen, C. and Pushak, N. 2008. *Building Bridges. China's Growing Role as Infrastructure Financier for Sub-Saharan Africa*. Washington, D.C.: World Bank.

Grimm, S. 2008b. Africa-China-Europe trilateral co-operation: is Europe naïve?. *EDC 2020 Opinion Paper*, 1, 1–2.

Grimm, S., Humphrey, J., Lundsgaarde, E. and John de Sousa, S.L. 2009. European development cooperation to 2020: challenges by new actors in international development. *EDC 2020 Working Paper*, 4, 1–43.

Guenther, B. 2008. The Asian drivers and the resource curse in Sub-Saharan Africa: the potential impacts of rising commodity prices for conflict and governance in the DRC. *The European Journal of Development Research*, 20(2), 347–63.

He, W. 2007. The balancing act of China's Africa policy. *China Security*, 3(3), 23–40.

Herbst, J. and Mills, G. 2009. Commodity flux and China's Africa strategy. *China Brief*, 9(2), 4–6.

Kaplinsky, R. and Morris, M. 2009. Chinese FDI in Sub-Saharan Africa: engaging with large dragons. *The European Journal of Development Research*, 21(4), 551–69.

Kiely, R. 2007. Poverty reduction through liberalization? Neoliberalism and the myth of global convergence. *Review of International Studies*, 33, 415–34.

Kragelund, P. 2009. Part of the disease or part of the cure? Chinese investments in the Zambian mining and construction sectors. *The European Journal of Development Research*, 21(4), 644–61.

Li, R. 2007. Zhengqu renshi fazhanzhong guojia de zhaiwu kezhixu wenti (Correct understanding of debt sustainability of developing countries). *World Economics and Politics*, 4, 63–72.

Marks, S. 2009. Chinas sicherheitspolitik in Afrika (China's security policy in Africa). *IPG*, 1, 74–89.

Mawdsley, E. 2008. Fu Manchu versus Dr Livingstone in the dark continent? Representing China, Africa and the West in British broadsheet newspapers. *Political Geography*, 27, 509–29.

Men, H. 2007. Strategic roadmap of China's idea evolution. *World Economics and Politics*, 7, 13–20.

Murithi, T. 2009. The African Union's transition from non-intervention to non-indifference: an ad hoc approach to the responsibility to protect?. *IPG*, 1, 90–106.

Oyejide, T.A., Abiodun, S.B. and Adeolu, O.A. 2009. China-Africa trade relations: insights from AERC scoping studies. *The European Journal of Development Research*, 21(4), 485–505.

Pang, Z. 2009. China's non-intervention question. *Global Responsibility to Protect*, 1, 237–52.

Pang, Z., Chen, Q. and Huang, Y. 2009. Guoji ganshe de guifan weidu (Reconstructing norms of international interventions). *World Economics and Politics*, 4, 6–15.

South Centre. 2010. The impact of the global economic crisis on industrial development of least developed countries. *South Centre Research Paper*, 28, 1–99.

Wissenbach, U. 2007a. The EU's effective multilateralism – but with whom? Functional multilateralism and the rise of China. *Friedrich-Ebert-Stiftung, International Politikanalyse*.

Wissenbach, U. 2007b. China, Africa and Europe: Africa's attractions. *The World Today*, 63(4), 7–9.

Wissenbach, U. 2009. The EU's response to China's Africa safari: can triangular co-operation match needs?. *The European Journal of Development Research*, 21(4), 662–74.

Yuan, P. 2007. A harmonious world and China's new diplomacy. *Contemporary International Relations*, 17(3), 1–26.

Zhou, H. 2008. China's foreign aid and 30 years of reform. *World Economics and Politics*, 339(11), 33–43.

Websites

Berger, B. 2008. *EU puts Africa ball in China's court*. [Online]. Available at: http://www.atimes.com/atimes/China/JJ30Ad01.html [accessed 3 October 2009].

Draper, P. 2007. *Europe, Africa and partnership agreements: in search of a developmental agenda*. [Online]. Available at: http://www.voxeu.org/index.php?q=node/442 [accessed: 3 October 2009].

Foster, V., Butterfield, W., Chen, C. and Pushak, N. 2008. *Building Bridges: China's growing role as infrastructure financier for Sub-Saharan Africa.* [Online]. Available at: http://siteresources.worldbank.org/INTAFRICA/Resources/ Building_Bridges_Master_Version_wo-Embg_with_cover.pdf [accessed: 3 October 2009].

Manji, F. 2008. *China: still a small player in Africa – monthly review.* [Online]. Available at: http://www.monthlyreview.org/mrzine/manji280408.html [accessed: 3 October 2009].

Newspapers

Jopson, B. 2009. Congo miners suffer as boom turns to bust. *Financial Times*, 9 March.

Wade, A. 2008. Time for the West to practise what it preaches. *Financial Times*, 24 January.

Command Papers

China's African Policy. 2006. Beijing: Ministry of Foreign Affairs of the People's Republic of China.

Global Europe: Competing in the World (Communication from the Commission to the Council, the European Parliament, the Economic and Social Committee and the Committee of the Regions). 2006. COM 567(2006) final. Brussels: European Commission.

Meeting of the Task Force on Africa's Partnership with Emerging Powers: China, India and Brazil. 2006. Addis Ababa: African Union Commission.

The Africa-EU Strategic Partnership. A Joint Africa-EU Strategy. 2007. Lisbon: The European Union and the African Union.

The EU, Africa and China: Towards Trilateral Dialogue and Cooperation (Communication from the Commission to the Council and the European Parliament). 2008. COM 654(2008) final. Brussels: European Commission.

Conclusion
China and the EU in Africa: Partners or Competitors?

Jing Men and Benjamin Barton

Despite the respective long-standing bilateral relations that exist between China, the European Union (EU) and Africa, their triangular interaction is a recent phenomenon. Due to the impact of globalization, a number of dramatic changes have occurred in the international political sphere. China's growing economic and political presence in Africa acts as a prime example in this respect. When looking back just over a decade, the concept of China's non-negligible presence in Africa offered little in terms of credibility. Nowadays, China's growing stature in a wide range of different sectors in Africa (business, investment, foreign aid, security, development, infrastructure, regional integration) has led to its establishment as one of Africa's major external actors. As Chapter 1 outlined, China's bilateral relations with Africa run much deeper than commercial exchanges, the Chinese government and Chinese businesses have cemented their rising status by engaging in a wide range of areas with African partners and by taking great risks. Chapter 2 complements this viewpoint as it highlights the extent of the depth of China's involvement in Africa by focusing on four specific cultural affinities that have solidified China's historic emergence as a reliable and trustworthy partner for African states.

China's establishment as one of Africa's main strategic partners has not suited everyone. The EU and its member states' initial reactions to China's growing appeal in Africa were disdainful at best. This defensive reaction was in part due to the realization that China could offer an alternative to EU policies on different fronts, which could potentially put European interests at risk (in terms of investments, political affiliations, development objectives and value systems). It was this strong reaction that in part heightened the attention towards China's growing role in African political circles. On the other hand, the EU has more recently shown its resolve and determination to engage China in Africa, instead of simply constantly chastising the Chinese on their strategic choices in Africa (such as with its support for Sudan and Zimbabwe). The European Commission's 2008 paper on triangular dialogue and cooperation is evidence of the EU's pragmatism.[1]

---

1 For more information, see the European Commission's Communication on trilateral dialogue and cooperation at: http://eur-lex.europa.eu/LexUriServ/LexUriServ. do?uri=COM:2008:0654:FIN:EN:PDF.

The EU's ambiguous and often contradictory stance is endemic of its current strategic relations with the African continent – although both sides have advocated moving the relations more towards a fairer and equitable balance, as seen at the Joint Africa-EU Summit in 2007,[2] little evidence has surfaced to support this evolution. On the other hand, as this book has demonstrated throughout, change is possible whether it be in terms of policies or concepts. In addition, to the surprise of many, China has been showing the most potent signs of developing its Africa strategy beyond purely commercial objectives. As demonstrated in Chapter 7 and 8, China has understood the importance of protecting its positive image in Africa – this is considered as a *sine qua non* for Chinese foreign policy-makers. In effect, the more China's positive image is consolidated among Africa's political elites, the further China's economic aspirations are fulfilled, the better it is for China's internal development, and the more influence China will exert in Africa. Yet, as Sara van Hoeymissen and Jianxiang Bi demonstrated in their respective chapters, China is reconsidering its approach towards its policy on national sovereignty. There is a tendency that China is becoming more cooperative in peacekeeping and peacemaking actions based on the principle of responsibility to protect. As these two respective chapters outline, this evolution has proved to be a stimulating and multifaceted development with China firmly respecting the framework of international law, whilst proactively engaging itself on the ground in order to certify its presence as an actor dedicated to 'doing good' for the continent at large. It is this dualistic paradigm that interestingly serves as the greatest indication that China is not only willing to make concessions in order to better its international reputation, but also that it is showing a greater degree of commitment to international governance at large. This perspective not only applies to its humanitarian ambitions, but also to its business dealings with Africa where China is now establishing special economic zones in certain African countries. As Martyn Davies outlined, one of Beijing's objectives is to help foster stronger regional economic integration amongst some of the least developed countries. This further development will serve to reinforce its presence as a vital economic actor in Africa – a point thoroughly extrapolated by Martyn Davies' interpretation of the link between China's economic prosperity and Africa's real Gross Domestic Product (GDP) growth.

While Beijing attaches great importance to its international image building, its foreign policy is oriented towards sustaining a long-term approach. As pointed out in Chapter 6, Beijing is ready to make political compromises when necessary. In that chapter, Taylor centres on Beijing's fear of scorning the reputation it has incrementally built for itself in Africa. Although China's record regarding the protection of human rights and its dealings with African authoritarian regimes is far from perfect, the chapter casts aside any lingering doubts surrounding Beijing's re-evaluation of its need to better strategize when selecting its African partners or

---

2   For example, see the Joint Africa-EU Strategy Partnership, available at: http://ec.europa.eu/development/icenter/repository/EAS2007_joint_strategy_en.pdf.

potential business investments. The necessity to preserve a positive image of itself has prompted a more selective and cautious approach by Beijing, especially in cases where certain African countries are known for their human rights abuses. As Ian Taylor indicates, this political reassessment is necessary for China if it is to not jeopardize its relations with Africa over the long-term.

Whether consciously or not, China has somehow fallen into a competitive paradigm with the West, and the EU in particular, due to its astronomical rise in importance in Africa. This has caused concern. As Taylor exposes, the human rights issue remains a serious concern for Europeans in China's African policies. Due to their different understandings and policies in values, the EU and China have different approaches in Africa. In the meantime, the EU has adopted a firm line on China's progressive importance, by stressing the importance of the sustainability of China's interactions with the continent. The EU has almost expected for China to respect European values (good governance, human rights and democracy promotion) when dealing with its African partners. Although China has now become an undeniable feature in African politics, the EU remains perhaps Africa's most crucial foreign partner in terms of the depth of their historical relations.

While the EU and China are both active in Africa and the two sometimes are viewed from the lenses of competitors, Zhang Xinghui illustrates in his chapter that China does not withhold the intension to overthrow European interests. To the contrary, in line with the title of Chapter 3, China is seeking to achieve a delicate balance between fulfilling its own needs and maintaining its strategic partnership with the EU and its member states. These two respective chapters constitute an important reflection of the delicate strategic choices which Beijing faces in Africa. In its policy-making for the African continent, Beijing has to consider its self-interests, those of its African partners and of other strategic partners. To act in an egotistical manner in Africa will not serve China's self-interests and thus will not allow it to sustain its influence there.

In reaction to China's increasing influence in Africa, the EU demonstrates its pragmatism by seeking areas for cooperation. Chapter 4 and 5 pay homage to the EU's strive for multilateralism by providing concrete examples where the EU has sought to involve China in the fight against piracy or small arms and light weapons, to which the Chinese government has responded with timid yet progressive intent. These two distinct areas have either proven as concrete steps towards future cooperative engagement between the EU and China in Africa, or as a channel through which the two can concretely work in symbiosis – a feat which would be a definitive added-value, as demonstrated by Thomas Wheeler. It is at this stage that this book has proven the rapidity with which changes are made, both at the policy-making and academic level.

Where ten years ago potential cooperation between these three actors came across as an illusion, it now pertains to being the most optimal approach for the EU, China and Africa to work together. Notwithstanding the current lack of cooperative projects held between the three, the trilateral dialogue is a first step in the progress towards coordination and exchanges between the two major actors in Africa. If the EU and China are to fulfil their set targets for the African continent, now more than ever, they will need to work together. As Chapter 11 and 12 illustrates, areas for complementarity and coordination are aplenty whether it be in terms of helping to construct Africa's vital infrastructural needs or in terms of establishing concrete three-way political cooperation as a means of seriously boosting Africa's development process. Nevertheless, as always, it is the political will and dynamism shown on both sides which shall determine whether the EU and China can coordinate for Africa's good – a relationship that will prove fundamental in bringing the African continent out of its perpetual obscurity.

Index

Page numbers in *italics* refer to figures and tables.